INVESTING IN CORPORATE BONDS AND CREDIT RISK

Investing in Corporate Bonds and Credit Risk

FRANK HAGENSTEIN,
ALEXANDER MERTZ AND JAN SEIFERT

palgrave
macmillan

First published in 2004 by
PALGRAVE MACMILLAN
Houndmills, Basingstoke, Hampshire RG21 6XS and
175 Fifth Avenue, New York, N.Y. 10010
Companies and representatives throughout the world

PALGRAVE MACMILLAN is the global academic imprint of the Palgrave Macmillan division of St. Martin's Press, LLC and of Palgrave Macmillan Ltd. Macmillan® is a registered trademark in the United States, United Kingdom and other countries. Palgrave is a registered trademark in the European Union and other countries.

ISBN 1–4039–3469–X

This book is printed on paper suitable for recycling and made from fully managed and sustained forest sources.

A catalogue record for this book is available from the British Library.

Library of Congress Cataloging-in-Publication Data

Hagenstein, Frank
Investing in corporate bonds and credit risk / Frank Hagenstein, Alexander Mertz, and Jan Seifert.
p. cm.—(Finance & capital market series)
Includes bibliographical references and index.
ISBN 1–4039–3469–X (alk. paper)
1. Bonds. 2. Investments. 3. Credit—Management. 4. Risk management. I. Mertz, Alexander, 1973– II. Seifert, Jan, 1971– III. Title. IV. Finance and capital markets series

HG4651.H23 2004
332.63'234—dc22 2004048937

10 9 8 7 6 5 4 3 2 1
13 12 11 10 09 08 07 06 05 04

Printed and bound in Great Britain by
Antony Rowe Ltd, Chippenham and Eastbourne.

Contents

List of Tables

List of Figures

Preface

This book covers various topics related to credit risks. The last couple of years was driven by a volatile and changing world of corporate bonds. Strategic asset allocation for corporate bonds in general and the use of quantitative techniques (in particular) has become more and more important. Therefore credit managers have to use structured credit products and derivatives for positioning and hedging.

Looking forward the challenge for being successful in managing credit portfolios will be a split between top-down and bottom-up analysis. A permanent overlay of risk management tools is needed for generating an attractive risk-adjusted performance.

Special thanks are due to Viktor Hjort (Credit Strategist from Morgan Stanley) for his input in Chapter 7.

Thanks are also due to colleagues at Union Investment: Anja Mikus (MD of Fixed Income Portfolio Management) and Martin Marinov (Macro Strategist) for their helpful comments in Chapter 3 and Peter Varga (Credit Fund Manager) for his input on convertibles in Chapter 5. We gratefully acknowledge significant support by Thomas Bossert (MD of institutional portfolio management) who provided us with the description of an asymmetric risk management for corporate bond portfolios in Chapter 11.

Finally we are very grateful to Matt King (Head of European Quantitative Credit Strategy) from Citigroup for the foreword and his careful pre-reading of various chapters.

Foreword

Investing successfully in credit represents a considerable challenge. Over the past few years, the asset class has grown enormously. So too has the range of derivative instruments and modelling techniques which ought to aid portfolio management. Yet coping with the day-to-day realities of portfolio management – the fear that another undetected accounting scandal might undermine a whole year's returns, the difficulty of making up for losses with gains elsewhere, the illiquidity of the asset class – remains as difficult as ever. Somehow much of the literature on credit portfolio management remains too academic to be easily applicable in practice.

In this book, Hagenstein, Mertz and Seifert steer a careful path between the best of theory and practice. Drawing upon years of buy-side experience of running corporate bond portfolios in both high grade and high yield, and illustrating with numerous examples, they provide a practical guide to successful portfolio management in cash, and to the workings of the myriad of derivative instruments (single name and tranched) now widespread in the market.

I have personally not seen any single volume elsewhere which provides such a comprehensive guide to successful investing in credit.

Matt King
Director, Head of European Quantitative Credit Strategy
Citigroup Global Markets Limited

CHAPTER 1

Introduction

1.1 BACKGROUND

In the last ten years the investment world has changed dramatically. The equity bubble of the second half of the 1990s that created so many millionaires was financed by corporate credit. New technologies, mergers and acquisitions and share buyback programs were financed primarily by the issuance of corporate bonds. As a consequence the market value of the European corporate bond market quadrupled between the end of 1996 and April 2003. Now, after the equity bubble has burst, investors are looking for alternatives. Because of their spread over government bonds corporate bonds provide an attractive yield in the current low-interest rate environment. But the consequences of the excesses of the 1990s have weighed heavily on the market. The confluence of the bursting of the equity bubble and the 2000/2001 recession that was caused by overinvestment led to exceptionally high default rates. Balance sheet irregularities and corporate malfeasance as in the cases of Enron, Worldcom and Ahold have caused excessive volatility and have made issuer selection, in this period, the key in the investment process.

Therefore the demand for protection has increased rapidly. The credit derivatives market has benefited from this need. It has promoted the efficiency of corporate financing by bringing together the two sources of external financing: the corporate bond market and the market for bank loans. Credit default swaps (CDS) provide the opportunity to trade and evaluate credit risk in an isolated manner. They also make it possible to create short positions in the credit markets by buying protection without owning the underlying. The success of the market for collateralized debt obligations (CDO) is closely tied to the popularity of credit derivatives. Often CDS serve as the collateral for a CDO. The valuation of synthetic credit derivatives requires not only an assessment of the fundamental situation of each company, but also a thorough understanding of the default correlations of the constituents in the basket. Because of its relatively low correlation with other asset classes CDOs have gained more and more popularity especially among the institutional investor base.

With the increasing volume and liquidity of the credit market new players have entered into the arena. Hedge funds and speculators look for arbitrage opportunities between the different capital market instruments of one issuer. Mispricings and other market inefficiencies seem to be decreasing. These developments require a sound understanding of the market dynamics and the market drivers. Traditionally, credit investors have made money through a simple buy-and-hold strategy. In the low default rate environment of the early- and mid-1990s they earned the carry of the bonds they invested in by avoiding the few names that blew up. But this strategy only works fine when default rates are low and credit spreads are declining. The harsh market environment stretching from 1997 to autumn 2002 was characterized by increasing leverage across most companies and sectors, widening credit spreads and finally soaring default rates. Clearly, in this period earning carry was not enough.

In the meantime investors have understood that the risk/return profile of credit instruments is asymmetric. Whereas the return potential is somewhat limited there is a small probability of realizing a significant loss in the case of a default of the company that was invested in. Therefore detailed analyses of the macroeconomic environment, industry trends and fundamental company data are required to support an active, disciplined investment process. Qualitative and quantitative analyses complement each other to form a comprehensive picture. Despite the vast variety of information sources, the validation and weighting of the different pieces of information lies in the hands of the portfolio manager. Nevertheless, cases of fraud show that even the best analyses sometimes cannot protect investors from incurring losses. Professional investors minimize this risk by diversifying their portfolios broadly. The years 2000–02 have shown that disciplined realtime risk management should be an integral part of any structured investment process for credits. The evolution of the credit derivatives market boosts the efficiency and the growth of the corporate bond market as a whole. But as a consequence, deviations from fair value will become fewer and shorter, meaning that the struggle for outperformance versus benchmark indices or peer groups will become more demanding. The structured investment process presented in this book hopefully will provide the tools to generate consistently advantageous risk/return profiles for credit portfolios over the medium to longer term.

1.2 ORGANIZATION OF THE BOOK

In the course of Chapter 2 we will provide an overview of the whole investment process that will be developed in this book. We will also spend some time on two basic concepts of every active management process. First, the concept of diversification will be redefined to include three dimensions, then the fundamental law of active management will be introduced. Since every step of the investment process can be supported by quantitative as well as qualitative analyses, the merits and pitfalls of each research concept will be discussed at this early stage of the book.

Chapters 3–5 focus on the three basic pillars of a structured investment process for credits:

- the research process of the strategic asset allocation is top-down driven. It results in recommendations for the portfolio beta, that is the aggressiveness of the portfolio versus the benchmark index, and in the case of mixed portfolios or pure government portfolios, the weighting of corporate bonds.
- the selection of the sectors and spread classes are the main tasks of the tactical asset allocation. In this step the research process combines top-down and bottom-up elements.
- issuer and issue selection are the last steps of the investment process. They are based on fundamental analyses and relative value considerations.

When the investment universe is extended to include asset classes that are not comprised in the benchmark, large opportunities for outperformance arise. However, the peculiarities of the high-yield market, the natural extension of the investment universe for investment grade investors, require a slightly modified investment process. Therefore the particular focus of Chapter 6 is on bond covenants, an issue that is of minor relevance in the investment grade universe. The popularity of credit derivatives has grown immensely during the last five years. They are not only efficient tools for hedging credit risk, but also a possible source of outperformance. CDS and CDOs form a major part of Chapter 7. Chapter 8 presents a brief introduction to the most popular credit benchmarks as well as exchange traded funds (ETF) that track credit indices. Keep in mind that the first step to outperformance is a profound knowledge of the benchmark.

Chapter 9 deals with the role of ratings in the investment process. Questions like 'Are ratings the best indicator for credit quality?' or 'What influence do changes of the rating outlook have on credit spreads?' are discussed.

Portfolio optimization in a Markowitz framework is a basic feature of many investment processes. Chapter 10 introduces two alternative approaches that account for the asymmetric risk profile of corporate bonds. Skewness and leptokurtosis are typical characteristics of time series of credit returns. Nontrading and nonsynchronous trading in less liquid segments of the credit universe, for example, the high-yield sector, distort conventional estimates of volatility. Therefore, the weights of illiquid sectors that are obtained by most optimization approaches are significantly too high. We will provide a desmoothing algorithm that deals with this problem. The results of a backtesting indicate that our alternative frameworks deliver portfolios with a more favorable risk/return profile than those obtained by Markowitz optimization.

In a low-return environment and with the equity meltdown still in mind, total return concepts have gained dramatically in importance. There is virtually no investment company that does not try to offer a proprietary total or absolute return product. Credit as a whole is an interesting asset class for total return managers, because well-diversified portfolios exhibit astonishingly low volatility compared to government bonds of the same average maturity, for example. Usually in economic downturns, credit spreads widen and government yields decline. In upturns, investors reward better fundamentals on the company level with lower spreads, while at the same time government yields are mostly on the increase. The relatively young market for credit derivatives, too, provides a playfield for total return investors because it offers several products that show low correlations with traditional asset classes. Chapter 11 discusses some total return concepts that are based on credit.

Risk management is relevant for all kinds of credit investing. In the last chapter we will define the demands for a sophisticated risk management tool for credit portfolios and discuss the assumptions underlying two alternative concepts. Although ex ante risk models help to identify sources of risk, they do not protect investors from losses through single issuer credit events. Therefore sufficient diversification is essential for the management of credit portfolios. In the portfolio context dependency of default plays a major role, especially with respect to absolute return products like CDOs.

1.3 SETTING FOR CREDIT MANAGEMENT

The focus of this book is on the investment process for credit portfolios and the different aspects of its practical implementation by portfolio managers. But usually when the portfolio manager enters the arena, his playfield is already prepared. The definition of investment idea, performance goal and benchmark selection are carried out before the launch of the portfolio. Because those decisions heavily impact the degrees of freedom of the portfolio manager, he should attempt to get involved in the product development. The decisions made in this phase are usually irreversible. So to a certain degree the success of the product from a marketing as well as a performance perspective is essentially determined without direct participation of the portfolio manager.

Especially, the choice of the investment universe and the benchmark have a material impact on the risk-return characteristics of a credit portfolio. From a portfolio manager's point of view, the other important points are

- investment goal
- investment horizon
- risk tolerance or risk budget and
- restrictions.

Who defines the investment goal, depends on whether the portfolio is managed on behalf of private or institutional investors. If the product is targeted at private investors the definition of the investment goal and universe are usually chosen to suit a broad class of investors. Institutional portfolios are more focused and therefore often are exposed to a lot of restrictions. Whereas rating triggers apply to mutual funds as well as to specialized funds, upper limits for the weighting of financial issuers would be an example for a specialized fund.

The issue of benchmark selection will be tackled in detail in Chapter 8. Hence, in this context we can concentrate on the consequences of benchmark selection during the process of product development. In the past, narrow liquid benchmark indices normally outperformed the broad market during credit rallies. In times of financial distress the opposite was true. So the use of large cap indices as a benchmark tends to result in a more volatile portfolio performance. This is due to the lower diversification, higher liquidity and better replicability of large cap indices.

CHAPTER 2

Investment Process

2.1 BASIC STRUCTURE OF AN INVESTMENT PROCESS FOR CREDIT PORTFOLIOS

This chapter introduces a structured investment process for credit portfolios as seen in Figure 2.1. It comprises three central pillars that will be discussed in great detail in Chapters 3–5. In Chapter 3 we will start with the assessment of the global environment for credits. Generally, the analysis of macroeconomic factors like GDP growth, central bank policies as well as the level, trend and migration velocity of default rates, to name only some of the most important variables, supports the decision about the weighting and structure of corporate bonds in mixed portfolios or the aggressiveness of a pure corporate bond portfolio. Market drivers like swap spreads, the correlation with equity-market performance and volatility and the shape of the yield curve, and last but not least, technical factors like flows of funds and corporate bond issuance also help to derive the strategic asset allocation. Comparisons are drawn relative to other asset classes and relative to the historical performance of corporate bonds in a similar market environment. In the context of pure corporate bond portfolios the portfolio beta or the aggressiveness of the portfolio relative to its benchmark is determined. For mixed portfolios or even portfolios with government benchmarks, additionally, the weighting of corporate bonds is fixed.

The selection of industries and spread classes is based on top-down as well as bottom-up criteria. The questions that have to be answered at this stage are: Do high spread assets, for example, look cheap or rich relative to less risky investments? Which sectors or industries offer the most value for a certain time horizon? Empirical studies show that there are two main drivers that influence the level of spreads: credit quality and maturity. Therefore the investment universe should be divided in buckets by a spread and a maturity factor. It should be noted that in our investment

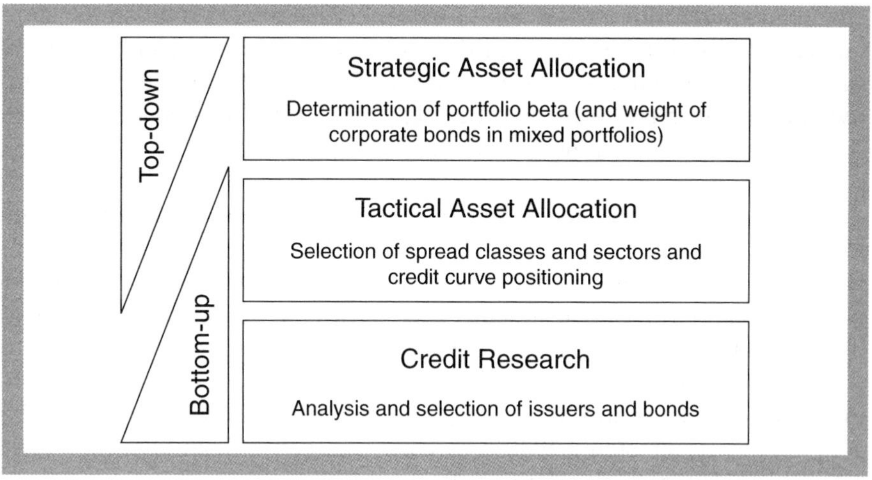

Figure 2.1 Structured investment process for the management of credit portfolios

Source: Union Investment

process spread classes, or in other words risk classes, take the role of ratings. In our view spread and spread volatility are realtime indicators for credit quality, whereas ratings tend to lag changes in company fundamentals. Nevertheless, ratings play a role, because usually constraints in the investment policy are closely linked to ratings. A typical example is that many mutual funds are not allowed to invest in speculative grade issues. In the case of a downgrade below BBB-/Baa3 they might become forced sellers. The partial change in the investor base creates high volatility for fallen angels and rising stars, resulting in investment opportunities, but also a lot of downside risk.

Traditionally credit investors have put a strong emphasis on fundamental analyses of the issuers. Consequently, the company selection is based to a large extent on the bottom-up approach. The fundamental analysis incorporates information from the cash flow and income statement, balance sheet and financial ratio analysis, business strategy, competitive environment and management quality. The fundamental analysis on the company level has to be accompanied by relative value analyses, that is by comparing a company's credit spreads versus its peer group and historical spreads. In 2001 and 2002 equity-based models for the valuation of corporate bonds gained tremendous popularity. Reasons for this were the high correlation between equity-market performance and implied volatility of equity options on the one hand, and corporate bond spreads, on the other hand. During this period, the strong relationship held almost across all sectors and issuers. While the analysis of balance sheet data and evaluation of management skills requires a profound knowledge of the company, its competitors and industry trends, structural models rely solely on a mathematical relationship between equities and corporate bonds. Hence, they are easy usable tools that can save a lot of time. But in our discussion of qualitative and quantitative research processes at the end of this chapter we will show that equity-based models work only in particular stages of the credit cycle.

Any corporate bond team has to divide its human resources between top-down and bottom-up research. The strengths and weaknesses of the sector specialists and the fact that performance can be measured against a corporate benchmark, a government benchmark or a mixed benchmark will determine the appropriate mix. If the performance is measured against a government benchmark the top-down approach will be assigned more importance because, in the first step, a global picture for credits has to be assessed. It can be stated that even corporate bonds with weak financial ratios and balance sheets relative to their peer group can add dramatically to the performance of a portfolio if, for example, the economy is in a growth period (positive credit environment). A fund with a corporate benchmark should allocate a large part of the fixed-income department to the bottom-up-driven process of industry and company selection. On the other hand, one has to consider that the addition of a few corporate bonds in a fund with a government benchmark can cause a high tracking error versus the peer group and the benchmark whereas the chances for an underperformance remain significant because of lack of diversification. Instead, corporate bond funds should be considered as a suitable admixture for funds with a government benchmark. The accompanying risk of the fund performance versus the benchmark has to be evaluated by the fund management.

Especially when corporate bonds are included in portfolios with a government benchmark, risk management plays a major role in the investment process. The failure of ex ante apparently safe companies like Worldcom or Swissair provided a painful lesson for many investors. The particularity of corporate bonds lies in the asymmetric risk/return profile. A high probability to achieve a relatively small outperformance versus riskless instruments is contrasted by a small likelihood of incurring substantial losses. Because of the limited return potential of corporate bonds a sophisticated approach to managing downside risk is highly recommended. Only if capital losses are minimized the potential benefits of corporate bonds can unfold. Sufficient diversification on the sector and issuer level therefore is one key to success in corporate bond portfolio management. Combining various sources of information, for example top-down and bottom-up analyses or qualitative and quantitative methods, provide a comprehensive overview of the risks and opportunities of certain investment ideas. This increases the likelihood to create a consistently advantageous risk/return profile. Hence, careful analysis is not only one of the pillars of a state-of-the-art investment process for corporate bonds, but implicitly a first step towards risk management.

2.2 DIVERSIFICATION OF IDEAS

The performance of most portfolio managers is measured against a benchmark index. Active management exposes investors to beta, which is defined as portfolio volatility relative to the market, and to alpha, the value added by the portfolio manager's luck or skill. Sharpe (1991) observes that the market as a whole is made up of all market participants, and therefore the average return of all participants equals the return of market, before fees and costs. After fees and costs, however, the average return of all market participants is below market return. Consequently, to beat the market consistently, investors need to have special skills. Interestingly, if one asks market participants what active return they expect to earn, 90 percent of them say they expect an excess return of 1–1.5 percent. Obviously, this contradicts conventional wisdom.

A good starting point for the analysis of active management concepts is the Evans–Archer diagram depicted below. As portfolios become more diversified portfolio risk declines until it asymptotically reaches a level that is known as undiversifiable, systematic or market risk. Portfolios are usually managed against fully diversified benchmark indices that are designed to reflect market performance and market risk as good as possible. In other words, the performance of broadly diversified benchmark indices represents the reward to market risk.

The component above the horizontal line in Figure 2.2 is usually known as idiosyncratic, unsystematic or diversifiable risk. In this context we use

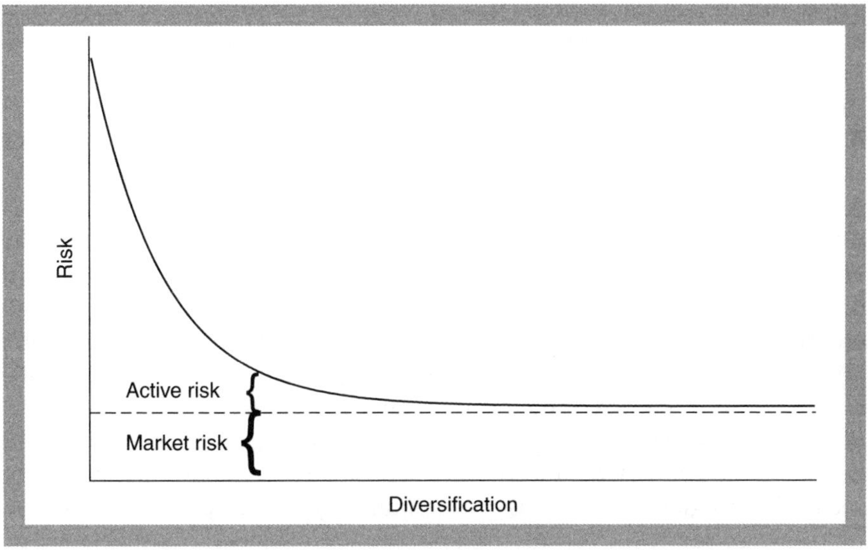

Figure 2.2 Evans–Archer diagram of risk versus diversification
Source: Union Investment

the term active risk because it is the risk of an active manager who deviates from the benchmark in order to beat the market. Establishing the right portfolio structure requires skill or the portfolio will underperform the benchmark. Active risk therefore means accepting a certain amount of idiosyncratic risk over and above market risk in order to add value through active management. However, as idiosyncratic risk is diversifiable, it is usually not rewarded, except from luck. Consequently the unconditional expected return of taking on active risk is zero. If a portfolio manager has special skill in active management, his conditional expected return, however, is proportional to skill and hence positive.

Grinold (1989) introduced an interesting concept that relates the excess return generated by the portfolio manager to the risk he incurs relative to the benchmark. In this framework the manager's opportunities can be described by the ex ante information ratio IR, defined as the ratio of expected active return divided by active risk, that is

$$\mathrm{IR} = \frac{E(R_\mathrm{A})}{\sigma_\mathrm{A}},$$

where R_A denotes active return and σ_A denotes active risk. If the benchmark is the riskfree rate, the ratio is identical to the Sharpe ratio. The original form of the "Fundamental Law of Active Management" suggests that

$$\mathrm{IR} = \mathrm{IC}\sqrt{N}.$$

Consequently, the information ratio depends on the information coefficient IC and the number of independent decisions in the actively managed portfolio. The information coefficient IC is defined as the correlation of the forecasts with the actual outcomes. Combining both formulas, the fundamental law reads

$$E(R_\mathrm{A}) = \mathrm{IC}\sqrt{N}\sigma_\mathrm{A}.$$

The expected active return consequently depends on skill, breadth and the amount of risk that is taken by the portfolio manager. Grinold (1989) and Thomas (2000) highlight the approximate nature of the fundamental law and recommend its use as a strategic tool. The lesson from the fundamental law is that the value added by active management is determined by the quality of the decisions of the portfolio manager as well as the diversification of investment ideas. The law therefore encourages managers to exploit independent sources of information whenever available. Whereas very focused strategies often are easy to explain they may lead to a high volatility of excess returns. Diversifying not only with respect to asset classes or sectors, but also with regard to risk factors and sources of information is likely to produce consistently favorable risk/return profiles, especially over the medium to longer term.

Assuming that a portfolio manager acts in a way that is mean-variance efficient the value added, VA, is proportional to the information ratio squared. Expressed in terms of skill and breadth the portfolio manager's ability to add value is

$$\text{VA} = \frac{\text{IC}^2 \cdot N}{4\lambda_R},$$

where λ_R represents the level of risk aversion. Consequently, to double his information ratio or the value added for a given level of active risk, the portfolio manager must double his skill, or quadruple the number of independent bets in the portfolio. Figures 2.3 and 2.4 illustrate this relationship. The more independent decisions are made the lower is the skill required to achieve a target information ratio. If the number of independent trade ideas is very low, for instance because the portfolio manager chooses to implement only strategic duration bets, a high level of skill is required to generate a favorable risk-adjusted return. Clarke, de Silva and Thorley (2002) point out that portfolio managers often face constraints that reduce the degree to which trade signals are transferred into active weights. Typical constraints for real-money investors would include "no short sales" and maximum leverage restrictions. In practice, the observed transfer coefficients lie between 0.3 and 0.8. If the transfer coefficient is 0.5 only 25 percent of the variation in realized excess return, that is, tracking error, is attributable to

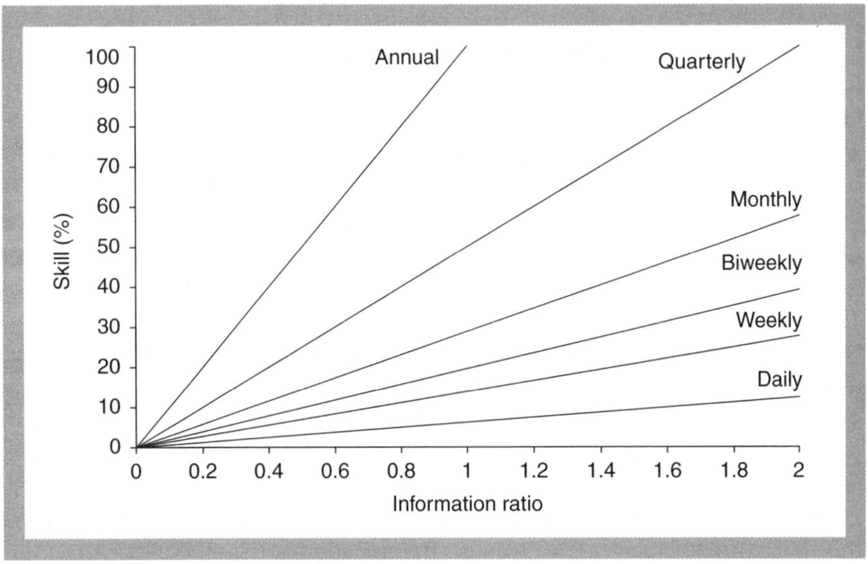

Figure 2.3 Skill required to achieve a certain information ratio depends on the frequency of the implementation of independent trades

Source: J.P. Morgan

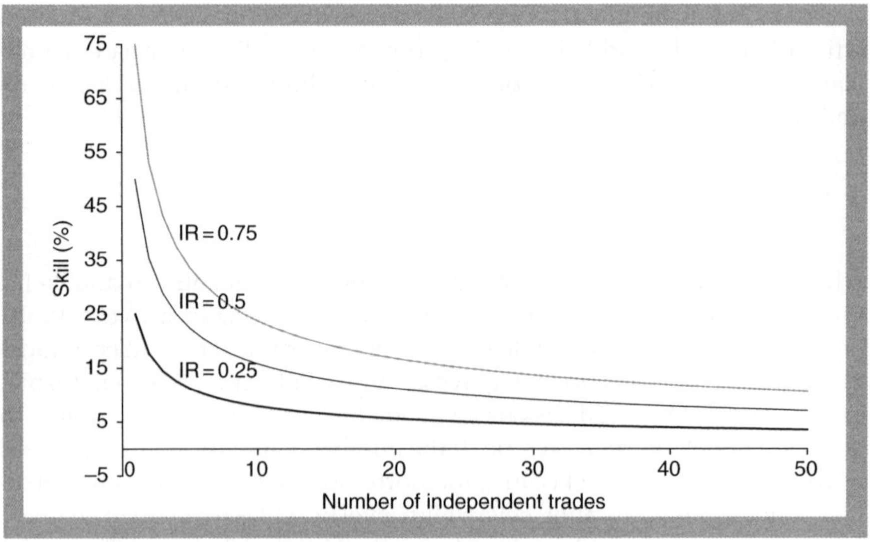

Figure 2.4 A given information ratio is achieved by various combinations of skill and breadth

Source: J.P. Morgan

the success of the signal. The remaining 75 percent are due to constraint-induced noise. The success rates, or skill levels, that are required to achieve a certain information ratio is therefore the higher, the more restrictions exist. Managers with substantial constraints will experience frequent periods where the investment ideas are successful, but performance is poor. Conversely, there will also be periods when performance is good although the quality of return forecasts is poor. Portfolio managers who may only take long positions, for example, government bond managers who are allowed to diversify into corporate bonds temporarily, face a particularly disadvantageous situation, because the number of potential trades is limited. Thus, the required success rate is significantly higher than the one of an investor with an aggregate benchmark who is able to benefit from overweight as well as underweight positions.

In practice, it often proves difficult to assign an accurate level of skill to a certain portfolio manager as well as to estimate correctly the number of independent trade ideas. Nevertheless, before launching a major research project, improving the technical infrastructure or optimizing internal processes to increase skill, a quick calculation of this sort may be valuable, considering the costs and the uncertainty of success related to these measures. From a cost and a portfolio management perspective, broadening the spectrum of investment ideas is often more promising.

Traditionally, credit investors have primarily diversified investments within an asset class. The fundamental law of active management suggests that this is not enough. Trade ideas on the issuer level should be complemented by sector and, if permitted, asset allocation bets. Diversifying into risky asset classes like high yield, for example, may not necessarily increase portfolio volatility if correlations with the core portfolio are low enough. In addition, active management of duration, yield and credit curve positioning and currency risk can add value. Finally, a combination of various sources of information helps to generate a variety of independent trade ideas. Remember that the frequency of deviating from the benchmark has substantial impact on the expected information ratio and excess return.

2.3 QUANTITATIVE ANALYSES

The bear market for credit between 1997 and mid-2002 has put a new focus on valuing corporate credit. The debt-financed equity bull market of the second half of the 1990s was accompanied by historically high default rates and investigations of the management and reporting of corporate balance sheets. Obviously the standard approach of using rating agency credit ratings to gauge credit risk is no longer sufficient. As a consequence, quantitative approaches have recently gained popularity, particularly structural models based on equity-market inputs. Quantitative models can be used as a tool to provide warning signals or to determine whether the spread on a corporate bond adequately compensates the investor for the risk. Due to the current low-yield/low-return environment the number of investors interested in credit products has grown worldwide. Credit models like KMV or CreditGrades have been developed to meet the growing investor demand. These enhancements of the Merton model are able to incorporate company-specific details and can include subjective credit analyst views. With respect to the rapidly expanding credit derivatives market, quantitative models provide critical inputs for valuation and hedging. Default correlation, a major driver for the valuation of credit portfolio products, can be modeled in both structural and reduced form models. Finally, quantitative credit models have become indispensable tools for the risk management of financial institutions. Although various quantitative models are used by credit investors, two approaches for modeling default have gained widespread acceptance: structural models and reduced-form models. Both of these methods provide estimates of default probabilities or fair market spreads.

The traditional fundamental approach and structural models generally are based on the same set of balance sheet inputs. But while the fundamental approach used by most credit analysts requires thorough company and industry knowledge and is therefore rather costly and time-consuming, equity-based models are an efficient means to screen broad universes of credit issuers. However, structural models allow to incorporate credit analysts' forecasts to take account of qualitative information that is not yet reflected in the balance sheet. Projections can be used to create more realistic estimates of the default threshold or to generate different scenarios with respect to future liabilities.

2.3.1 Structural models

In the structural approach, assets and liabilities of a company are modeled simultaneously. Thus, structural models are based on fundamental company data, focusing on its balance sheet and asset value. Default occurs when the value of the firm's assets falls below its liabilities. Consequently, the required inputs comprise the firm's liabilities, usually taken from its balance sheet, market value of equity and (implied) equity volatility. Since equities are typically more liquid than corporate bonds, one may argue that equity prices tend to reflect the value of a company's assets more accurately. Using information from the equity markets allows fixed income instruments to be priced independently, without requiring credit spread information from related fixed income instruments. However, if equity prices become irrationally inflated or deflated, as we have experienced during the equity hype of the late 1990s, they may be misleading indicators of actual asset values. Generally it is assumed that one can reasonably infer asset values from equity prices. An option pricing model is then used to derive the volatility of the firm's assets. Although it is generally possible to model financial institutions in the structural framework they should be treated with caution, since it is difficult to assess their assets and liabilities. Furthermore, since financial institutions are highly regulated, default may not occur even if the value of assets falls below the firm's liabilities.

The Black–Scholes (1973) option pricing model and Merton's work on the pricing of corporate debt (1974) lay the foundations for the structural model. Merton's model establishes a relationship between the market value of a firm's assets and the market value of its equity. Consider a firm whose operations are financed exclusively by a zero coupon bond maturing at time T with a face value of X, and equity. Denote the market value of the firm's assets at time T by $V_\alpha(T)$. Then the company pays off its liabilities in full, if the market value of its assets exceeds the face value of the zero coupon bond, that is $V_\alpha(T) \geq X$. In this case, the shareholder's value is

Table 2.1 Stylized balance sheet

Assets	Liabilities
Assets	Debt
	Equity

Source: Union Investment

$V_\alpha(T) - X$. Conversely, if the value of the firm's assets is lower than the face value of debt, $V_\alpha(T) < X$, the company cannot repay its liabilities in full and defaults. The creditors take over the firm and the equity becomes worthless. Figure 2.5 shows the pay-off profiles for debt- and equity holders at maturity of the liabilities.

Thus, the zero coupon bond is equivalent to a long position in a risk-free zero coupon bond and a short put on the assets of the company. Similarly, equity may be considered as a call option on the assets of the firm. The strike price of both options equals the face value of debt. Using the Black–Scholes option pricing model we are able to derive the market value and the volatility of the firm's assets. According to Black–Scholes the market value of equity, V_ε, and the market value of assets are related by

$$V_\varepsilon = V_\alpha N(d_1) + e^{-rT} X N(d_2)$$

with

$$d_1 = \frac{\ln (V_\alpha / X) + (r + (\sigma_\alpha^2/2))T}{\sigma_\alpha \sqrt{T}}$$

and

$$d_2 = d_1 - \sigma_\alpha \sqrt{T},$$

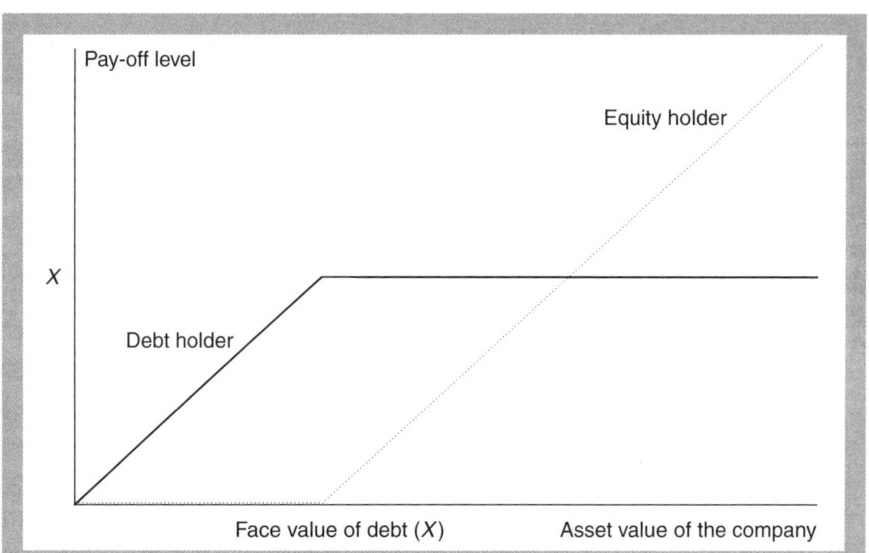

Figure 2.5 Pay-off patterns for debt- and equity holders at maturity of the liabilities

Source: Union Investment

where σ_α denotes asset volatility, r is the risk-free rate, and $N(\cdot)$ is the normal distribution. For equity volatility the condition

$$\sigma_\varepsilon = \frac{V_\alpha}{V_\varepsilon} N(d_1)\sigma_\alpha$$

holds. Simple balance sheet theory suggests that $V_\alpha = D + V_\varepsilon$, where D represents the market value of debt. Consequently, if asset value is known, the market value of debt can be inferred easily. Since the face value of debt and its maturity are known, too, we can now determine the yield of the zero coupon bond and its spread over the risk-free rate. However, it should be noted that the original Merton model tends to underestimate short-term spreads because of the assumption that asset value follows a continuous lognormal process. Using this assumption the probability of falling below the default threshold in a short period of time is usually very low. Therefore, commercial models make adjustments in order to model short-term spreads more accurately.

To estimate the probability that the market value of assets will be lower than the face value of debt, we need to make an assumption about the behavior of the firm's asset value. Black and Scholes posit that the market value of the firm's asset follows a stochastic process:

$$dV_\alpha = \mu V_\alpha \, dt + \sigma_\alpha V_\alpha \, dZ,$$

where μ denotes the drift of the market value of assets, and dz represents a Wiener process. Using η to denote the random component of the firm's return at time t we obtain

$$\ln V_\alpha^t = \ln V_\alpha + \left(\mu - \frac{\sigma_\alpha^2}{2}\right)t + \sigma_\alpha \sqrt{t}\eta.$$

The probability of default is then described by the expression

$$P\left[\ln V_\alpha + \left(\mu - \frac{\sigma_\alpha^2}{2}\right)t + \sigma_\alpha \sqrt{t}\eta \leq \ln X_t\right]$$

$$= P\left[-\frac{\ln (V_\alpha/X_t) + (\mu - (\sigma_\alpha^2/2))t}{\sigma_\alpha \sqrt{t}} \geq \eta\right],$$

where

$$\frac{\ln (V_\alpha/X_t) + (\mu - (\sigma_\alpha^2/2))t}{\sigma_\alpha \sqrt{t}}$$

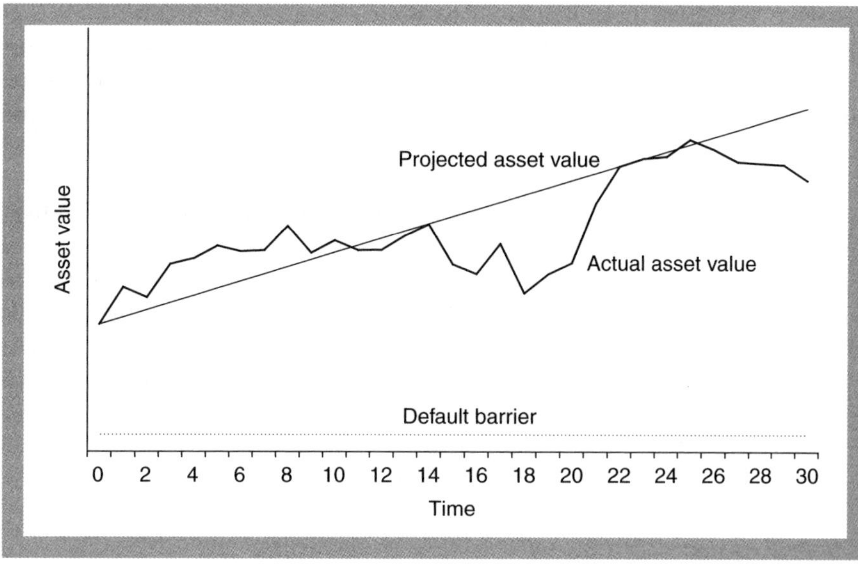

Figure 2.6 Projected and realized asset value in the Merton model

Source: Union Investment

represents the number of standard deviations that asset value is separated from the default barrier (see Figure 2.6). KMV calls this expression "distance to default". In the Black–Scholes–Merton framework the expression above is equivalent to d_2. Consequently, the risk neutral probability of default is $N(-d_2)$. It is also possible to compute the expected recovery rate under the risk-neutral measure. Conditional on the default of the company, debtholders may expect to recover an asset value of

$$V_\alpha \frac{N(-d_1)}{N(-d_2)}.$$

As we have pointed out for short-term spreads expected recovery value may be too high for short-term liabilities due to the assumptions of the model. Commercial implementations of the original structural model are more sophisticated, in order to produce more accurate spreads, default probabilities and recovery rates even for short time horizons. While in pure diffusion models with a barrier overnight debt is quasi-riskless, the introduction of a jump process captures the fact that default could be triggered by a sudden, unexpected event. Thus, the jump process is appropriate to model the possibility of the firm defaulting instantaneously due to the arrival of negative information with respect to, for example, litigation or fraud.

Additional features of commercial applications include, for example, time-varying default barriers, continuous monitoring of the default threshold, the use of alternative option pricing models and different assumptions for the behavior of asset values. They typically incorporate short-term and long-term liabilities, convertible debt, preferred equity and common equity, although this substantially enhances complexity of the model. Hence, structural models are well suited for handling different securities of the same issuer, including bonds of various seniorities and convertible bonds. Even the behavior of the company's management can be incorporated into a structural model. A typical example is a "target leverage" model, in which the initial capital structure can be adjusted. The level of debt fluctuates over time depending on changes in the firm's value, so that the ratio of debt to assets is mean-reverting. Nevertheless, it is hard to model a firm that is close to its default threshold, since management often chooses to adjust the capital structure in this situation. Over one-year horizons, however, commercial implementations of structural models have a consistently good track record with respect to the prediction of defaults.

2.3.2 Reduced-form models

The second kind of models that we want to highlight is "reduced-form models." Unlike structural models, they are based on information from the credit market, such as asset swap spreads or credit default swap spreads. Thus they are capable of capturing valuable information regarding the probability of default that is contained in bond and credit default swap markets. This is particularly helpful when insufficient or no balance sheet data is available. In the reduced-form framework, default is modeled as a surprise event. Rather than modeling the value of a firm's assets, here the probability of default is derived directly from market data. The interested reader may note that this approach is similar to the way interest rates are modeled in order to price fixed income derivatives.

The reduced-form approach aims to model the hazard rate, $h(t)$, which is equivalent to a forward probability of default. The hazard rate reflects the marginal probability of default over the next small time interval, given that the company has survived until time t. Denoting with τ the time to default, the hazard rate is defined as

$$h(t) = \frac{P(\tau \leq t + \Delta t | \tau > t)}{\Delta t}.$$

Hazard rates can be inferred from current default swap spreads or asset swap spreads and therefore reflect the current estimate of market participants for the default probability of an issuer. Although the hazard rate represents an instantaneous measure for the forward probability of default, the probability of default over any time horizon can be derived. If one assumes a constant hazard rate, the probability of an issuer defaulting in the next t years is

$$1 - e^{-ht}.$$

Figure 2.7 illustrates the path of cumulative default probability for a hazard rate of 4 percent. The probability of the company defaulting in the next 5 years, for example, is $1 - e^{-0.04 \times 5} = 18.12$ percent.

One can show that under the assumption of a constant hazard rate, the premium of a credit default swap approximately equals

$$h \cdot [1 - E(RR)],$$

where $E(RR)$ denotes the expected recovery rate. If the expected recovery rate is 30 percent and the credit default swap trades at a premium of 280 bp, the market participants expected hazard rate is implicitly, $h = 2.8$ percent/ $(1 - 0.30) = 4$ percent.

To demonstrate the basic functionality of reduced-form models we have assumed that hazard rates are constant. Practical implementations, however, attempt to model hazard rates. Historical experience shows that market-implied default rates typically overestimate default probability.

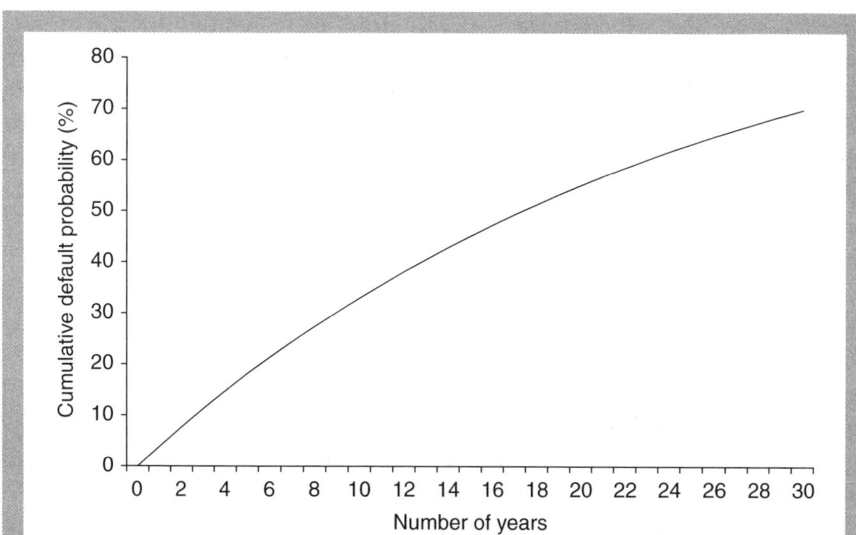

Figure 2.7 Cumulative default probability assuming a hazard rate of 4 percent

Source: Union Investment

Various reduced-form models try to mitigate this problem by incorporating jumps that occur at random times. Typically, hazard rates are calibrated to a term structure of credit default swap spreads or asset swap spreads. The model easily allows to generate correlated hazard rates, which lead to correlated defaults. Although reduced-form models are sensitive to assumptions with respect to the correlations between hazard rates, they are a convenient tool for running simulations to value credit portfolio products. Even if hazard rates are highly correlated, default events may not necessarily be highly correlated. Hence, attention has to be paid to which particular process hazard rates are assumed to follow. Models with jumps have proven to be more reliable with regard to this problem.

2.3.3 Factor models

The third and last type of quantitative credit models that we want to mention briefly are factor models. In contrast to both the structural and reduced-form models, the factor model does not attempt to model default. Rather, linear regression is used to assess the relative richness or cheapness of individual credits. The factor model attributes current spreads of a broad universe of issues to certain common factors that should be appropriate to explain differences in credit spreads. Credit quality, for example, may be represented by a rating and a leverage factor. Debt to EBITDA ratios have proven a particularly reliable indicator for future relative spread movements. Duration and implied equity volatility of the issuer as well as a dummy variable for the sector might be further explanatory variables. The residual from the regression is taken as an indicator for the richness or cheapness of individual securities. Empirical studies show that factor models may be a valuable tool to generate relative value ideas, especially for short time horizons.

2.3.4 Conclusion

In determining if quantitative approaches may add value, and which model is best suited, both investment horizon and performance targets as well as credit-specific characteristics should be considered. We would distinguish those investors who are concerned with mark-to-market fluctuations from those who are focused on absolute return to maturity. The latter may find the long-term signals provided by credit analysts, rating agencies and quantitative models to be more relevant than market expectations that are reflected in credit spreads and implied default probabilities. In the portfolio context, quantitative tools are particularly helpful to determine the risks associated with correlated defaults. Absolute return investors enjoy more freedom to implement relative value trades than those investors that may not deviate substantially from a given benchmark index.

With respect to the analysis of a specific issuer, it is important to consider how far the market value of the firm's assets is away from its default threshold. When the value of the assets approaches the default barrier, fundamental issues such as the likelihood of capital structure changes, possible corporate actions and potential changes in the business model determine credit valuation. Generally, the value of credit analysis rises with an increasing level of leverage because the probability of default is primarily related to management options, such as the above-mentioned. Credit analysts typically do not only rely on balance sheet analysis, but rather introduce metrics like debt-to-EBITDA ratios in order to measure a company's ability to service its debt from operations. Furthermore, credit analysts' views on the probability and timing of potential capital structure changes are essential in determining valuation. If the magnitude and likelihood of a change in the capital structure is high, then it will dominate any valuation of a credit. Yet, quantitative models help to estimate the impact of capital structure changes on the valuation of a particular issuer.

The management option to alter the capital structure establishes the link between structural models and fundamental credit analysis. It may be remembered that in the Merton framework the strike price of both the call and the put option on the firm's assets changes when the capital structure of a company changes (see Figure 2.8). This is undoubtedly one of the

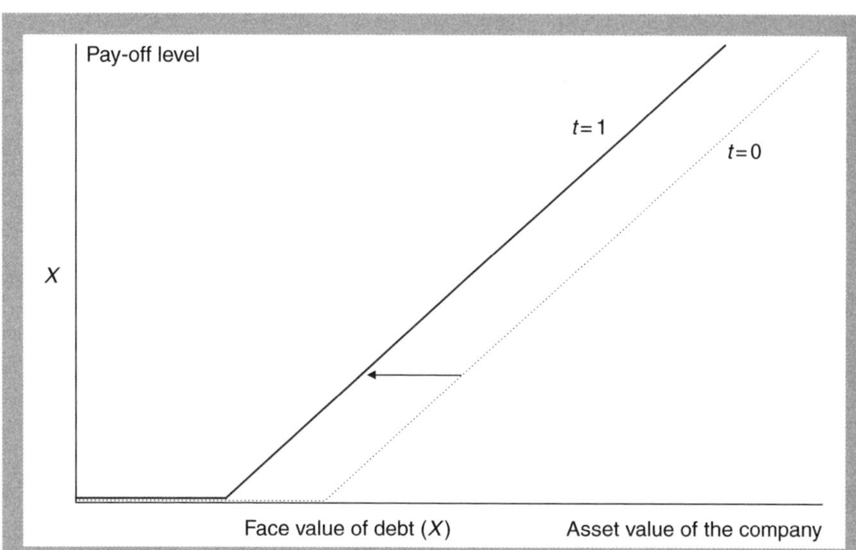

Figure 2.8 Option of the management to alter the capital structure

Source: Union Investment

strategic risks a credit analyst has to evaluate. But there are further points that potentially may have a strong impact on credit spreads, but cannot be captured by quantitative models. Pension liabilities, off-balance-sheet items and litigation risk, which have been major drivers of credit spreads recently, are typical examples. Therefore, we feel that it is most promising not to concentrate on a purely quantitative or a purely fundamental approach. Combinations of both may prove particularly insightful. Undoubtedly, none of the analyzed approaches works in every environment. But experienced and sophisticated managers will be able to select the best method for a given investment situation.

CHAPTER 3

Strategic Asset Allocation

3.1 OVERVIEW OF THE TOP-DOWN RESEARCH PROCESS

Strategic asset allocation is the first step in the investment process for credit portfolios. At this stage, all analyses are from a top-down perspective. In other words, the medium to long-term outlook for credit quality and the future direction of credit spreads is assessed on an aggregate basis, that is, for the credit market as a whole. The research process therefore focuses on three main subjects: the macroeconomic environment for credit, valuation and technical market drivers (see Figure 3.1). The weighting of these aspects, however, differs according to the market environment, the investment universe and the risk/return profile of the portfolio for which the top-down analysis is performed. Due to the increased business risk of non-investment grade companies, changes of the macroeconomic environment are particularly important for high-yield investors, whereas credit spreads

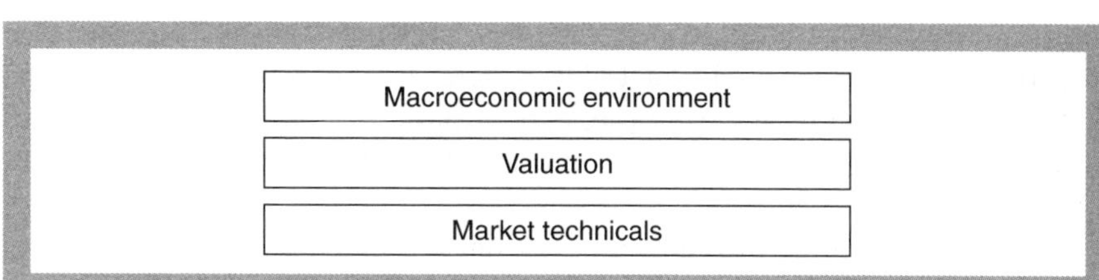

Figure 3.1 Structure of the research process of the strategic asset allocation

Source: Union Investment

in the investment grade corporate bond market are frequently influenced by technical factors like the issuance of cash bonds or CDOs. Valuation aspects with respect to past performance in similar stages of the business cycle and in relation to other asset classes tend to have a high influence for investment grade as well as for high-yield bonds.

The macroeconomic analysis of corporate bond markets typically is based on aggregate measures of growth, employment, interest rates and monetary policy. The impact of changes of these variables on corporate revenues and cash flows and thus on credit risk depends on financial and operating leverage and on the ratio of earnings or cash flows to net interest payments, that is, some measure for interest coverage.

The subject of valuation can be analyzed from various perspectives. Investors usually tend to compare current spreads with historical spreads. However, it is highly recommended to consider the stage of the credit cycle between then and now, when doing this. The results also should be adjusted for different compositions of the credit universe and a potential rating drift over time. Fundamental models for credit spreads implicitly take changes of the economic environment and consequently of the average ratings of the issuers into account. In other words, the outcome of this kind of models is a fair spread for corporate bonds with respect to the economic environment.

With the growth of the European credit market since the mid-1990s corporate bonds have gained acceptance as an own asset class. From an asset allocation perspective the focus is clearly on the relative valuation of one asset class compared to others. Beside the convenience of use and its sound theoretical foundation, this is one of the reasons for the immense popularity of equity-based models for the valuation of corporate bonds. The comparison of the risk premia of corporate bonds and equities is a similar approach to identify temporary divergences between those asset classes from a top-down perspective.

However, often market movements cannot be explained by fundamental factors or inefficiencies between markets. Market participants frequently cite changes of the risk appetite as an explanation for spread changes. Although risk appetite or risk aversion are clearly no valuation indicators, they should be considered in conjunction with the analysis of inter-market dependencies because the impact of this factor is not limited to one market. A rising risk appetite, for example, can explain widening corporate bond spreads, declining equity markets and a devaluation of emerging market currencies.

Similar to a change of risk appetite, market technicals also can lead to temporary distortions in credit markets. As with every market, prices for corporate bonds are driven by supply and demand. A substantial rise in issuance activity, or declining flows into corporate bond funds, therefore, can also cause a widening of credit spreads.

As a result of the above-mentioned research process the portfolio manager should be able to align the portfolio structure with the medium- to long-term investment goals on an ongoing basis. The primary control mechanism for pure credit portfolios is the portfolio beta, or in other words, the aggressiveness of the portfolio. Similar to the beta factor of an equity portfolio, it measures the systematic or market risk of the portfolio. Among corporate bond managers, it is common use to define the corporate portfolio beta as the degree of spread variability of the portfolio versus a broad benchmark index. If the portfolio manager decides to increase the aggressiveness of his portfolio, he might decide to add weight to cyclical, higher leverage sectors at the expense of lower beta sectors. The admixture of subordinated bonds from the financial sector, or of high-yield bonds and convertibles helps to increase the risk profile of the portfolio relative to the index, because these higher beta asset classes usually are not comprised in the benchmark.

3.2 MACROECONOMIC ENVIRONMENT

While the focus of equity markets is on growth, corporate as well as government bond markets primarily reflect the boom and bust of the economy. Especially bond markets have proven a reliable indicator for future recessions. Long-term government bond yields are driven by market participants' expectations for growth and inflation. Short-term interest rates, conversely, are closely linked to monetary policy, which in turn primarily targets price stability. At the height of an expansion there are usually concerns about rising inflationary pressures, leading central banks to tighten monetary policy. As a consequence the prospects for future economic growth falter and long-term inflation expectations fall. A strong yield curve flattening or even an inversion indicates that the economy faces a downturn. Conversely, a steep yield curve can be taken as a signal that the outlook for future growth is better than the current environment.

The performance of credit is the second bond market indicator for the state of the economy. A rise in credit spreads reflects the investors' perception that credit risk is rising. Usually this expectation is confirmed by an increasing number of insolvencies and bankruptcies. The years 1997–2000 are brilliant examples for the decoupling between credit and equity markets. Whereas equity markets boomed in expectance of high growth rates and a sustained rise in profitability, credit spreads widened because of the economy-wide rise in leverage. This example shows that credit spreads are a good indicator for the vulnerability of the economy and for risk aversion. At the risk of stating the obvious, credit spreads do not only reflect the risk of default, but also potential mark-to-market losses because of rating migration and risks associated with their lower liquidity compared to government bonds. In practice it is difficult to isolate default risk and the risk premium of corporate bonds.

According to the Merton model, credit quality deteriorates as the leverage of the firm or the volatility of the firm's assets increases. Hence, aggregate credit spreads can be modeled as a function of gearing in the corporate sector and asset volatility. Although changes of the capital structure have a substantial influence on the credit quality of an issuer, they must be considered individually on the company level. Since the ability to service debt depends on cash flow generation, some attention will be devoted on how to capture the latter at the macroeconomic level through activity variables. In order to sort out the impact of the economic cycle on credit markets, some major macroeconomic indicators will be discussed.

Since long histories are required to capture the behavior of credit spreads over several business cycles, economists usually define the credit spread as the yield differential between Moody's Baa corporate bond index and long-term treasury bond yields. Historically, the index consisted of 75–100 bonds with a minimum amount outstanding of US$100 million, an initial maturity of at least 20 years and a liquid secondary market. According to Bevan and Garzarelli (2000) there are three points that question the representativeness of this yield differential as a long-term indicator of credit risk. The first problem is known as index refreshing. It results from the fact that the index keeps the credit quality of the issuers constant, thus measuring the yield on subsequent samples of corporate bonds that satisfy the construction criteria. Since the rating of the index is held constant, the aggregate probability of default risk is broadly stable, too. Therefore, our measure for credit spreads is more an indicator of the overall appetite for lower investment grade credit risk than for default risk.

The second problem is caused by the inclusion of callable bonds in the corporate bond index. Prior to the mid-1980s, most corporations issued only callable bonds. Part of the variation in spreads, therefore is caused by a change in the price of the underlying option that the issuer holds. Declining yields imply a rise in the value of the call option that the issuer holds and hence induce a slightly negative correlation between credit spreads and treasury yields.

The last problem stems from the fact that corporate bonds and treasury bonds are taxed differently. In several parts of the United States, corporate bonds are taxed at the federal, state and local levels, while treasury bonds are only subject to taxation at the federal level. An increase in risk free rates increases the tax advantage of treasuries over corporate bonds, thus motivating investors to require a higher spread for credits. The taxation bias induces a slightly positive correlation between treasury yields and corporate bond spreads. However, the magnitude of the distortion is hard to quantify because it depends, among others, on the state income tax rate faced by the marginal investor.

3.2.1 Economy-wide indicators

3.2.1.1 Economic activity

Since 1970, the credit spread for Baa rated US corporate bonds versus treasuries varied in an extremely broad range. The tightest spread levels were reached at the end of the 1970s, but the double-dip recession in 1980 and 1981/82 led to a massive spread widening. Corporate bond spreads peaked at 400 bps, a level that was reached again after the equity bubble burst and the US economy went through a recession in 2000/2001.

In general the corporate bond spread simply reflects the risk premium that investors demand in order to invest in corporate bonds. In this respect it is similar to the equity risk premium. The corporate bond spread has to compensate investors for different kinds of risk:

- default risk,
- migration risk, and
- liquidity risk.

While liquidity risk is primarily a function of the willingness and ability of banks and brokers to provide liquidity and of investors' readiness to take on risk, in other words, risk appetite, the other two points are related to the economic environment. The companies' ability to generate sufficient cash flows to service their liabilities is central for the probability of default and is reflected in ratings. In general slowing economic growth, usually coupled with lower private consumption due to weak growth of labor income and rising unemployment undermines the profitability of the corporate sector. In this context, it is worth remembering the definition of a recession. Market participants often define recessions in terms of two consecutive quarters of decline in real GDP. The National Bureau of Economic Research (NBER) which is responsible for dating recession periods, however, claims that recessions are characterized by a significant decline in economic activity spread across the economy, lasting more than a few months, normally visible in real GDP, real income, employment, industrial production and wholesale–retail sales.

Numerous empirical studies confirm that the economic cycle is an important determinant for the performance of credit and government bond markets. They find that credit spreads are negatively correlated with GDP growth, an observation that is supported by Figure 3.2. Historically, spreads tightened during the early stages of economic expansions, and spreads widened during economic recessions. Crabbe and Fabozzi (2002) note that during the ten economic cycles since the end of the Second World War, the Baa–Aaa quality spread typically already widened in the months leading

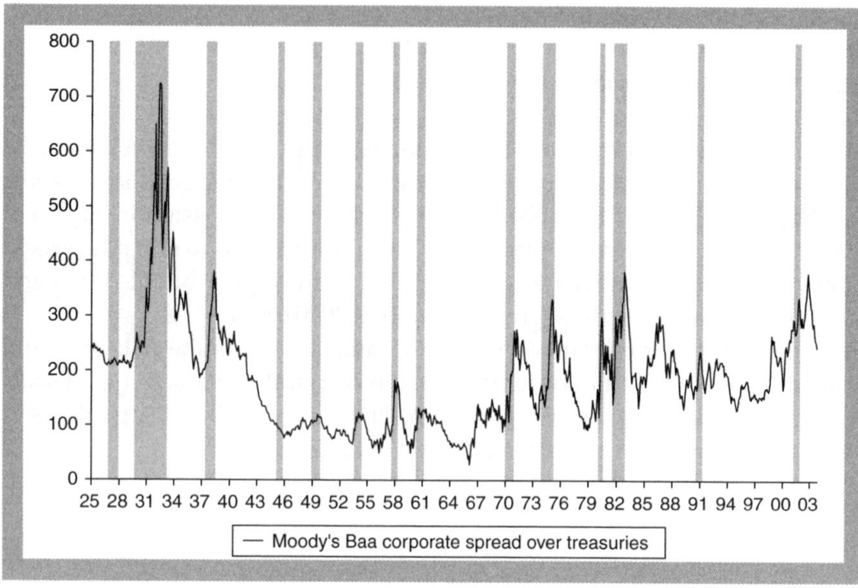

Figure 3.2 Moody's Baa corporate bond spread versus long-term treasury bonds

Source: Moody's

up to a recession. After a recession began, spreads usually continued to widen, peaking approximately 10–14 months into the cycle. The magnitude of the spread widening as well as the duration of the spread widening, however, varies from cycle to cycle, depending primarily on the duration of the recession period and the magnitude of the economic downturn. The fact that credit spreads tend to widen before the business cycle peaks indicates that corporate bond investors often anticipate future economic developments. Focusing on macroeconomic activity variables, therefore, is not sufficient to predict changes in corporate bond spreads. Investors should carefully analyze leading economic indicators as well as any evidence that corporate profitability slows or leverage increases. Both factors result in a reduced ability to generate cash flows and weakens credit quality, resulting in a higher risk of default.

Although the close relationship between credit spreads and economic activity has held most of the time since 1950, the late 1990s witnessed a significant decoupling. Companies expected long-term stable and high growth rates, driven by new technologies like internet and mobile communication. Coupled with a sustained rise in profitability, an idea strongly promoted by the Fed, this expectation caused companies to invest heavily and to leverage their balance sheets. In this period maximization of shareholder value was the credo of many managers. Despite strong economic growth credit markets punished the rise of financial and operating leverage that was

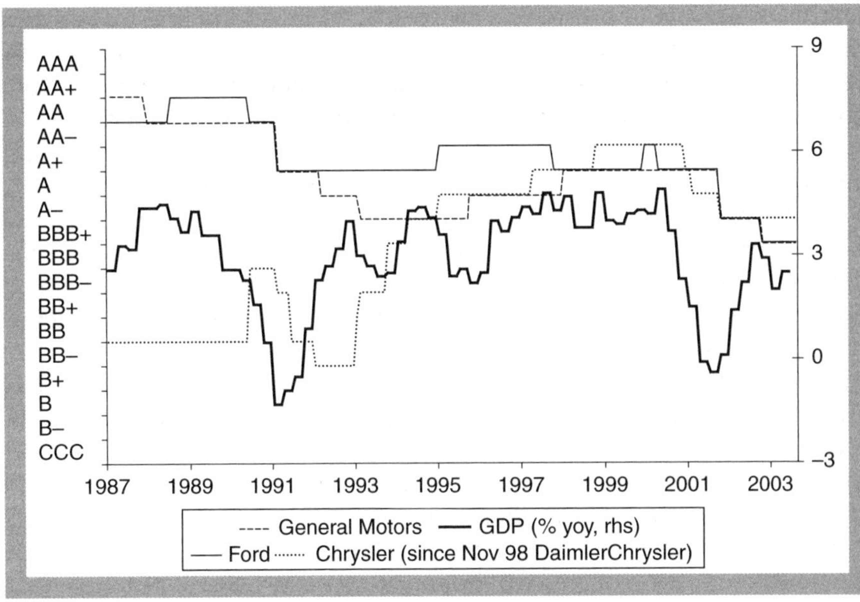

Figure 3.3 Dependency of US big three automotive manufacturers' ratings from the business cycle

Source: Union Investment

observable across most industries and companies with widening credit spreads. Excessively high default rates in 2001 and 2002 showed that market participants anticipated the rise in systematic risk quite early. The sustained equity downturn and cases of fraud added to the woes of the credit markets.

Figure 3.3 shows the strong long-term relationship between US GDP growth and the credit quality of the US automobile industry. Because of the cyclical nature of their business, that is the dependence of corporate revenues and earnings on private consumption, and the high level of fixed costs in the automotive sector, credit ratings of the big three US car manufacturers Ford, GM and DaimlerChrysler are strongly dependent upon the state of the US economy. Hence GDP growth is a good leading indicator for the rating trend in the automotive sector. During periods of economic growth consumer confidence rises and car manufacturers improve their profitability by increasing car sales numbers, which leads to better credit profiles and tighter spread levels. Markets often anticipate falling credit risk and reward improvements in the credit profile by requiring lower risk premia for the bonds of the issuers.

3.2.1.2 Interest rates

Globally, the low interest rate environment in the first years of the new millennium has spurred investors' interest in credit as a way to boost returns. However, one has to be aware that there is a correlation between the level of interest rates, the slope of the yield curve and credit spreads because both the yield curve and credit spreads reflect the state of the economy. Since they are driven by expectations about the same underlying factor, the relation between the yield curve and credit spreads has an impact on top-down driven asset allocation and duration decisions.

In the past, credit spreads have been closely correlated with interest rates. There is typically a negative correlation between spreads and the level of interest rates. As interest rates increase due to an improving outlook for future economic growth and rising price pressure, credit quality tends to improve because firms have opportunities to strengthen their future earnings and cashflows. Similarly, a flatter money market slope (2 years–6 months) is usually positive for credit spreads because it indicates better economic conditions. In a difficult economic environment, such as at the trough of the recession, the money market curve tends to be very steep and credit usually underperforms treasuries, especially at the long end.

Similar to the level of interest rates itself the slope of the yield curve also is an indicator for the economic environment. Generally, the slope of the yield curve is seen as a good proxy for future economic growth and corporate profits. Steep yield curves imply that future rates are expected to be higher than at present. A steep 2s10s slope and a further steepening of the 2s10s slope in the past often have been followed by positive excess returns of corporate bonds. Usually, one observes a steepness in this part of the curve at the end of a recession and at the start of an expansion. When the expansion finally materializes the curve flattens, and inflation concerns cause central banks to raise interest rates. In this environment, credit usually suffers, and investors should be particularly cautious when overweighting cyclical credits.

3.2.1.3 Central bank policy

Monetary policy, too, appears to be an important indicator for corporate credit spreads. Let us assume that the economy is at the brink of deflation. Generally, deflation tends to be accompanied by a rise in bankruptcies. When corporate revenues and earnings are weak, highly leveraged borrowers have difficulties to meet their obligations. In this situation central bank easing paves the way for future economic growth. The traditional channels by which a lowering of the federal funds rate tends to stimulate faster growth in real and nominal GDP are: (1) lower debt cost of capital, (2) higher stock prices, (3) dollar weakness, (4) consumer durables, including automobiles, and (5) housing. Hence, it lowers the equity cost of capital and bolsters consumer confidence through the wealth effect. Figure 3.4 shows that Baa credit spreads usually reach their peak when the Fed has done approximately two-thirds of the interest rate cuts.

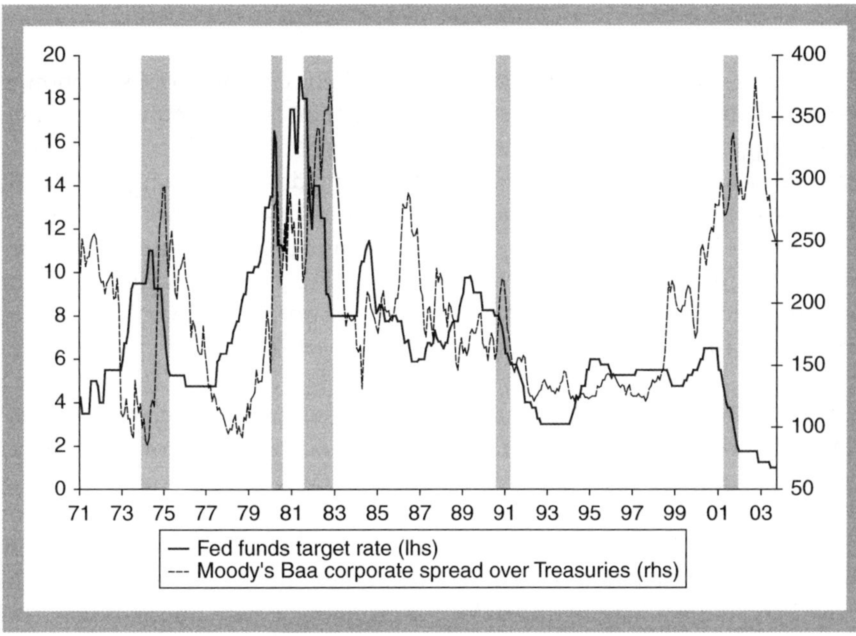

Figure 3.4 Moody's Baa corporate bond spread versus Fed Funds Target Rate

Source: Moody's and Federal Reserve

Interestingly, the relationship between equity and bond markets differs in deflation-risk periods and inflation-risk periods. In inflation-risk periods, rising inflation rates push up long-term interest rates, reflecting the fear that aggressive monetary tightening will depress future earnings and hence stock prices. Thus, in periods of rising inflation risk, government bond prices and stock prices tend to fall. In deflation-risk periods government bond prices and stock prices usually go in opposite directions, because fixed income markets benefit from the expectation of falling interest rates, while equities suffer from the worsening profit outlook and increasing default risk. Credit spreads tend to benefit from rising inflation because it becomes easier for companies to pay down their debt. Deflationary periods usually lead to a spread widening across the whole credit market, hitting consumer-related industries the hardest. However, long-term interest rates seem to have a minor influence on fluctuations of credit spreads in the short term. Companies that borrow at a fixed rate are immune to changes in yields and spreads over the life of the borrowing. Yet, there is a refinancing risk, when debt has to be rolled over. Conversely, when companies borrow at floating rates, they are directly affected by changes in money market rates, which are primarily driven by monetary policy.

3.2.1.4 Employment

For decades economists have analyzed the behavior of various economic indicators during the business cycle. Employment is commonly seen as one of the lagging indicators for the state of the economy. However, there is a leading indicator for the labor sector that coincides with changes in credit spreads. For example, for most of the time since 1968 there has been a close relationship between credit spreads and the index of help-wanted advertising. Falling demand for work force usually coincides with widening credit spreads, indicating falling profits in the corporate sector. Cost-cutting and restructuring measures are typically undertaken in this phase of the economic cycle.

So far, we have examined the impact of several of the most closely watched indicators for the overall state of the economy on corporate bond spreads. Arguably, only monetary policy and market indicators like the slope of the yield curve are true leading indicators for the performance of credit markets. When the GDP figures are published, the credit markets usually have anticipated what the outcome will be. Accordingly, employment is not only a lagging indicator for economic performance, but also at best a coinciding indicator for credit spreads.

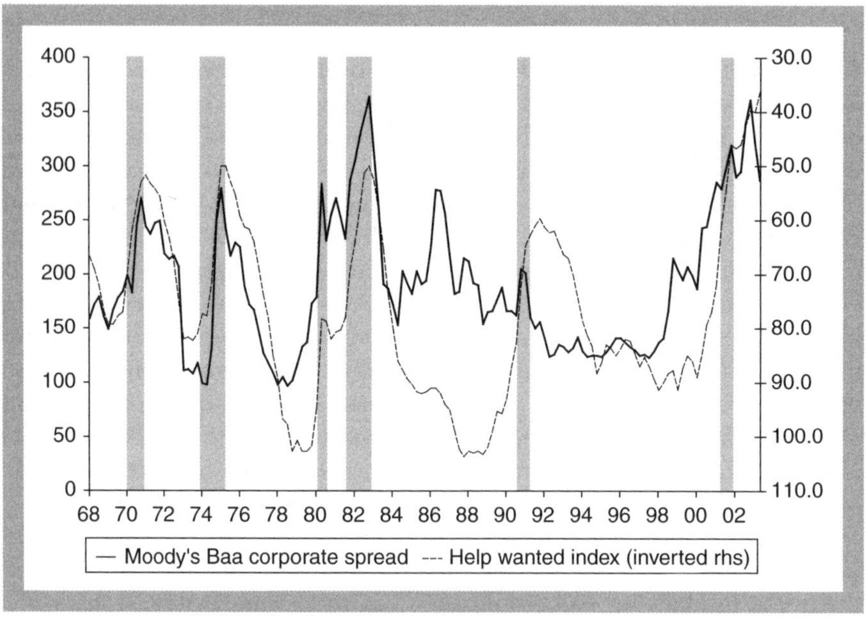

Figure 3.5 Moody's Baa corporate bond spread and index of help wanted advertising

Source: Moody's and Conference Board

3.2.2 The corporate sector

3.2.2.1 Financial leverage

Having discussed some of the most influential economy-wide factors for the performance of corporate bonds, we will now examine specific indicators for the state of the US corporate sector. Traditional metrics of leverage focus on the debt-to-equity ratio. The rationale behind this is that a company's assets are funded by a combination of debt and equity. Since the value of a company's debt remains relatively stable over time, the debt-to-equity ratio is extremely sensitive to fluctuations in the market value of equity in the short to medium term. High equity valuations, for example, lead to a significant underestimation of leverage. Using historical cost for equities can help to mitigate this problem. Yet, the issuance of new equity at inflated valuation levels still distorts the metric. Figure 3.6 highlights the volatility of equity-based measures of leverage.

Financial ratios that reflect a company's ability to repay its liabilities tend to measure credit risk more adequately. This ability depends on

- the overall level of interest-bearing liabilities,
- the real-interest rate that has to be paid on this debt, and

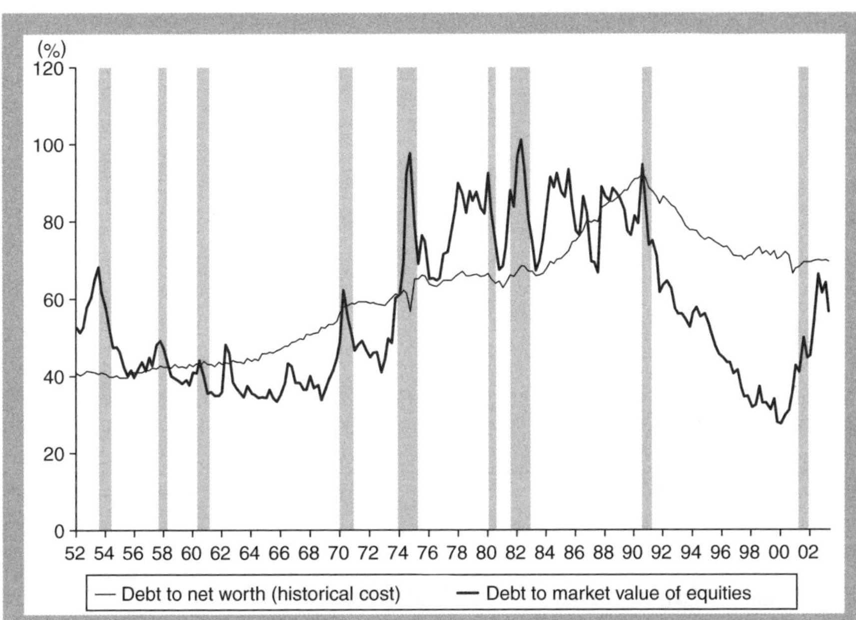

Figure 3.6 Equity-based metrics of leverage
Source: Federal Reserve and J.P. Morgan

- the company's capability of generating sufficient cash flows to repay its liabilities.

Generally, in growing economies the nominal level of debt rises over the years. This is mostly because of inflation and a steady growth in balance sheets. The long-term upward trend has accelerated sharply since 1980, coinciding with the sustained fall in short- and long-term interest rates and inflation rates. Since then, the steadily falling level of interest rates has allowed companies to take on significantly higher levels of debt than before. Despite record debt levels, interest payments have remained manageable. To gain a better insight in the debt burden, we have graphed the level of credit market instruments outstanding relative to the GDP of the nonfinancial corporate sector. The second line in Figure 3.7 shows the level of indebtedness in real terms, that is, after adjustment for the price deflator of the nonfinancial corporate sector. Both measures exhibit a cyclical pattern that is overlaid by a long-term uptrend. Usually indebtedness rises in the first stage of a recession and is cut back consequently at the end of each recession and the following years, reflecting the companies' efforts to restructure their businesses and clean up their balance sheets. In the later years of an expansion top-line growth usually slows and companies tend to increase their leverage to boost return on equity and to finance future growth, for example, through acquisitions.

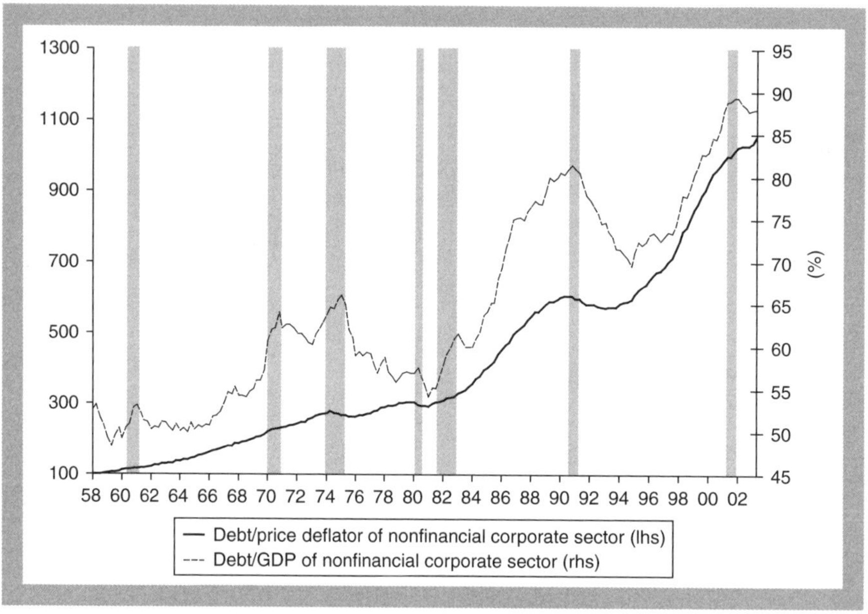

Figure 3.7 Level of indebtedness of the US nonfinancial corporate sector

Source: Federal Reserve and Bureau of Economic Analysis

So far, we have identified a close correlation between credit spreads and future economic activity. When the economy is growing, usually each sector benefits from that growth. In the labor sector, economic growth typically leads to falling unemployment and rising wages. Historically, the corporate sector has benefited particularly during economic expansions. Not only did corporate profits grow in those periods, but also they increased faster than national income. This is reflected by a rising share of national income that usually goes to the bottom-line of the corporate sector during economic expansions. In other words, corporate profitability rises. In recessions, conversely, the labor sector as well as the corporate sector suffers. The problems of the corporate sector become evident by a declining ratio of profits to GDP. Hence, corporate profitability and thus the companies' abilities to generate cash flows to service their liabilities are highly cyclical. Figure 3.8 illustrates that the cyclical nature of corporate profits and cash flows explains variations in corporate bond spreads extremely well. In our view the most objective measure for the ability of companies to service their liabilities is free cash flow. As a proxy for the overall free cash flow that is generated in the US corporate sector, the flow of funds statistics provides a measure that is known as internal funds.

Yet, free cash flow numbers are not available for all companies. European firms, for example, historically have published only profit figures. Therefore,

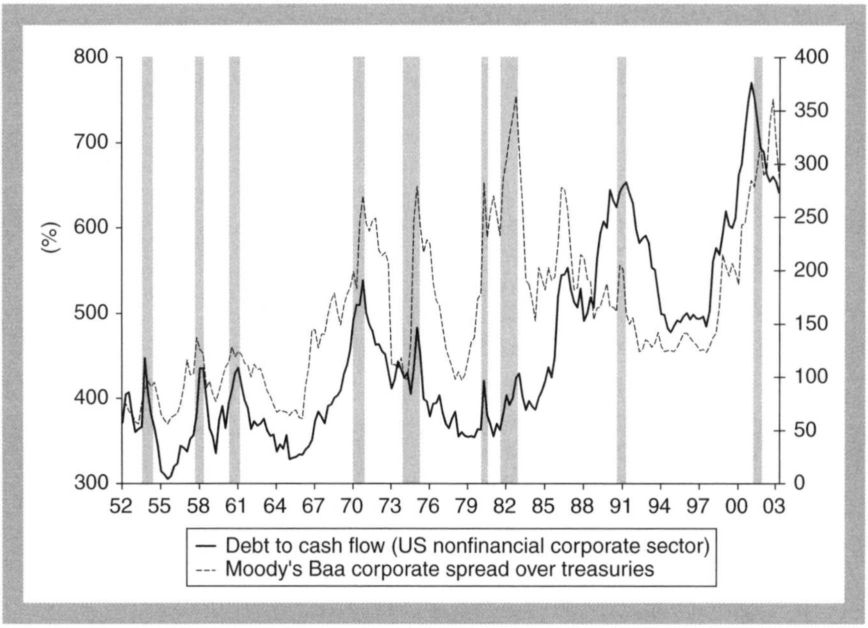

Figure 3.8 Ratio of credit market instruments to internal funds for the US nonfinancial corporate sector

Source: Moody's and Federal Reserve

we also look at EBIT and EBITDA figures. Of these two the latter is preferred because it deducts cash that is needed to maintain the operations. Specifically, on the macro level we use pre-tax profits with inventory adjustment and capital consumption adjustment, and add net interest payments to end up with an aggregate measure of EBITDA. The ratio of debt to EBITDA behaves similar to the debt to cash flow metric, albeit it is considerably more volatile (see Figure 3.9). Part of this volatility is induced by the degrees of freedom related to the accounting of depreciations and amortizations. To forecast profits, one should look at margins and the macroeconomic prospects for growth. Popular proxies for profit margins are the difference between annual percentage changes in the GDP deflator and unit labor costs, and Merrill Lynch's corporate misery index.

While the choice of the most appropriate measure of corporate leverage is an arbitrary task, empirical studies indicate that the financing gap is able to explain a lot of the variance in credit spreads. It is defined as the difference between capital expenditures, including outlays for inventories, and the amount of cash that corporations need to raise in order to finance their investment plans, expressed as a percentage of nominal GDP. The rapid rise in this metric was a powerful warning sign at the end of the 1990s that capital spending was overextended. As one usually observes at the end of recessions, the financing gap has not only closed after the 2001 recession,

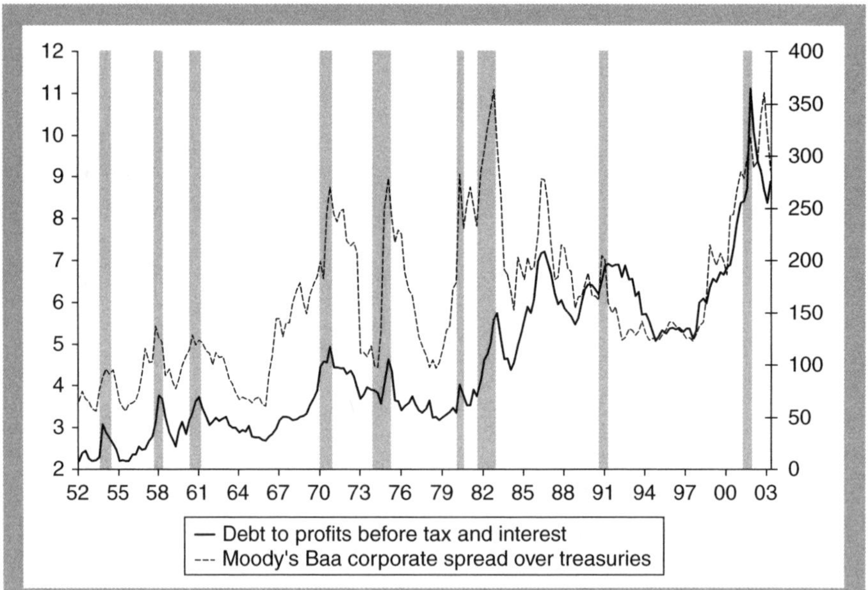

Figure 3.9 Ratio of credit market instruments to pre-tax profits of the US nonfinancial corporate sector

Source: Moody's and Federal Reserve

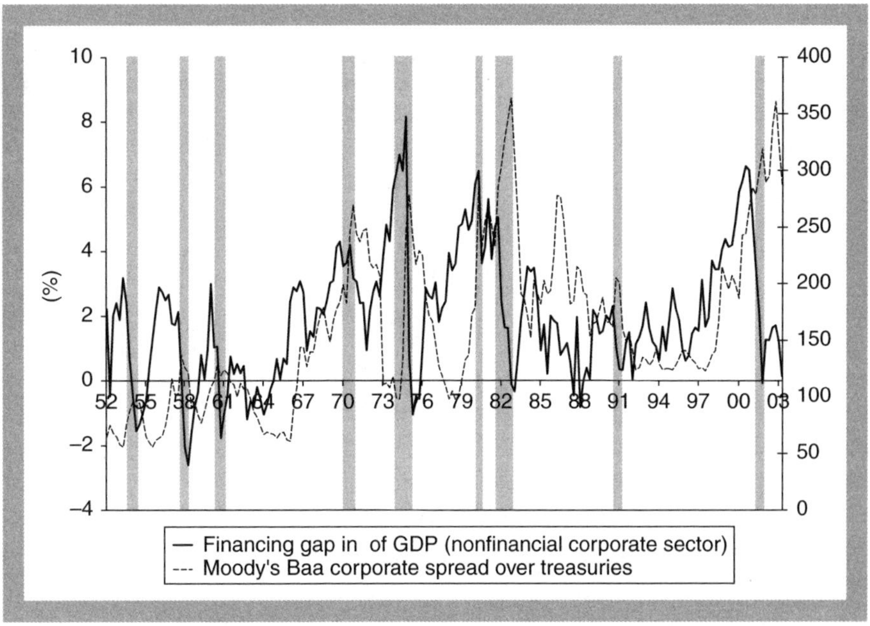

Figure 3.10 Percentage points of capital expenditures of the US nonfinancial corporate sector that are not covered by internal funds versus Baa corporate spread over treasuries

Source: Moody's and Federal Reserve

but fell substantially below its long-run average (see Figure 3.10). In 2003, after-tax cash flow exceeded capital outlays, which is a rare occurrence. In the past, this was usually a good sign for capital spending. Intuitively, the US Treasury replaced the corporate sector as a financier for business spending. Via tax cuts it provided the corporate sector with capital, thereby raising after-tax cash flow, and reducing the requirement for external financing through corporate debt issuance. The increasing amount of Treasury supply, combined with deleveraging in the corporate sector contributed significantly to corporate spread tightening between autumn 2002 and 2004.

3.2.2.2 Interest coverage

Having focused on indicators for the overall level of leverage so far, we will now switch to metrics that relate the ability to generate cash flows and profits to the interest burden. This helps to better capture liquidity problems in the short term, but goes at the expense of understanding the longer term vulnerability of the corporate sector due to leverage. Although Figure 3.11 seems to show a long-term upward trend in the ratio of net interest payments to cash flows, one can argue that the level reached in 2003 roughly

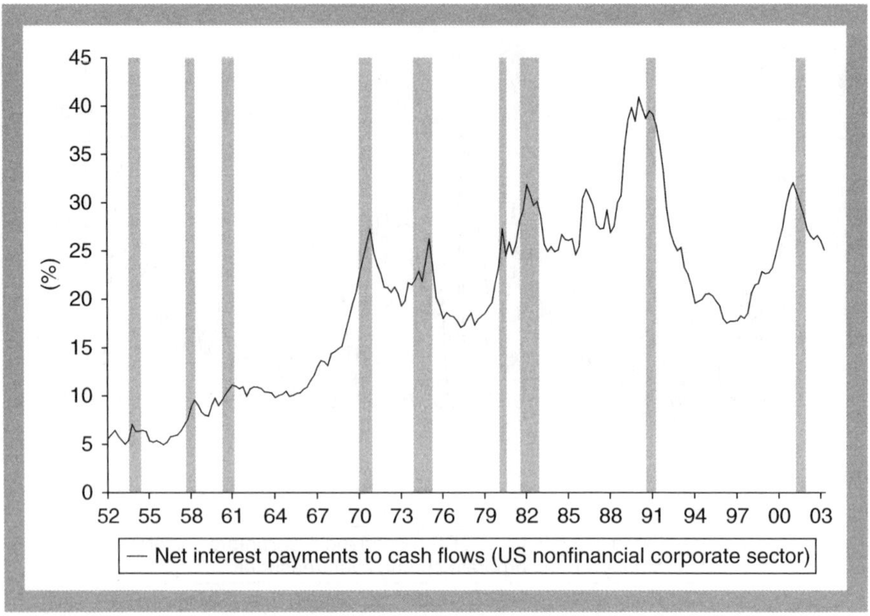

Figure 3.11 Ratio of net interest payments to cash flow for the US nonfinancial corporate sector

Source: Moody's and Federal Reserve

represents the average over the last 35 years. The rise in the overall level of indebtedness in this period has coincided with significantly falling interest rates, keeping the interest burden for the companies on a manageable level.

Like the ratio of net interest payments to cash flows, interest coverage, defined as the ratio of profits to net interest payments, has remained in a range since 1970. Again, as one might expect, when net interest payments are better covered by the level of profits, creditworthiness improves, and credit spreads tighten. But interest coverage in 2003 was still near its cyclical low, indicating weak profitability in the nonfinancial corporate sector and a lack of top-line growth (see Figure 3.12). Considering the fall in yields, the low level of interest coverage is problematic. Partially it results from the fact that not only the companies' liabilities are interest-rate sensitive, but also the value of a part of the assets depends on the level of interest rates.

3.2.2.3 Operating leverage

Corporate bond markets typically reward companies for stable revenues and earnings. However, empirical evidence shows that in times of high risk appetite and positive expectations for future economic growth, companies

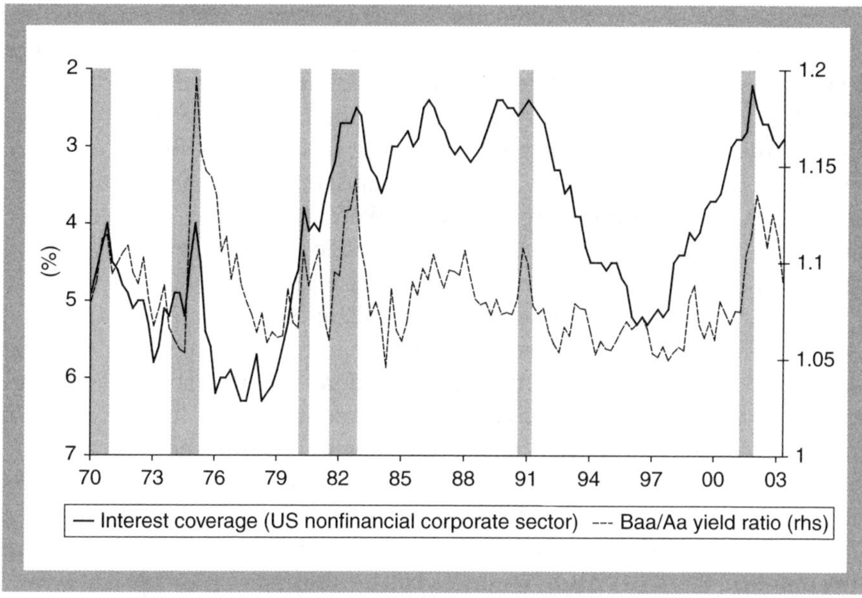

Figure 3.12 Ratio of profits before tax and interest of the US nonfinancial corporate sector to net interest payments versus Baa/Aa yield ratio

Source: Moody's and Federal Reserve

with rather volatile revenues tend to outperform. That is because when there is a lot of optimism on revenue growth, companies with volatile revenues usually benefit the most. Similarly, for companies with a history of high earnings volatility, the probability for a margin expansion is particularly high as the economy recovers. Therefore, if the market expects a cyclical recovery, corporate bonds from cyclical sectors tend to outperform due to the companies' high degree of operating leverage.

Operating leverage is the idea that companies can make more money from each additional sale if they do not have to increase fixed costs to produce more. In general, operating leverage refers to the fact that a lower ratio of variable cost per unit to price per unit causes profit to vary more with a change in the level of output than it would if this ratio was higher. So operating leverage is a function of fixed unit costs and output. The benefits of operating leverage unfold when business picks up. Then the existing workforce, plant and equipment can produce more without additional costs. Profit margins expand, and profits boom. Obviously, the profit of a business with a high degree of operating leverage varies more, everything else remaining the same, than do those profits of businesses with less operating leverage. Greater variability of profits, of course, means that the credit risk is higher. Conversely, with a lower level of operating leverage, the business shows poor growth in profits as sales rise, but faces a lower risk of loss as sales decline.

For the last couple of years the broad economy has experienced an extraordinarily high level of operating leverage and consequently since 2000, companies have cut costs. The best evidence of that elevated level of operating leverage is the very low rate of industrial capacity utilization. Despite the modest improvement since 2001, utilization is still at levels not seen since the 1982 recession. On the one hand, that is a sign that businesses continue to suffer from overcapacity. Looked at it another way, however, the low-but-improving rate of capacity utilization is an indication that profits may grow above average in the future (see Figure 3.13).

Investors can also see low capacity utilization as good news since it means there is little near-term risk of demand getting ahead of supply, sparking inflation. And that means the Federal Reserve should not have to raise interest rates aggressively for quite some time. Large amounts of unused production capacity acts as a buffer that diminishes the inflation risks implicit to rising demand. The other clear sign of the high level of operating leverage in the US corporate sector is the jump in productivity. Of course, for productivity increases and low capacity utilization to work through to corporate profits, business sales still need to pick up. Therefore, final demand has to increase. For the economy to really soar, businesses have to start spending on hiring workers, new technology and capital

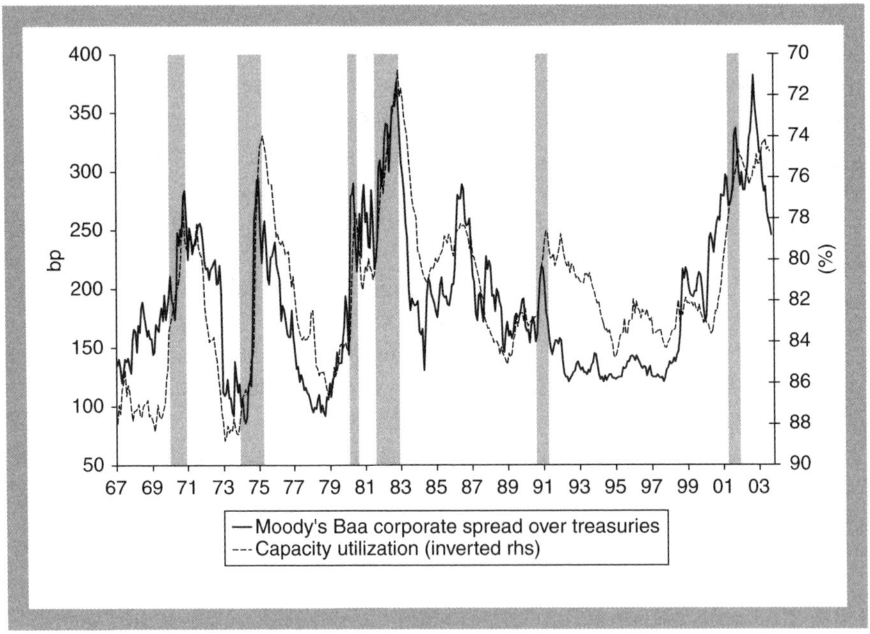

Figure 3.13 US total industry capacity utilization versus Moody's Baa corporate spread over treasuries

Source: Moody's and Federal Reserve

improvements. And usually will, once the evidence clearly shows that profits are perking up.

On the macroeconomic level, capacity utilization rates are a good indicator for the level of fixed costs of the corporate sector, because the higher the utilization rates are, the less the costs of maintaining the infrastructure to generate one unit of output will be. Furthermore, an increase in industrial output hints at rising revenues and solid cash flows for the companies. This strengthens the companies' abilities to service their debt. Therefore, credit spreads tend to tighten when capacity utilization and industrial production increase (Figure 3.14). Yet, rising cash flows tend to invoke business investment, particularly when capacity utilization rates are above average. Historically, levels above 80–82 percent have been a threshold above which the willingness to invest has increased significantly.

Like capacity utilization rates, industrial production is a coincident indicator for the state of the economy. Across the business cycle, credit spreads tighten when industrial production grows, and sell off when the economy is doing poorly. Usually, when the economy is doing well, default rates tend to fall and the more positive sentiment usually leads to a lower level of risk aversion. Therefore credit investors settle with lower spreads than in times of poor economic performance.

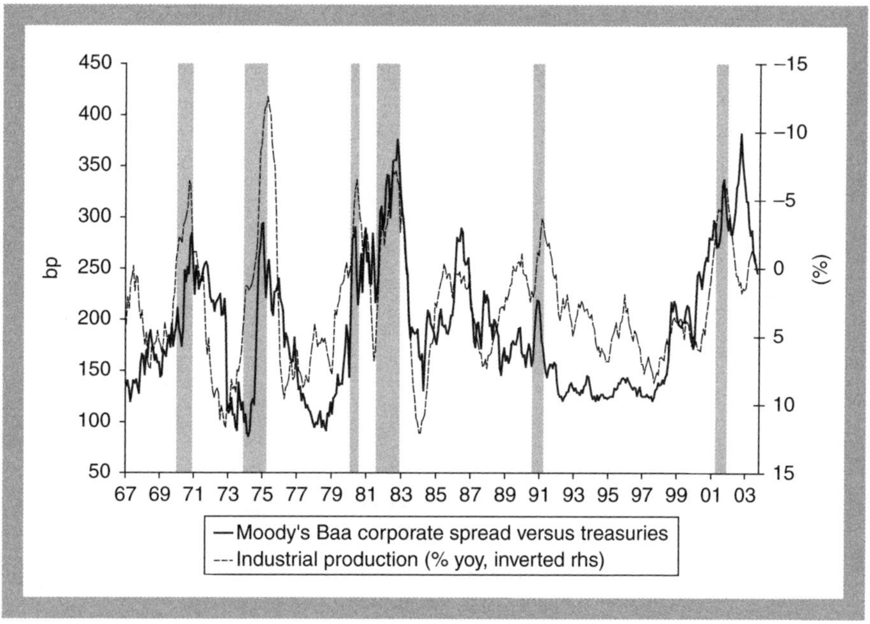

Figure 3.14 Annual change in US industrial production versus Moody's Baa corporate spread over treasuries

Source: Moody's and Federal Reserve

3.2.3 The credit cycle

Overall, the analysis suggests that credit spreads are highly correlated with the business cycle and that there is a leverage cycle that is closely related to macroeconomic activity variables. While carry-driven strategies may work most of the time, a thorough understanding of the leverage cycle helps to anticipate a harsh credit environment, even before it is reflected in GDP growth and equity performance. As the years 1997–2000 have shown, information from the equity markets is clearly not sufficient as an indicator of business and financial risks in the corporate sector. Most companies go through a regular cycle of leveraging and deleveraging, which is related to the profit and Capex cycle. Especially trends in mergers and acquisitions have a significant impact on the performance of credit markets. Figure 3.15 displays a stylized leverage cycle. Consequently, the concept of "safe" and "risky" companies loses its allure. Companies from sectors like utilities or noncyclical services that are considered safe today may increase leverage and be more risky tomorrow. On the other hand, highly leveraged companies may decide to deleverage and thus lower their business risk, like the European telecom sector in 2002 and 2003. Although the profit cycle is more pronounced in cyclical sectors, a credit cycle may be observed across virtually all industries. Credit markets react to this dynamic process through spread tightening and spread widening, thus causing investors mark-to-market profits or losses.

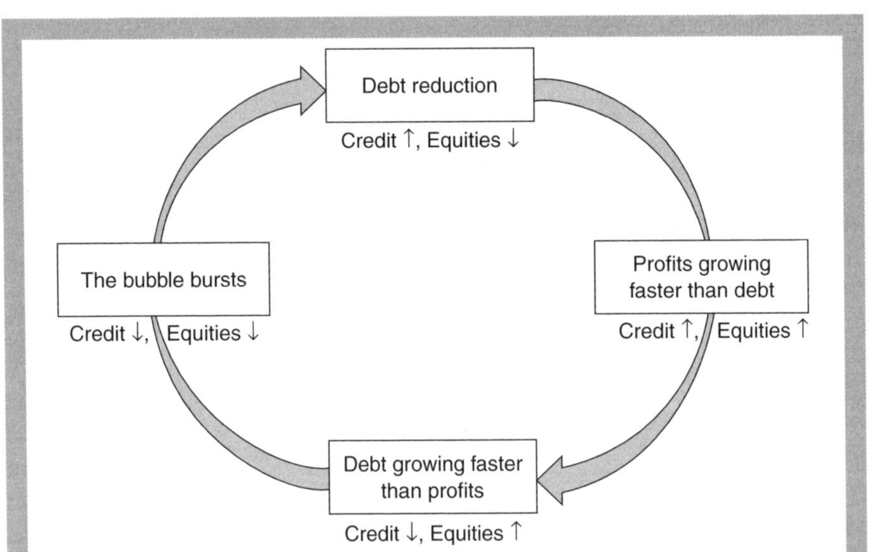

Figure 3.15 Stylized leverage cycle and performance in credit and equity markets

Source: J.P. Morgan

Considering the importance of dynamic credit risk modeling, the analysis of the relationship between the two major indicators for credit risk, that is default rates and credit spreads, and the business cycle is central for the understanding of the risks associated with investing in corporate bonds. Especially investors that tend to hold securities to maturity, investing in high yield, or running structured portfolios are concerned about avoiding defaults. While default rates generally are a function of the credit cycle outlined above, their current level is not necessarily reflected in credit spreads. In order to judge the attractiveness of the current spreads, one need to not only forecast the future direction of default rates, but also to see whether they are sufficient to cover potential future losses. The sensitivity of the corporate bond market to economic downturns depends particularly on the distribution of the credit quality of the issuers and on the ratio of cyclical companies to noncyclical companies.

The rating agencies provide the most accurate data on historical default rates. Based on their data, empirical studies by Wilson (1997), Nickell *et al.* (2000), Bangia *et al.* (2002), Allen and Saunders (2003), and others suggest that default rates tend to be higher in recessionary periods. As might be expected, default rates usually peak at the end of recessions and fall when the economy is expanding. A closer look at history shows that default rates reached their highest levels in the 1930s, peaking at 9 percent in 1932. Since then they have never come close to that level. From 1940 to 1970 they were extremely low, hardly ever exceeding 1 percent. Moody's themselves note that in the 1973 recession, the default rate was close to zero because only the best issuers had been able to access the capital markets in the previous years. In the early 1990s and at the beginning of the new millennium default rates rose significantly, reaching their peak at about 4 percent. Thus, the default cycle has mirrored the business cycle very well in the past 15 years. Yet one difference is not reflected in this figure. On a dollar-weighted basis, the 2002 default rate for speculative grade issuers was nearly twice as high as in 1991, causing painful losses for many investors. Furthermore the 2002 default rate for US investment grade issuers reached more than 1 percent on an issuer-weighted basis and almost 3 percent on a dollar-weighted basis. This is substantially above the 30-year average of the investment grade default rate, which is about 25 basis points. Clearly, investment grade defaults are supposed to happen very infrequently.

Intuitively, the described long-term pattern contrasts with the much more cyclical behavior of credit spreads. Yet it should be noted that a large part of this deviation has to be attributed to changes in the databases of the rating agencies and the average quality of recent new issuance. When the database contains more investment grade companies, default rates naturally tend to be lower, and vice versa. Furthermore, historical data on default rates does not only reflect the broad credit cycle, but also changes in companies' preferences towards bank debt and corporate issuance. When banks' lending standards are particularly restrictive, especially companies with a lower credit quality may prefer to finance their business by issuing corporate bonds. For the high-yield market there is empirical evidence that the average maturity of outstanding debt is correlated with the probability of default. In other words, default probability changes over the life of a bond. While at the date of issuance the company has sufficient capital, there is often considerable uncertainty about the viability of the business model and future economic success. Together with the 1990/91 recession the enormous volume of junk bonds issuance that took place in the late 1980s is responsible for the peak in default rates in 1991. Consequently, default rate data provided by the rating agencies is not a very pure indicator of credit conditions through time.

Fama and French (1989), Stock and Watson (1989), and Chen (1991) examine the correlation between credit spreads and the business cycle. They find empirical evidence that corporate bond spreads are good predictors of future economic growth. Based on empirical data from 1933 to 1997, a recent study by Koopman and Lucas (2003) reveals two different types of cycles. On the one hand, there is a cycle with a frequency of about 6 years, where a positive correlation between credit spreads and default rates, and a negative correlation between spreads and economic growth can be observed. On the other hand, a second cycle with a duration of about 11 years shows a positive link between spreads and business failures, and a negative correlation between GDP growth and both spreads and default rates. However, constraining the analysis on the post Second World War era no significant correlations between credit spreads, default rates and the business cycle could be found (see Figure 3.16).

With regard to the above-mentioned problems, rating migrations seem to be a more reliable indicator of changes in credit quality than default rates. Given that the risks of downgrade as well as default vary over time, the question is whether credit spreads compensate investors adequately. Since the sample for the calculation of rating transition matrices is much broader than for default rates, they are less likely to be biased by changes of the rating agencies' universe. To measure changes of credit quality over time, the ratings drift, that is the number of upgrades minus the number of downgrades, as a proportion of the total number of entities rated, can be a valuable indicator. A sample of high-quality issuers, however, will tend to have more downgrades than upgrades, and vice versa. Hence, variations of the ratings drift partly reflect changes in average credit quality over time. As one would expect, credit spreads tend to rise when the ratio of upgrades to downgrades becomes worse (see Figure 3.17).

The question, however, is, whether the credit spreads widen enough to compensate investors sufficiently for the deterioration of average credit quality that is reflected by a falling ratings drift. While predicting the direction of spread changes may help to make money on a mark-to-market basis,

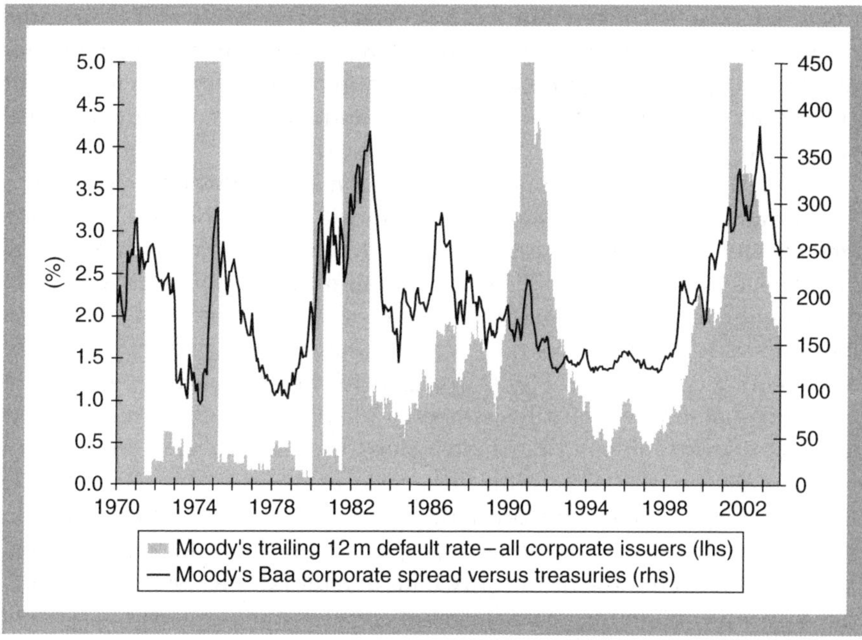

Figure 3.16 Baa corporate spread over treasuries versus trailing 12-month default rates

Source: Moody's

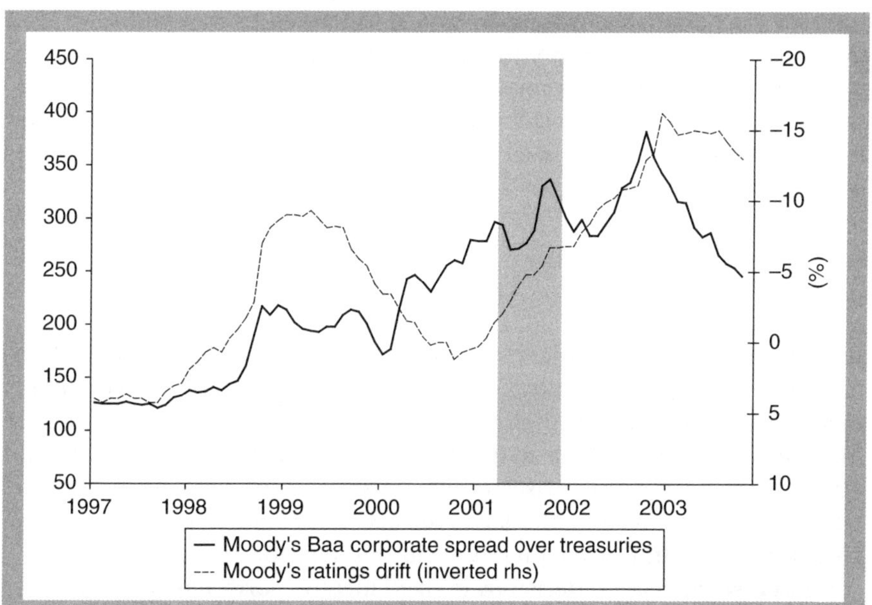

Figure 3.17 Moody's ratings drift ([upgrades – downgrades]/number of rated issuers) versus Moody's Baa corporate spread over treasuries

Source: Moody's

it is not adequate for buy-and-hold investors. They have to estimate the magnitude of the spread widening that corresponds to an observed deterioration of credit quality. Hence, the focus is purely on credit risk, while credit spreads also incorporate liquidity premia, and are influenced by technical factors and market sentiment.

The spread needed to compensate for default risk depends upon future default rates, recovery rates and ratings transition probabilities. The rating agencies publish their forecasts of future default rates based on historical data. Usually required spreads come out significantly lower than current spreads for investment grade companies. For high yield, however, observed spreads tend to be too low, given the actual risk of default. While over the long term buy-and-hold strategies may earn an excess return over government bonds for pure investment grade portfolios, this strategy is not appropriate for high-yield portfolios. Here, investors need to focus much more on the process of selecting the right companies and avoiding the blowup names. A look at historical data shows that market spreads tend to overshoot at the end of credit cycles, especially in the wake of a recession. For example, even if the historically high default rates of 1990/91 had persisted over the following years, investors should have required a BBB credit spread of only 115 bps for medium-term bonds. At that time the average market spread for BBB-rated issues, however, peaked at more than 180 bps. Consequently, the market was much too bearish in 1991. Conversely, in 1997, at the beginning of the severe bear market for credit, spreads were too tight for the period of downgrades and credit blowups that followed. Note that these observations apply for bonds with a maturity of roughly 4 years. While the cushion is not as comforting as for shorter maturities, even at the long end the spread levels reached in recessions provide sufficient protection, even when assuming that default rates stay high for a sustained period of time.

3.3 VALUATION

Besides market fundamentals valuation is the major driver of market performance for the longer term. The other two drivers that are commonly mentioned in investment literature, technicals and market sentiment, are more likely to explain short- to medium-term fluctuations of credit spreads. The subject of valuation arises on every level of the investment process. Generally, it is a question of relative attractiveness of one investment *vis-a-vis* another one. In this chapter, we will outline four approaches that may support asset allocation decisions in fixed income portfolios with an aggregate benchmark as well as help to determine the beta of a pure credit portfolio.

3.3.1 Fundamental models for corporate bond spreads

A popular approach to estimate the credit risk of an issuer is the use of z-scores. In this context, Altman's five components framework has attracted particular interest. On the company level, it is based on the five metrics depicted in Table 3.1.

Replacing the company-specific metrics by macroeconomic factors yields a fundamental model for the credit market. Because of the required minimum history and data reliability we will focus on the US market. Data for this procedure is taken from the flow of funds statistics and the national accounts of the United States.

The ratio of working capital to total assets measures the net liquid assets of a firm relative to the sum of financial and tangible assets. We isolated net liquid assets for the US nonfinancial corporate sector from the flow of funds statistics by subtracting mortgages, consumer credit, trade receivables and miscellaneous assets from total assets and subsequently adding inventories, trade and tax receivables. Figure 3.18 shows the working capital ratio over time. The large fall in 1974 is due to a significant decline in the value of trade payables. Usually, the ratio of working capital to total assets falls in a recession. But there also seems to be a secular downtrend in this ratio.

A common measure for profitability is the ratio of retained earnings to total assets. We defined retained earnings as undistributed profits, that is, after-tax profits minus dividend payments. Like the working capital ratio, the profitability measure is on a downtrend in the longer term. During recessions the profitability of the companies usually declines. It is worth noting that the latest recession in 2001 marks an exception with respect to the ratio of internal funds to total assets. Whereas the profitability declined like in any other recession before, the cash flows of the companies on average improved in this period due to rigorous cost cutting in the corporate sector.

Table 3.1 Factors of the Altman *z*-score model

Metric	Interpretation
Working capital to total assets	Net liquid assets relative to the firm's assets
Retained earnings to total assets	Profitability relative to size
Earnings before tax and interest to total assets	Profitability relative to the firm's assets
Market value of equity to total debt	Inverse of leverage
Sales to total assets	Sales generating capacity of a given asset base

Source: Altman [1968]

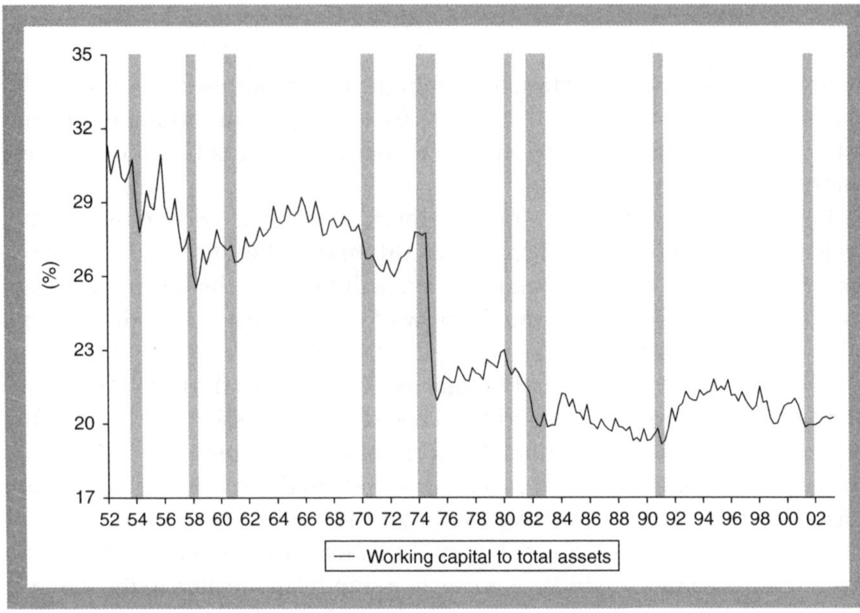

Figure 3.18 Ratio of working capital to total assets for the US nonfinancial corporate sector

Source: Federal Reserve

A second metric for profitability is the ratio of earnings before tax, interest depreciation and amortization (EBITDA) to total assets. Using data from the national accounts of the United States we define earnings before tax and interest as pre-tax profits with inventory valuation and capital consumption adjustment plus net interest. This metric follows a similar path as the ratio of retained earnings to total assets, although on a higher level and with a higher volatility (see Figure 3.19).

Measuring the extent to which a firm's value can decline before its book value becomes negative and a firm becomes insolvent, the ratio of market value of equity to total debt represents the inverse of leverage. We have defined the value of equity as the market value of outstanding equities, total debt is defined as total credit market instruments. Figure 3.20 illustrates that the tremendous equity bubble of the late 1990s has collapsed, but nevertheless the equity-to-debt ratio stays above the level reached in the 1970s and 1980s. Because of its higher volatility, the ratio is largely driven by the equity performance. As a result the equity-to-debt ratio usually rises at the end of a recession because equity markets already anticipate stronger economic growth while many companies still deleverage their balance sheets. Here again, the 2001 recession makes an exception. About one-and-a-half years after the end of the recession in November 2001 equity markets finally marked their lows.

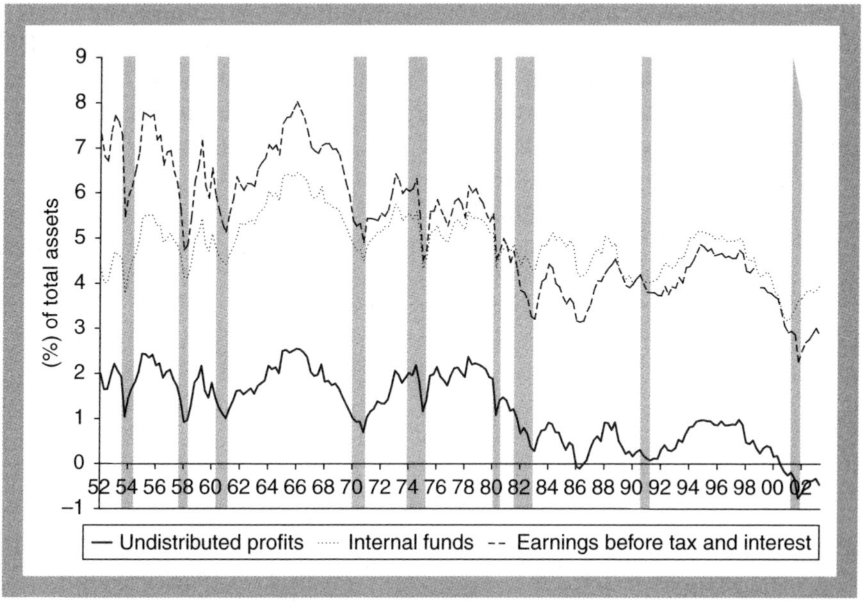

Figure 3.19 Undistributed profits, earnings before tax and interest and internal funds versus total assets for the US nonfinancial corporate sector

Source: Federal Reserve

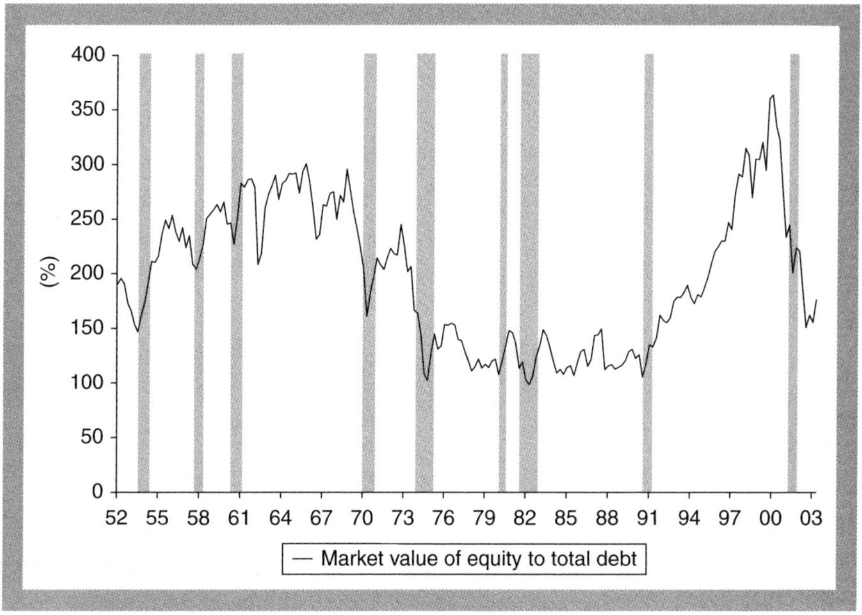

Figure 3.20 Market value of equity outstanding to total credit market instruments of the US nonfinancial corporate sector

Source: Federal Reserve

Finally, the ratio of sales to assets is an asset turnover ratio that measures the sales-generating capacity of a given asset base. Taking the nominal GDP of the nonfinancial corporate sector as a measure for sales, Figure 3.21 shows that the ratio has started to turn up at the beginning of 2001. This pattern is normally consistent with periods of recovery. However, it should be noted that this ratio is near its historical low.

To gauge the financial health of the corporate sector, we combine the five metrics of the Altman model applying the original weighting scheme. Accordingly, the *z*-score is calculated as

$$z = \frac{1.2 \cdot \text{working capital} + 1.4 \cdot \text{retained earnings} + 3.3 \cdot \text{EBIT} + \text{sales}}{\text{total assets}} + 0.6 \cdot \frac{\text{equity}}{\text{total debt}}.$$

A *z*-score below 1.8 signals that the company is in financial distress and the probability of default is high. The "grey" zone, indicating medium risk, ranges from 1.8 to 3. Scores above 3 are associated with "safe" companies.

Figure 3.22 illustrates that the *z*-score for the nonfinancial corporate sector has collapsed dramatically since 2000, resting well below the critical level of

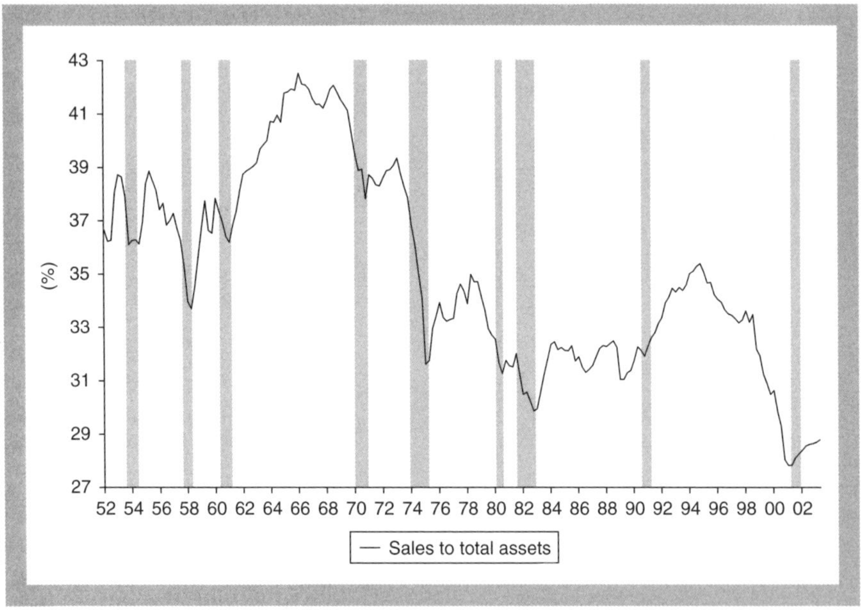

Figure 3.21 Nominal GDP of the US nonfinancial corporate sector to total assets

Source: Bureau of Economic Analysis and Federal Reserve

1.8 since the second quarter of 2002. For an individual firm this signals that the company is likely to fail within 2 years. On the macro level it indicates a high probability of rising default rates and widening credit spreads. Three points stand out from Figure 3.22:

- based on macroeconomic data the z-score has never been in the safe zone;
- the average score since 1952 is about 2;
- in the 1970s and 1980s, the *z*-score was permanently in the distress zone implying that corporate America should have gone bankrupt, but clearly it survived.

This leads to the conclusion that the weighting scheme is no longer appropriate to capture the vulnerability of the corporate sector. The relative importance of the individual factors changes over time. Therefore, it is necessary to adjust the weighting scheme on a regular basis, for example by using a regression methodology.

Figure 3.23 shows the results of two linear regression models based on Altman's five indicators for the health of the corporate sector. In both models the factors are combined in a way so as to minimize the squared

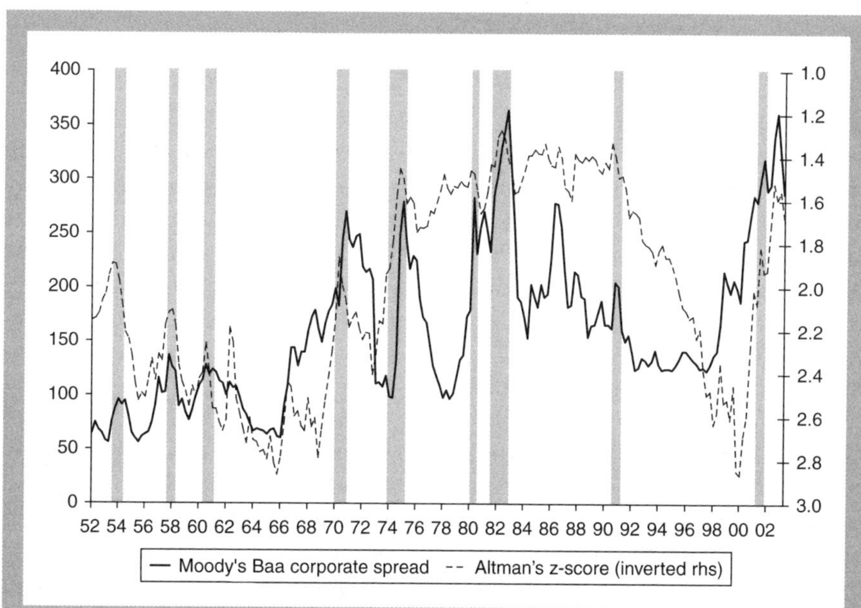

Figure 3.22 Moody's Baa corporate bond spread versus Altman's *z*-score

Source: Moody's and Union Investment

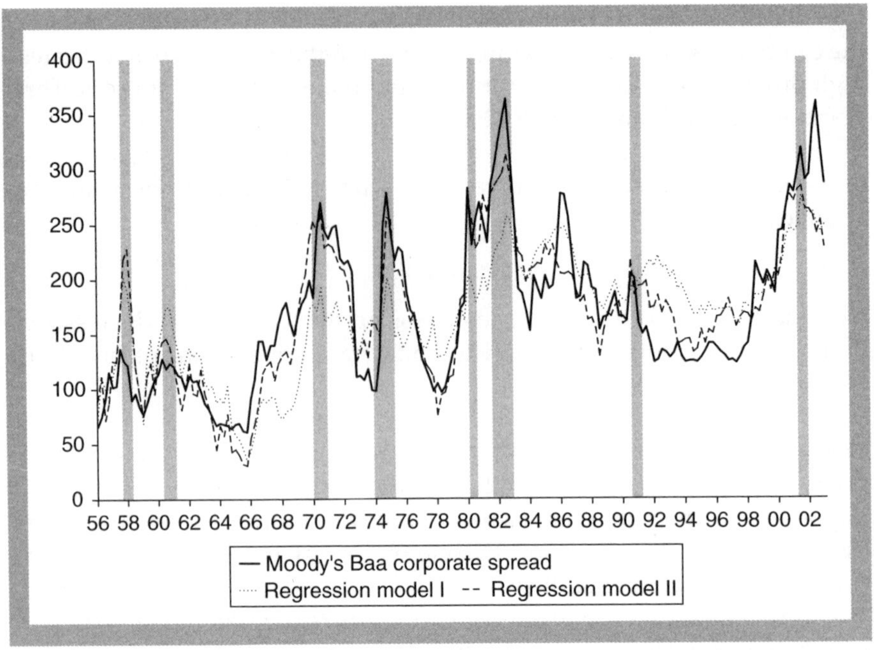

Figure 3.23 Moody's Baa corporate bond spread versus two fundamental models based on Altman's five indicators for the health of the corporate sector

Source: Moody's and Union Investment

regression residuals (OLS regression). Regression model I fully relies on the five Altman factors. The second fundamental model includes as a sixth variable the oil price to capture the effect of oil price shocks on the economy and on credit spreads. Furthermore, some of the independent variables are lagged. Obviously, the fitted time series of the second model tracks the historical Baa corporate bond spread even better than the original model.

3.3.2 Equity prices and volatility

One of the most widely used indicators to value corporate credit is the equity market. The Merton model formalizes the relationship between leverage, equity prices, equity volatility and credit spreads. While the model permits an assessment of the relative valuation of equity and credit, it makes no explicit statement about which of the markets is currently priced correctly, or if both markets are in disequilibrium. In addition, focusing solely on equity prices and volatility neglects the effects of changes in leverage. However, equity-market performance contains information about the future state of the economy, the future cash flows and risk premium in the market. Stronger cash generation benefits corporate bonds since creditworthiness improves and the required risk premium is lower. Furthermore, as the equity cushion increases through rising equity prices and more IPOs and equity volatility decreases, default probabilities and spread levels tend to fall.

Generally, equity-based models for credits have to be analyzed in the context of the leverage cycle. When the level of debt remains constant, equity as well as credit investors both benefit from rising equity prices, driven, for example, by increasing earnings estimates. When leverage is rising like, for instance, between 1997 and 2000, equities tend to perform well while credit spreads widen at the same time. Conversely, deleveraging through rights issues or asset disposals, cost cutting and dividend cuts provide a favorable environment for credit, but not for equities. As Figure 3.24 shows, there is undoubtedly a relationship between equity prices and credit spreads. Yet, this relationship varies over time, depending on the current and the expected fundamental environment in the future. Models that only relate credit spreads to equity prices therefore need to be interpreted cautiously. Assume, for example that the management of a company signals its willingness to concentrate on the creation of shareholder value. Then the probability of leveraging increases substantially. If there has been no decoupling, credit investors should take that as a sign to be rather bearish.

Clearly credit and equity investors tend to look at the corporate sector from different angles. While the focus of equity markets is primarily on

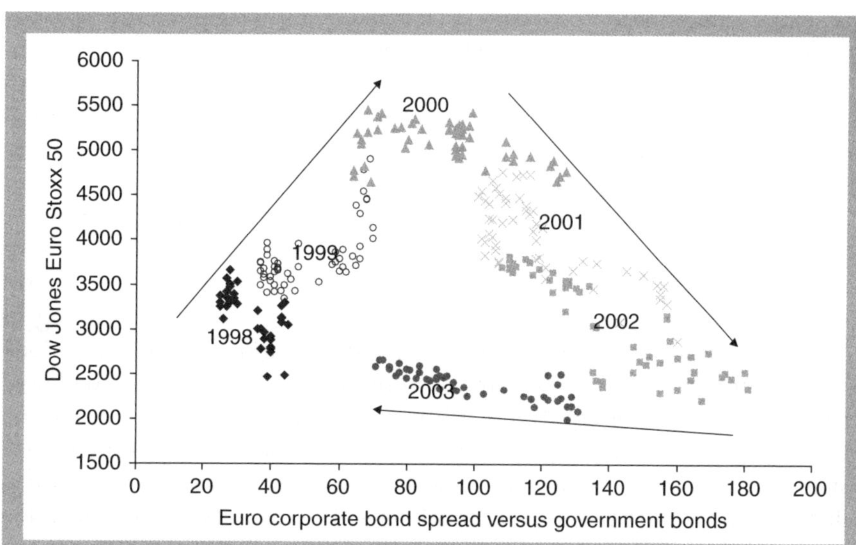

Figure 3.24 Euro corporate bond spreads versus equity-market performance

Source: J.P. Morgan

earnings growth, credit investors rely on debt-related factors to make their decisions. However, if one combines both perspectives the result is a stylized debt–equity cycle that may support both parties in the process of decision-making. The four phases of the cycle depend on the degree of earnings growth (high or low) and changes in leverage (rising or falling). Changes in leverage reflect the companies' efforts to change their capital structure as well as their ability to generate cash flows. As an example we will examine the last complete debt–equity cycle that reached from 1991 to 2003.

After the 1990/91 recession the US corporate sector underwent a period of massive restructuring. Balance sheet repair, rights issues to repay debt, asset disposals and measures to improve cash flow generation led not only to falling leverage, but also to low earnings growth rates. During this first phase of the debt–equity cycle, the 'repair phase' credit usually outperforms equities. It lays the foundation for higher growth rates due to an improved ability to generate cash flows. The subsequent recovery period is beneficial for equity markets as well as credit markets, as the years 1994–97 have shown.

Phase 3 is characterized by high growth and rising leverage, as during the years 1997 to mid-2000. In this period M&A activity was rapidly accelerating, driven by a major focus on the creation of shareholder value. While earnings grew in this period, aggregate measures of corporate profitability like the ratio of after-tax profits of the nonfinancial corporate sector to GDP already declined. Deteriorating free cash flow measures also signaled heightened risk in the corporate sector. As one would generally expect in the expansion phase, equities performed well while credit spreads widened. In general, the high level of debt accumulated during the expansion makes companies vulnerable to economic downturns. Low growth and rising leverage increase the risk of defaults and rating downgrades, and are generally negative for credit as well as equity markets. The years 2000–02 are a typical example for this phase.

Figure 3.25 shows that credit spreads historically have been negatively correlated with 3-year rolling equity-market returns, as we would have expected from the Merton model. Indeed, there seems to be a longer term debt–equity cycle. But the chart also reveals a significant decoupling of equity and credit during the 1990s. Since equity-market performance alone is only temporarily able to explain variations of credit spreads, we will now analyze the impact of equity volatility on spreads. However, most of the time equity prices and implied volatility tell the same story. When stock prices are falling, demand for protection increases, and thus volatility, which is simply the price of protection, rises. The result is a strong negative correlation between equity prices and option-implied volatility. Yet the times, when both markets tell different stories, are the most interesting.

The level of implied volatility is a widely used indicator for risk appetite, and, on the individual company level, for the uncertainty related to future

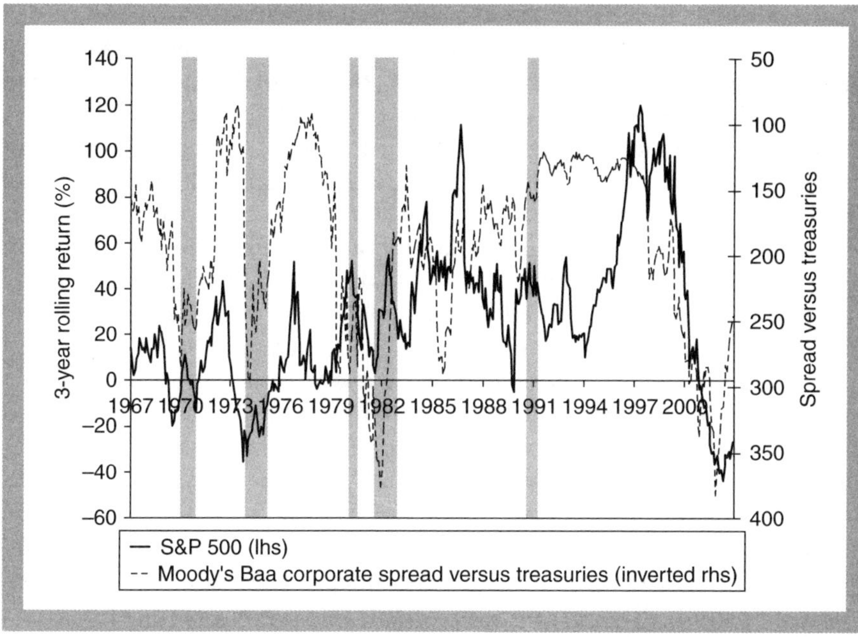

Figure 3.25 Three-year rolling equity-market returns versus Baa corporate spread versus treasuries

Source: Moody's, S&P's and Union Investment

earnings. It is also considered a good measure of equity-market risk, because the higher the implied volatility the higher the price of equity options, and thus the higher the cost of insuring against equity-market downturns. Corporate bond spreads reflect the compensation that the investors demand for taking on credit risk. While the debt and equity markets' estimates of risk, as explained by the Merton model, tend to move together, temporary disconnections do occur. The combination of low levels of implied equity volatility and wide credit spreads suggests the potential for the credit spreads to tighten, as the divergence in the equity and credit market eventually gets corrected. Conversely, when implied equity volatility appears high relative to credit spreads, credit markets are more optimistic about business risks in the corporate sector. The decoupling in the second half of 2003, however, was not an indication that credit spreads were rich relative to implied equity volatility. Rather credit markets were faster to cash in on the reduced risks in the corporate sector because of the massive balance sheet deleveraging, especially in the telecom sector. Corporate managers were selling off assets, issuing equity and keeping cash for the debtholders, as opposed to using the cash to buy back stock for the first time in 10 years. By the end of the year, equity volatility came down significantly, closing the gap in the assessment of risk.

The correlation between the debt and equity markets' measures of risk has been extremely strong over the recent years. External shocks, for example the tragic events of September 11, 2001, the LTCM disaster in 1998 or the Asian crisis, have a substantial impact on credit spreads as well as on implied equity volatility. Figure 3.26 illustrates the relationship between implied volatility of call options on Dow Jones Euro Stoxx 50, and the spread versus government bonds of the MSCI Euro corporate bond index. One way of interpreting implied volatility on an equity index is as the compensation that the investors receive for taking on equity risk. The index of credit spreads represents the additional yield investors demand for holding corporate debt over benchmark government debt. While there have at times been brief periods of divergence, these two risk measures typically move together. For example, in 1993/94 banks in the United States cleaned up their balance sheets by writing down nonperforming assets, causing the VIX index, representing the implied volatility of put and call options on the S&P 100, to fall to a historical low just above 10 percent. The decline in implied equity volatility triggered a credit spread rally. A similar thing happened in 2002. Average credit spreads collapsed by half, as did option-implied volatility. So the decline in volatility was a major driver of credit spread tightening. However, one tends to find that when implied volatility

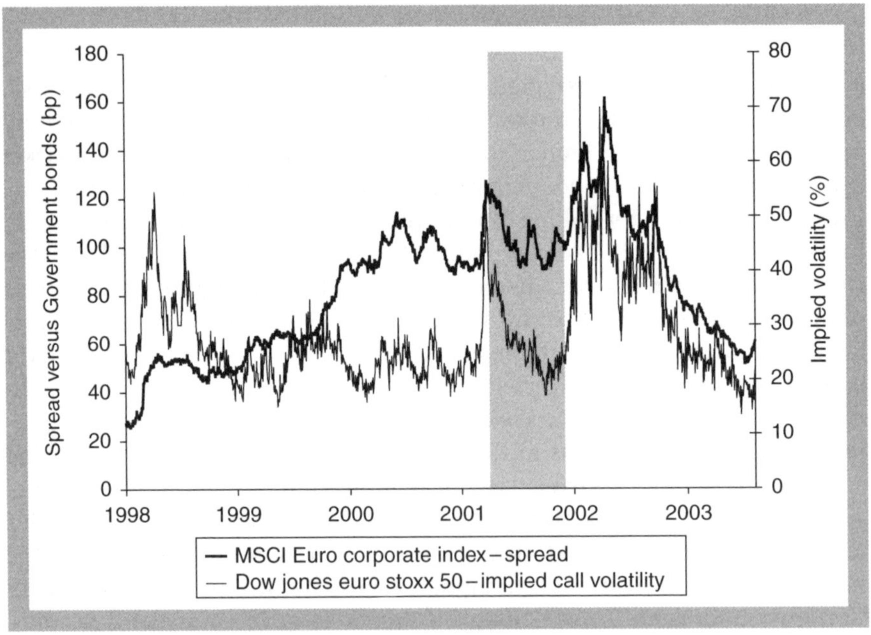

Figure 3.26 Euro corporate bond spreads versus Dow Jones Euro Stoxx 50 implied volatility of at-the-money call options

Source: MSCI and Dow Jones

falls below a certain threshold the effect of small changes on spreads is rather subdued.

Remember that corporate bonds can be replicated by the combination of a riskless bond and a short put on the assets of the company. Since lower rated bonds generally are closer to at-the-money than higher rated bonds, it can be expected that the increase of equity-market volatility leads to a widening of the spread differential between issues of different rating classes. This is due to the fact that the sensitivity of the bonds to changes in volatility is different. Options that trade close to at-the-money levels react more strongly given a change in volatility compared with options, which trade far out-of-the-money. The above-described relationships can be witnessed particularly well during crash scenarios in equity markets. In 1990/91, the rise in equity volatility, which was initiated by numerous profit warnings by companies, was a leading indicator of credit spreads. Figure 3.27 shows that the subsequent rise in implied equity-market volatility led to a steepening of the yield differential between high and lower rated credits. Baa and Aa rating classes are chosen to illustrate this relationship because for these rating classes the bond universe offers sufficient breadth and liquidity.

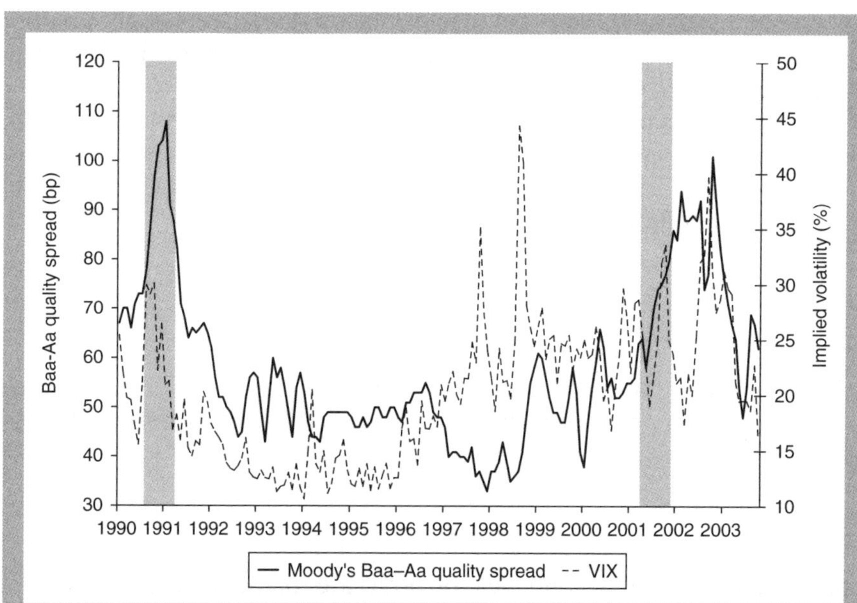

Figure 3.27 Moody's Baa–Aa spread differential versus implied equity volatility for the S&P 100

Source: Moody's and S&P's

3.3.3 A risk premia approach

The rapid growth of the European corporate bond market since 1997 has promoted the acceptance of corporate bonds as a separate asset class. Therefore, identifying relative value not only between equities and government bonds, but also relative to corporate bonds, has become a central task of asset allocators. But, of course, this analysis is also relevant from the perspective of a pure fixed income investor. Not only does it help to assess the outlook for credit spreads in general, but also to decide on the beta or, in other words, the aggressiveness of a pure corporate bond portfolio relative to its benchmark. Although it has been common use to compare equities and government bonds, it is far less common to compare equities and corporate bonds.

One approach to identify relative value between the above-mentioned asset classes is to compare risk premia. For corporate bonds this is equivalent to the spread over government bonds. The comparison versus equities requires the estimation of the equity risk premium, that is the difference between the expected rate of return on the stock market and a risk-free interest rate, usually long-term government bond yields. While there are differences in the sector structure of the equity and corporate bond markets, for example with respect to technology exposure, the equity credit premium may nevertheless provide valuable insights into the relative valuation of both markets. This is because risk factors such as economic growth, risk aversion and implied equity volatility influence both markets in a similar manner.

The equity risk premium is derived from the Dividend Discount Model. It states that the current stock price is equivalent to the present value of future dividends. Assuming a constant real rate of dividend growth, g, the equity risk premium is defined as

$$P = \sum_{t=1}^{\infty} \frac{D(1+g)^t}{(1+r)^t} = \frac{D}{r-g},$$

where D denotes the current dividend and r the real rate of return required by equity-market participants to invest in stocks. Rewriting the equation as

$$r = \frac{D}{P} + g$$

and subtracting the real bond yield on both sides of the equation shows that the equity risk premium is equal to dividend yield plus real dividend growth minus real bond yield. To calculate an ex ante equity risk premium real long-term dividend growth has to be estimated. Numerous studies show that real dividends should grow with the same rate as real GDP over the long term. For the US economy, trend growth is typically estimated to lie between 3.5 and 4 percent over time, depending on the assumptions for productivity and population growth. To graph the equity risk premium we also need to estimate the real long-term bond yield. In order to adjust the nominal yield on 10-year treasury securities for inflation, we subtract the expected inflation that is published by the University of Michigan. This time series reaches back to 1978, whereas data on inflation-linked treasury securities is only available since 1997.

Whenever the equity risk premium falls below current spread levels, there is a quasi-arbitrage opportunity between corporate bonds and equities. After a long period with a positive equity credit premium, the picture changed in 1999, signaling the height of the equity bubble. The interpretation of this was that expected returns on corporate bonds versus equities were extremely attractive. While corporate bonds actually outperformed equities by far between 2000 and 2002, those years were characterized by a massive widening of credit spreads. Due to the bursting of the tech bubble and the credit spread tightening since fall 2002, the gap has closed.

While portfolio managers are mostly concerned about fluctuations of market prices in the short term, private investors tend to compare expected returns over the longer term. Since Moody's Baa corporate bond index is based on bonds with a minimum maturity of 20 years, it is possible to approximate the probability of corporate bonds outperforming equities

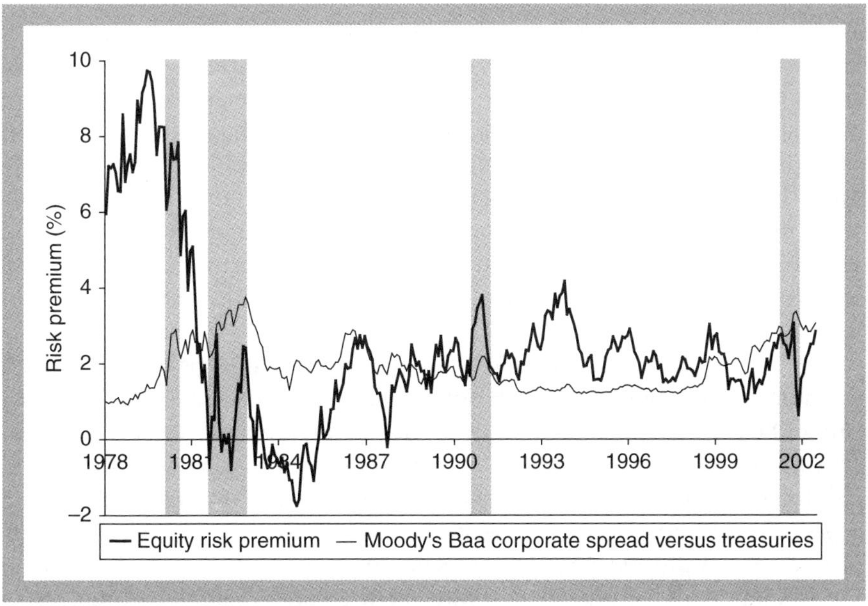

Figure 3.28 Ex ante equity risk premium for the US stock market and Moody's Baa corporate spreads versus treasuries

Source: Moody's and Union Investment

over this period. Using the current risk premia of equities and corporate bonds and historical default probabilities to estimate corporate bond excess returns, the probability of equities outperforming corporate bonds is given by

$$P = \phi\left[\sqrt{T}\left(\frac{r - i}{\sigma} - \frac{\sigma}{2}\right)\right],$$

where $\phi(\cdot)$ is the normal density function, T is time, σ denotes equity volatility and $r - i$ is the ex ante risk premium, or the difference between the equity risk premium and current corporate bond spreads. The ex ante equity credit premium equals

$$r - i = \frac{D}{P} + g - \left(Y + S - S \cdot (1 - R) \cdot p_d\right),$$

where S denotes spread and Y real bond yield. Assuming a constant recovery rate of 40 percent and a 1-year default probability for Baa-rated bonds of 0.15 percent, one can calculate the probability of equities outperforming corporate bonds over time.

3.3.4 Risk appetite

The corporate bond market is a leading indicator of economic activity. However, its forecasting power is obviously not perfect, because – like equity markets – credit spreads sometimes predict recessions that do not occur subsequently. After the 1987 stock market crash, for example, credit spreads widened significantly. A similar observation could be made in 1998, following the LTCM hedge fund crisis and Russia's default. Yet, both events were not followed by a recession. The spread widening rather mirrored increasing risk averseness of investors. In general, risk appetite or risk aversion refer to market participants' willingness and ability to invest in risky assets.

Market participants often cite changes in investors' risk appetite as a possible explanation for developments in global financial markets that cannot be explained by changes of market fundamentals. Indeed, financial crises often seem to coincide with abrupt shifts in market sentiment from risk tolerance to risk avoidance. While fundamentals undoubtedly remain of significant importance, these shifts are likely to reflect the effective risk attitude as manifested through the behavior of active investors. But behavior similar to that induced by shifts in the fundamental preferences of investors over risk and return can also reflect changes in the composition of active market players or tactical trading patterns. Theoreticians like Kumar and Persaud (2001) argue that investors' risk appetite not only changes over time, but also that these changes can be measured. If included in fundamentally based econometric models, risk appetite can lead to more accurate forecasts of market developments. Tools that track the dynamics of investors' willingness to take on risks can lead to a better understanding of the functioning of financial markets. In particular, they can supplement the risk management of institutional investors. Sophisticated models therefore aim to distill a measure for risk appetite from a broad spectrum of sufficiently liquid assets. By taking various assets from across the global risk spectrum, a comprehensive comparison of the returns that they have offered relative to risk can be made.

Geopolitical risks like war and terror can create stress scenarios for all risky asset classes. The geopolitical situation has a strong impact on the risk aversion of investors. The events of September 11, 2001, provide a tragic example after which investors bought safe haven assets such as government bonds and gold at the cost of risky asset classes. Very risky and illiquid asset classes are particularly sensitive to changes in risk appetite. In times of growing risk appetite, more volatile and hence riskier assets perform well as investors become more willing to tolerate risk in exchange for higher expected returns. When risk appetite is falling, the reverse happens as risk premia rise and funds flow to safer assets. Consequently, special attention has to be paid in periods of high uncertainty. The most important indicators for risk aversion should be observed regularly. Among the most common indicators are implied volatilities and put/call ratios on equity options and options on interest rate future. The relative performance of growth and value stocks or high and low beta stocks can also help to estimate risk appetite. Gold and oil prices, too, often react quickly to changes in the geopolitical environment. Intermarket comparisons of the performance and volatility of different asset classes not only indicate changes in the risk-loving attitude of investors, but also contain valuable information about the relative attractivity of certain markets. However, some of the above-mentioned indicators may temporarily be distorted through demand and supply dynamics, or through a lack of liquidity.

The cyclical nature of risk appetite is shown in Figure 3.29. Changes in risk appetite seem to depend on the level of risk appetite in the preceding month. Up- and downswings of risk appetite are driven by investors' perceptions. If risky assets have outperformed for some time, investors tend to expect a continuation of this outperformance. Conversely, during times of underperformance of risky assets, investors apparently recall the downside risks associated with higher yielding assets. At the height of the equity bubble in March 2000, for example, riskier assets had been performing better than safer assets, whereas at the 'panic' low in October 2002, riskier assets had been performing worse. It should be noted that reversals seem to become more and more likely as risk appetite reaches extreme levels. For

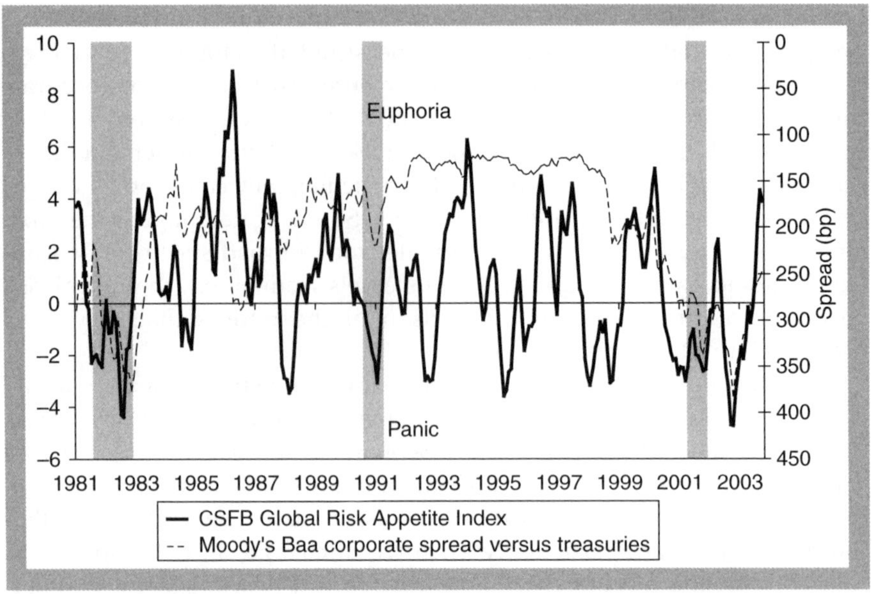

Figure 3.29 Baa corporate bond spreads and CSFB Global Risk Appetite Index

Source: CSFB and Moody's

example, having made a panic low CSFB's Global Risk Appetite Index usually reenters the euphoria zone in roughly 12–18 months. This index is calculated as the slope of a weighted regression of the returns of a broad range of assets from across the global risk spectrum against their historical return volatility. At a 'euphoric' peak as in March 2000, riskier assets had been performing a lot better than safer assets, whereas at a 'panic' low such as October 2002, riskier assets had been performing worse. Kindleberger (1978) describes the periods when the risk appetite reaches extremes as 'distress'. He notes that in the extreme zone there appears to be an increased probability that events, which normally would be ignored by financial markets, trigger a reversal of the cycle.

Tversky and Kahneman (1974, 1979) and Shiller (1998) argue that the assumption of rational, utility-maximizing behavior of investors is frequently violated in real life. They also show that these anomalies can be predicted and that they result from the use of simple heuristics to facilitate the process of decision-making. Sophisticated investors can benefit from this fact if they are able to predict changes in the direction of risk appetite correctly. In particular, reversals in risk appetite often correspond with turning points in the direction of spreads. Risk appetite indicators may also be a useful tool for major asset allocation decisions such as stocks versus bonds, value versus growth stocks or emerging markets versus developed markets.

3.4 MARKET TECHNICALS

3.4.1 Market structure

The assessment of the macroeconomic environment results in a judgement of the stage of the business cycle and the leverage cycle. Valuation indicators help to form an opinion on the future direction of credit spreads. However, the magnitude of a change in spreads essentially depends on the market structure, especially the average credit quality and the share of cyclical sectors. Lower average quality of the issues or a higher portion of cyclical industries typically results in a higher volatility of credit spreads, and therefore higher mark-to-market risk. Rational investors should require an additional risk premium for investing in a more volatile market, as an additional spread provides a cushion against adverse market movements.

A comparison of the sector structure of the Euro and US dollar corporate bond markets shows that the share of financials is much higher in the Euro market (see Table 3.2). While financial companies are somewhat cyclical, especially with respect to changes in the interest-rate environment, they are usually considered a rather defensive sector. The same holds true for the utility sector. Thus, it becomes very clear that the Euro corporate bond market as a whole is less exposed to the economic environment than the US market. However, we have not analyzed the industrial sector so far. Here, the picture is mixed. While the Euro market has a higher weight of automotive companies, the other cyclical sectors, such as basic industries, capital goods, consumer and services cyclical, media and technology, generally have a higher share in the US market.

From the industry structure it becomes obvious that the average credit quality of the issuers in the US investment grade market is lower than in the Euro corporate bond market. The current rating of the Euro market is A+, whereas it is only A− in the US market. Over the last 5 years this differential has fluctuated between 1 and 2 notches. This helps to explain the wider spreads generally observed in the US corporate bond market (see Figure 3.30). Additionally, US corporate bond spreads have been substantially more volatile than their Euro peers. Especially in times of weak equity markets and rising implied equity volatility the US market tends to underperform. This is due to the fact that lower rated bonds are usually closer to the default threshold. Therefore, the put option on the assets of the company is more sensitive to changes in equity price and volatility.

But the more cyclical character of the US market and the lower average credit quality of the issuers are not the only reasons that explain the spread

Table 3.2 Structure of the markets for Euro and US Dollar denominated investment grade corporate bonds as of October 2003 (in percent)

	Euro corporates (%)	USD corporates (%)
Financials	45.3	33.4
Banking	33.8	15.9
Brokerage	1.8	6.4
Finance and investment	5.1	8.0
Insurance	4.6	3.1
Industrials	45.2	60.2
Automotive	10.1	7.7
Basic industry	3.1	4.0
Capital goods	3.2	4.8
Consumer cyclical	1.2	3.2
Consumer noncyclical	6.2	8.1
Energy	2.1	8.1
Media	1.1	5.7
Real estate	0.6	1.9
Services cyclical	2.8	4.0
Services noncyclical	0.1	0.9
Technology and electronics	0.7	2.4
Telecommunications	14.0	9.5
Utilities	9.6	6.4
Utilities	9.6	6.4

Source: Merrill Lynch

differential. Another reason is the different investor base. It was already pointed out that the European corporate bond market is still young, while the US market is well developed and has attracted a broad base of institutional investors. Those investors are usually very concerned about mark-to-market losses, and therefore their decisions are driven by short-term considerations. Furthermore, hedge funds have been very active in the US corporate bond market over the last years. Both issues have helped to increase volatility. However, with the growing liquidity of the European corporate bond market and the increased professionality of investors, this differential probably will diminish.

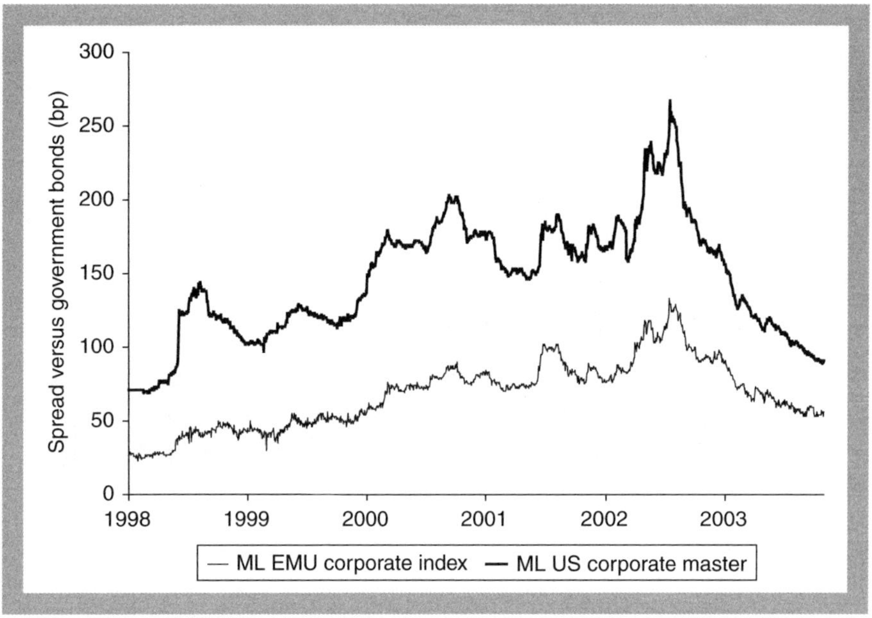

Figure 3.30 Spread versus government bonds for Euro and US$ investment grade corporate bonds

Source: Merrill Lynch

3.4.2 Issuance activity

The high correlation between M&A activity and equity market performance clearly shows that M&A was a major driver of the equity bubble of the late 1990s. Sometimes even mergers that did not create synergies were rewarded by rising stock prices on the side of the overtaking parties. It was obvious that not every merger was going to increase operating profitability. Yet, the degrees of freedom in goodwill accounting helped to grow earnings per share without actually increasing profit levels. At the height of the equity bubble, investors encouraged companies to use their own overvalued equity to pay for the overvalued assets of another company (see Figure 3.31).

But a lot of this M&A frenzy was financed by debt. Consequently, the balance sheets of many companies deteriorated rapidly. Doubts, if the exuberant profit expectations would be fulfilled, and concerns about company leverage initiated the decline in equity markets. The bubble burst when investors realized that they were not compensated for the downside risks associated with investing in overvaluated tech companies. When a few of the TMT newcomers began to struggle, investors had to acknowledge that there was no free money to be made in TMT IPOs. Highly leveraged

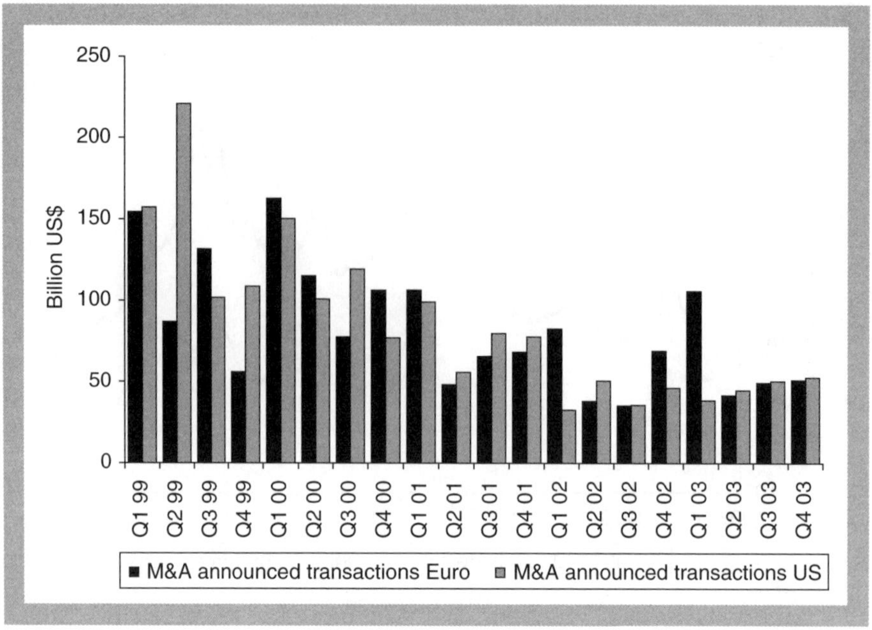

Figure 3.31 Volume of announced mergers, acquisitions or divestitures involving either a European respectively US target or acquirer

Source: Bloomberg

balance sheets caused serious problems for some of the brightest stars of the equity hype, and for some of the big companies. Actually much of the equity bubble was concentrated on large cap companies.

Figure 3.32 highlights that in the last 20 years there were two periods, when US companies substituted equity by debt, especially by issuing corporate bonds. Consequently, between 1984 and 1990 and in the second half of the 1990s leverage rose dramatically. It also stands out that there were various periods when banks' lending standards were extremely restrictive and one period, namely since 2000, when activity in the commercial paper market slowed down. Both events spurred corporate bond issuance in the past. If the usual pattern of the credit cycle holds, equity buybacks remain subdued until the economic expansion gains ground. As long as companies are willing to repair their balance sheets, net corporate bond issuance is also expected to be low. The analysis of the maturity structure of outstanding US and Euro corporate bonds shows a massive amount of redemptions for 2004 and 2005. On the other hand, while supply should remain weak during this period, demand for US financial assets by foreign residents is expected to remain strong. It is primarily driven by European investors and Asian central banks that pour huge amounts of money into the US capital market (see Figure 3.33). A potential shift in the balance of

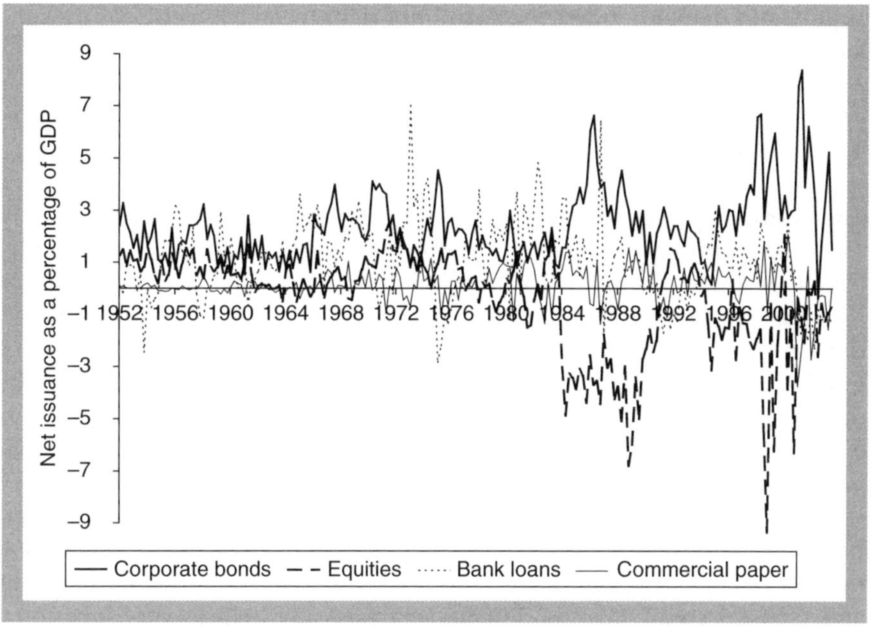

Figure 3.32 Net issuance of the US nonfinancial corporate sector

Source: Federal Reserve

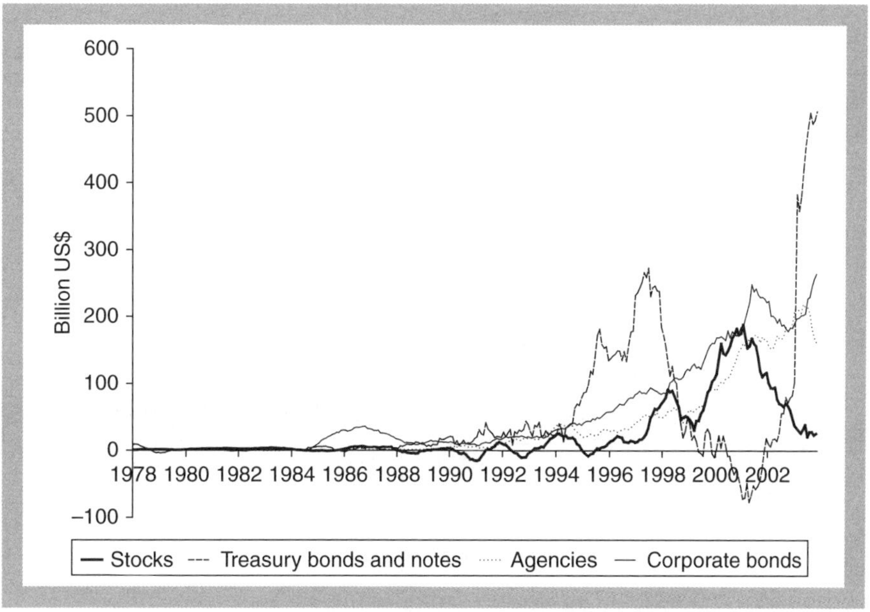

Figure 3.33 Rolling 12-month net foreign purchases of US financial assets

Source: US Treasury

supply and demand, however, is an important technical factor for the outlook for corporate bond spreads.

3.4.3 Flows of funds

The overall sentiment of investors towards the asset class corporate bonds is mirrored in mutual fund flows. Monthly and weekly statistics, for example, from Investment Company Institute, AIG and Trim Tabs, track the net flows into the major asset classes and their subcomponents. They also give an indication about the portion of cash held in mutual funds. The published numbers can help to explain movements in credit spreads that are not directly related to changes in the fundamental environment for credit. For example, they partly reflect risk appetite of investors. This is especially true, when looking at flows into high-yield bond funds. Major shifts in the asset allocation of institutional investors can also be observed from the data. Yet, published information on mutual fund flows tends to be behind the curve, in other words it is a lagging indicator for the activity of market participants and thus for credit spreads. But the analysis may help to spot long-term trends in the relative attractiveness of different asset classes (see Figure 3.34).

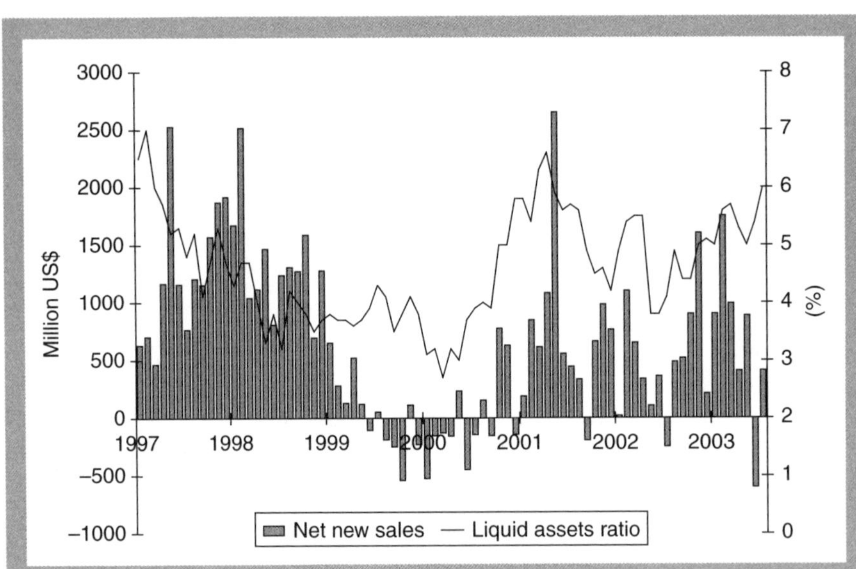

Figure 3.34 Net new sales and liquid assets ratio of US investment grade corporate bond funds

Source: Investment Company Institute

CHAPTER 4

Tactical Asset Allocation

4.1 OVERVIEW

The tactical asset allocation in credit portfolios combines top-down- and bottom-up analyses in order to arrive at medium- to short-term investment decisions (see Figure 4.1). In this step of the investment process three major subjects are tackled:

- Spread class selection,
- Sector allocation, and
- Credit curve positioning.

When making a decision about the allocation of resources to different spread classes, elements of the top-down analysis clearly have a substantial impact, since the assessment of the fundamental and technical environment for credit and the valuation relative to other asset classes have significant influence on the positioning within the credit asset class. Conversely, credit curve decisions are usually implemented on a sector or, probably even more frequently, on a single issuer basis. Although elements of the bottom-up analysis clearly influence the positioning on the credit curve, there are also some economy-wide indicators that have to be considered. Therefore, and with respect to the time horizon of investment decisions and their potential impact on active portfolio performance, the three above-mentioned issues should constitute an own step in a structured investment process for credit portfolios.

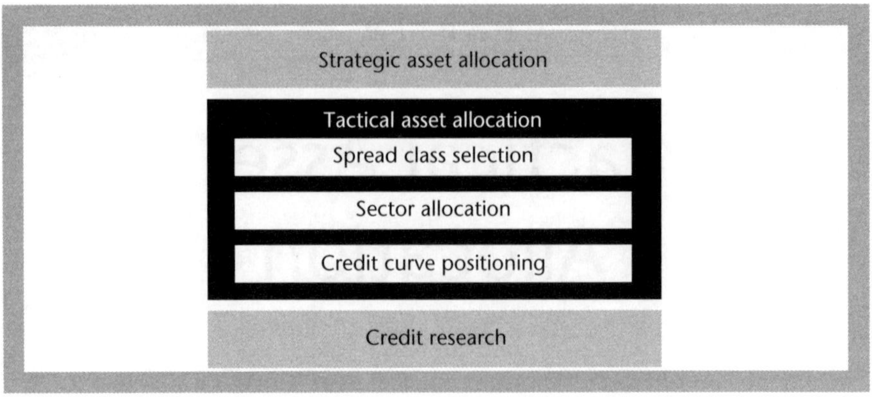

Figure 4.1 Structure of the tactical asset allocation
Source: Union Investment

4.2 SPREAD CLASS SELECTION

The risk profile of a credit portfolio, in absolute terms as well as relative to a benchmark index, is largely determined by the weighting of different risk classes. Of course, the allocation of capital to riskier asset classes not only increases risk, but also offers ample opportunities for outperformance. From a top-down perspective there are various methods to split the corporate bond universe in different risk classes. Here the three most popular approaches are introduced: dividing the universe by rating classes, by degrees of subordination or by the degree of cyclicality of the different industries.

4.2.1 Rating classes

While in a single name context ratings are often criticized for being lagging indicators of credit quality, classifying bonds by rating is one widely used method to reflect the behavior of different risk classes in credit markets. Many market participants argue that spreads themselves and spread volatilities are more timely indicators of an issuer's credit risk than ratings. They consequently prefer to split the universe in spread class buckets. The disadvantage of this method is that it leads to relatively unstable compositions of the individual buckets and is less convenient, because the major index providers do not calculate indices based on spread classes. Since the different rating buckets constitute the corporate bond market as a whole, there is clearly a correlation between overall market fluctuations and the spread changes of the different rating subportfolios.

Investors require a premium for taking on credit risk. Not only does this premium, in other words the credit spread, have to increase with decreasing credit quality, but one also expects a higher sensitivity of spreads to changes of the fundamental environment for lower rated credits. As pointed out in Chapter 2, the assets of a company with a higher degree of leverage are nearer to the default threshold than those of a firm with a conservative balance sheet structure. In terms of the structural model the short put option on the assets of the issuer moves nearer at-the-money with decreasing credit quality, causing the delta to rise. Hence, a falling value of the assets, for example, in periods of a deteriorating economic environment and consequently declining equity markets, leads to a larger change in the credit spread the lower the credit quality of the issuer is.

Figure 4.2 is representative for the characteristics of different risk classes compared to the corporate bond market as a whole, because it covers the boom of the late 1990s as well as the first recession of the new millennium in 2001. Both were reflected in equity markets, first by the technology bubble between 1997 and early 2000, then by the eventual correction of the excesses until the equity markets bottomed in March 2003. The chart shows that none of the rating buckets could decouple from the general trends in the credit market. However, BBB-rated corporate bonds tend to suffer more when credit spreads widen and to benefit particularly from a positive trend in the corporate bond market. AAA-rated bonds conversely have the lowest sensitivity to market fluctuations.

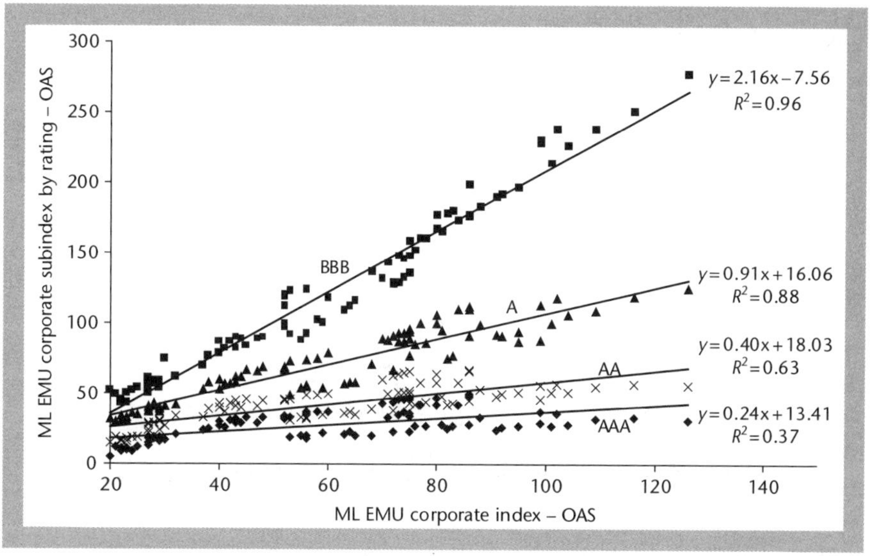

Figure 4.2 Sensitivity of different rating buckets to spread changes in the Merrill Lynch EMU corporate index in the period Dec. 1996–Feb. 2004

Source: Merrill Lynch and Union Investment

Another point stands out from Figure 4.2. BBB-rated corporate bonds obviously have a very high correlation to fluctuations of credit spreads in general. Although they made up on average only 25 percent of the Euro investment grade market, the influence of lower rated bonds on market spreads is substantial. Higher quality bonds, on the other hand, exhibit lower correlations to market spread changes. One reason is that their impact on the market direction is less pronounced because they are less volatile. But the second reason is probably more important. Euro corporate bonds are typically valued against swaps, that is the spread versus government bonds consists of two components: the swap spread and the spread over swaps. As a consequence changes of swap spreads have an influence on the spread of a corporate bond versus duration-matched treasuries. The higher the credit quality and the lower the spread of an issuer, the higher is the fraction of the benchmark spread that is due to the swap spread.

4.2.2 Degrees of subordination

A second method to slice the corporate bond universe, especially the financial sector, is by different degrees of subordination. Chapter 5 discusses the characteristics of different types of bank debt in detail. In summary, Tier 1 preferred, Upper Tier 2 and Lower Tier 2 differ from senior bank debt in two major dimensions: with respect to loss absorption and interest deferral

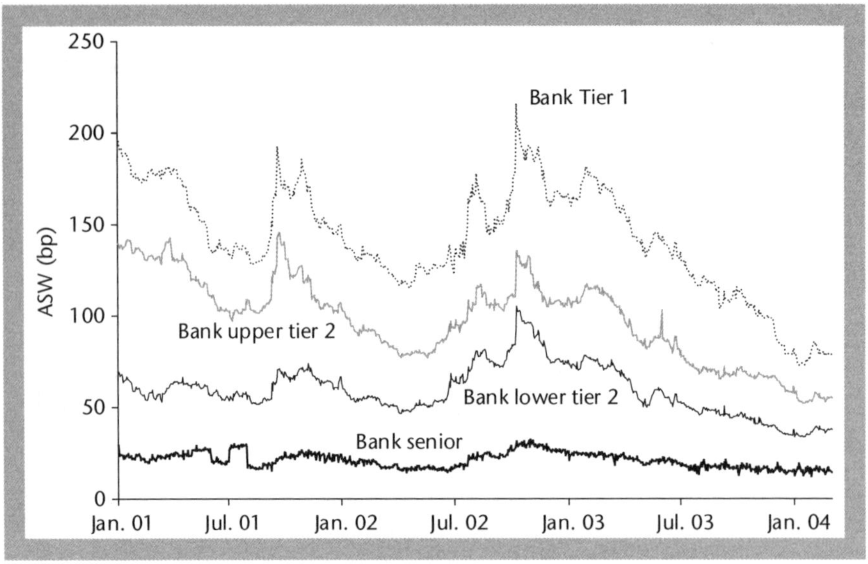

Figure 4.3 Spread history of different types of Euro bank debt
Source: J.P. Morgan

features. Both Tier 1 and Upper Tier 2 capital are able to absorb losses. But while missed interest payments are canceled immediately for Tier 1 issues they are repaid at a later date for Upper Tier 2 bonds. On the other hand, Lower Tier 2 debt contains no loss absorption features.

As a consequence each of the mentioned types of bank capital represents its own risk class. Investors clearly have to be compensated to carry the additional risks compared with senior bank bonds. Figure 4.3 shows that on average the spread differentials between senior bonds and Lower Tier 2, Lower Tier 2 and Upper Tier 2, and Upper Tier 2 and Tier 1 tend to be roughly equal. But one should note that spread volatility also increases significantly when moving to more subordinated types of bank debt. Again, this can be explained by the Merton model. Since Tier 1 and Upper Tier 2 bonds are designed to absorb losses before holders of senior bonds and Lower Tier 2 suffer a loss, the strike price of their embedded short put option is closer at-the-money than that of senior and Lower Tier 2 bonds. Hence, in absolute terms the delta of the short put is higher, causing larger changes of the value of the option and consequently spreads, when fundamentals change.

Besides fundamental developments the risk appetite of investors is a driver of the spread differentials between various risk classes. Risk appetite in general describes the willingness of market participants to invest in risky assets as opposed to risk-free assets. Clearly, risk appetite is an unobservable factor but there are various indicators that are designed to extract a measure for risk appetite or risk aversion from market data. More details on

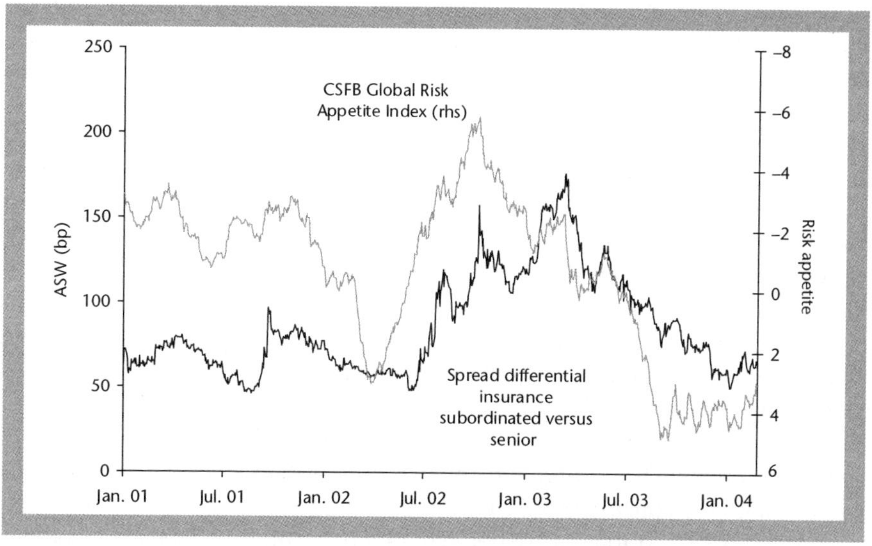

Figure 4.4 Spread differential between senior and subordinated Euro insurance bonds versus risk appetite

Source: J.P. Morgan, CSFB, and Union Investment

this subject are provided in Chapter 3. With respect to the performance of subordinated bonds versus senior bonds, there is an impact of risk appetite. Figure 4.4 shows that spreads usually widen when risk appetite falls and tighten when risk appetite increases. From this chart there seems to be a lead–lag relationship between risk appetite and subsequent credit spread changes. If the leading character of risk appetite holds for the future it may provide valuable trading signals for subordinated financials.

4.2.3 Cyclical versus noncyclical sectors

Finally, while the subjects of industry analysis and the identification of relative value between sectors are covered in more detail below, it should be noted that the sector allocation has a substantial influence on the risk profile of a corporate bond portfolio. Sectors differ not only with respect to the goods or services they produce, but also with respect to their sensitivity to the economic environment. Therefore, investors usually distinguish between cyclical and noncyclical sectors. In general, cyclical industries are those where the ability to generate revenues and cash flows is closely linked to the business cycle. Usually, this is due to the fact that the companies in those sectors produce goods or services for private consumption or that belong in the category of capital expenditures. Typical examples of cyclical sectors therefore are the automotive and the capital goods sector.

The breakdown of real GDP in its components highlights the importance of private consumption and investment for the state of the economy. In Q4 2003, personal consumption and investment accounted for 87 percent of US real GDP, that is, these components are major drivers of the economic cycle. Although the National Bureau of Economic Research (NBER) that is responsible for dating recessions employs a variety of indicators to determine the peak and trough of an economic cycle, recessions are usually characterized by declining private demand. Figure 4.5, however, illustrates that this was not true for the 2001 recession. The consumer held up very well, taking on even more debt and thus stretching his balance sheet to the limit. Tax rebates and incentives like the zero percent financing in the automotive sector supported the high level of consumption additionally, so that the indebtedness of private households reached record highs while the savings rate plunged to extremely low levels by historical standards. This combination explains not only the limited downturn of retail sales during the 2001 recession, but also the sluggish recovery compared to former recessions.

Although the consumer sector did surprisingly well, the spreads of cyclical sectors widened massively between the beginning of 2000 and October 2002. Apart from external shocks such as September 11, 2001, there are two economic explanations for this observation. First, the corporate sector increased its leverage dramatically between 1997 and 2001, for the benefit

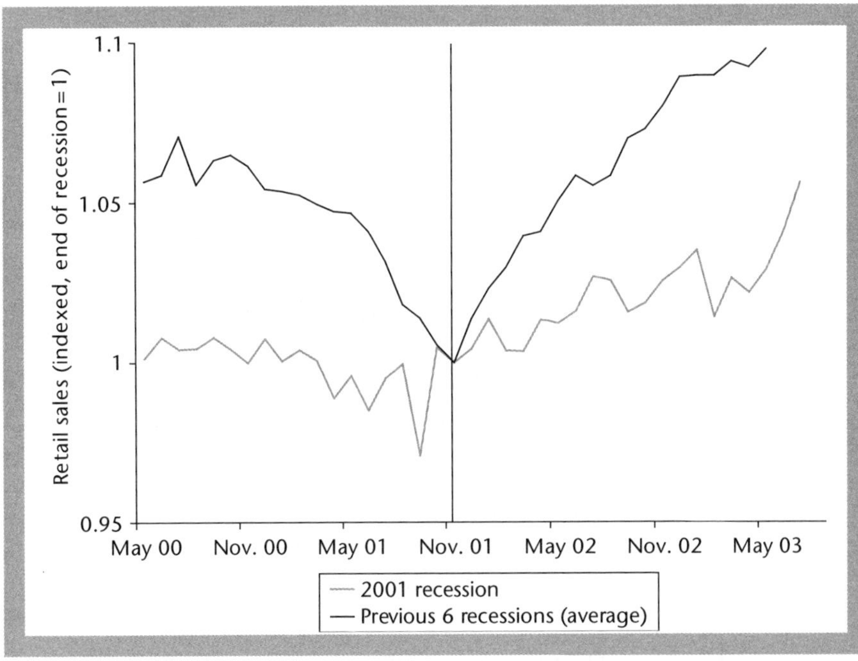

Figure 4.5 Retail sales around the 2001 recession in comparison to the previous six recessions

Source: National Bureau of Economic Research

of shareholders and at the cost of bondholders. The high level of leverage made companies vulnerable to economic downturns. Second, the recession that finally occurred in the United States was not typical in the sense that it was not driven by a lack of private demand, but it was rather driven by overinvestment, overcapacities in many industries and as a consequence there was a decline of business investment. The capital goods sector was directly affected by this development and credit spreads widened substantially. The automotive sector, conversely, suffered rather from speculations that the consumer might break away one day. Additionally, the incentive programs weakened profitability in the already fragile automotive sector further and funding gaps in the pension plans materialized following the burst of the equity bubble.

On the other hand, noncyclical sectors like banks and utilities performed reasonably well in 2001, as Figure 4.6 shows. The steepening yield curve helped banks to increase their interest margins and thus to offset the costs associated with the declining credit quality in the customer base. The utility sector again justified its safe haven status that is based on the utility companies' strong ability to generate cash flows.

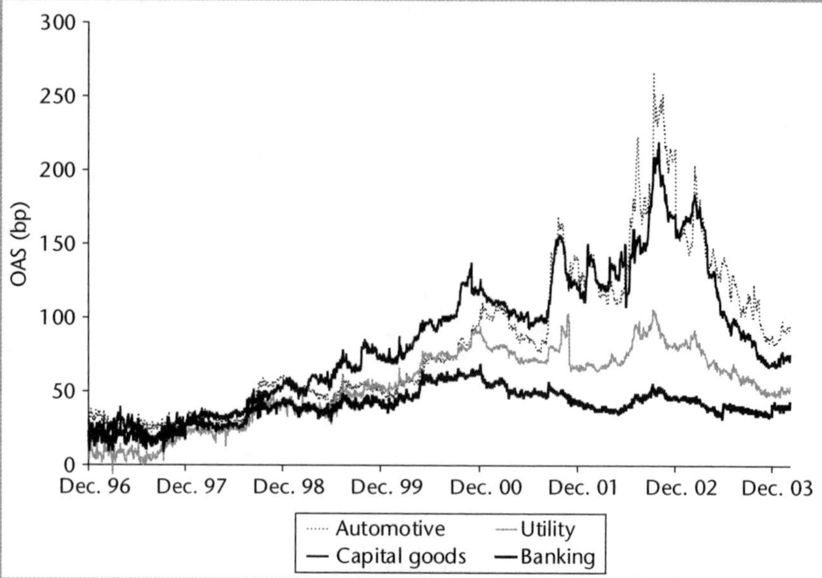

Figure 4.6 Spread history of different industry sectors of the Euro corporate bond market

Source: Merrill Lynch

4.3 SECTOR ALLOCATION

4.3.1 Industry analysis

The sector selection is one of the most important performance drivers in a corporate bond portfolio. The overweighting and underweighting of different industries is a key element in a corporate bond strategy. The weighting of sectors in a corporate bond portfolio is the result of controlled deviations from the benchmark. They are based on the analysis of the operating environment of specific sectors, a bottom-up analysis of the respective companies and the risk-return profiles of bonds from a specific sector. It is advantageous to set up a corporate bond team by sectors because this structure allows an in-depth coverage of all sectors and the understanding of the competitive environment as well as the market positions and management strategies of single companies out of each sector. An industry consists of a group of firms which offer products that are close substitutes for each other.

Industry analysis consists of estimating the industries' earnings streams and their volatility under consideration of industry-specific economic cycles. An industry's expected growth versus GDP growth and capacity utilization worldwide give indications for the industry's cyclicality. Figure 4.7 summarizes the key elements of an industry analysis. They will be discussed in detail in the following sections.

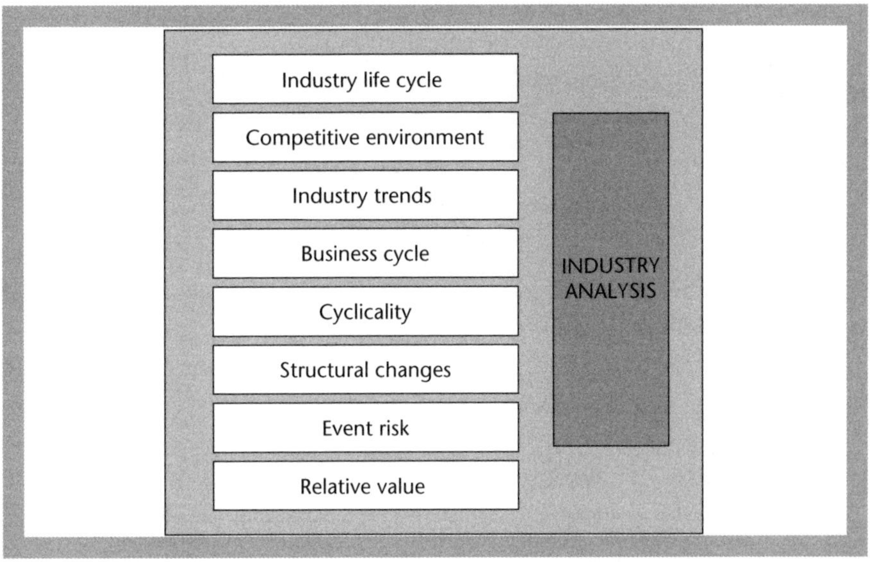

Figure 4.7 Structure of the industry analysis
Source: Union Investment

Generally, trends in demand, supply, pricing and profit margins determine the outlook for an industry. Careful analyses help to assess which of these key indicators have a major impact on investor behavior at present time and which will be the indicators to watch in the future.

4.3.1.1 Industry life cycle

The analysis of an industry's life cycle is useful for making projections about profit margins, earnings growth, trends in sales and profitability. To simplify things it is quite common to reduce the entire life cycle of an industry to 5 stages (Figure 4.8). Such a 5-stage model is described by Reilly and Brown (2003). A brief description of the different stages will follow next.

- Pioneering development: A modest sales growth is accompanied by small or negative profit margins and profits. The firms face high R&D costs. Most recent examples are high-tech companies or internet-based companies with unproven business models. Most of the financing is obtained through venture capital or private equity.
- Rapid accelerating growth: Demand for products and services grows and due to only few competitors, profit margins are high. Firms experience substantial backlogs and production capacity is being built up. At this

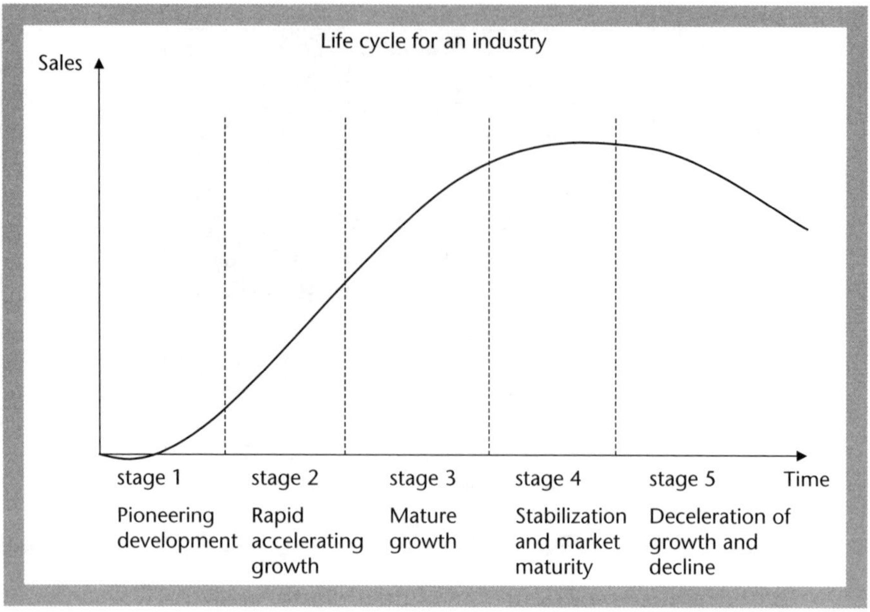

Figure 4.8 Life cycle of an industry
Source: Reilly and Brown, 2003

stage successful companies will be able to access the capital markets for further financing.

- Mature growth: An increasing number of competitors enter the market. The demand for the industry's goods and services is satisfied, prices decline and profit margins begin to decline. At this stage financial discipline is important because future earnings might be lower due to competition. Companies with sustainable debt levels will benefit in the long run.
- Stabilization and market maturity: The growth rate of the industry declines to the growth rate of the aggregate economy and profit growth will vary by industry due to different competitive structures. Competition will result in lower profit margins. In this stage industry trends will contribute to the development of aggregate credit quality.
- Deceleration of growth and decline: Sales growth declines because of changes in demand and new substitutes. An increasing number of companies start to generate losses. The industry experiences a negative credit trend.

For a fixed income investor the best investments will be in sectors whose life cycle is in stages 3 and 4. Stage 1 is characterized by high business and financial risk. The rewards can be substantial but fatal losses can occur as well. The traditional financing sources for early stage industries are venture capital, private equity followed by the equity market. In stage 2 an industry will experience accelerating growth in sales and profits, but it can be assumed that all generated funds will be reinvested to grow the business, and financial discipline will not be a priority to management. Bondholder unfriendly corporate actions across the industry will increase the downside potential for corporate bond investors.

Corporate bond investors should target industries with a balanced business risk and financial risk profile. In mature industries cash flows become increasingly predictable and capital expenditures of companies tend to stabilize. In such an industry the task is to select those companies who succeeded in controlling their cost structures and operate at efficient levels. Those sectors will show a stable credit trend. Structural changes might push a whole industry into a declining stage. Companies out of those industries will experience structural losses, hence their credit metrics will deteriorate. Management will have no options available to stop this trend.

In a next step the competitive environment of an industry has to be analyzed. The 5-Forces diagram by Michael E. Porter summarizes best the interaction of an industry with its economic environment (Figure 4.9). An understanding of those relationships is essential for the projection of credit trends in a sector. The competitive environment determines profit margins and the pricing power of companies.

- Competition within the industry: The competitiveness of an industry can be expressed by the concentration of competition, product differentiation and exit barriers.

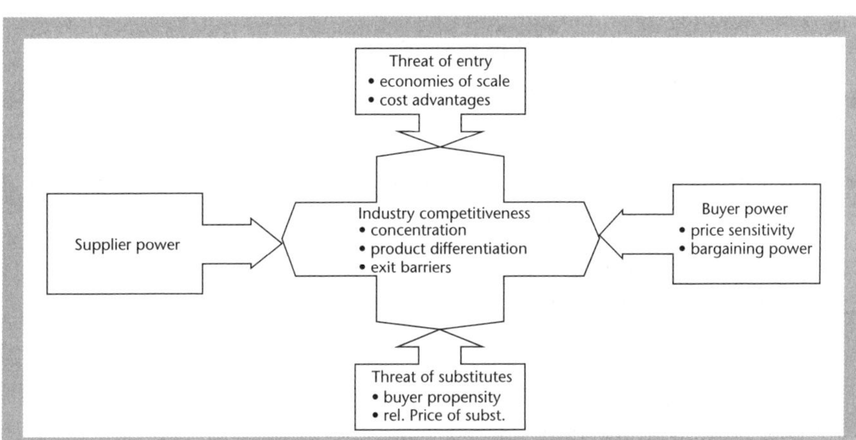

Figure 4.9 5-Forces diagram
Source: Porter

The various types of competition can be grouped as follows:

- Pure monopoly: Only one company provides a certain product or service in an area (e.g. post office, local utility companies). It is a result of regulation, patent, license or economies of scale. Earnings are highly predictable since competition is almost nonexistent and the degree of regulation is very high.
- Pure oligopoly: A few companies produce the same commodity (e.g. oil, steel). There is enough market share for every competitor. Profit margins will depend on the economic cycle and the cyclicality of industries.
- Differentiated oligopoly: A few companies produce partially differentiated products (e.g. cars, computers). The differentiation occurs along lines of quality, features, styling or services. Here it is important to evaluate the different business models of the companies. Profit margins will vary across different industries and companies.
- Monopolistic competition: This industry consists of many competitors able to differentiate their products and services (e.g. food, beverage).
- Pure competition: Many competitors offer the same product and service (e.g. commodity market). The degree of product differentiation gives an estimate about the margin structure of an industry. A low product differentiation is accompanied by an intense price competition which results in low profit margins.

Exit barriers are also important as they vary widely across industries depending on the amount of sunk costs. These are costs a company will not recover when it exits a business.

- Power of supplier: Integration potential

Industry dynamics might be changed, for example, by vertical integration of suppliers.

- Threat by new competitors: High entry barriers can decrease the threat by new competitors. Entry barriers can result from:
    - Economies of scale
    - Product differentiation
    - Cost advantages
    - Capital needs
    - Access to distribution channels
    - Technology know-how
    - Access to raw materials
    - Location advantages
    - Government subsidies

  - Learning curve/product experience.

- Threat by substitutes: The quality or price of substitutes poses a threat to an industry since those substitutes may induce a structural change of an industry.
- Power of buyers: Price sensitivity and bargaining power of buyers have a great effect on the profitability of industries. The automobile industry is a good example at this point. The build-up of overcapacities created a buyers market.

4.3.1.2 Macroeconomic environment

After analyzing industry life cycles and the competitive environment of industries the macroeconomic environment has to be incorporated in the industry analysis process. For this purpose the focus will be on business cycles and the cyclicality of industries.

Figure 4.10 shows a long history of corporate profits as a percentage of GDP across several economic cycles. Corporate profits tend to fall long before the economy goes through a recession. Corporate profits usually reach their bottom towards the end of a recession. They start to rebound with rising economic activity. During the last expansion, which was one of the longest and that stretched through the 1990s, corporate profits started to deteriorate already in 1998. Sharply rising equity valuations, a focus on shareholder value and an undisciplined build-up of leverage induced a decline in profits when the earnings growth trend reversed. Every business cycle will be different from past cycles so the task is to identify evolving trends in order to make reliable projections about future performance.

Corporate spreads and profits showed a close relationship during past economic cycles (see Figure 4.11). Deteriorating profits as a percentage of GDP go along with wider credit spreads. Market phases with improving profits are accompanied by tighter credit spreads.

The business cycle sets the parameters for the sector rotation strategy. Sectors with a high cyclical component will outperform at the early stages of an economic expansion while noncyclical sectors will tend to underperform during an expansion phase relative to the market. The cyclicality of a sector allows predictions about the development of earnings across business cycles. For example, the business of IT hardware companies depends on the capital expenditure (CAPEX) plans of other companies. In an economic slowdown when CAPEX is scaled back or postponed, IT hardware companies run a higher risk of being downgraded due to a deterioration of their credit protection measures. The most recent examples are the telecommunications equipment companies Alcatel and Ericsson. Both suffered from the lack of demand by telecommunications companies in 2002.

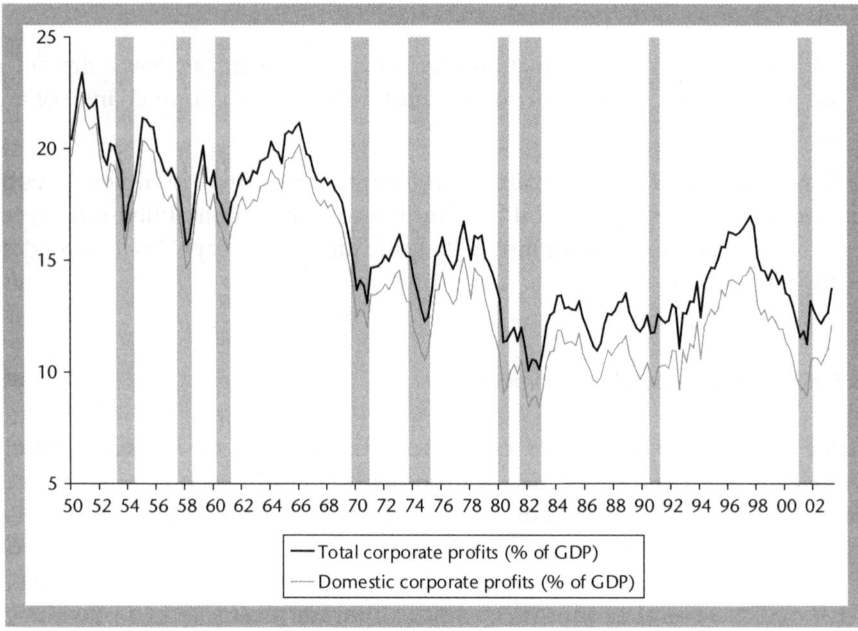

Figure 4.10 Total and domestic corporate profits as a percentage of GDP 1950–2003

Source: Union Investment

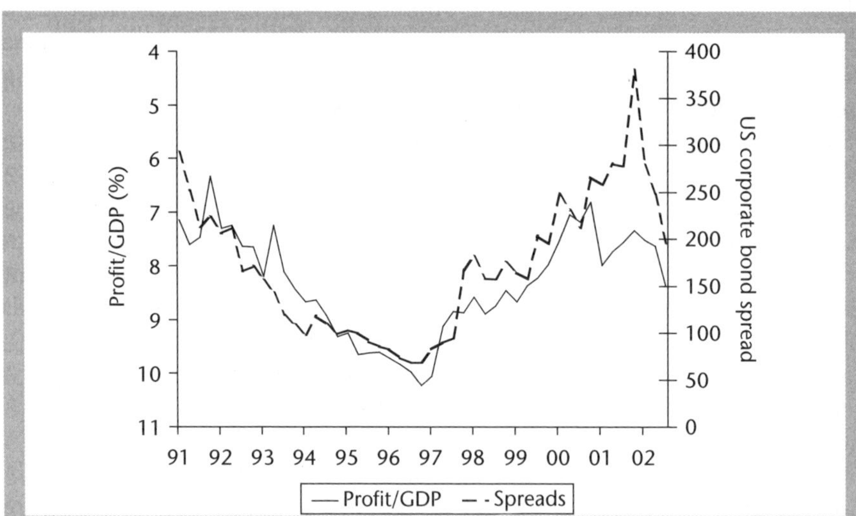

Figure 4.11 US corporate bond spreads and corporate profits as a percentage of GDP 1991–2003

Source: Union Investment

The defensive character of noncyclical sectors pays off during stages of weak economic growth. Figure 4.12 shows at what stage in the economy cycle the different industries reach their profit peaks relative to the market. This is a basis for a sector rotation strategy but the profit cycle is not the only selection criterion.

Banks show a profit rebound in the early phase of a recovery because the countercyclical Fed policy that is often observed in this economic environment results in low interest rates. A steep yield curve helps banks to increase their interest margins.

Automobile manufacturers usually realize a profit rebound at the early stages of an economic rebound because consumer confidence improves and induces a higher demand for discretionary products. In this phase favorable financing is also available and especially car manufacturers can substantially increase their sales through financing initiatives like zero-percent financing and large discounts for new car sales. Cyclical industries like automobiles have a high operating leverage which means that they will benefit at the early stages of economic recovery because they experience a rise in sales. Also industries with high financial leverage benefit from rising sales volume. Fixed financial costs like interest expenses determine financial leverage.

Capital goods, paper, and metals and mining companies realize their respective profit peaks at the later stages of an economic expansion as they produce goods and services whose demand is closely tied to economic activity. Additionally business peak cycles are accompanied by inflation as demand exceeds supply and for example, basic material industries experience higher profit margins in this environment because their production

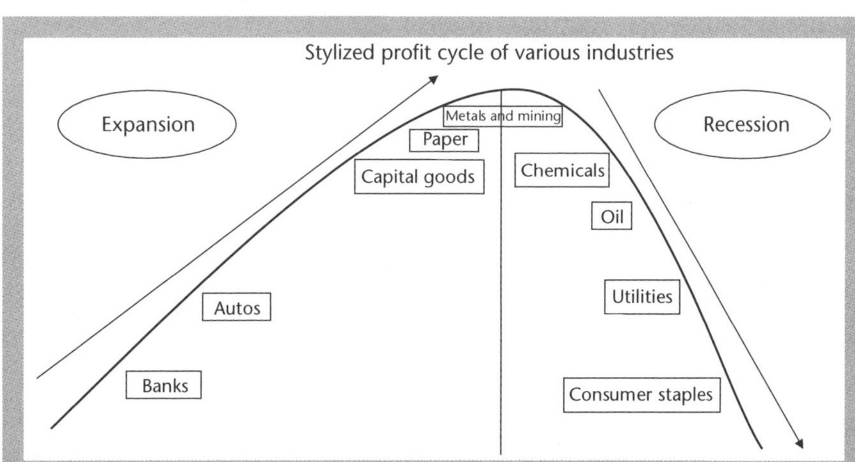

Figure 4.12 Profit cycle of various industries
Source: National Income and Product accounts and Union Investment

costs are not significantly affected by inflation and, on the other side, they can increase prices for the finished products. Industries with a high operating leverage benefit as well because their costs are fixed in nominal terms and revenues increase with inflation. The fixed costs in a company's operating structure determine the operating leverage. Generally, it can be said that industries with a high fixed cost base and high inventory costs, for example, the paper and the aluminum industry, are always under pressure to keep capacity utilization rates high because decreasing capacity utilization rates will have an immediate adverse effect on profitability.

Oil companies' relative profits also peak during a recession because an economic downturn is usually accompanied by high oil prices. Utilities have a noncyclical business profile and they are subject to regulated pricing. They will realize their profit peaks relative to the market during a later stage of an economic downturn.

Consumer staples is a noncyclical sector and hence the profit peak relative to the market is reached towards the end of a recession. Profits are not robust but consumers cut spending on large discretionary purchases while the demand, for example, for food and beverages remains relatively stable across the whole economic cycle.

Figure 4.13 groups sectors according to their change in profits during recession and recovery. The profits of cyclical sectors will fall in recessions and rise during a recovery. On the other side, the profit cycle of defensive companies is countercyclical. Profits will rise in recessions and they will tend to fall in recoveries. Some industries experience structural gains which means that their profits rise during recession and recovery. Other industries suffer from structural losses which means that they realize falling profits in recession and in recovery as well. Those are industries which reached a declining stage in their industry life cycles.

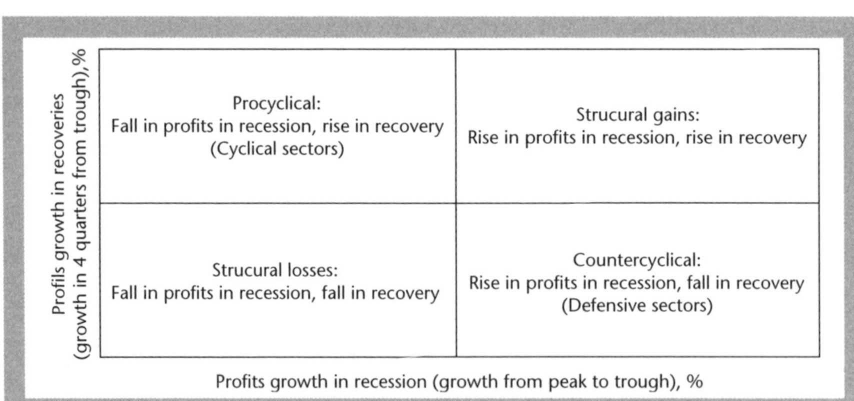

Figure 4.13 Stylized profit cycle

Source: ABN Amro

Figures 4.14 and 4.15 show the profit cycle of various industries since the 2001 recession. In the upper left quadrant we can distinguish between cyclical industries in terms of their loss in recession and gain in recovery. Some industries experience a rise in profits in recovery which is less than the profits lost in recession. Other companies are able to generate profits during a recovery which more than compensate for the profit losses during a recession.

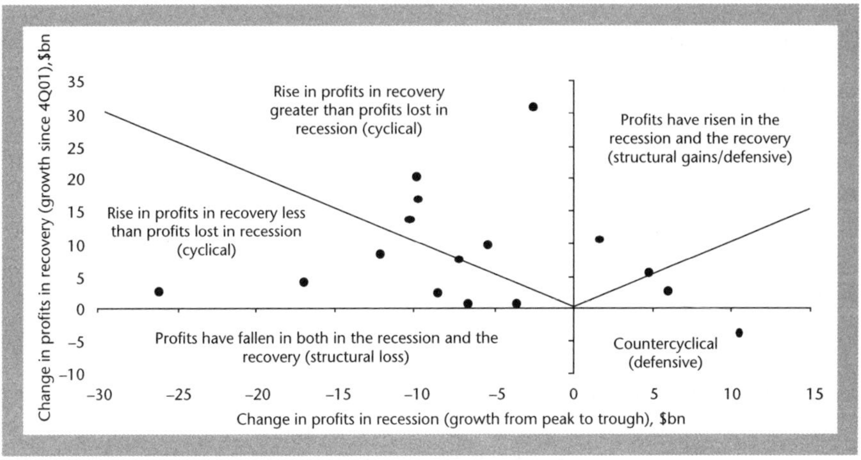

Figure 4.14 Profit cycle since the recession March until November 2001

Source: ABN Amro

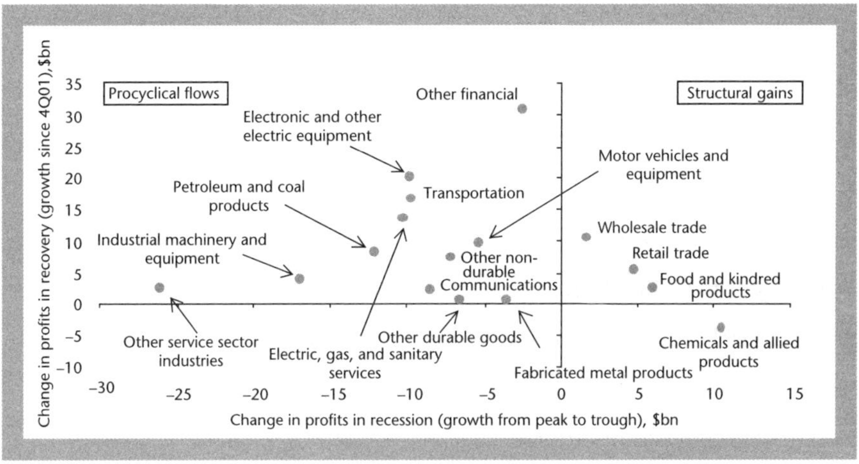

Figure 4.15 Change in profits in recession and recovery for selected industries

Source: ABN Amro

Industries with structural losses have to be avoided because their profits will fall in recession and recovery as well. Defensive industries with structural gains will experience a rise in profits during the whole economic cycle.

Industry trends have to be monitored and projections about future trends have to be made because they will influence the profitability of an industry. Some major industry characteristics are:

- Pricing and cost structures (evolution over time)
- Domestic and international competition
- Technological change (pace and adaptability)
- Asset values
- Upcoming financing needs
- Potential liabilities
- Political and regulatory environment
- Government support
- Current state of regulation/deregulation.

Structural economic changes of industries are important in the sector selection process for corporate bond investors because they determine how an industry functions and will allow to make projections about the development of the credit quality of specific industries. It has to be determined whether certain changes in industry dynamics occur which have a material effect on the evolution of the industry structure. Examples of some driving forces for change are:

- Long-term changes of growth patterns
- Changes in the customer base (demographics)
- Changes in production costs
- Product innovation
- Changes to production processes
- Structural changes of supplementary industries
- Changes of government policy
- Exits and new competitors.

Figure 4.16 shows a value chain for various industries divided by raw materials, intermediate goods, finished goods and services. It shows how the

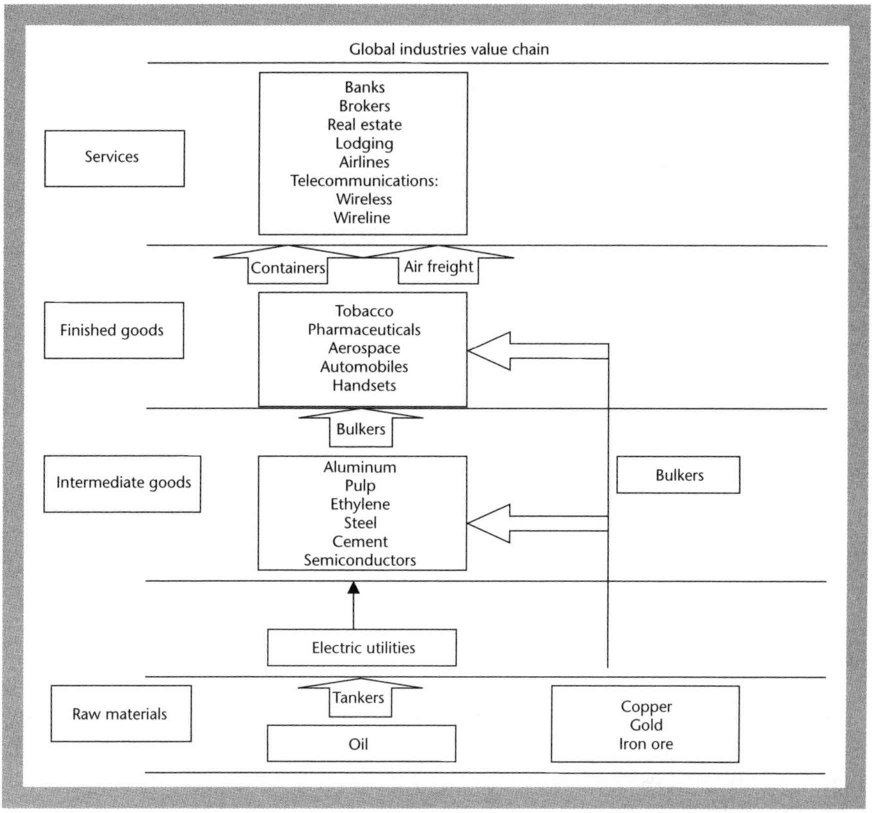

Figure 4.16 Global industries value chain

Source: UBS Warburg

different sectors interact. Intersectoral dependencies have to be considered in a sector rotation strategy.

Next, some examples of industry value chains will be presented. Figure 4.17 shows the value chains for telecommunications wireless and electric utilities as examples for noncyclical sectors. Wireless operators interact with equipment suppliers and their biggest cost positions are for subscriber acquisition, advertising and interconnection fees. Their customer base is divided into business clients and individual consumers. The success of a wireless operator will depend on the control of all parts of the value chain. This includes the costs for acquiring new customers, maintaining the existing customer base, the bargaining power with equipment suppliers, network costs and interconnection fees. The earnings situation will depend on the market power and degree of competition.

Fuel costs represent a big cost block for electric utilities hence their profitability depends to a large extent on raw material costs. Electric utility

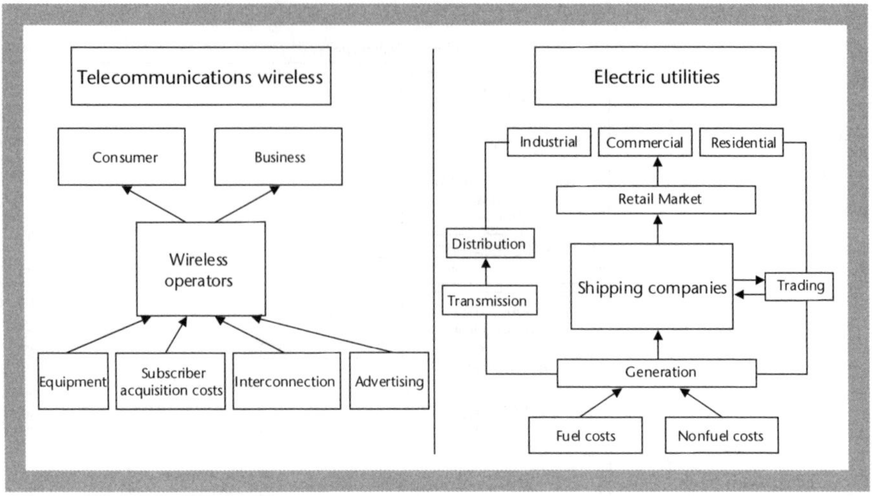

Figure 4.17 Value chains for telecommunications wireless and electric utilities
Source: UBS Warburg

companies can diversify across the business segments generation, transmission, distribution and trading. The customer base is divided as industrial, commercial and residential.

Figure 4.18 shows the value chain for the automobile industry representative for a cyclical sector. The various component makers interact with suppliers from the steel, textiles and basic materials industries. The car manufacturers assemble all parts together and finished automobiles are shipped through various distribution networks to the final consumer. Own financial services companies support the sales process. A vertical integration will increase the car manufacturers' ability to control the entire value chain. Production costs are a major component for the success of car manufacturers.

If a new technology or regulatory/deregulatory forces change the structure of an industry's value chain the companies within this industry will try to adapt to the new situation. This means that management will change its business strategy in order to remain competitive. As a result, the capital structure may change which has a direct effect on credit quality.

Telecommunications companies serve as a good example at this point. They used to be fixed-line operators. The introduction of new wireless technology changed their business models since they had to adapt their strategies to the new technological landscape. Capital expenditures were massively increased for the building of new wireless networks and the competition intensified for new wireless customers since the telecommunications market was liberalized, and alternative providers were allowed to compete

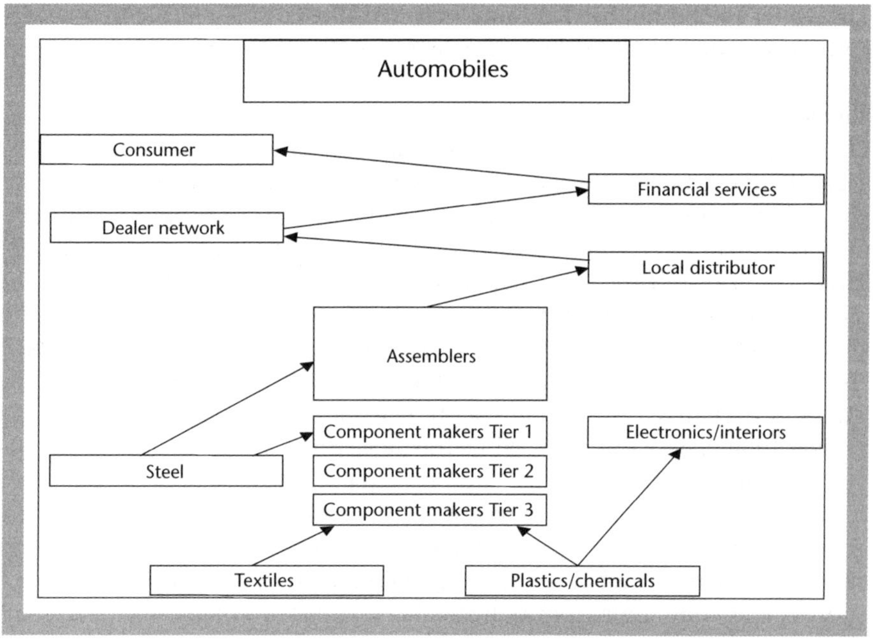

Figure 4.18 Value chain for the automobile sector
Source: UBS Warburg

with the incumbent telecommunications companies. Additionally government regulators in Europe asked for billions of dollars in fees for wireless licenses (3G). These technological and regulatory changes resulted in a tremendous increase of leverage for most of the telecommunications companies and a repricing of credit risk in this sector occurred that was accompanied by a negative industry rating trend (from AA− to BBB+).

Another example for the changing landscape of an industry is the electric utilities sector. This market undergoes a liberalization process which is in different stages according to the various jurisdictions. Changes of the regulatory environment have an impact on the development of credit quality. The business models became riskier as the competition in the sector increased, M&A activities picked up considerably and some utility companies got involved in the risky energy trading business. Formerly low risk and stable cash flows generating businesses turned into higher risk (e.g. energy trading) and more volatile cash flow businesses.

4.3.1.3 Specific risks

The major risks faced by industries can be categorized by currency risk, event risks and the risk of rating changes in cases where rating agencies take a negative stance towards a whole industry. As a last point technical factors will be highlighted because they can substantially influence the performance of bonds issued by companies from the same industry.

Currency risk

Credit spreads are also affected by fluctuations of exchange rates, with the USD/EUR exchange rate being the most influential one. The depreciation of the dollar that started in 2002 could potentially affect European corporate issuers if it slows economic growth and reduces demand for their products. However, a rise of the euro against the dollar could move the ECB to cut rates and thus would impact credit spreads via the interest rate channel. The dollar weakness is mainly due to a large current account deficit, low levels of interest rates and slowing equity capital inflows. Of course, sustained fluctuations of exchange rates can impact the business of corporate borrowers as well as financial institutions. While this does not necessarily lead to significant changes in credit quality and subsequent rating actions in the short term, especially companies with a weak financial profile may find the currency issue an unwelcome challenge. A forward-looking active currency management may be based on three main factors: US inflation, European growth and comments from policymakers. However, many companies are not able or willing to manage their currency exposure actively. In this case, significant changes in exchange rates will affect companies in three ways: via transaction risk, translation risk and import competition risk.

Transaction risk arises when a company has a currency mismatch between its costs and revenues, that is, revenues are generated in one currency while costs are denominated in another, the reporting currency. The sustained depreciation of the US dollar since February 2002, for example, has negatively affected the P&L and cash flow statements of European exporters. Although it proves difficult to obtain a breakdown of the cost structure of a company by currency, the automotive sector and the aerospace sector seem to be hit most by transaction risk.

Therefore, many companies try to offset at least a part of their currency exposure via natural hedging. That is, they try to match currency flows that result from exports and imports of goods and services. A high degree of flexibility with respect to input factors and capacity utilization of plants in different regions also provides an effective hedge against adverse currency movements. Another possibility of reducing currency risk is through derivatives, primarily forward exchange contracts and currency options. In our experience most companies that are significantly exposed to currency risk use some form of derivatives hedging. Yet, most contracts are set up for a period of 1–2 years at most. In the long term, it is difficult for companies to assess their demand for hedging because they have no reliable information about the future demand for their products and services so that the future cost and earnings situation is unknown. For longer term trends in exchange rates, natural hedging usually is more effective. Credit analysts often lack a thorough insight in currency hedging strategies, especially with regard to derivatives hedging. Since they are hardly able to assess the true currency exposure in the short term, they tend to prefer the longer term and more transparent natural hedging strategies.

When financial accounts are converted from one currency to another, translation risk arises. Typically, the financial accounts of foreign subsidiaries have to be translated back in the reporting currency to be included in the consolidated financial accounts. Since most companies do not hedge translation risk, significant changes in exchange rates during the reporting period can cause volatility in revenues and operating income. Usually companies present constant exchange rate revenues as an addition to reported revenues, to allow investors and creditors to analyze the effect of currency fluctuations.

However, a secular depreciation of the US dollar positively affects those European companies with part of their liabilities denominated in US dollars. Not only the amount of debt shown on the balance sheet is reduced, but also the associated interest burden is lessened. In terms of credit ratios, the issuance of debt in a currency, in which part of the revenues are generated, can provide an effective natural hedge against exchange rate volatility. For example, if profits of a European company operating in the United States were reduced by a weakening US dollar, it may be offset by a contemporaneous reduction of the level of US dollar denominated debt. In this case, credit ratios as well as interest coverage ratios could remain constant or even improve. It should be noted that revenues and earnings typically accrue gradually, hence they are translated at average exchange rates, while balance sheet figures are usually determined at the end of reporting period spot rates.

The third effect of currency fluctuations refers to the fact that the appreciation of the local currency attracts imports from abroad. Usually, the import competition effect only becomes apparent, when the currency appreciation has been sustained for some time. While companies are quick to cite the impact of exchange rate movements on revenues, profits and liabilities, the longer term effects with regard to market share and prices are hard to quantify. Ultimately increased competition through cheaper imports can cause earnings erosion in the domestic markets. On the other hand, European car makers benefited from the weak Euro in 2000 and 2001 through increased exports to the United States.

Although in the age of globalization, currency fluctuations may have an impact on most companies earnings, some sectors are more vulnerable to the currency issue than others. In general, the industrial, and here most notably the capital goods sector, and the automotive sector are particularly exposed. Especially from a longer perspective, the impact varies on the company level, when (natural) hedges are taken into account. While the European utilities and telecom sector have a relatively low exposure to the US dollar, they are more impacted by fluctuations of emerging market currencies.

Being one of the most global sectors, the automotive sector is particularly exposed to currency movements. Significant changes of major exchange rates therefore may have a material impact on earnings. Yet, some manufacturers are better positioned than others due to a number of factors that do not only relate to natural or derivatives hedging. A well-filled model pipeline, restructuring plans, cost reduction issues and a high degree of flexibility in the use and sourcing of raw materials and intermediate goods may outweigh negative effects due to currency fluctuations. With regard to transaction risk, those companies that have no foreign exchange exposure or are hedged, either naturally or through derivatives, clearly have the lowest risk. In terms of translation risk, companies whose assets and liabilities are well matched have the lowest risk and will have the lowest volatility of operating profits.

During the 2002/03 US dollar weakness, revenues and to a lesser extent operating profits of most European industrial issuers suffered significantly due to substantial US operations. However, exposure to US markets varies across industries.

The paper sector is only mildly exposed, since in general companies generate no more than 20 percent of their revenues in the United States. The more internationally oriented technology and chemical companies like Siemens, Philips and Akzo generate about 30 percent of sales in the United States, and have substantial further sales outside the Euro area. Yet, the impact on operating income is reduced by the fact that a significant part of costs accrues in US operations. Additionally, most industrial companies engage in hedging activities. Among the companies with a high exposure to currency risk are UK companies FKI and Pearson that both generate more than 60 percent of sales in the United States. When the US dollar depreciates significantly, these companies are hit hardest.

With respect to their vulnerability against currency movements, companies from the consumer sector benefit from their broad geographic diversification. It appears to be common policy to match assets and liabilities in the various regions to minimize overall currency risk. However, while transaction risk is accounted for, companies tend to leave translation risk unhedged. But many of the well-known European consumer companies like Nestle and Unilever have been able to raise funds in US dollars. Thus US dollar denominated debt exceeds assets and earnings. During the US dollar weakness those companies have seen their debt and interest burden diminish faster than their earnings. UK tobacco companies tend to finance a significant part of their business with Euro denominated debt, leaving them exposed to a strengthening of the Euro versus Sterling.

European telecom companies have their operations primarily in Europe. Therefore, exposure to foreign currencies is very limited with the exception of Telefonica's exposure to Latin America and Deutsche Telekom's US subsidiaries. While in other industries an appreciating Euro increases competition, it appears that this effect should be negligible for the established European telecom services companies. The barriers of entry seem to be high enough to guarantee broadly stable market shares in the coming years. Since many of the telecom companies have a material fraction of their debt in US dollars, they would benefit from a strengthening Euro.

It is in the nature of financial institutions to have exposure to a variety of currencies. Exchange rate risk is therefore translational rather than transactional. By and large, long-term currency risk is primarily taken in the form of subsidiaries. Currency fluctuations change the value of the equity invested, hence are reflected in the balance sheet rather than in the P&L. Of the larger European banking groups, ABN Amro, BNP Paribas and Royal Bank of Scotland have substantial retail banking operations in the United States. In the insurance sector, Aegon, AXA, ING Verzekeringen and Prudential stand out in terms of US exposure.

Event risks

The occurrence of event risks is almost unpredictable hence they are hard to quantify. Most of the event risks can be associated with the creation of shareholder value. This can be share buyback programs, an aggressive acquisition strategy, or isolated, risky projects which change the capital structure of a company in favor of shareholders. A wealth transfer takes place from bondholders to shareholders of a company. This kind of event risk can be reduced by regular meetings with management. Unfortunately many event risks are out of control for management and sometimes the effects are not isolated for a specific company but have an effect on the entire industry (Table 4.1). In the past good examples can be found for various industries. Many capital goods companies are facing asbestos claims which weigh heavily on their financial profiles. Especially in a market phase with increased risk aversion these topics are brought up and heighten the negative sentiment of market participants against sectors with increased asbestos liabilities. The telecommunications sector faces new challenges through wireless technologies. European state regulators set license fees for wireless spectrum which reached billions. This changed the financial profile of the incumbent telecommunications companies. The utilities sector goes through a liberalization process accompanied by increasingly riskier business models. The tobacco sector is always a litigation target and the healthcare and pharma sectors face a lot of regulatory risks.

Rating Risk

The rating outlook of both rating agencies (S&P and Moody's) can be another criterion to choose between industries. If companies with a positive rating outlook outweigh the companies with a stable or negative rating outlook within an industry, it can be a good indicator for favorable industry dynamics, even if we have to recognize that ratings are sometimes lagging indicators for credit quality. A diversified portfolio should overweight the

Table 4.1 Selected Industries and their main event risks

	Event risks		
All sectors: Industry	Share buyback programs and extra dividend payments		
Automobile	Strategy/ globalization	Consolidation	Product liability
Consumer goods	Leveraged buyouts	Globalization	Fragmentation
Tobacco	Litigation	Consolidation	Regulation
Telecommunications	Strategy/execution	Licenses/technology	Consolidation
Industrials	Geographic Expansion	Consolidation	Litigation
Utilities	Deregulation/Privatization	Consolidation	Geographic expansion

Source: Union Investment

industries with a positive rating outlook and underweight industries with a negative rating outlook if the whole credit market experiences a "Flight-to-Quality." During a market phase with a higher risk appetite, fundamental factors like the rating trend in a specific industry might not be the primary decision criterion for a sector positioning and other factors like valuation will play a bigger role.

Figure 4.19 highlights the credit spread for BBB-rated US corporate bonds and the amount of issuers being on negative credit watch by either Moody's or S&P. Periods of declining amounts of issuers being on negative watch are consistent with spread tightening and vice versa.

A major reason why sectors experience significant shifts in their average ratings is the degree of cyclicality. Noncyclical sectors usually have a stable credit trend whereas cyclical sectors are heavily dependent on economic cycles and their rating outlooks move in tandem with the economy even though it has to be pointed out that the rating agencies try to rate through the economic cycle, meaning that cyclical swings should be incorporated in a company's rating. Macroeconomic dynamics can drive the negative credit trend of industries and single companies, affecting their credit spreads even more than company-specific problems and risks. At this stage we want to point out that external shocks, which endanger geopolitical stability, can bring the whole economic system in disorder. After the tragic events of 11 September 2001 the airline and leisure industries were hit the hardest and a spread widening of 360 and 185 bps respectively was recorded. An average widening of 30–40 bps across all other sectors occurred in the short term, whereas the cyclical industries like automobiles showed higher spread movements than noncyclicals.

Technical factors

Technical factors have to be considered in the decision process regarding the weighting of various sectors in a corporate bond portfolio. First of

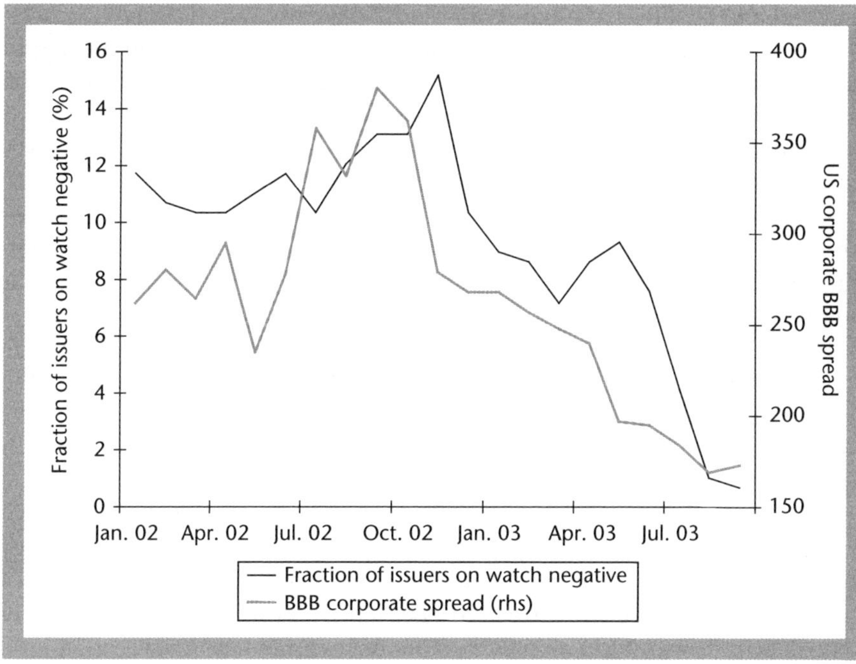

Figure 4.19 Amount of issuers on negative credit watch and US BBB corporate bond spread in basis points

Source: Moody's and Union Investment

all, projections about the expected net new issuance volume have to be made. All redemptions in an industry are known and the projected financing needs of all companies within an industry add to the total expected issuance from a specific sector. In the past, the largest issuance volume has been concentrated in the automobile, telecommunications and utility sectors. It has to be evaluated whether the new issuance volume can be absorbed by the market or whether it will put pressure on spreads. The general risk appetite/aversion of market participants and the prevailing sentiment towards the various sectors will give a hint about the demand for certain sectors. Another important factor is liquidity because it will vary substantially between sectors. Furthermore if investors want to express a certain view on different maturity buckets within a portfolio the choice might be limited to a few frequent borrowers who have bonds in all maturity buckets outstanding. Those companies are usually concentrated in the automobile, telecommunications and utility sectors.

4.3.2 Relative value

Sector fundamentals have to be put in perspective to valuation. The relative value approach is a common method for sector rotation strategies. It supplements the fundamental analysis of the sectors and improves the decision to overweight or underweight specific sectors. In a first step the aggregate spread levels of sector indices are compared with their respective spread volatilities. Typically the spread volatilities (annualised standard deviation of daily spread changes) will increase with an increasing spread level of the different sectors. This procedure allows to identify sectors whose risk-return profile relative to the whole market is attractive (overweight) or unattractive (underweight). This approach can also be applied on the company level but a lesser weight should be assigned to the results for lower rated credits which require an in-depth credit analysis in the first place.

Figure 4.20 shows the different sector volatilities in relation to aggregate spread levels. It can be stated that senior banks were less volatile than the telecommunications and automobile sectors. Especially the automobile sector and subordinated insurance increase the risk profile of a portfolio due to higher volatility and offer more potential to outperform/underperform the corporate benchmark if an overweighting is targeted. Services noncyclical and technology appear unattractive in Figure 4.20 as they offer a relative low spread and a high spread volatility. The media, telecom and services cyclical sectors have an attractive risk-return profile and consequently should be overweight in a portfolio. The different spread volatilities of the

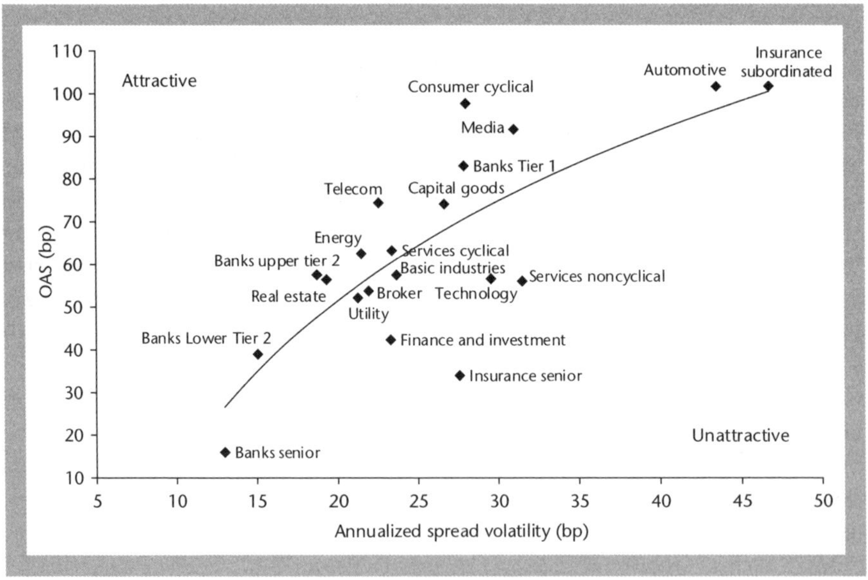

Figure 4.20 Relative value chart, spread volatility on *x*-axis and spreads on *y*-axis for different sectors

Source: Merrill Lynch and Union Investment

sectors lead to divergent investor behavior regarding risk aversion /appetite, which in return results in different risk premia (spreads).

The rating differences between the various sectors have to be considered as well because in this example we compare AA-rated financials with low A/high BBB-rated telecommunication and automobile companies.

Spread volatility is one of the most important underlying drivers of nominal spreads. Investing in more volatile sectors requires a higher compensation (higher option adjusted spread) because it is more difficult to target projected returns. There is a close relationship between aggregate spread levels and aggregate spread volatility. Periods of tight spreads are accompanied by lower spread volatility. When spreads tend to widen the spread volatility will also increase (Figure 4.21).

Sector betas are used as a measure of risk and signal the systematic risk of a sector. Corporate bond betas are computed on the basis of spreads and are, like the equity betas, useful indicators for the assessment of the different risk profiles of various companies and sectors. A high beta indicates an above average investment risk, because it depends on the average leverage level of issuers from a sector. The change in betas over time reflects the change in relative risk of a sector versus the overall market.

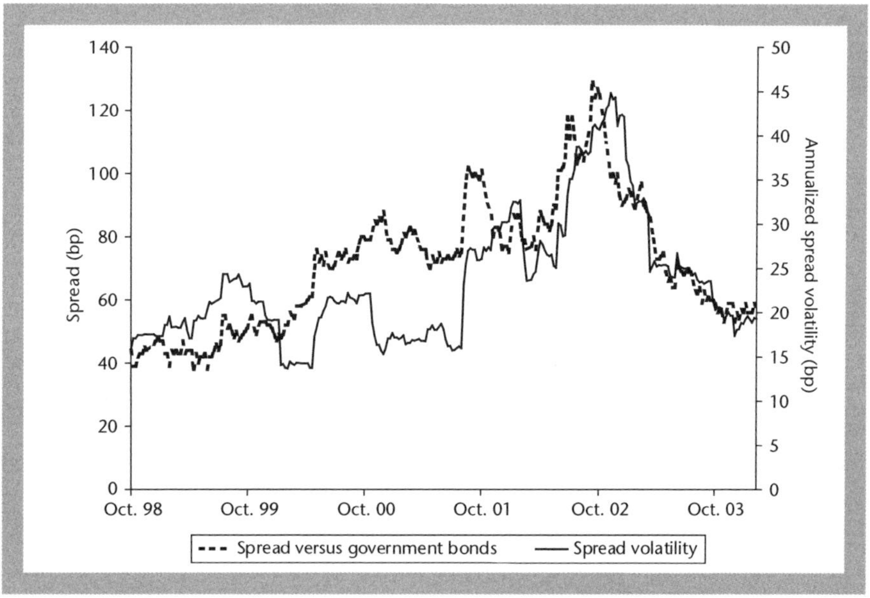

Figure 4.21 Spread volatility and spread level for the European investment grade market

Source: Merrill Lynch and Union Investment

4.4 CREDIT CURVE POSITIONING

4.4.1 Macroeconomic drivers of the slope of the credit curve

Many government bond investors believe that deviations of treasury yield curve steepness from the traditional range or a fair value obtained by regression analysis are only temporary. That is, they expect yield curve steepness to be mean reverting. From a theoretical point of view there is strong support for this hypothesis. In the early stages of the business cycle, that is at the beginning of an expansion, monetary policy is easy and short-term interest rates are still low. But an improving outlook for future economic growth leads to rising long-term interest rates and a steeper yield curve. The later stages of the expansion are characterized by rising inflationary pressures and consequently central bank tightening. The most impressive example for this experience were the seven interest rate hikes by the Fed between January 1994 and January 1995, that led to a sell-off in the treasury market and were accompanied by a massive flattening of the yield curve. When the tighter monetary policy begins to unfold its influence on price growth, this is usually followed by weakening economic growth. In this economic environment yield curves steepen again, because short-term interest rates tend to price in room for central banks to cut interest rates.

Figure 4.22 points to the fact that the steepness of the yield curve follows a certain pattern over the business cycle. The 1991–2001 economic cycle is

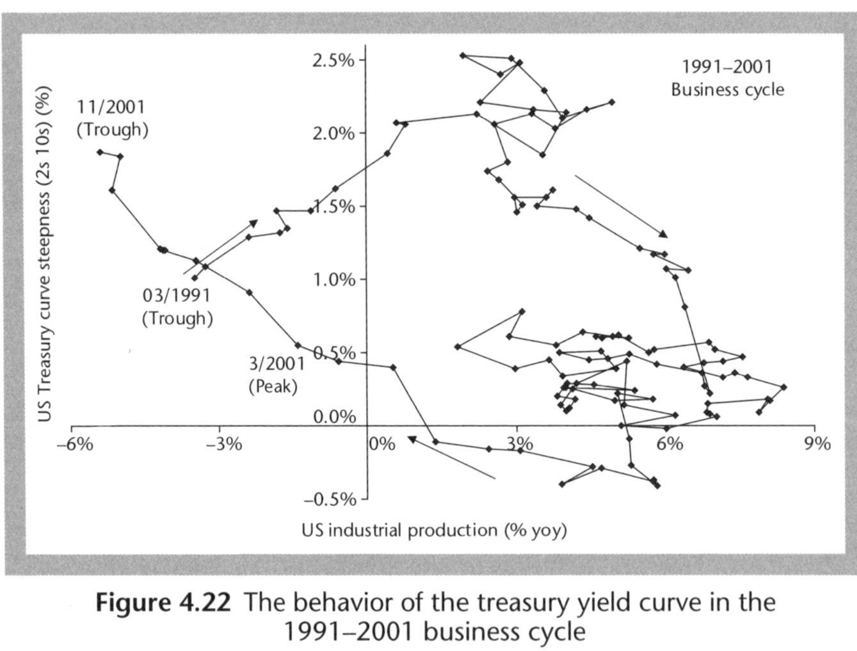

Figure 4.22 The behavior of the treasury yield curve in the 1991–2001 business cycle

Source: Bloomberg and Union Investment

representative for past economic cycles in the sense that it displays the usual pattern for the correlation between yield curve steepness and industrial production. But it is special because it comprises the longest economic expansion in the United States since the NBER started dating recessions back in the 1850s.

The management of the yield curve is a central element of fixed income portfolio management, even for corporate bond investors. However, many of them tend to take no or rather small active exposures with respect to duration and the positioning on the yield curve. Consequently, active positions with regard to sector and issuer exposures are responsible for a large part of the out- or underperformance versus the benchmark index. Since corporate bonds as an asset class clearly depend on the boom and bust of the economy, it seems natural that not only the spread level but also the slope of the credit curve may – similar to the slope of the yield curve – be related to economic activity. The question then is if taking active positions on the credit curve can attribute to the performance of a corporate bond portfolio.

The sensitivity of corporate bonds to the economic environment essentially depends on their time to maturity. In the short term, default risk for investment grade corporate issuers is primarily due to nonsystematic factors, for example, cases of fraud or litigation. Over longer term horizons, conversely, systematic factors tend to have a higher impact on the default probability of corporate issuers. Changes in the economic environment and business risks in the sense of adverse industry trends or increasing competition are major drivers of credit risk and hence for spreads in the longer term. Therefore, one would expect the spreads of long and intermediate investment grade corporate bonds to be more sensitive to indicators of economic activity than short-term bonds. This implies that credit curves should flatten when the economic outlook improves. Rising confidence in the corporate sector additionally spurs investors' willingness to take on more spread duration. Consequently, in periods of spread tightening investors should expect credit curves to flatten. In other words, as Figure 4.23 illustrates, the slope of the credit curve and the level of credit spreads are positively correlated for investment grade issuers.

In Chapter 3, a positive relationship between different measures of financial leverage and the level of corporate bond spreads was shown. Additionally there is evidence for a strong impact of operating leverage and indicators for economic activity on corporate bond spreads. Clearly, rising utilization rates and a growing industrial production are a healthy environment for the corporate sector. In this period, credit spreads should tighten across the credit curve. Since there is a high correlation between corporate bond spreads and various indicators for the state of the economy, for example, industrial production or capacity utilization, those factors might also hint to future changes of the credit curve. But, although the theoretical

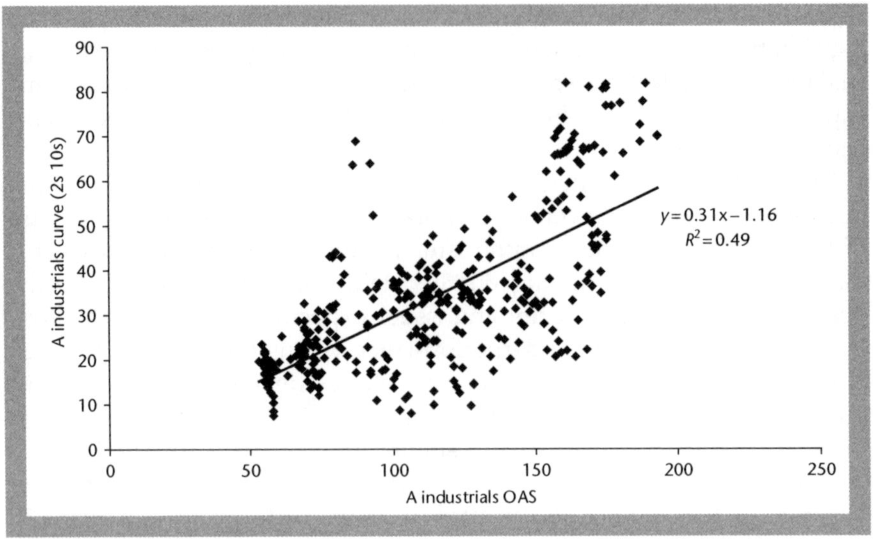

Figure 4.23 Slope of the 2s10s credit curve for A-rated US industrials versus spread levels in the period Jan. 1997 until Nov. 2003

Source: Merrill Lynch and Union Investment

argument is compelling, the correlation between the shape of the credit curve and macroeconomic variables is weak.

It has to be considered that indicators like industrial production are published only once a month and with a significant time lag. In other words, more timely available indicators of the market participants' expectations for future economic growth such as yield curve steepness should be able to explain variations of the credit curve better. As pointed out before, the yield curve usually experiences a bear steepening in the early stages of the business cycle and a bull steepening in the later stages of the business cycle, that is during recessions. While the first period is usually characterized by tightening credit spreads and flattening credit curves, the opposite is true for economic downturns. Therefore the relationship between yield curve and credit curve changes depends on the stage of the business cycle. At the beginning of an expansion one should expect a negative correlation between yield curve and credit curve steepness (Figure 4.24), but when economic growth slows down the correlation should turn positive (Figure 4.25).

Empirical evidence supports the hypotheses above. In the early stages of the economic expansion after the 1990/91 recession the yield curve steepened, driven by an improving economic outlook, and credit curves at the same time flattened. The higher confidence of investors in the ability of companies to generate sufficient cash flows led to declining risk premia for longer term corporate bonds. Conversely, during the 2001 recession, both

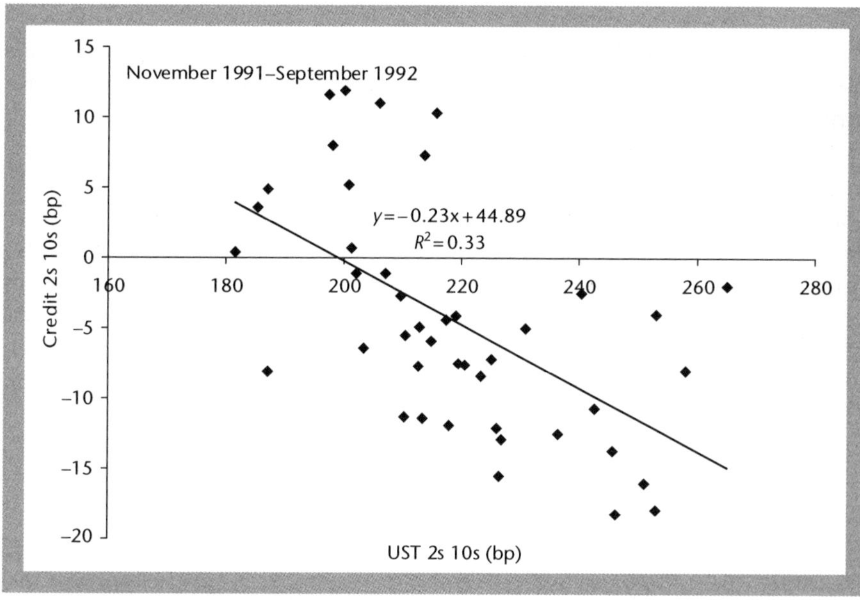

Figure 4.24 Slope of the credit curve for A-rated US industrials versus slope of the yield curve during the early stages of the economic expansion after the 1990/91 recession

Source: Morgan Stanley and Union Investment

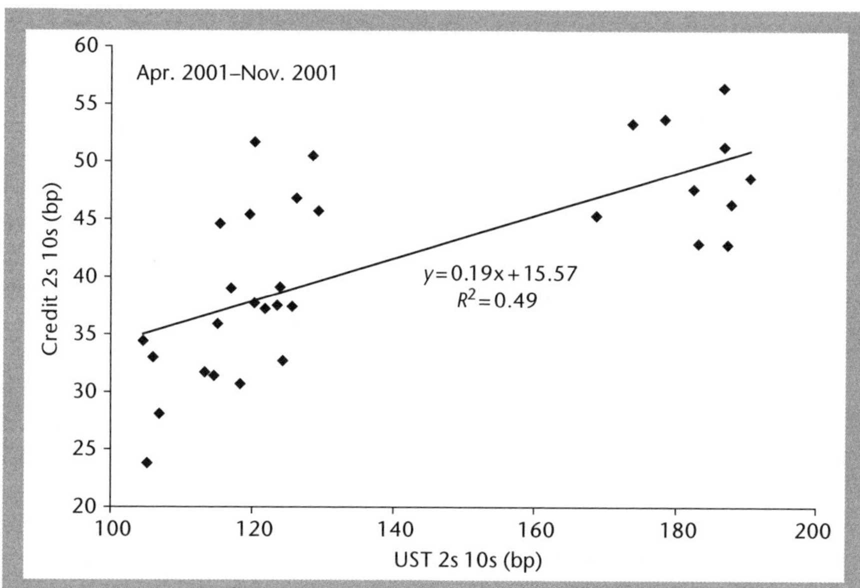

Figure 4.25 Slope of the credit curve for A-rated US industrials versus slope of the yield curve during the 2001 recession

Source: Morgan Stanley and Union Investment

yield and credit curves steepened. While government bond markets were driven by falling inflationary pressures and monetary easing, corporate bond investors shortened their spread duration, causing risk premia for longer term corporate bonds to rise.

In January 2003, the European corporate bond market established a new segment. France Telecom, Telecom Italia, RWE and Telefonica were the first companies to issue benchmark size Euro denominated 30-year bonds. Since then investors have ample opportunities to set up credit curve trades for Euro corporate bond portfolios, even at the long end of the curve. Analysis of the behavior of the 10s30s credit curve is difficult because of the limited history, but experience shows that the long end of the credit curve is temporarily influenced by the level of 30-year government bond yields.

4.4.2 Spot and forward credit curves

Investors often analyze yield curves for government bonds in terms of forward rates. As Ilmanen (1996) points out forward rates in treasury markets can be viewed as break-even yields. In this framework forward rates indicate the yield changes that are required for every single maturity along the yield curve in order to generate the same return over the holding period. For an upward sloping yield curve, for example, yields would have to rise across the curve, but in a nonparallel fashion. It is important to consider that the forward yield curve reflects mathematically implied yields, but not necessarily expected future government bond yields. From a theoretical perspective longer term bonds should contain a risk premium to compensate the investors for the increased price volatility associated with holding longer term bonds in comparison to short-term bonds.

Similar analyses as for government yield curves can be done for corporate bond yield curves. The holding period return of a corporate bond is composed of the coupon income, the price change due to the change in the underlying government bond yield, and the price change due to the spread change. As pointed out before, corporate bond investors tend to take only small active positions with respect to the yield curve. They rather manage their credit curve exposure actively. Therefore, they are most interested in the analysis of the last component, price changes due to changes in spreads. If one assumes that the government yields move to their forward rates, holding period returns of a company's bonds with different maturities are not affected by the performance of the government bond market. As a consequence corporate bond returns in this case only depend on initial spreads and spread changes over the holding period. The forward spread curve then reflects the break-even spreads, that is the spreads that have to be observed at the end of the holding period in order that all bonds along the credit spread curve achieve the same return.

It is important to note that upward sloping credit curves imply a widening of spreads, flat credit curves imply stable spreads and inverse credit curves imply tightening spreads. Again, as with government bonds implied spreads differ from expected future spreads. Longer term corporate bonds should not only contain a premium that compensates investors for accepting higher price volatility, but also for taking on additional credit risk.

A second observation with respect to forward credit curves is related to the slope: The steeper a credit curve is, the larger is the implied spread widening. If the spread widens less or more than indicated by forward spreads over the holding period, certain bonds will perform better than others. Portfolio managers who have a strong view on the spread changes they expect for an issuer's bonds may benefit from this fact. If, for example, they expect the bonds of an issuer with an upward sloping credit curve, as France Telecom in Figure 4.26, to widen less than implied by forward spreads, they would prefer to own longer term bonds, because the additional carry should overcompensate the capital loss due to the expected spread widening. Another example for credit curve trades based on forward CDS spreads is presented in Chapter 7.

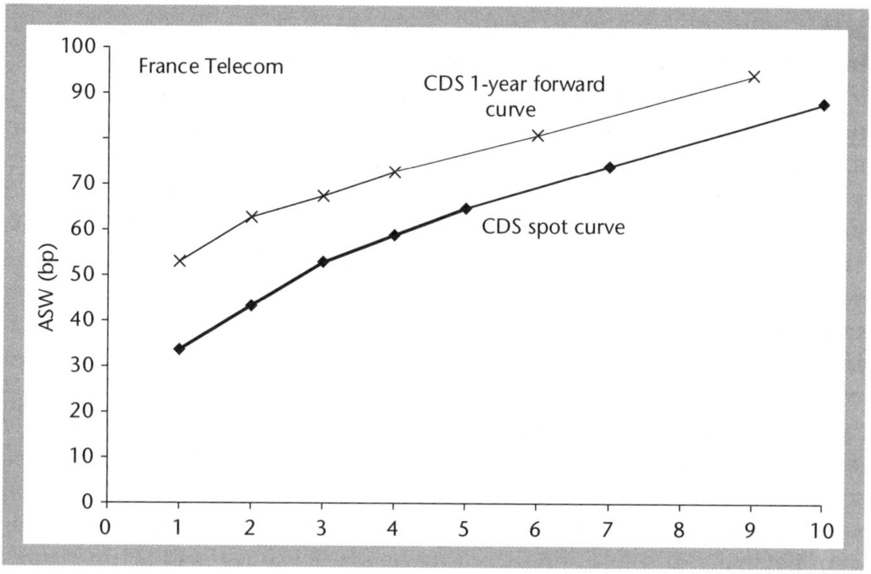

Figure 4.26 France Telecom CDS spot and forward curve in 1 year on Mar. 17, 2004

Source: Bloomberg and Union Investment

More complex trades can be implemented when two issuers are considered. Assume that issuer A has a steeper credit curve than issuer B, implying a larger spread widening in the future. If an investor expects just the opposite to happen eventually, he could set up the following box trade:

- Buy long-term bonds of company A and short-term bonds of company B, and
- Sell short-term bonds of company A and long-term bonds of company B.

A detailed description of how to set up credit curve trades without altering the duration exposure of the portfolio is given in the following sections.

4.4.3 Credit curve strategies

4.4.3.1 Credit curve trades with one issuer

In most cases portfolio managers do not expect the spread change to occur that is priced in forward spreads. If this view is strong enough, and if the portfolio manager has proven his skill in predicting corporate bond spread changes, he may decide to bet against the market, in other words to take an active position with respect to the credit curve. Several different ways to implement such trades will be discussed subsequently.

The first trade is simply a bond swap on an issuer's credit curve. If an investor expects the credit curve to flatten more than implied by forward spreads over the holding period, he may switch out of short-term bonds into longer maturities. In order to keep the duration exposure constant, a part of the proceeds of the sale of the short-term bonds would have to be kept in cash. Although this trade can be constructed to be duration-neutral, the performance over the holding period relative to the benchmark depends on changes of the shape of the yield curve. A yield curve steepening can lead to the underperformance of the long bonds even if the credit curve flattens.

When a steepening of the credit curve is expected that is not fully reflected in forward spreads a portfolio manager would have to sell the long bonds and buy short-term bonds. However, in order to keep duration constant, he would have to put more cash to work in the short-term bonds than he receives from selling the long bonds. Since real money managers such as mutual funds and insurance companies are not allowed to borrow and to leverage their positions, setting up a credit curve steepener involves taking a duration view, because the investor implicitly ends up being short duration.

4.4.3.2 *Credit curve trades with two issuers*

However, there is an alternative way to benefit from a steepening credit curve. If an investor expects issuer A's credit curve to steepen more than implied by forward spreads and issuer B's credit curve to flatten at the same time, he could switch from company A's long bonds into company B's long bonds. Whenever company B has a bond outstanding with a longer maturity than the bond that is sold, the trade can be set up on a duration-neutral basis. Crabbe and Fabozzi (2002) point out that the return from this strategy over a 1-year horizon is approximately equal to

$$\text{Return} = \text{spread differential} - \text{duration} \cdot \text{change in spread differential},$$

assuming roughly equal durations for both bonds. But it should be noted that this trade is not a pure bet on an issuer's credit curve. Even if the credit curves behave as expected and the trade turns out to be profitable, taking another position may have been more beneficial in absolute terms and with respect to the individual credit curves of the two involved issuers. This is true, for example, if the spreads of company A and B widen significantly across their credit curves. In this case the capital loss due to the spread widening can exceed the profit of the bond swap. Being positioned at the short end of the credit curve then would have been a better strategy from an absolute return perspective.

A way to avoid the shortcomings of the above-described credit curve trade are duration-neutral box trades. Essentially, the trade consists of two legs. The investor buys the long-term bond of issuer A and sells the long-term bond of issuer B. Additionally, he sells short-term bonds of the first issuer and buys short-term bonds of the second issuer. Consequently, the trade benefits from a flattening of issuer A's credit curve and a steepening of issuer B's credit curve. This trade, of course, can be constructed to be duration neutral. Yet, there are myriad possibilities to do this. Assuming that no borrowing and leveraging are allowed the duration of the combined trade will always lie between the durations of the second shortest and second longest bond. While the position is insensitive to changes in the yield curve, its performance in general depends not only on changes of the credit curve but also changes of the level of spreads.

If an investor only has a view that the credit curves of two issuers will converge, but is not sure whether this will happen at wider or tighter spread levels, he would like to construct the box trade in a way that makes it insensitive to parallel shifts of the credit curves. In order to achieve this goal the trade has to be proceeds neutral. Additionally, the cash has to be invested in each bond of the two involved issuers in a way that equal spread changes of the long and short bond of an issuer cause the same capital gain or loss. Crabbe and Fabozzi (2002) show that in mathematical terms these two conditions can be expressed as:

$$V_{\text{A, long}} + V_{\text{B, short}} = V_{\text{A, short}} + V_{\text{B, long}}$$
$$V_{\text{A, long}} \cdot D_{\text{A, long}} \cdot \Delta S_{\text{A}} = V_{\text{A, short}} \cdot D_{\text{A, short}} \cdot \Delta S_{\text{A}}$$
$$V_{\text{B, long}} \cdot D_{\text{B, long}} \cdot \Delta S_{\text{B}} = V_{\text{B, short}} \cdot D_{\text{B, short}} \cdot \Delta S_{\text{B}},$$

where $V_{\text{A, long}}$ denotes the market value of the longer bond of company A, $D_{\text{A, long}}$ the bond's duration and ΔS_{A} the parallel shift of the credit curve of issuer A. Solving for $V_{\text{A, long}}$ yields the following results:

$$V_{\text{A, long}} = \frac{(V_{\text{A, long}} + V_{\text{B, short}}) \cdot D_{\text{A, short}} \cdot (D_{\text{B, long}} - D_{\text{B, short}})}{D_{\text{A, long}} \cdot D_{\text{B, long}} - D_{\text{A, short}} \cdot D_{\text{B, short}}}.$$

It is worth noting that the spread-neutral box trade is almost independent of the spreads, except for the minor impact of spreads on duration. Remember that this trade is designed to protect investors from spread changes that might adversely impact their credit curve trade. Yet, often portfolio managers not only have a view on the relative changes of the credit curve of the two issuers but also on the direction of spreads. In this case the spread-neutral box trade is not optimal. The investor would rather choose a longer or shorter duration, depending on his view on the direction of spreads.

4.4.4 Combining sector and credit curve views

Having evaluated the risk and return potential of different sectors, the investor is confronted with the question of how to implement a bullish or bearish view on a particular sector. Essentially, the answer depends on how an investor manages his risk exposure in a certain sector. There are two ways to increase the risk budget allocated to a sector: increase the weighting or the spread duration. Table 4.2 illustrates this. The fourth

Table 4.2 Index characteristics of the Merrill Lynch EMU Corporate Index and the subsector automotive per Feb. 29, 2004

	Weight (%)	Modified duration (%)	Sensitivity
Automotive	8.30	3.86	0.32
ML EMU Corporates ex Automotive	91.70	4.63	4.25
Total	100.00	4.57	4.57

Source: Merrill Lynch

column, sensitivity, is obtained by multiplying sector weight and modified duration. Thus, it measures the impact of a 1 bp change in the spread of a certain subsector on the performance of the whole portfolio. In our example a tightening of 10 bp in the automotive sector, *ceteris paribus* would result in a positive excess return for the Merrill Lynch EMU Corporate Index of 3.2 bp versus duration matched government bonds.

Overall exposure to the automotive sector can be increased in two ways. To double the portfolio sensitivity to changes of automotive spreads the investor could double the sector weight, double spread duration or combine both strategies in an adequate ratio. Assuming that the overall interest rate sensitivity of the portfolio shall not be changed, each strategy requires adjustments to the automotive subportfolio as well as to the rest of the portfolio. Table 4.3 illustrates the trades that are caused in a portfolio worth 100 million Euros if the investor wants to double the portfolio sensitivity to spread movements in the auto sector.

While both strategies yield portfolios that have the same sensitivity to parallel shifts of the credit curve, they usually yield very different returns in real world scenarios. Not only will capital gains differ when the credit curve moves in a nonparallel way, but returns from carry differ also when the yield pickup from extending duration is not equal to the yield pickup from increasing the allocation to the sector. Of course, these presumptions are rarely met in reality. Increasing the allocation to a high beta sector like automotive usually generates more carry than extending duration. Therefore, over the long run, this strategy has proven more successful. The allocation strategy is also more intuitive with respect to the allocation of capital to different risk or spread classes.

Of course, the allocation of resources to different risk classes within sectors also has a significant impact on portfolio performance. In the automotive sector, for example, companies like BMW and Toyota are low beta names, whereas Ford and General Motors bonds are the high beta issuers.

Table 4.3 Alternative strategies to change the portfolio exposure to a certain sector

Double the weight of the automotive subportfolio:

(a) Buy 8.3 million automotive bonds with an average modified duration of 3.86%.

(b) Sell 8.3 million non-automotive bonds with an average modified duration of 3.86%.

Double the modified duration of the automotive subportfolio:

(a) Adjust the composition of the automotive subportfolio so that its average modified duration increases to 7.72%.

(b) Adjust the composition of the rest of the portfolio so that its average modified duration falls to 4.28%.

Source: Union Investment

With the decline of default rates and credit blowups in 2003 and 2004, more and more portfolio managers have realized that the concentration on idiosyncratic risk yields unsatisfactory results in a more favorable environment for credit. Increasing allocation and spread duration may sometimes not be enough to outperform the market during a rally. The use of betas can help to correct this error. The concept originally stems from the equity markets where it is used to describe the portion of the variation in asset returns that is due to market fluctuations. In credit markets beta analysis should only be applied to credit returns, that is the part of a bond's return that is solely due to changes of the spread versus the swap curve. For a well-diversified portfolio systematic risk, which is captured by the beta, is the major part of credit risk. On a single issuer basis, however, idiosyncratic risk prevails, especially for lower rated credits. Since market data for individual bonds contain a lot of noise, regressions to obtain betas versus the market index should also be done on the sector level. If the portfolio manager is bullish on the credit market, he will tend to overweight higher beta sectors and issuers. This methodology adds a third dimension to the process of tactical positioning, supplementing the decisions on the sector allocation and spread duration.

CHAPTER 5

Credit Research

5.1 INTRODUCTION

This chapter is divided into two parts. The first part will present a framework for the fundamental analysis of an industrial company which involves the borrower's capacity to repay, the underlying collateral, key factors that affect the earnings situation of a company and traditional ratios to assess the strength of cash flows from operations and the ability of a company to service all debt obligations as well as all limitations of such ratios. The approach presented can be applied to investment grade and high-yield issuers. The latter require further analysis steps like debt structure and company structure, which will be pointed out in this chapter as well. In the second part, we will discuss the analysis for banks.

5.2 THE BOTTOM-UP APPROACH FOR INDUSTRIAL COMPANIES

Traditional credit analysis is a bottom-up approach which focuses on the selection of companies. The credit quality/risk has to be determined and the two following questions have to be answered:

- Is the issuer able to make the coupon payments?
- Will the company value at maturity be large enough to pay back the principal?

During highs and lows of market cycles psychological and technical factors tend to push asset prices to extremely elevated or depressed levels. At those times it is appropriate to focus on credit fundamentals and detect companies where such moves were not justified. Credit analysis should be able to identify opportunities to add substantial yield by assuming only little higher credit risk at the same time. The following paragraphs describe a possible way of analyzing the credit risk and investing in corporate bonds.

The main anchors of credit analysis are cash flows, asset value, profitability, management assessment and covenants. Every company has to be able to generate positive cash flows in the long run. Companies with permanently negative cash flows will face liquidity constraints at some point in future. Another focus lies on balance sheet strength. The value of assets is very important for bondholders because they can be pledged against liabilities. For particularly high leveraged companies a situation might evolve where asset sales are the last option for deleveraging. The management assessment is another important factor for credit analysis particularly for assigning probabilities to various event risks. Finally, covenants have the main purpose of limiting event risk in terms of a company undertaking bondholder-unfriendly actions. Figure 5.1 outlines the main factors, which have to be incorporated in the credit analysis. Another focus lies on the equity-market performance and the implied volatility of a company's stock. We can identify periods where equity and corporate

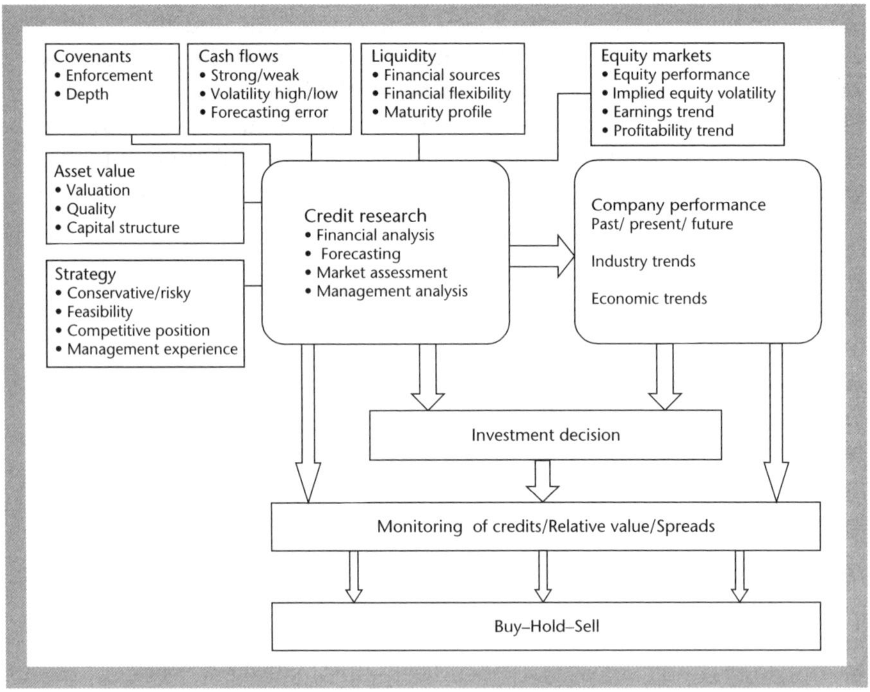

Figure 5.1 Bottom-up approach for industrial companies

Source: Union Investment

bonds move in the same direction and times where they decouple; in distressed cases the decoupling will be permanent because equity will have no value and the remaining value will reside with debt.

The various steps of the analysis do not apply to banks and financial institutions; these differ from other companies, because they are highly leveraged due to the nature of their business, as their main business is to manage their assets. An indepth analysis of the credit risk of banks will follow at the end of this chapter.

There are several documents which can be used to assess the credit quality of a company. These are the 10K (Annual Statement), 10Q (Quarterly Statement) and the annual report and quarterly financial report presented to the shareholders. If a company has a public offering of a new security it has to provide a prospectus. Every prospectus has a section where all current and potential risks to the company have to be disclosed. Regulated companies like utilities and banks must also prepare documents for regulators. Besides useful financial data, the annual report contains the shareholder's letter where the management discusses business strategies.

As the first step the financial risk of a company has to be assessed. As the next step the business risk has to be defined and its effect on the financial risk has to be explained because various business strategies will result in different finanical profiles. The third component is event risk which is partly influenced by management, but also external factors which are out of the control of management (Figure 5.2). The trend in a company's financial risk profile is determined to a large extent by the underlying business. The analysis of business risk deals with the stability, quality and predictability of a company's business throughout the entire economic cycle, for example, cash flows and earnings of car manufacturers depend to a large extent on the economy and investors will require higher risk premia in weak economic periods which results in the spread widening for bonds issued by car manufacturers. In this case a comparable analysis of an issuer's market position versus its peers and the ability to manage weak economic periods

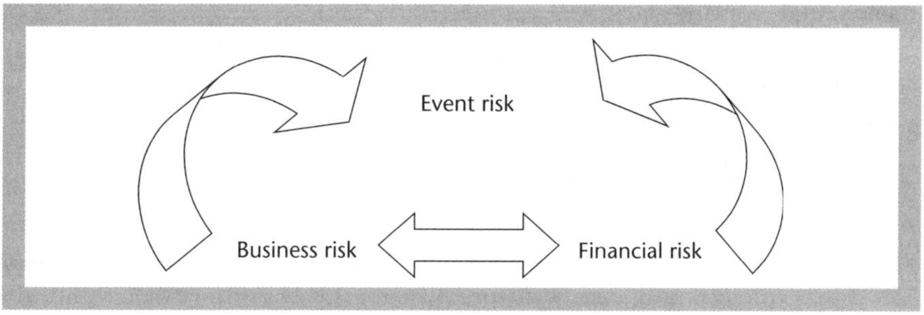

Figure 5.2 Dimensions of corporate credit risk
Source: Union Investment

in the past should be incorporated in the dynamic part of the credit analysis. The evaluation of a company's future prospects of being a profitable business and the ability and willingness to improve the financial risk profile is a very important part in the investment decision process. The quality and experience of management is of particular interest because the compatibility of the business strategy with the financial profile of a company is fundamental for successful companies. Financial and nonfinancial factors like strategic management decisions (feasibility of the business plan) and the competitive environment set the parameters for the improvement of credit quality in the future. Management has always the option to surprise market participants with the announcement of unexpected company actions which will alter the capital structure. The change of a previously announced strategy is a major component of the event risk. It is impossible to quantify event risk for a company hence it is a subjective factor in the valuation process. Typical examples are:

- Mergers and Acquisitions
- Share buyback programs
- Focus on new business segments
- Leveraged Buy-outs
- All actions which result in an increased leverage.

Credit investors also face other event risks which are out of control for management and we will discuss this topic later in the chapter. The subjective assessment of a credit analyst can provide valuable information about future changes of an issuer's credit quality and hence the performance of bonds.

As the next step the capital structure and covenants have to be analyzed which is particularly important for high-yield issues. Sometimes bonds of issuers with a negative credit trend have coupon step-up language which means that bondholders will receive, for example, 25 bp in the case of 1 notch downgrade by one rating agency. This way a company can show committment to its current rating and bondholders have some protection in the case of a downgrade.

In a final step a relative value analysis has to be conducted in order to make a final investment decision based on the fundamental analysis results. Analysts and portfolio managers are used to express their views relative to a chosen average, for example, statements like bond *X* should trade 15–20 bp wide to bond *Y* are quite common. At this point spread volatility and the liquidity of single bonds have to be considered in the final decision-making process.

5.2.1 Financial analysis

The financial analysis uses the information from the income statement, the balance sheet and the cash flow statement to compute various financial ratios. The purpose of the financial statement analysis is to evaluate the firm's financial decision-making process and operating performance.

Nevertheless, we have to recognize that the information value of individual data items from the financial statements is quite limited. Financial ratios have to be examined in the context of the firm's history, the industry, major competitors and the state of the economic cycle. Furthermore, it has to be pointed out that the assessment of the financial situation of a company should not be static, but a dynamic analysis has to support the investment process. Financial numbers of a company have to be forecasted by the implementation of scenario analysis (e.g. worst case – base case – best case). By this means it can be shown whether a company will succeed in future and sales-, investment- and financing-plans will help to assess the dynamic liquidity position of a company.

5.2.1.1 Income statement

The income statement shows the revenues, expenses and income of a company for a certain period of time. Table 5.1 highlights some important positions from the income statement, which are used to compute the profitability ratios and most importantly EBITDA (earnings before interest, taxes, depreciation and amortization) as a measure of cash flows from

Table 5.1 Income statement according to US–GAAP

	Revenues
–	Cost of goods sold
=	**Gross profit**
–	Selling and administrative expenses
=	**EBITDA**
–	Depreciation and amortization
=	**EBIT**
–	Interest expense
–	Taxes
=	**Net income before extraordinary items**
±	Extraordinary gains/losses
=	**Net income (net earnings)**

operations. It is important to assess whether net income has been determined based on conservative accounting policies or on liberal accounting policies which might not reflect economic reality and hence result in lower quality of earnings. High nonrecurring income as well as nonrecurring costs will bias the trend in earnings. An overstatement of revenues will distort profits. Revenue recognition practices vary across industries.

EBITDA can be a good determinant of cash flows and it is the most commonly used measure for a company's credit quality, for example, by computing coverage and leverage ratios. However, the use of EBITDA as a single measure of cash flows can be misleading, hence other factors have to be considered. The following are some critical points:

- EBITDA ignores changes in working capital and overstates cash flows in periods of working capital growth.
- EBITDA says nothing about the quality of earnings and can be a misleading measure of a company's liquidity.
- EBITDA can be manipulated through aggressive accounting policies relating to revenue and expense recognition, asset write-downs, excessive adjustments in deriving "adjusted pro-forma EBITDA" and by timing asset sales.
- EBITDA does not take into consideration the many unique attributes of different industries.

If some start-up companies (e.g. most of the noninvestment grade European telecommunications companies) have negative EBITDA, the computation of current financial ratios becomes almost meaningless and one has to focus on the growth trend, for example, whether the EBITDA loss narrows or widens over time. When computing the leverage ratio for these companies EBITDA can be replaced by PP&E (Property, Plant and Equipment). The ratio (Total Debt/PP&E) is a limited measure for leverage, hence debt protection.

5.2.1.2 Balance sheet

Every balance sheet is grouped by assets, liabilities and stockholder's equity. The balance sheet information in Table 5.2 is a basis for analyzing the sources of earnings. If assets are overstated, earnings will also be overstated because they will not include those charges required to reduce the assets to their proper valuations. Consequently, when liabilities are understated, earnings will be overstated. The asset quality depends on factors like changes in industry and economic conditions, and changes in the operations of the firm.

Table 5.2 Balance sheet positions according to US–GAAP

Assets	Liabilities
Current assets:	**Current liabilities:**
Cash + marketable securities	Accounts payable
Accounts receivable	Debt with maturity < 1 year
Inventory	**Long-term debt:**
	Bank debt with maturity > 1 year
Long-term assets:	Bonds with maturity > 1 year
Property, plant and equipment	**Stockholder's equity:**
Investments	Preferred and common stock
Intangible assets (Goodwill)	Additional paid-in capital
	Retained earnings
Total assets	**Total liabilities**

Table 5.3 Main working capital ratios

Ratio	Definition
Asset turnover	Working capital/sales
Accounts receivable days	(Receivables/sales) * 360
Inventory turnover	Cost of goods sold/average inventory
Accounts payable days	(Payables/cost of goods sold) * 360

Source: Citibank

Assets can be divided into different risk classes, for example, the future realization of accounts receivable has a higher degree of probability (lower risk) than the future realization of goodwill. A current asset is expected to be converted into cash during the operating cycle of a business. By analyzing the balance sheet one has to be aware of the existence of off-balance-sheet items. They are not disclosed in the balance sheet but have an effect on the financial situation of a company.

The optimal debt/equity ratio depends on many variables like capital costs of other companies in the industry, the access for further debt financing and the stability of earnings. Another important measure for the company's financial situation which can be drawn from the balance sheet is the working capital need, defined as the difference between current assets and current liabilities. Working capital must be related to other financial statement elements such as sales or total assets (Table 5.3). The management of working capital is important for cash flows because it shows how efficiently a company manages its cash. It is defined as:

Working capital = Accounts receivable + inventory – accounts payable.

The amount of cash, marketable securities and noncore assets help to assess the liquidity situation and the financial flexibility of the company as well.

Property, Plant and Equipment are of particular interest to bondholders in case of financial distress, because the proceeds from asset sales are used to service the debt obligations.

Pension liabilities are an important topic in the analysis of corporate balance sheets and hence play an important role in the evaluation of corporate bonds. The two main pension schemes are:

- Defined contribution: the employer pays into a designated pension fund for the benefit of the employee. After the contribution the employer has no further obligation to the employee.
- Defined benefit: the employer agrees to pay to the employee an annuity (or lump sum) of a defined amount at retirement. This pension represents an ongoing liability for the employer.

Credit risk is associated with rising pension expenses, cash contribution and rising unfunded pension liabilities. Falling asset returns increase pension costs because unfunded pension plans require cash contributions. Therefore, less cash is available for investments and deleveraging. While dealing with pension schemes we have to consider jurisdictional differences which create discrepancies in financial flexibility and different accounting standards. Unfunded pension plans became an issue for the capital markets in 2002 due to a multiyear equity bear market that significantly lowered the value of pension assets. At the same time historically low bond yields increased pension liabilities. Finally, rating downgrades associated with pension liabilities highlighted the credit risk inherent in unfunded pension plans. The main points which have to be considered in credit analysis are summed up below:

- Unfunded pension liabilities have earnings, cash flow and balance sheet consequences dependent on the jurisdiction.
- Unfunded pension liabilities have debt-like characteristics.
- Company characteristics have an impact on the size of liabilities. Mature companies and workforces will cause higher cash outflows as well as heavily unionized workforces.

- The actuarial assumptions made to calculate pension liabilities can misrepresent the funding status. It is in the interest of a company to keep discount rates (for future pension obligations) higher and assume also higher expected returns on pension assets in order to inflate earnings.

5.2.1.3 Cash flow statement

A statement of cash flows has to provide information about the cash receipts and cash payments of a company during a period. Furthermore, it will provide insight into the investing and financing activities of the company. The cash flow statement is a central tool in credit analysis for corporate bonds because it will help creditors to assess:

- the ability to generate future positive cash flows;
- the ability to meet obligations and pay dividends;
- reasons for differences between income and cash receipts and payments;
- both cash and noncash aspects of a company's investing and financing transactions.

A main focus is on future operating cash flows because the debt service capability, CAPEX and working capital needs have to be covered by operating cash flows, particularly if a short-term financing on the capital markets proves to be problematic. The uncertainty of projected future cash flows is higher for companies with a more volatile earnings trend. Overall, companies with high leverage will experience a high increase in their credit risk and widening in spreads when only a minor decrease in their cash flows occurs. The short-term refinancing risk increases with increasing short-term debt, increasing working capital needs and a higher CAPEX. An improvement of operating cash flows reduces the refinancing risk.

The development of cash flows from operating, investing and financing activities should be monitored on a quarterly basis and the cash position at the beginning of the period is compared to the cash position at the end of the period (see Table 5.4). A projection of the cash flows will help to determine the future liquidity situation of a company.

In Table 5.5 the FASB (Federal Accounting Standards Board) has listed the following as examples for cash flows from operating, investing and financing activities.

Noncash investing and financing activities must be distinguished from activities that involve cash receipts and payments and reported separately because they might have a significant effect on future cash flows of a

Table 5.4 Cash flow statement according to US–GAAP

±	Operating cash flow
±	Investing cash flow
±	Financing cash flow
=	Change in cash
+	Cash beginning of the year
=	Cash at the end of the year

Table 5.5 A classification from cash in- and outflows from operating, investing and financing activities

	Operating	Investing	Financing
Cash inflows	Receipts from sale of goods and services	Principal collections from loans and sales of other entities' debt instruments	Proceeds from issuing stock
	Sale of loans, debt or equity instruments carried in trading portfolio	Sale of equity instruments of other enterprises and from returns of investment in those instruments	Proceeds from issuing debt (short term or long term)
	Returns on loans (interest)	Sale of plant and equipment	Not-for-profits' donor restricted cash that is limited to long-term purposes
	Returns on equity securities (dividends)		
Cash outflows	Payments for inventory	Loans made and acquisition of other entities' debt instruments	Payment of dividends
	Payments to employees and other suppliers	Purchase of equity instruments of other enterprises	Repurchase of entity's stock
	Payments of taxes	Purchase of plant and equipment	Repayment of debt principal, including capital lease obligations
	Payments of interest		
	Purchase of loans, debt, or equity instruments carried in trading portfolio		

Source: Federal Accounting Standards Board

company. These are for example:

- Acquiring an asset through a capital lease
- Conversion of debt to equity
- Exchange of noncash assets or liabilities for other noncash assets or liabilities
- Issuance of stock to acquire assets.

Every company has to generate enough operating cash flows in the long run in order to grow and continue its business. The operating cash flows should be adjusted by the following positions in order to make them comparable over time and to other companies:

- Cash flows from interest rate expenses are included in the operating cash flows even though they should belong to the cash flows from financing.
- Income taxes are included in operating cash flow. Correctly, they are affected by financing decisions (e.g. deductibility of interest rate expenses of debt-financed projects) and investing decisions (e.g. tax credits for certain investment projects).
- Interest income and dividend income are considered as operating cash flow but they are the result of investment activities.

The cash flows from investing activities can be a measure of management's risk appetite and also the current phase of the business plan. Cash flows from financing give an insight into the company's ability to access the capital markets or alternative financing sources. It can be stated that bonds of companies which generate permanent positive free cash flows will on average outperform bonds of companies with negative free cash flows.

Operating cash flows can be computed in two different ways which will be illustrated next.

The direct method (Table 5.6) derives the net cash provided by or used in operating activities from the components of operating cash receipts and payments.

The indirect method (Table 5.7) derives the net cash provided by or used in operating activities by adjusting net income (loss) for the effects of transactions of a noncash nature, any deferrals or accruals of past or future operating cash receipts or payments, and items of income or expense associated with investing or financing activities.

Table 5.8 shows a possible way to compute the free cash flows from operations for a company.

Table 5.6 Cash flows from operating activities (direct method)

	Cash received from dividends
+	Cash received from interest
+	Cash received from sale of goods
=	**Cash provided by operating activities**
–	Cash paid to suppliers
–	Cash paid for operating expenses
–	Cash paid for interest
–	Cash paid for taxes
=	**Net cash flows from operating activities**

Table 5.7 Cash flows from operating activities (indirect method)

	Net income before taxation and extraordinary item
+	Depreciation of property, plant and equipment
+	Amortization of preoperative expenses
–	Investment income
+	Interest expense
=	**Operating income before working capital changes**
–	Increase in accounts receivable
–	Increase in inventory
–	Decrease in accounts payable
=	**Cash generated from operations**
–	Interest paid
–	Income taxes paid
=	**Cash flow before extraordinary item**
±	Proceeds/expenses from extraordinary items
=	**Net cash from operating activities**

If a company is currently not free cash flow positive the analyst has to focus on short-term liquidity and make projections about the future cash burn rate (uses of cash) and evaluate if it is sustainable with the sources of cash.

Table 5.8 Computation of free cash flow from operations using the indirect method

	Net income
+	Depreciation
+	Interest expense
=	**Operating income before working capital changes**
−	Increase in accounts receivable
+	Decrease in inventories
−	Decrease in accounts payable
=	**Cash generated from operations**
−	Interest and income taxes paid
=	**Net cash from operating activities**
−	CAPEX
=	**Free cash flow**

5.2.1.4 Financial ratios

The rating agencies Standard & Poor's, Moody's and Fitch Ibca use some of the financial ratios from Figure 5.3 as a basis for their rating decision when evaluating the credit quality of a company. There is a variation in the average ratio size across the various industries so that a company's ratios should be compared only with the peer group. The main financial ratios can be divided into the following categories:

- Coverage
- Leverage
- Profitability
- Cash flows/liquidity.

Profitability ratios explore the causes of a change in earnings. The way a company manages its assets and debt has a direct effect on its profitability. By understanding the causes one can better project future profitability and hence the ability to service debt. In the long run, every company has to generate free cash flows from operations. Short-term liquidity is essential for every company to stay in business.

An in-depth analysis of the whole capital structure is thus required prior to computing the leverage ratios. Many issuers (all rating classes) have convertible bonds outstanding. Especially when a company's stock price is

Coverage:

EBITDA/Interest

EBIT/Interest

(EBITDA – CAPEX)/Interest

(EBIT + fixed charges)/fixed charges

(EBT + $Interest_{cash}$ + $Rent_{lease}$)/$Interest_{cash}$ + $Rent_{lease}$

Leverage:

Total debt/EBITDA

(Total debt – Cash)/EBITDA

Total debt/(Total debt + Market cap)

Long-term debt/Total assets

Profitability:

EBITDA/Sales

EBIT/Sales

Sales/Total assets

Operating profit/Sales

Net income/Sales

ROA = EBIT * (1 – tax)/Total assets

ROE = Net income/Book value equity

Cash flows/ Liquidity:

Operating cash flow/Net revenues

Operating cash flow/Total debt

(Operating cash flow + Cash)/Current liabilities

Funds from operations/Total debt

(Funds from operation-CAPEX-change in Working capital)/Total debt

Current Ratio = Current assets/Current liabilities

Sales/Average Accounts receivable

Figure 5.3 Major financial ratios

Source: Union Investment

falling, a redemption of the convertible bond will be the most likely scenario (conversion option expires worthless). Under such circumstances the convertible bonds have to be considered as "pure" debt instruments. Leverage will decline when cash flow growth from earnings outpaces debt growth.

Figure 5.4 shows a relationship between leverage (here, total debt/EBITDA) and spreads for selected European investment grade bonds ex financials. Generally, it can be said that an increasing leverage is accompanied by wider spread levels.

There is no valid scoring model for the exact evaluation of financial risk, which implies that the probability of default or development of credit quality is a nonquantifiable process. Generally, the default probability rises with increasing financial risk and decreasing rating class. The evaluation of the financial situation of a company should be a synthesis out of the following factors:

- Financial flexibility; variability of CAPEX; working capital intensity
- Profitability
- Liquidity; cash position; lines of credit; vendor financing
- Access to capital markets under a stress scenario
- Refinancing risk; debt maturity

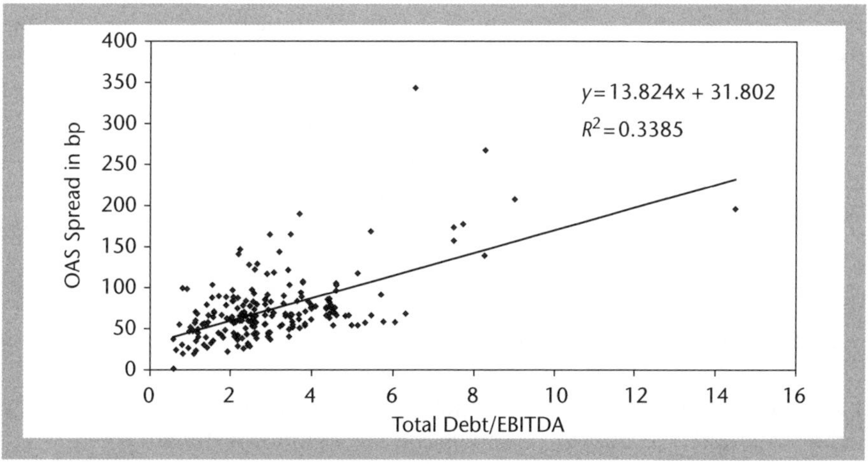

Figure 5.4 Leverage and spread levels for selected European investment grade bonds (Merrill Lynch EMU Corporate Index ex financials) on February 13th 2004

Source: Union Investment and Bloomberg

- Balance sheet structure (leverage, capital structure, coverage)
- Financial decisions and risk appetite
- Financial profile (dividend policy; share buybacks; IPOs)
- Merger and acquisition potential
- Nonstrategic assets
- Accounting approach (aggressive or conservative).

Countless numbers of financial ratios were used to determine the probability of financial distress. This effort is complicated by the fact that various reasons for financial distress are reflected in different financial ratios. The deterioration in the following ratios proved to be a good indicator – several months before the occurrence of default:

- Cash flow / total debt
- Net income / total assets
- Debt / total assets
- Sales / total assets
- Working capital / total assets
- Current assets / current liabilities.

It is almost impossible to standardize an approach for detecting financial distress by monitoring a set of financial ratios due to the fact that every industry has its own dynamics and every default case is unique by itself. Credit trends like the evolution of leverage, coverage, EBITDA growth and the growth of operating margins proved to be very reliable indicators of the performance of companies and also the performance of whole industry sectors. Deteriorating margins are equivalent with problems in the core business and will result in weaker debt protection measures (coverage + leverage) over the course of time. The trend in the ratio cash flows / total debt proved to be a very good indicator of financial distress as well.

5.2.1.5 Company's liquidity position

Liquidity is a measure of a company's financial flexibility. It has to be acknowledged that liquidity profiles can vary significantly across different industries. In general a company has four options to repay maturing debt:

- Cash position
- Operating cash flow

- Refinancing
- Asset sales.

The following points have to be considered when evaluating the liquidity position of an issuer:

- Cash position and marketable securities and the strength and availability of cash flows
- Ability to raise capital (equity and debt) in the short term
- Undrawn bank facilities (focus on covenants, material adverse change clauses)
- Available vendor financing
- Ability to control working capital as a means of improving cash flows (especially under a stress scenario)
- The scaleability of the business plan in order to reduce or postpone CAPEX
- Value of non-strategic assets which can be sold (timing and asset value under a stress scenario)
- Asset securitization
- Direct and contingent obligations of a company.

Particularly in assessing the quality of bank lines the presence of "material adverse change" clauses is important. Such a provision enables the lender to hold back or cancel earlier committed bank lines if the borrower's financial condition or operational position has deteriorated significantly and the circumstances which led to the new situation were previously unknown.

The following factors have to be considered in the analysis:

- The issuer's cash flows matched against its short-term debt maturity profile
- The issuer's ability to manage its working capital and capital spending
- Funding diversity through regular global market access and/or securitizations.

The rating agencies emphasize the liquidity situation of an issuer in their credit rating assessment. Especially cyclical companies can experience short-term liquidity problems, which can lead to financial distress, particularly if a company relies heavily on short-term debt. An appropriate cash management is an important factor for the success of a company. In general, every company has to find a match between its investment function and financing function.

A sensitivity analysis of the issuer's sources and uses of cash which considers issuer-specific factors and broad market disruptions has to be performed. The analysis tests the issuer's ability to cover its cash needs under scenarios with increasing degree of stress. It is useful in understanding an issuer's sensitivity to unforeseen adverse events, its vulnerability to a restriction of external funding and the time period over which an issuer could withstand a stressed environment.

The financial analysis of a company is not sufficient to evaluate its credit quality but other qualitative factors like the market (business) risk and the assessment of the management quality have to be incorporated into the analysis framework. Execution risk and "bad news" about operating problems can result in a high volatility of spread movements because the future earnings prospects and cash flows are negatively impacted and hence the ability to repay outstanding debt in a timely manner. This leads us to analyze factors affecting the outcome of the business strategy.

5.2.1.6 Capital structure

Every company tries to optimize its capital structure. The underlying business determines the appropriate leverage. In general, there is a pecking order in the financing decision of every company. Internal financing (retained earnings) is the first form of financing that the management has to consider. If a company is dependent on external financing it will use bank financing before issuing bonds or convertibles. The last form of financing is represented by equity issuance either in an IPO or seasoned issuance (e.g. rights issue) (Figure 5.5).

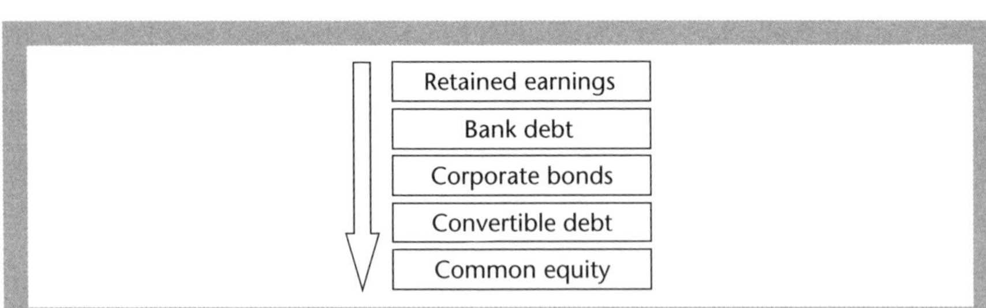

Figure 5.5 Financing hierarchy

Source: Union Investment

Companies with long-term stable cash flows can increase their leverage without jeopardizing their balance sheet strength. Growth-oriented companies on the other hand should consider a high portion of equity in the capital mix in order to maintain a solid balance sheet structure.

Financial leverage (bank debt and bonds) up to a certain point (optimal debt–equity mix) can increase EPS (earnings per share) and ROE (return on equity) but the volatility in EPS will increase as well. As a rule of thumb a debt/capitalization (sum: debt + equity) ratio of around 40 percent is considered to be the optimal capital mix by computing the theoretical equity price.

The following three points shall support the thesis that industrial companies have little incentives to maintain a very conservative capital structure reflected in a AAA or AA-rating category.

- The information asymmetry between management and investors favors debt financing over equity financing. If management expects an increase in the stock price it would give away a "free lunch" to new shareholders by issuing equity instead of bonds. If management expects a decline in the equity price and tries to sell equity prior to the fall, it could turn out difficult to sell equity at a fair value because investors might anticipate the decline in the stock price.
- An unlevered company will increase its value by taking on debt. This is true because dividend income is fully taxed whereas the interest costs are deductible from corporate taxes. Nevertheless, it is important to notice that an increased gearing (ratio debt/equity) results in a higher risk of financial distress. The following formula clarifies this point:

  Value of firm = Value of equity + Value of tax shield − Cost of distress.
- Every company faces individual capital costs. The task is to find the right mix between debt and equity so that the value of the firm is maximized. Market weights should be used to compute the weighted average cost of capital (WACC):

$$\mathrm{WACC} = \frac{\mathrm{D}}{\mathrm{V}} \cdot r_{\mathrm{D}} + \frac{\mathrm{E}}{\mathrm{V}} \cdot r_{\mathrm{E}},$$

where D denotes debt, E is Equity and $\mathrm{V} = \mathrm{D} + \mathrm{E}$ the value of the firm. r_{D} and r_{E} denote the cost of debt and equity, respectively.

By choosing the capital structure the risk and costs of capital have to be considered (see example below). Capital costs represent a break-even point (costs have to be covered in order to stay in business in the long run). All projects with IRR (internal rates of return) lower than the capital costs are not profitable and should be avoided.

- Cost of long-term debt:

$$\text{Cost of debt} = \frac{\text{Annual coupon of a new bond}}{\text{Principal} \cdot (1 - \text{floatation costs})}$$

$$\text{Cost of debt} = \frac{9}{100 \cdot (1 - 0.0018)} = 9.16\%$$

Adjusted for taxes (40%) : $0.0916 \times (1 - 0.4) = 5.5\%$

- Cost of preferred stock:

$$\text{Cost of preferred stock} = \frac{\text{Preferred dividend}}{\text{Market price of preferred} \cdot (1 - \text{floatation cost})}$$

Issue price: 100
Dividend: 11

$$\text{Cost of preferred stock} = \frac{11}{100 \times (1 - 0.04)} = 11.46\%$$

- Cost of common stock: assumption of a constant dividend growth rate

$$\text{Cost of common stock} = \frac{\text{Dividend} \cdot (1 + G)}{\text{Price of Stock} \cdot (1 - \text{floatation cost})} + \text{constant growth rate}$$

$$\text{Cost of common stock} = \frac{2 \times 1.07}{16 \times (1 - 0.05)} + 0.07 = 14.39\%$$

The CAPM (Capital Asset Pricing Model) is also used to compute the cost of an equity issue:

Expected risk premium on stock = beta · expected risk premium on market
$r - r_f = \beta \cdot (r_m - r_f)$,

where r is the rate of return, r_f the risk-free rate, r_m the market return and β the systematic risk of the stock. It has to be considered that various assumptions of the CAPM appear to be unrealistic many times.

5.2.1.6.1 The optimal capital structure. Every company has to find an "optimal" capital structure. Generally management's objective is to maximize the value of the firm. The cost of capital of a firm changes with leverage.

A simple measure of how much debt and equity a firm is using is to look at the debt to capital ratio:

$$\text{Debt-to-capital ratio} = \frac{\text{Debt}}{\text{Debt} + \text{equity}}$$

Debt has a tax benefit as the interest payment is tax deductible (tax benefit = tax rate · interest payment). The costs of debt frequently discussed in economic literature are bankruptcy costs, agency costs and the loss of future flexibility. The cost of debt will depend on:

- The general level of interest rates
- The default risk premium
- The firm's tax rate.

Cost of equity = Risk-free rate + beta · risk premium
After-tax cost of debt = (Risk-free rate + default spread) · (1 − tax)

The cost of capital matters because the value of a firm equals the present value of cash flows to the firm discounted back at the cost of capital. If the cash flows to the firm are held constant and the cost of capital is minimized, the value of the firm will be maximized. With increasing debt levels the cost of equity will increase because equity will become riskier with a rising beta, and the cost of debt will increase with increasing debt levels as well because default risk will go up (Figure 5.6).

Optimal debt ratios will vary with certain firm-specific and macroeconomic factors. It can be said that a low variance in earnings and lower intangible asset values support higher debt ratios. Higher default risk premiums imply lower optimal debt ratios and vice versa. One fundamental principle of an optimal debt–equity mix is to make the cash flows on debt match up

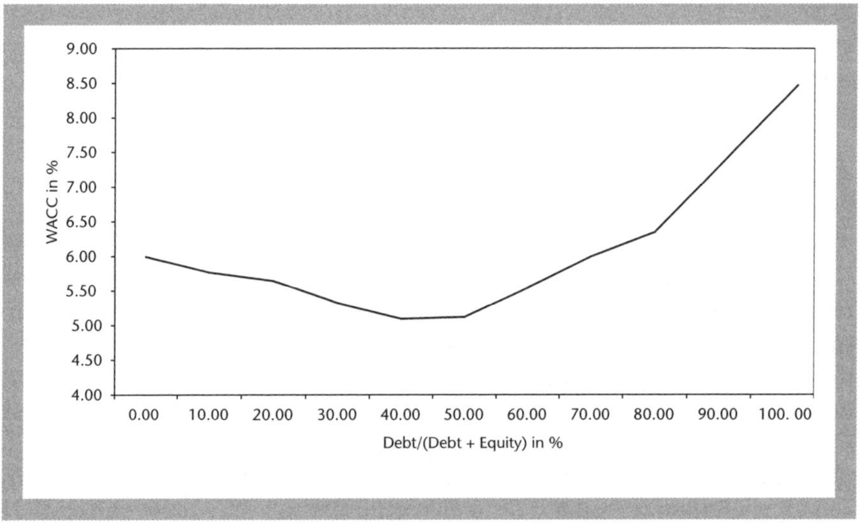

Figure 5.6 Change in weighted average cost of capital with an increasing leverage

Source: Union Investment

with the cash flows that the firm makes on its assets (e.g. duration and currency mix). Hereby the risk of default is reduced, debt capacity and the value of the firm is increased.

In the case of an underlevered firm, the management should ask itself if the firm has good projects. If this is the case then it makes sense to finance those with debt otherwise dividends should be paid to shareholders or share-buybacks commenced. Here the problems might start for a company which uses extensive debt financing. If previously good projects turn bad, earnings will not be sufficient to support the high debt levels. As a consequence the firm's debt profile deteriorates. If a firm is a takeover target then a reasonable strategy would be to increase leverage quickly. On the other hand, in an over-levered firm that has good projects, management should fund those through equity or retained earnings. If the overlevered firm has no projects to finance then retained earnings should be used to pay off debt, dividends should be cut and possibly new equity issued. If such a firm runs the risk of bankruptcy then deleveraging through asset sales or renegotiation with lenders should be the appropriate strategy for management.

The next paragraphs are dedicated to convertible debt securities. They can be added to fixed income portfolios for yield enhancement purposes. Depending on their structure rating agencies consider convertible bonds either as equity or debt.

*5.2.1.7 Convertible bonds**

There are several reasons for companies to issue convertible bonds. One is to capture the high implied equity volatility in the market (companies issuing convertibles are sellers of the equity call option, so they can save on the coupon payments as they can issue the convertible at a higher volatility level). Another very popular reason to issue this type of securities is to liquidate cross holdings. Especially in the European market exchangeable bonds are a common way for companies looking to monetize their equity holdings in other firms. Convertible bonds generally can save money for the company, as the coupon payment on these securities is below 50 percent of the coupon of straight bonds with same maturity, so companies are able to increase their leverage without affecting the interest costs in the P&L statement. Convertible new issues can have a significant effect on the corporate bond market. The main players in the convertible bond markets are hedge funds (leveraged investors), who buy the convertible new issues, sell the delta-weighted equity position in the name and buy CDS protection to separate the cheap implied volatility in the option value. This causes a widening in the CDS level of the issuer. However, particularly

* Thanks are due to Peter Varga for his input on Convertible bonds.

during 2003, many of them let the credit portion of the convertibles unhedged, expressing their view on the credit market (being long credit).

Plain vanilla convertible bonds are fixed income securities with an embedded equity call option (Figure 5.7). The price of this instrument changes over time with the underlying stock price of the equity option, equity volatility, credit quality and interest rates. The main difference to other fixed income securities is the incorporated equity call option. This option gives the convertible security holder the right, to convert the bond into a given number of shares of a predetermined security at a previously set date. If it is not converted until maturity, the convertible will be redeemed at a fixed price (100 percent).

Most convertibles pay a regular coupon which is lower than that of a comparable fixed income security (in some cases as low as 0 percent) because of the embedded option value (the bonds are issued at 100 percent, so the lower coupon compensates for the equity option value). Because of this lower coupon the main source of return of a convertible bond is the capital gain. Convertibles also have a fixed maturity (if not converted) and mainly the US-issues have call and/or put dates. Opposed to the normal fixed income securities, convertibles can have a negative yield to maturity (YTM) in cases when the call option is near the money. This could be very important for fixed income investors, as it could adversely impact the YTM of their portfolios.

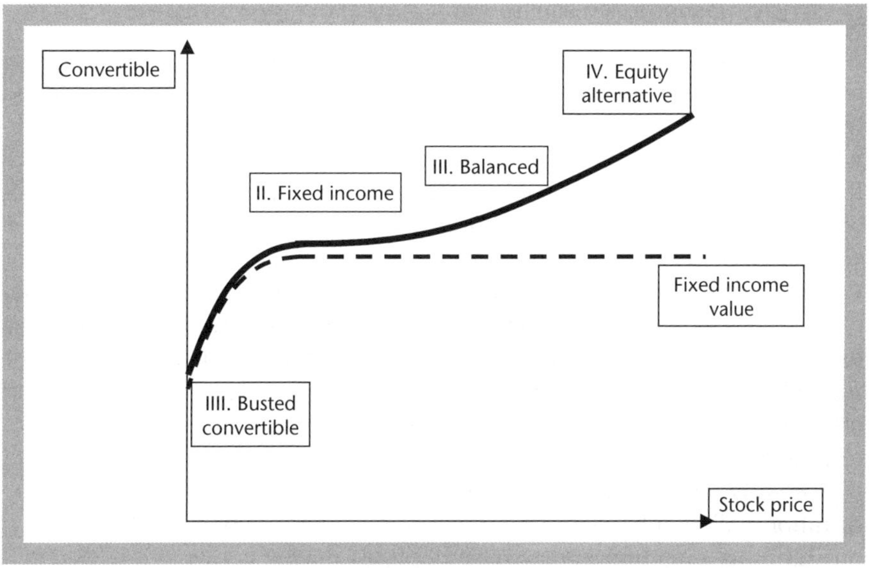

Figure 5.7 The different life cycles of a plain convertible bond
Source: Union Investment

Before examining the behavior of a typical convertible bond in the different life cycles, the inputs impacting the pricing of convertibles have to be analyzed. Depending on the territory the convertible bond is trading, the following factors will have a different weight explaining the movement:

***Delta-effect* (*Equity price sensitivity*)**: The stock price has a dual impact on the price of a convertible security. Obviously it will have an impact on the price of the embedded call option (higher stock price means higher option value and higher convertible value) especially in the "balanced" and "equity alternative" territory, where the sensitivity of the option to the stock price (common name: delta, which shows the percentage change in the option price caused by a 1 percent change in the share price) is greater than zero. It could have also a spill-over effect on the fixed income value of the convertible in a distressed situation, where the credibility and the potential survival of the issuer is questioned. In this situation the falling share price and the diminishing market capitalization of the company will have a negative impact on its cost of capital, hence on the cost of debt.

***Vega-effect* (*Implied equity volatility*)**: Rising equity volatility will have a positive effect on the price of the convertible bond as it impacts the option component of it. This impact will be strongest in the "balanced", or in the "equity alternative" territory. Implied equity volatility is also an important part of the Merton option model-based approach of valuing corporate debt, mainly for issues with lower credit quality or in the "Busted convertible" zone. The common definition of the option price sensitivity to the equity price volatility is "vega," which shows the relative price sensitivity of the option value to a 1 percent move in the implied equity volatility. The "vega" is always positive.

***Credit risk of the issuer* (*spread duration*)**: Issuer credit risk impacts the price of the convertible bond throughout its whole life cycle. As we mentioned before, the credit risk will have a positive correlation to the implied equity volatility and to the share price of the issuer. The spread duration shows us the sensitivity of the convertible bond to the movements in the CDS levels of the issuer. The impact of the spread duration or in general the duration will decrease as the security moves up in the equity sensitive territory. Convertible bonds are priced using CDS, so the holders of bond floor convertibles gain or loose versus the straight bonds because of movements in the basis (spread between CDS and the asset swap level of the bond). The following example shows the effect of the share price on the CDS (and implicitly on the value of the VNU 06 Convertible) in the case of VNU (Figure 5.8).

Sensitivity to changes in government yields: Like spread duration, the duration will also have an impact on the convertible bond as long as it is outstanding. This impact however depends on the equity sensitivity and maturity of the issue (also like in the case of the spread duration), the shorter the maturity and the less equity sensitive the issue is, the lower will

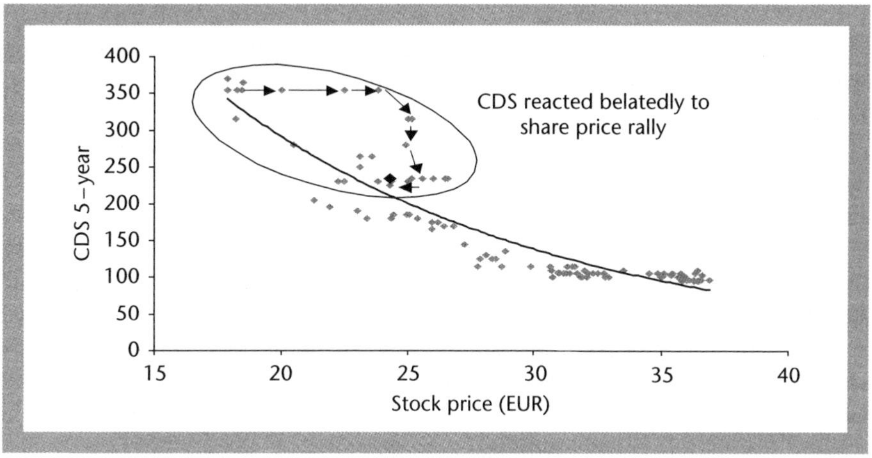

Figure 5.8 VNU 5-yr CDS versus stock price, Mar. 18, 2002 to Sep. 04, 2002

Source: Goldman Sachs

be the reaction on any yield movement of the convertible bond. On the other hand, the implied equity volatility and the debt/equity ratio do not have any effect on the "normal" duration of the security.

Conversion price, stock dividend: These two factors have a very simple and straightforward effect on the convertible security. The higher the conversion price of the issue (option) relative to the actual market price of the shares for exchange the lower is the option value and with that the bond value. Stock dividends, if they are unexpected could adversely impact the near- or at-the-money option value, because they represent an opportunity cost for the holder of the option unless the issue prospectus effectively handles this problem.

Redemption price and coupon: The price of the convertible bond will be positively influenced by a higher redemption price, because a higher redemption price means *ceteris paribus* a higher bond price. The coupon of the convertible bond could have an important role in measuring the composition of the total return of a portfolio. Many investors have tax restrictions or current income objectives on their portfolios so the tax impact of higher coupons (also in the case of exchangeable bonds the capital gains) and the sufficient current income generation potential of the portfolio are important issues to consider.

Prospectus: This factor is mentioned last not because of less importance but it is not a market factor. An indepth examination of the convertible bond prospectus is very important especially in the case of US and Asian issues. Convertible bond investors have to be aware of a potential subordination of the issue, the diverse put or call structures and their impact on the price of the security. The dividend protection, the stock-split adjustments and the exchange rate impacts could present negative surprise for those investors without experience and reasonable care in investing in convertible bonds.

Table 5.9 gives a good summary about the behavior of convertible bonds in the different life cycles. Fixed income investors should only consider the first three parts of the curve.

Busted convertibles: Busted convertibles have already lost their equity sensitivity, so the only way that the equity market could impact the price of the bond is, when the survival of the issuer is questioned or if the issuer just emerged from a successful reorganization. In these cases the steep rise or decline in the equity price will impact the credit ratios and the refinancing opportunities of the company so the risk premium will be dramatically lower or higher as before. ABB is a good example. In 2002, ABB faced a distressed situation because of its asbestos liabilities, high short-term debt levels and a poor earnings trend. The convertible bond with 2007 maturity traded as low as 40 percent of par in line with the straight bonds. After the successful restructuring plan of the company the spreads recovered along with the equity price, but the holders of the convertible bonds earned an extra return (almost 40 percent in 15 months) over the straight bonds because of the sharp increase in the equity price.

Fixed income alternatives: Another way to benefit from bond floor convertible bonds is the basis play. Fixed income investors can buy the busted or bond floor convertible and underweight the straight bond in their portfolios, if the basis is too large compared to historical means or if the issuer exhibits a positive credit trend – then the basis usually decreases. As the CDS recovers relative to the ASW level of the straight bond, investors earn an excess return. Two excellent examples were offered by the convertible bonds of France Telecom and those of the Dutch telecom provider KPN in the past. In the case of France Telecom, the holders of the convertible with a 4 percent coupon and 2005 maturity earned a 6 percent (not annualized) excess return over the straight bond with the same maturity from October 2002 until December 2002 as the basis declined between the CDS and the straight bond. The reasons were the announced debt-reduction measures of the company. In the case of KPN, the convertible issue is a subordinated one and investors could have gained both from the declining positive basis and from the melt-down of the subordination premium.

Balanced convertibles: Fixed income alternative instruments could change into a balanced issue if the share price recovers sharply. Many bond floor convertibles experienced a kick-in in their deltas when equity markets recovered in 2003. Fixed income investors could select issuers with a stable credit trend and with bond floor convertible characteristics and underweight the straight bonds: this strategy is a convex one: investors earn an excess return in case of a positive equity-market sentiment and have almost nothing to lose (only if

Table 5.9 Behavior of convertible bonds in different life cycles

Busted convertible	Parity 0–40%	* Bond floor does not hold (a severe decline in the equity price and the soaring volatility have a spill-over effect)
	Equity prem. > 100%	* Mostly for high-yield investors, who can take more volatility and tracking error
	Delta < 10%	* Could be a reasonable alternative to straight bonds (ABB, Vivendi Universal etc.)
	Risk prem. < 5%	* Higher implied volatility without any positive effect on the option price (deep out-of the money option)
	Rho > 3%	
FI. alternative	Parity 40–80%	* Deep out-of-the money option without any adverse affect of the lower equity price (fundamentals not questioned)
	Equity prem. > 25%	* This bond could gain on:
	Delta 10–30%	* Steep rise in the share price (buy the cheap option)
	Risk prem. 5–25%	* Bond/Credit market rally (if the duration is high enough)
	Rho 2–3%	* But ...
		* Could cause a 5–10% negative performance versus straight bonds in case of a sharp equity decline
		* In the higher delta territory: volatility could have a significant effect on the option price
Balanced cv.	Parity 80–120%	* Asymmetric Risk/Return Profile (Gamma-Effect) – *ceteris paribus*: a very interesting territory
	Equity prem. 10–25%	* Share price + 20% → Convertible ~+ 12%
	Delta 30–80%	* Share price − 20% → Convertible ~− 10.5%
	Risk prem. 20–40%	* Mainly the area 30–60% delta, tracking error could be however very significant!
	Rho 1–2%	* Only for investors with a strong opinion about the equity market, option market (volatility)
Equity alternative	Parity > 120%	* Very equity sensitive
	Equity prem. 0–10%	* Not recommended for fixed income investors
	Delta > 80%	
	Risk prem. > 40%	
	Rho < 1%	

Notes: Parity: (Equity PX × Conversion Ratio)/Price of the convertible security

Risk Premium: (Price of the CV security − Bond floor)/Bond floor

Source: Union Investment

the basis widens) when equities do not perform. Besides the bond floor names, convertibles with a delta of no more than 50 percent offer a reasonable return enhancement and more importantly they can lower the volatility of the fixed income/credit portfolio through very low or even negative correlation to other fixed income products. Table 5.10 shows, that convertible bonds had a slightly negative correlation to plain fixed income products during the very volatile 7-year period since 1997. The correlation with credits should be somewhat higher, because during 2000–02 the equity market and the credit market experienced a high correlation.

Investors using convertibles with a delta ranging from 10 to 50 percent in order to enhance volatility adjusted performance should however have a longer term view (see Figure 5.9). In the short term, a severe decline of equity markets could negatively impact the position, but exactly in this delta range the gamma effect of the convertible could be quite significant. The gamma is the nonlinear factor in the movement of the convertible price caused by the change of the share price. The gamma shows the change in the delta of an option for a given small change in the equity price. Choosing convertibles with a high gamma could protect investors on the downside (but not eliminate it!) as the delta will decline with an increasing speed if the equity falls and vice versa.

Using the very common Markowitz framework for a further analysis of convertibles in fixed income portfolios, Figure 5.10 provides further evidence of the benefits of such positions between 1998 and the beginning of 2004.

One weakness in using the Markowitz-type analysis for convertible bonds is that the mean–variance framework assumes the normal distribution of returns. This assumption is not true for convertible bonds, as their return distribution depends on their equity sensitivity. Especially the return

Table 5.10 Correlation matrix among different asset classes (Dec. 97–Jan. 04)

	GSBB European convertible index (%)	DJ STOXX 600 index (%)	JPM European Govt bond index (%)	49% Europe equities/ 51% Europe Govt bonds (%)
GSBB European convertible index	100	80	11	85
DJ STOXX 600 index	80	100	−37	97
JPM European Govt bond index	−11	−37	100	−18
49% Europe equities/51% Europe Govt bonds	85	97	−18	100

Source: Bloomberg, Goldman Sachs Convertible Strategy estimates

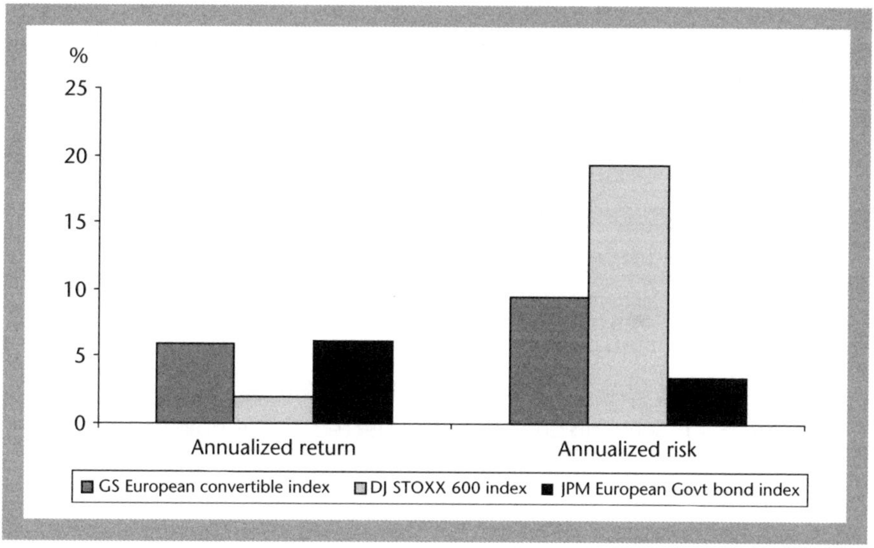

Figure 5.9 Convertibles are a valuable asset class compared to stocks or bonds (Dec. 97–Jan 04)

Source: Goldman Sachs Convertible Strategy estimates

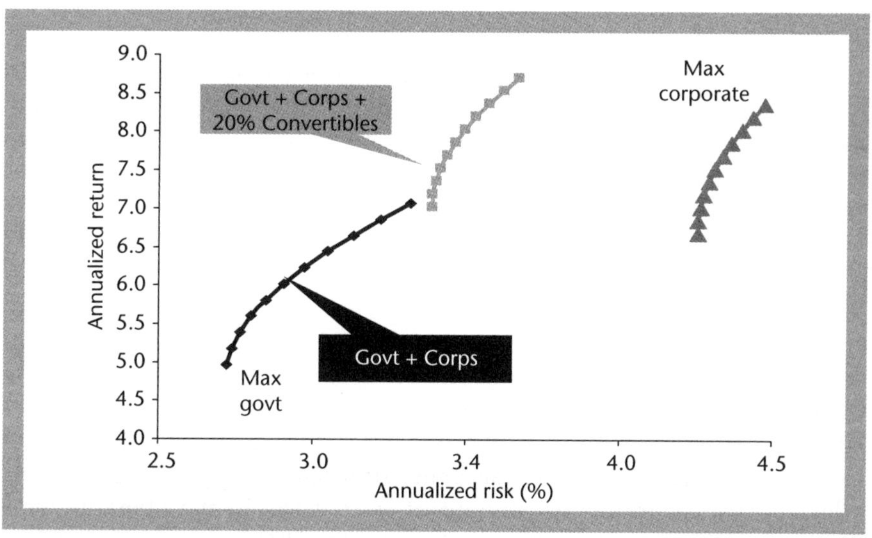

Figure 5.10 Convertibles in the Markowitz-framework

Sources: JPM indices; ML indices; UBSW indices; Bloomberg, Goldman Sachs estimates

distribution for high gamma convertibles has a fat tail on the right side but a relative small tail on the left side. This is a further argument for buying convertibles in the 10–50 percent delta range in fixed income portfolios. Under the consideration of a nonnormal distribution, the actual efficient

Name	Unicredito into Generali
ISIN	XSO182249846
Coupon	2.50%
Delta	41%
Duration	3.00
Price	103.25
Maturity	Dec. 19,08
Valuation Date	March 1, 04

	Yields		
Stock (%)	–	O bp (%)	+ (%)
10	7.78	6.04	4.39
0	4.19	2.50	0.89
–	1.00	−0.74	−2.58

Figure 5.11 Scenario analysis for a selected convertible bond issue

Source: Bloomberg, Union Investment

weighting for convertibles in mixed fixed income portfolios should be even higher than it is shown in Figure 5.10.

The following example shows a quick scenario analysis for a convertible bond issue, assuming changes only in the underlying share price and in the market yields (Figure 5.11).

Figure 5.11 shows that it pays off to own a convertible bond with a reasonable delta, if there is some volatility in both the fixed income and in the equity markets. Depending on the delta 7–10 percent increase in the share price compensates the investor for the loss of coupon relative to the straight bond in our example.

5.2.2 Market risk (business risk)

Market risk and business risk will have the same meaning in the following paragraphs. Market risk is the uncertainty regarding future earnings of a company and is determined by the industry to a large extent. The quality of earnings is impacted by the variability of sales. The operating leverage, which is a measure of the amount of fixed costs in the operating cost structure of a company, can be another source of the earnings variability. The higher the relative amount of fixed cost, the higher the operating leverage and hence the operating risk. The operating leverage can be expressed in an equation as the percentage change in operating earnings relative to the percentage change in sales.

The market risk determines the parameters for the financial risk of a company; hence the analysis of the market risk highlights main factors, which can have an effect on the credit quality of a company. A sensitivity analysis should make assumptions about the following factors, affecting the earnings situation of every company:

- Business plan/strategy
- Cost structure of the industry (operating efficiencies, R&D costs, labor costs)
- Marketing and distribution network
- Competition (domestic and global, position, product, price)
- Cyclicality of an industry
- Vulnerability to economic cycles (industry maturity, capacity utilization rates, supply and demand for major products and its production inputs–commodity prices)
- Business environment
- Growth potential
- Market share (customer relationship, competitive pricing)
- Industry structure/ industry trends/ life cycle of the industry (risk, financing need and profitability tend to decline over the life cycle of the industry)
- Own position in life cycle/ product mix/ product quality in relation to peer group
- Diversification of business units (revenue streams)
- Geographic diversification
- Political and regulatory environment (deregulation, liberalization, privatization, taxes, political stability, government guarantees and support etc.)
- Exposure to litigation
- Demographics
- Technology transfer
- Barriers of entry.

Coming back to the effect on credit spreads movements, it can be said that the spreads will tend to widen when one or more of the next points are true for a corporate bond issuer:

- A weak market position implies high investment costs in order to gain market share (costs resulting from the acquisition of new clients and external growth). The financial results will deteriorate in the short- and medium term. Generally, the cash requirements will be high when the market growth is high, independently of a low or high market share.
- Weak numbers in top-line growth are a good indicator of problems on the operations side of a company's business or a bad marketing strategy.
- An environment with a high degree of price competition allows a differentiation against the competitors only by increasing the product quality. The provision of value-added products results in a higher budget for R&D.
- Regulatory restrictions lead to an increase of operational risk.
- Products being in an early phase of their life cycle generally do not generate positive cash flows.
- Cyclical companies are always more impacted by economic downturns than defensive (noncyclical) companies.
- Negative industry trends (e.g. high energy costs, change in consumer behavior, overcapacity and regulations) impact the credit quality of all companies within a sector.

The SWOT analysis offers a convenient way to capture the operating risks of a company. The current strategy of a company is compared with the changes taking place in the business environment. This approach tries to incorporate the strengths and weaknesses as well as the opportunities and threats of a company in a single model (Figure 5.12) and helps to identify the major drivers for success and the major reasons for failure at the same time.

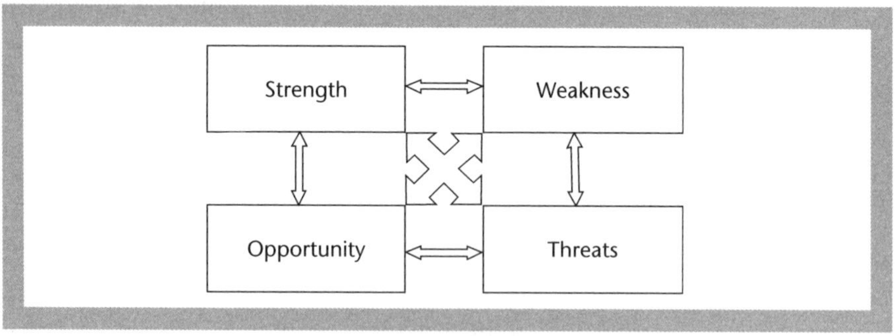

Figure 5.12 SWOT analysis

Source: Kotler

By forecasting future developments and changes in a company, analysts have to be able to recognize "weak signals" in the form of badly structured information as preliminary signs of discontinuities. This task is particularly difficult, because companies try to keep detailed information from the investors in their quarterly and annual reports and during one-on-ones they never give clear statements regarding operating margins in their business units, financial forecasts and liquidity positions. The focus of forecasts is on market development strategies, because sales growth is strategically very important particularly for external investors like creditors.

To evaluate the competitive position of a company we can use Michael E. Porter's Five Forces diagram as we have described already in Chapter 4. The same external forces determine the competitive position of a company. After defining an environment in which all companies from one industry have to operate, certain factors within an industry have to be analyzed in order to determine the success and failure of companies. These are:

- Degree of specialization
- Brand name
- Distribution channels
- Product quality
- Technological advantage
- Vertical integration
- Cost position
- Price policy.

Large diversified companies usually generate earnings and cash flows from various business units. Some businesses are strategically important and others can be considered as noncore businesses. According to the market attractiveness (measured by market growth rate) and the business strength (measured by relative market share) management has to decide about the allocation of their resources (Figure 5.13). For corporate bond investors the financial discipline of companies is a key investment consideration. Businesses in maturing markets with low growth rates but a solid market position will generate positive cash flows. These cash resources should be invested into projects in attractive fast growing markets where it is likely that the company will be able to achieve the necessary market size. If a situation occurs when a business burns a lot of cash and struggles to improve its market position then the prospects of contributing to the overall performance of a company shrink. It then depends on the management team to decide about a divestiture of such loss-generating businesses.

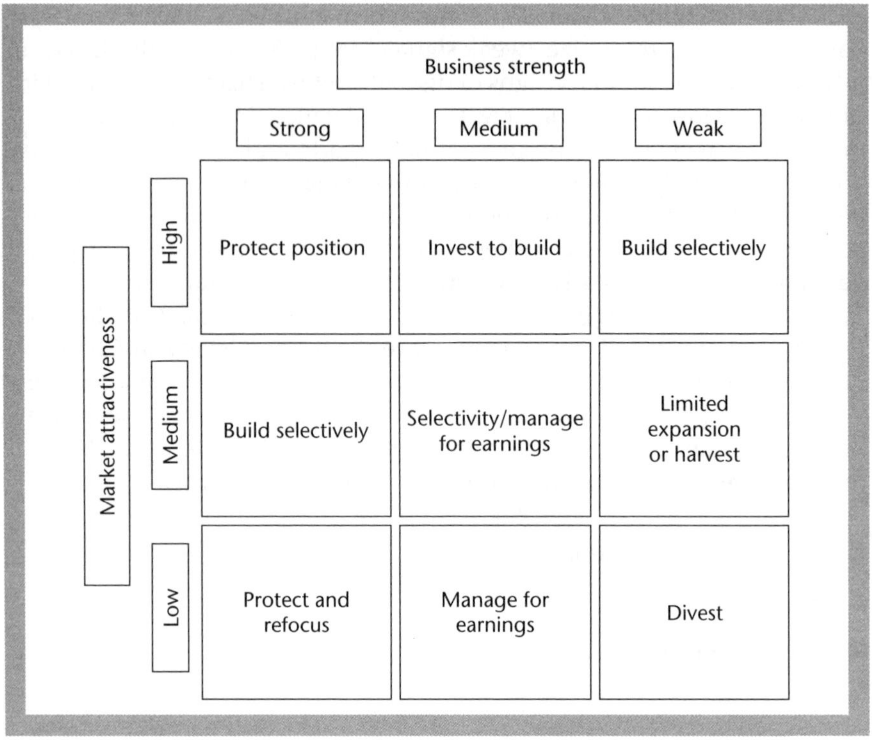

Figure 5.13 Multifactor Portfolio Matrix – each quadrant represents a business unit

Source: Kotler, pioneered by General Electric

Companies pursuing a bondholder friendly policy which are focused on balance sheet strength will reverse wrong strategic decisions early and take into account the small likelihood of selling a future top-performing business.

The company size has to be considered always when evaluating the credit quality of an issuer. The size of a company can be determined either by its total assets, market capitalization, sales or the number of employees. It can be argued that large companies usually have a better market position than small- and medium-sized companies because large companies are more diversified and have different income streams (product lines). These companies have a better access to the capital markets especially in a crisis scenario (slowing economy). The argument "too-big-to-fail" is particularly right for European issuers. In Europe, politics play a big part in business decisions and it is not an uncommon practice that a government steps in and bails out a distressed company when too many jobs are at stake.

5.2.2.1 *The management assessment*

The wrong strategic decision made at the wrong time can result in a serious deterioration in the financial profile of a company. A loss of investors' confidence in the management team can have a direct negative impact on the trading levels (spreads) of the bonds. A conservative management team is favorable for bondholders because too aggressive strategies usually favor only shareholders. A lot of companies have incentive systems in place in the form of employee stock option plans. Especially senior management is compensated on the basis of the company's stock performance. This easily leads to business decisions, which result in a wealth transfer from bondholders to shareholders. Bondholders do not necessarily participate in increasing equity prices if for example an aggressive growth strategy is largely debt-financed.

By evaluating the management team the following questions should be answered:

- To what extent do bondholders pursue the same goals as the management team?
- What is management's financial philosophy?
- Does management demonstrate enough commitment and what incentives systems are in place, for example, which employees qualify for a stock option plan?
- How successful is management in achieving their goals?
- How is the management performance monitored and how is compensation structured?
- Does management or the strategic investor have an exit strategy in place?
- Is the management team experienced enough in leading a highly levered firm?
- How flexible is the management and how fast can it adapt to a fast changing business environment?
- Is the management willing and able to adjust its business strategy to its financial situation?
- How is the decision process structured, for example, is there a strong management team in place or a strong equity sponsor, a strategic investor or are all important strategic decisions made by a single person?
- Are efficient information systems in place and available to support the management decisions at any time?
- Does the company implement an efficient cash management system and how are the company's resources controlled?

- Are there sufficient communication channels across all job levels in the company?
- How is job satisfaction measured?
- How effective is the public relations policy and how important are investor relations for the company, for example, is the management able to communicate the right business strategy?
- Does management assign the appropriate importance to execution risk and event risk and can the proposed strategy be implemented?

Once again the importance of management's integrity has to be pointed out because it is the management team which puts the business strategy in place and determines the risk profile of the company's business and hence to a large extent its performance. Figure 5.14 highlights some of the dimensions that the management has to consider by formulating the business strategy. Hereby the company can develop its local markets but can also choose to expand into new markets and diversify its product portfolio at the same time. A lot of noninvestment grade and lower investment grade issuers are global market leaders in their respective niche segments and

Market	**Product**	
	Present	*New*
Present	Market penetration Consolidation Status quo	Product development
New	Market development	Diversification
	Integration	Diversification
Local expansion	Low risk	Medium risk
International expansion	Medium risk	High risk

Figure 5.14 Business strategy
Source: Igor Ansoff and Citigroup

benefit from outsourcing trends of their large investment grade counterparts. The business risk increases with increasing market expansion and increasing product differentiation and vice versa.

5.2.2.2 Equity performance

The analysis of corporate bonds has to incorporate the stock performance of the particular issuer even though the asymmetric risk profile does not allow to participate in the growth of a firm. Due to the limited upside for corporate bonds and almost unlimited downside, when a credit actually begins to be distressed, market participants tend to worry about the value of the assets relative to the ability to pay off all debt. The relationship between a company's equity and debt starts to become nonlinear when the stock price falls below a certain threshold. The equity price is a good proxy for the value of the assets of a company. The following definition establishes a relationship between the equity price of a company and its leverage:

Leverage ratio = Total debt/(Total debt + Market capitalization)
Market capitalization = (number of common shares · equity price)

The deterioration of the ratio (Total debt/(Total debt + Market cap)) above the range of 60–70 percent will result in massive spread widening and is hence a very good indicator of worsening credit quality of a company. This ratio will especially deteriorate in times of falling equity markets (crisis scenario) and will bring additional pressure on the credit spreads.

At this point Ford serves as a good example (Figure 5.15). As long as Ford's stock price traded above a certain level (here: around \$14–\$15) the correlation between the stock price and credit spreads was low. As soon as Ford's stock price dropped below this range a threshold was passed where investors started worrying about the value of the firm and its ability to cover all indebtedness. Corporate bond investors began to demand a much higher risk premium because of the fear that their investment was not covered sufficiently by Ford's asset base. For the period between July 2002 and November 2003 Ford's stock traded in the range of \$6–\$13 and we find a very high correlation between Ford credit spreads and equity of −85 percent.

During those periods equity-based techniques work quite well in measuring and monitoring potential credit risk. We have to consider as well that the sensitivity of debt to equity also increases with the leverage of a particular company. The underlying business risk and asset volatility determine the level of sensitivity. Higher risk companies display a greater uncertainty about future earnings and cash flows hence have a higher volatility and will have a greater sensitivity to increasing leverage (here measured as total debt/(total debt + market cap)). The VIX Index is in certain periods a good measure for credit risk and works especially well for highly levered

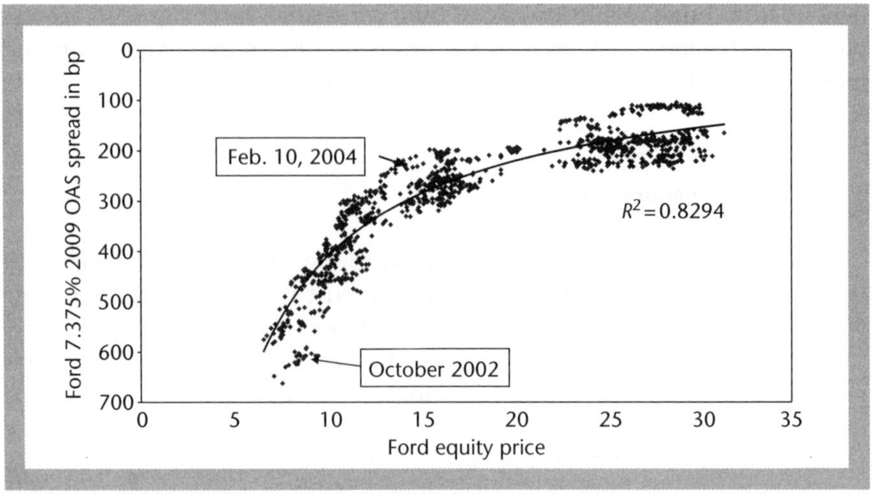

Figure 5.15 Ford equity price and bond spreads between Oct. 1999 and Jan. 2004

Source: Union Investment

companies. For Ford a high correlation of 90 percent was observed for the period October 1999 to February 2004 (Figure 5.16).

In February 2003, Ahold revealed accounting irregularities and both the equity market and bond market reacted very negatively to the news about fraud. Bonds began to trade on the expected recovery value but recovered since then as the equity value of the firm began to rise and it became apparent that the company would be able to survive in the long term (Figure 5.17).

WorldCom is another good example for the strong link between equity and corporate bonds when asset value drops below a certain threshold (Figure 5.18). In February 2002, WorldCom disclosed significant asset write-offs and accounting concerns persisted over the next couple of weeks. Finally, liquidity concerns pushed the company's equity and bond prices to distressed levels. WorldCom applied for Chapter 11 and the bonds traded down to around 15–20 cents on the dollar in July 2002.

5.2.2.3 Company selection

After completing all the steps in the analysis the results have to be put together in order to come up with an investment decision. Clearly many factors impact the credit quality of companies and perhaps most important are qualitative "soft factors" and their interpretation is very subjective. In Table 5.11 we summarize all important qualitative and quantitative factors and comment on what an investor should be focusing on. They consider fundamentals, technicals and valuation. The task is to bring all factors

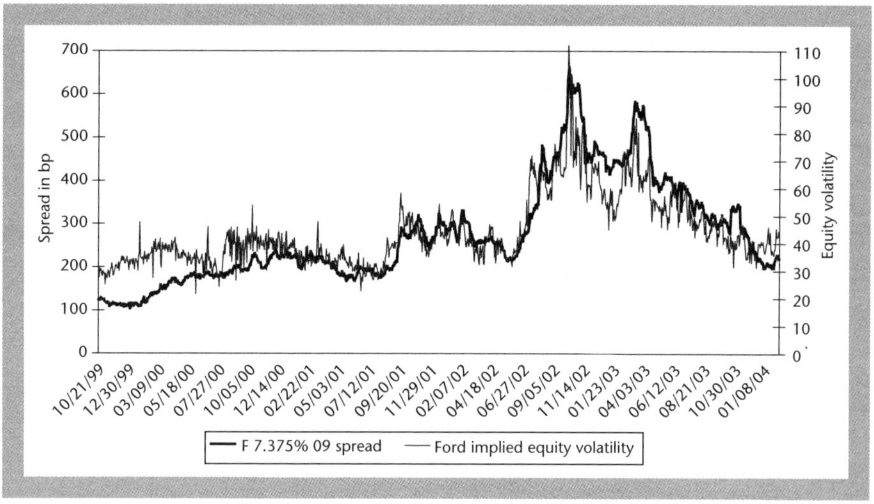

Figure 5.16 Ford bond spreads and Ford implied equity volatility between Oct. 1999 and Feb. 2004

Source: Union Investment

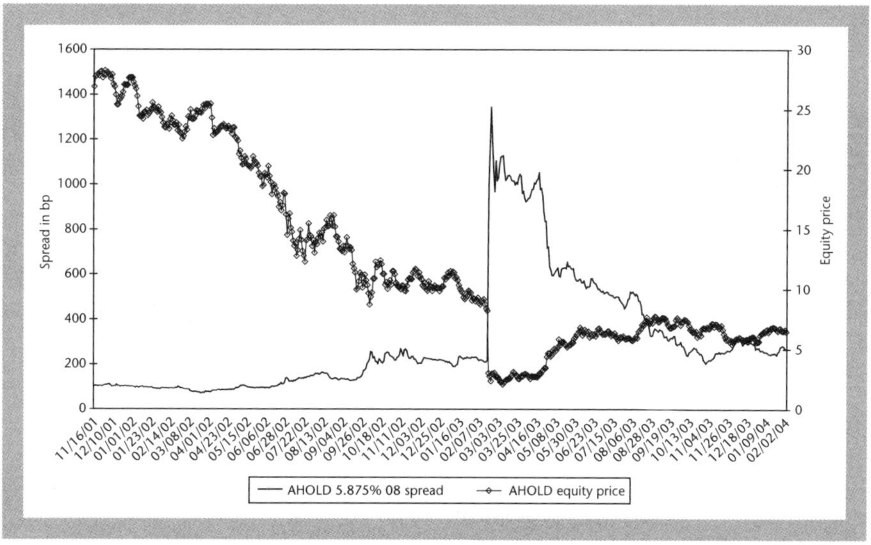

Figure 5.17 Ahold bonds and equity reacted sharply to the announcement of accounting fraud

Source: Union Investment

together and generate performance-enhancing investment decisions. For this purpose the various factors can be weighted according to their importance whereas the weights are set by the analyst. This means to pick a company with the highest outperformance potential out of a universe.

In the ideal case, investors will pick companies with the following fundamental characteristics and an attractive valuation versus the peer group so that high outperformance potential is given:

- Better and continuously improving average credit ratios than the peer group
- Commitment of management to a defensive financial policy and high credibility of the management team
- Positive outlook about future earnings

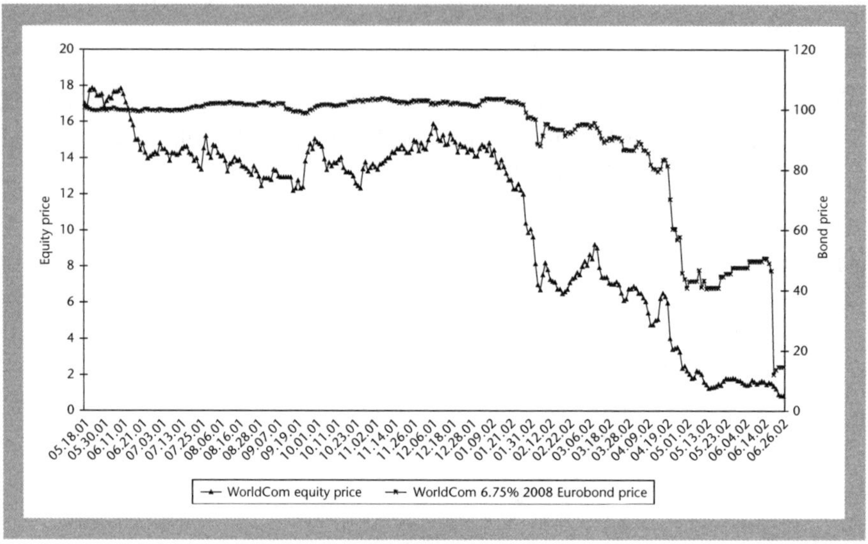

Figure 5.18 Relationship between Worldcom stock and bonds
Source: Union Investment

Table 5.11 Qualitative and quantitative factors applied in the company selection process

Factors	Comment
Industry trends	Focus on industry cycles, regulatory or environmental issues, capacity utilization rates, barriers of entry, competition
Market position	Market leader or niche strategy, trend in market share and costs involved in maintaining market share
Business risk	Technological innovations, high R&D costs, high sunk costs, high fixed costs
Event risk	Litigation, change in capital structure

continued

Table 5.11 continued

Factors	Comment
Financial/liquidity position	Short-term liquidity, access to the capital market, maturity schedule
Cash flow generation	Fluctuation of cash flows across the business cycle
Leverage	Leverage ratios in comparison to peers and within a rating class, trend in ratios
Coverage	Coverage ratios in comparison to peers and within a rating class, trend in ratios
Rating trend	Ratings history, outlook, is the company currently under review?
Management strategy	Disclosure of company strategy, experience of management team
CAPEX Plan	Timing and size of CAPEX to support business
Earnings	Fluctuation in earnings, does company permanently achieve stated earnings goals?
Operational performance	Focus on revenue growth, gross margin, SG&A as a percentage of sales, EBITDA trend and cash flows from operations
Quality of assets	Assets that serve as collateral, value of noncore assets that can be sold
Covenants	To what extent do they protect a bondholder without limiting a company's business plan, claim on assets and cash flows
Equity performance	Past equity performance relative to peers, firm value in perspective to overall debt level
Implied equity volatility	Perceived riskiness of future earnings
Secondary market liquidity	Particularly small issues have limited secondary market liquidity and therefore command an illiquidity risk premium
Fund flows	Determine demand for corporate bonds and hence the demand for high beta or low beta bonds
New issue supply	Net issuance will differ across sectors and companies, what volume can be absorbed without adverse effects?
Sentiment	Historical evidence shows that market psychology dominates at the top and bottom of market cycles whereas fundamentals and valuation play a subordinated role.
Relative value	Compare current trading level with past performance and with peer group, relative attractiveness versus other sectors and market, consider also spread volatility

Source: Union Investment

- Generation of free operating cash flows
- Operative outperformance versus peer group
- A solid market position in its core business areas
- A sound liquidity position and multiple sources of available financing
- Favorable outlook for the business cycle
- Spreads which offer a relative attractiveness versus peer group because all positive developments are not priced in the spreads yet.

5.2.2.4 Relative value

Analysts use many ways to demonstrate the relative attractiveness of a specific bond. Some examples follow next:

- Free Cash Flow: One of the risk metrics for corporate bond investors is cash generation. In a relative value framework companies can be grouped by the change in free cash flows and their respective spread levels. Companies with positive free cash flows and high spread levels have outperformance potential in the future.

The change in free cash flow can also be compared with leverage ratios like debt/EBITDA. Highly levered firms with corresponding higher yields but forecasted future increase in free cash flow have the potential to outperform.

- Sales: A good tool for evaluating companies is to put their sales figures in relation to CAPEX. Since CAPEX is an important determinant in balance sheet repair, we should look for companies with an expansion in sales and decreasing capital spending. Sales growth can also be put in relation to debt levels. The ideal company for bondholders will grow its sales and pay down debt at the same time.
- Return on invested capital (ROIC): ROIC is a measure of how efficiently a company spends money. For this purpose annual averages of ROIC can be plotted in a matrix versus the ratio of CAPEX/sales. Companies with high CAPEX/sales ratios and low returns on invested capital are poised to underperform at times when fundamentals are the main drivers of the credit market.

Figures 5.19 and 5.20 are examples for selecting a specific bond from the telecom and auto sector. First we plug all bonds from one sector in a matrix with modified duration on the *x*-axis and spread on the *y*-axis. By this

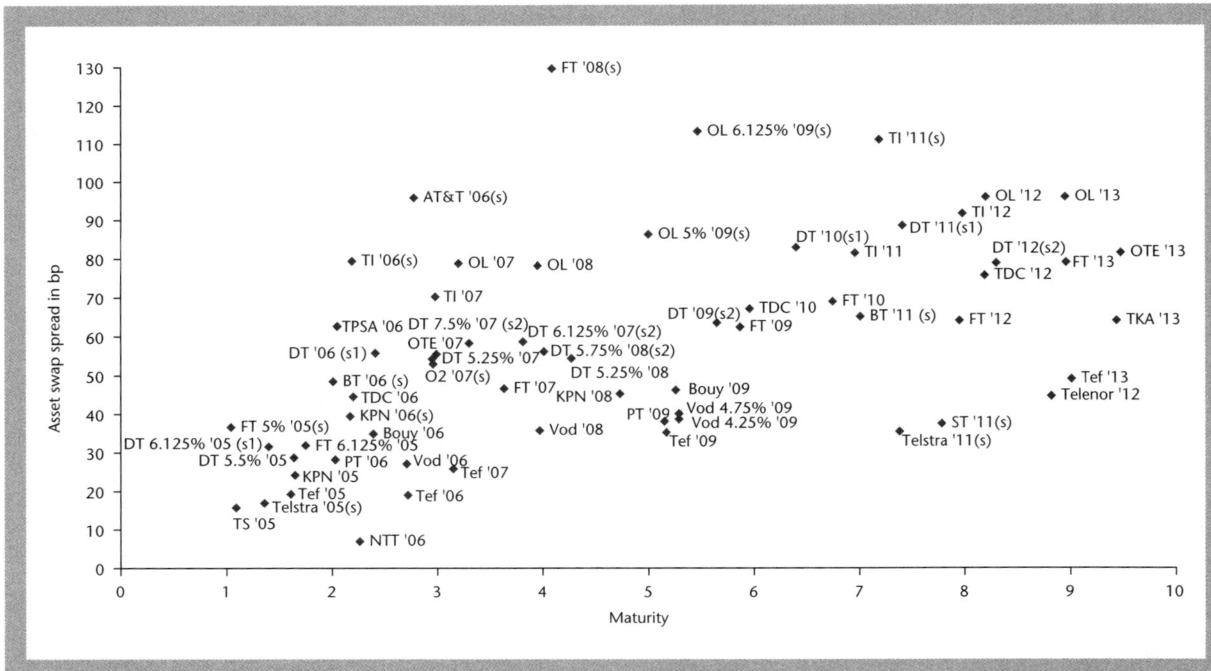

Figure 5.19 Selected Euro telecom bonds with 1–10 year maturity on Feb. 11, 2004

Notes: S = coupon step; S1 = coupon steps down by 50 bp at A-/A3; S2 = coupon steps up by 50 bp at BBB/Baa2

Source: Barclay's Capital

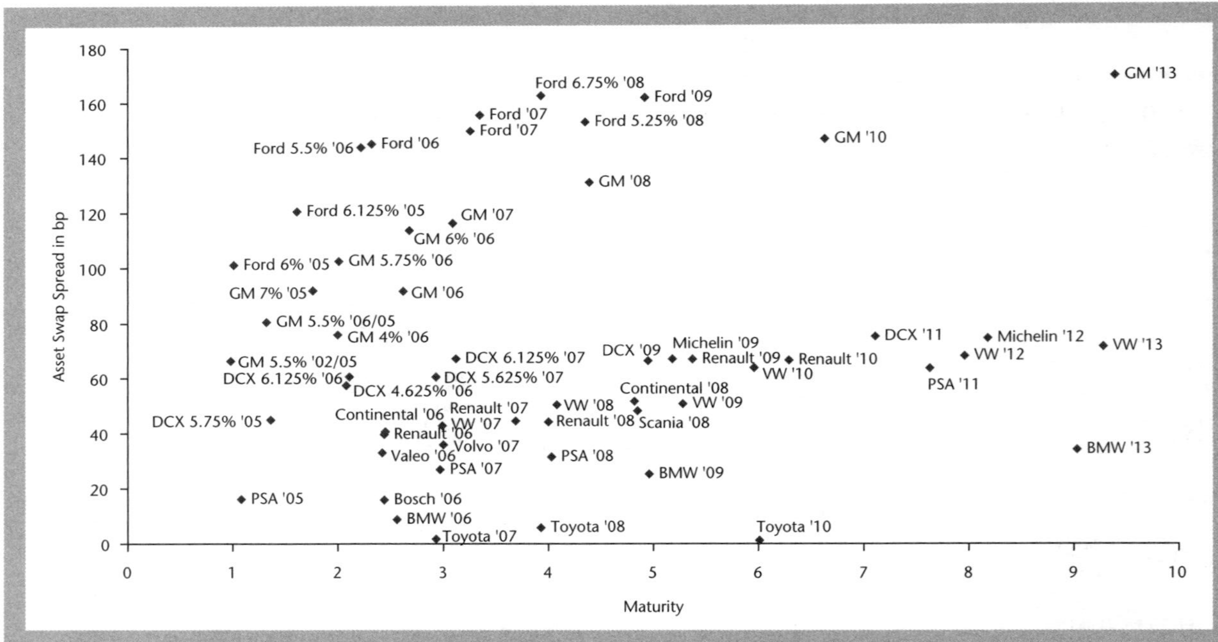

Figure 5.20 Selected Euro automobile bonds with 1–10 year maturity on February 11, 2004

Source: Barclay's Capital

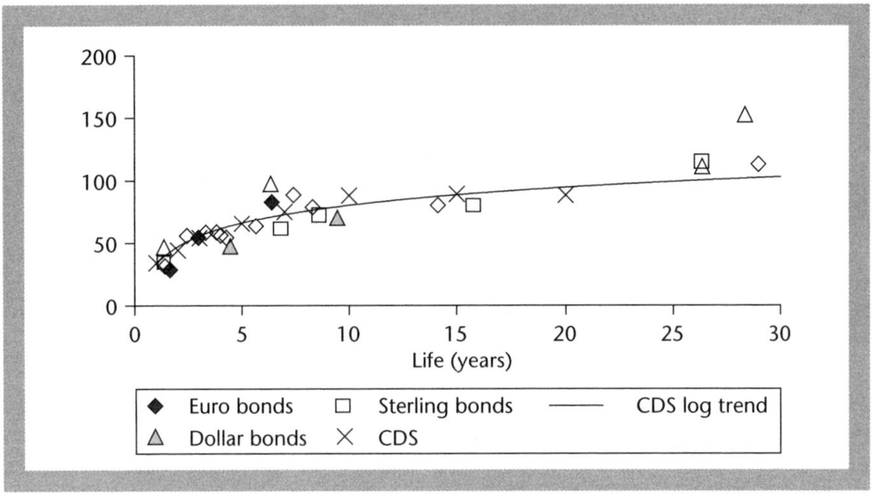

Figure 5.21 Deutsche Telekom cash bonds and CDS on Feb. 11, 2004

Source: Barclay's Capital

means one can see the different credit curves of all issuers within a sector and decide according to the risk appetite and risk profile of the portfolio about a specific company.

After making the decision on the company level, the bonds which offer the best value have to be selected. For this purpose all bonds of the issuer including credit default swaps are plotted in a diagram. This exercise is performed for Deutsche Telekom (Figure 5.21) and Ford Motor Credit (Figure 5.22). If investment restrictions allow to invest across currencies the investor has to decide about the relative attractiveness of bonds issued from an issuer in different currencies. The expectations about the curve shape in Euroland and the United States have to be incorporated in the decision process. At this point, we want to highlight that in the past US$ denominated bonds experienced a higher volatility than Euro denominated bonds from the same issuing entity. Therefore, it is justified that US$ bonds trade at a premium to Euro bonds of same maturity. Off-the-run bonds usually trade on a discount to on-the-run bonds but an investor has to consider the lower liquidity of those issues and evaluate whether the higher spread level compensates for this illiquidity. Sometimes technicals rather than fundamentals can drive the credit spread of single issuers so that one can position accordingly on the credit curve. Generally with increased uncertainty about an issuer it is appropriate to overweight the shorter maturities and underweight the long end of the credit curve. From a relative value perspective steep credit curves indicate value in the long end while flat credit curves favor the shorter maturities.

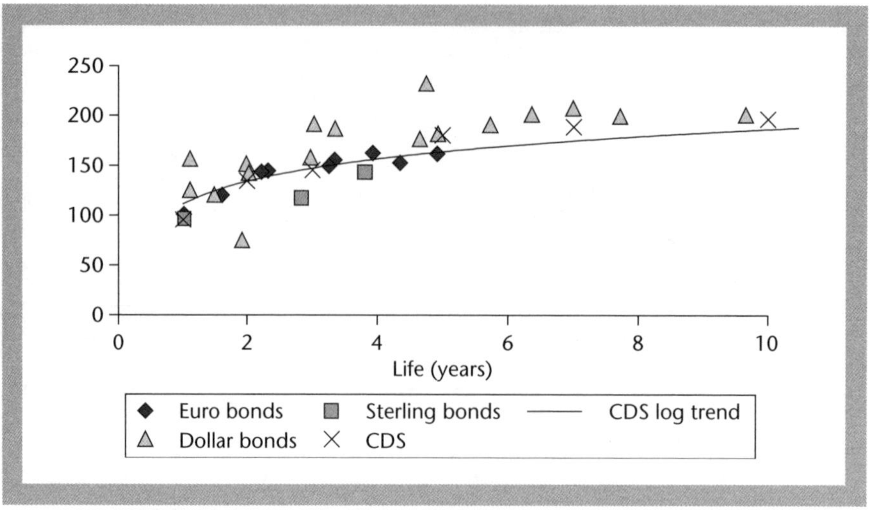

Figure 5.22 Ford motor credit cash bonds and CDS on Feb. 11th 2004

Source: Barclay's Capital

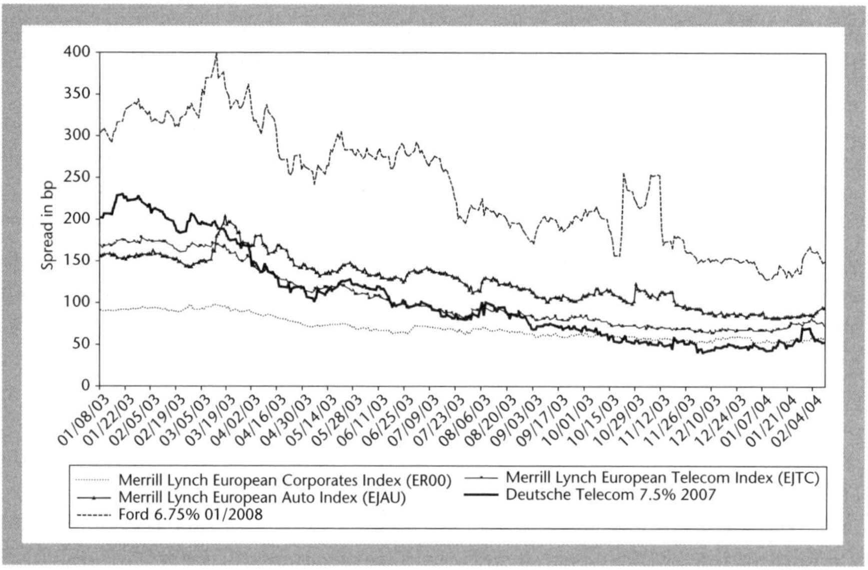

Figure 5.23 Single corporate bonds versus sectors and market index

Sources: Bloomberg, Union Investment

As a last step one can also draw historical charts for the chosen bond in order to see how it performed in the past versus the peer group and market index (Figure 5.23). This is helpful in deciding whether an investment at the current level still makes sense in a portfolio context. The spread volatility of single bonds is also an important characteristic for investing in corporate bonds. Tight spread levels usually go along with decreased spread volatility.

Figure 5.24 shows the spread change over a 1-month period for selected European automobile bonds. Keeping track of these movements helps to identify bonds which underperformed or overperformed the peer group. A mispricing can occur due to technical factors.

5.2.2.5 Event risks for companies

Event risks are almost impossible to quantify. Some event risks are reduced to a single company and others have an impact on the whole sector. Corporate bond and equity investors have to deal with events that have a negative or positive effect on their investments. Certain event risks are the result of management's option to change the capital structure of a company which is either bondholder-friendly or to the benefit of shareholders. Other risks can be of legal, regulatory or environmental nature and are out of control for management. Another source of event risks is a company's miscommunication with investors and unsatisfactory disclosure of certain company facts.

Table 5.12 summarizes possible event risks which can occur for a company.

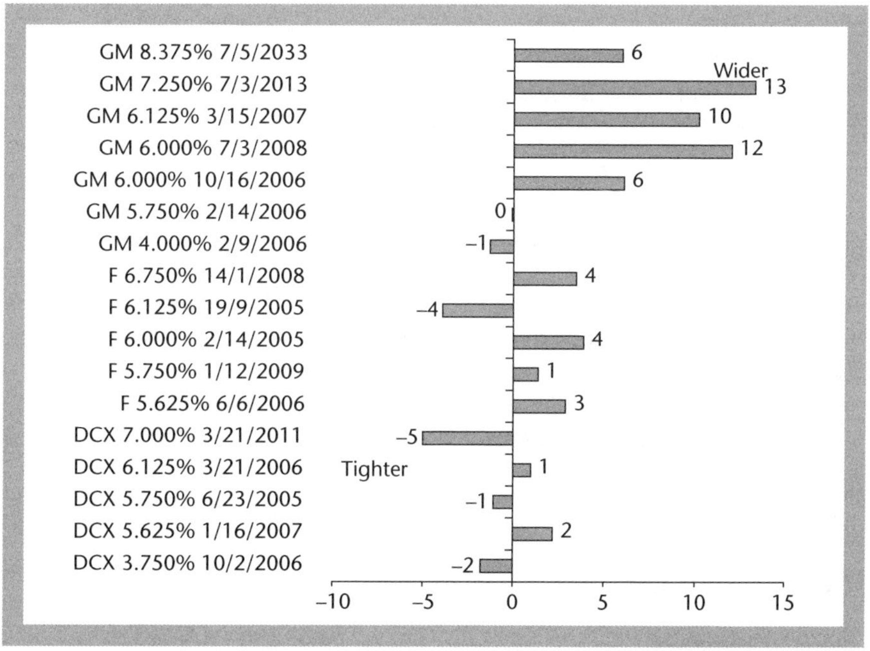

Figure 5.24 Monthly spread change for selected Euro automobile bonds (February 2004)

Source: BNP Paribas

Table 5.12 Major event risks for companies

Event risks	Comment
Litigation	Mostly related to Asbestos, Tobacco, Healthcare Products and Environmental.
Pension deficits	Large manufacturing companies with an aging work force are most likely to face underfunded pension plans.
Off-balance sheet liabilities	Those cash flow obligations are not reported on the balance sheet but affect a company's financial position. Examples are: operating leases, derivative financial instruments, nonconsolidated joint ventures and subsidiaries, project financing.
Rating triggers	In case of downgrade substantial repayments of debt can be accelerated and a company can face short-term liquidity constraints.
Cross default	The default of one entity causes a technical default at the parent company level. Poor disclosure.
Securitization	Improves liquidity but diminishes assets which could serve as collateral.
Covenants	Particularly poor disclosure of bank credit covenants. In the case of a covenant breach loan agreements have to be renegotiated.
Accounting irregularities	All companies can be subject to accounting fraud.
Mergers and Acquisitions	M&A activity depends on the business cycle and industry fundamentals.

Source: JP Morgan

5.2.2.6 Indentures of corporate bonds

After assessing the credit quality of a company by weighing financial, business and management risks, the investor has to focus on some specific features described in the prospectus for every issue. The main parts are:

- Ranking in the capital structure
- Covenants
- Optional redemption
- Change of control
- Use of proceeds.

Ranking in the capital structure: The following statements mainly refer to lower rated (BB-CCC) companies. Their bank debt usually ranks senior (one notch rating difference) to the bonds. The subordination in the capital structure can have a contractual or structural character. The contractual subordination is the typical form in the United States. The various jurisdictions in Europe make the enforcement of a contractual subordination in bankruptcy court difficult so the structural subordination was the favored form/structure for European high-yield deals. The priority of the claim of a debt investor is determined by the position within the capital structure. Industrial holding companies upstream cash from their subsidiaries. If those subsidiaries do not guarantee the holding company debt then it is structurally subordinated to all debt instruments residing at the subsidiary level including trade payables and lease obligations.

A holding company is the issuer of the senior notes which are effectively subordinated to bank debt and debt of the operating companies (Figure 5.25). This subordination can be alleviated somewhat through an upstream guarantee of the operating companies (subsidiaries). If more debt gets ahead of the bonds the rating difference between the issuer and the bond rating might increase to 2 notches.

The holding company conducts business through its subsidiaries (operating companies) and is dependent on the subsidiaries upstreaming the

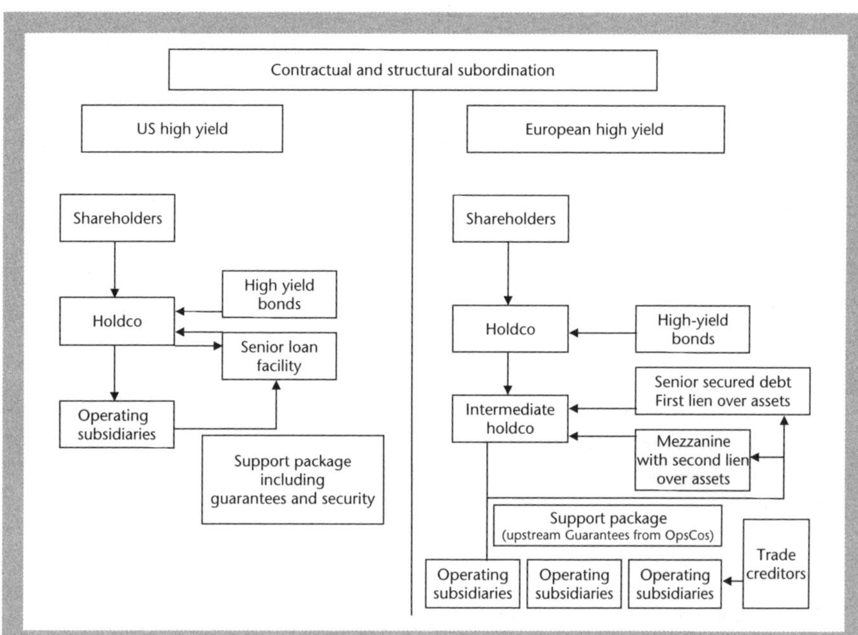

Figure 5.25 Contractual and structural subordination of high-yield bonds

Source: Fitch Ibca

cash flows through dividend payments. The implication for an investor is to make sure who is in control of the operating assets and what amount of debt actually ranks senior to the respective notes. A considerable equity cushion is always (especially during a crisis scenario) a credit positive for a bondholder because the increase in junior claims always improves the status of all other senior parties in the capital structure.

Table 5.13 shows that there are considerable differences in average recovery rates depending on seniority.

By analyzing the ranking of a bond within the capital structure it is possible to estimate recovery values in the case of distress. Especially for high-yield issuers it is also of importance to analyze the group structure of an issuer for restricted groups. Sometimes there might be legal restrictions for certain subsidiaries to upstream dividend payments to the holding company so that not all generated cash flows will be available to service the debt obligations.

Covenants: Covenants are part of a credit agreement between lenders and borrowers. Their purpose is to protect lenders by stating what the borrower must do in order to stay in compliance with the loan agreement. Covenants may protect the bondholder from certain event risks. One problem with covenants is that bank covenants are usually private information which is not disclosed by companies when issuing corporate bonds. If those covenants are breached bond investors come to know in the quarterly or annual filings so they should increasingly demand the disclosure of such covenants.

The following covenants are provided by most noninvestment grade issuers and investors in lower investment grade bonds should ask for similar covenant packages in order to avoid a wealth transfer to the equity holders. Attractive covenants represent value for the bondholders and have to be considered in the investment process. Only the most important covenants will be presented at this point. Generally, it can be argued that the covenant protection increases with a decreasing rating class.

Table 5.13 Average principal loss rate and recovery rate according to seniority as of Dec. 2003

Seniority	Number of issues	Average principal loss rate(%)	Average recovery rate(%)
Senior secured	216	47.1	52.9
Senior unsecured	839	59.8	40.2
Senior subordinated	725	67.0	33.0
Jr Sub and Discount notes	144	76.6	23.4

Source: CSFB

- Restrictions for the issuance of additional debt by coverage and leverage ratios. The most common are:
  (a) Fixed charge coverage ratio: (Funds from operations)/Total debt
  (b) Debt/EBITDA or Debt/Funds from operations
- Limit on asset sales. This can be of particular importance when a company faces financial distress and tries to sell noncore assets. This policy might not conform to bondholders' interests.
- Limit on dividend payments and share buy-back programs
- Limit on certain investments (e.g. outside the core business)
- Limit on lines and certain guarantees
- Limit on certain transactions with the operating companies
- A put option can be very valuable for the bond investor, for example when a company loses its investment grade status due to a large acquisition or a severe deterioration of its business fundamentals.

Optional redemption The issuer may redeem all or part of the notes at a specified price and time. This means that, for example, a company issues a bond with 10-year maturity and has the option to call the bond after 5 years. This option represents value to the issuer because depending on future interest rates and the required risk premium a company might considerably reduce financing costs by calling the outstanding bonds. Furthermore, most high-yield bonds have an equity claw-back clause in their indenture. This means that an issuer may redeem up to 35 percent of the aggregate principal amount of notes with the net proceeds of public equity offerings at the redemption price set in the indenture.

- Change-of-control: The change-of-control event occurs when, for example, a merger or acquisition leads to a change in the ownership structure. In most cases the bondholders have a put option.
- Negative pledge: The negative pledge restricts the issuers from using some or all of their assets as a guarantee for other indebtedness.
- Cross default: The cross default clause is a mechanism which links the credit quality of one bond to other securities issued by the same parent company. In the case of an issuer's bond default, a default will be triggered at all other bonds and loans within the capital structure.
- Carve outs: Carve outs weaken the protection of bondholders. They represent exceptions for actions previously forbidden by the covenants.

If a company is in danger of breaching one of their covenants or has to renegotiate a bank facility in order to stay in accordance with existing covenants, the credit spreads will widen immediately because major problems are anticipated in the future.

Use of proceeds from bond offering: Another important point which should be considered in the evaluation of a new bond issue is the use of proceeds, because for bond investors there is a major difference between, for example, the refinancing of outstanding debt (bonds and bank debt), CAPEX, general corporate purposes, acquisition financing or the financing of a share buy-back program. A transfer of wealth from bondholders to shareholders can occur. It is important to analyze the driving force behind a new bond offering. The use of proceeds will be determined by a company's needs in the first place but will also fluctuate with general economic conditions.

5.2.2.7 Coupon step-ups

Coupon step-up language

Especially lower investment grade (A-BBB) companies that have the risk of an imminent rating downgrade due to negative industry trends and firm-specific problems should include this clause in the covenant package. In the case of a downgrade the bond investors would receive a higher coupon payment (e.g. 25 bp per notch and rating agency). This way the companies can demonstrate their commitment to the current rating and the bondholder gets a fair compensation in the case of a downgrade.

Options pricing theory is applied to compute the value of the coupon step-ups and the swap spread is adjusted accordingly. The coupon step-ups are increasingly important in industries with a negative rating trend like, for example, the European Telecoms in 2001/02. The spread differential between the bond with a coupon step-up and the credit curve of the issuer without step-ups is equal to the market value of the coupon step-up (Figure 5.26). The market value is computed with a binomial model by assuming historical or subjective ratings migration expectations.

5.2.2.8 Corporate bonds and defaults

It is difficult to identify all variables, which lead to the default of a specific company. The monitoring of the company's ratings is not a good way because the rating agencies tend to react with a lag of sometimes a couple of months when the financial situation of a company deteriorates. A and BBB companies can reach the spread levels normally seen at the CCC level. Some points, which might be an indication for upcoming financial distress are as follows:

- A new accounting firm or banking relationship is in place
- A management conflict escalates and is discussed publicly

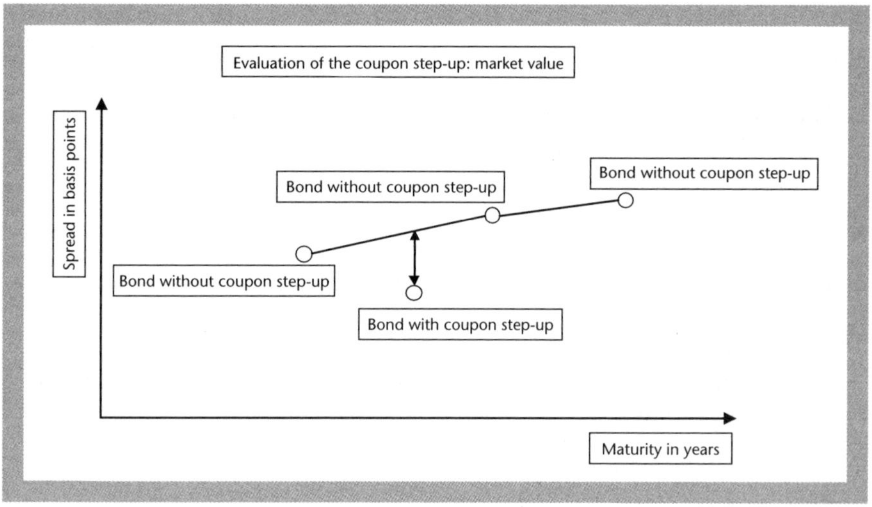

Figure 5.26 Coupon step-up

Source: Union Investment

- Members from top management leave on short notice
- The banks cancel or reduce credit lines
- The budget for R&D is capped
- A large depreciation of assets takes place
- The financial ratios deteriorate over a period of 6–36 months before the default occurs
- The equity price has a negative trend.

Companies which are likely to achieve a successful turnaround will have the following attributes:

- Balance sheet restructuring through, for example, a rights issue or convertibles
- Rebalancing of debt instruments towards more long-term debt
- The equity price recovers and keeps a positive trend
- New sources for working capital are available
- Operating income is generated during restructuring
- Sales growth is positive and the operating margins are at least constant (remember that in the short term, restructuring efforts will cause operational dislocation)

- Administrative costs and production costs can be kept under control
- Streamlining of operations
- The focus remains on the core business and noncore assets are sold successfully (increase liquidity in the short term, but may be leverage-neutral or negative)
- Downsizing of business through workforce reduction
- Top-line growth and a controlled geographic expansion
- Cash flows are generated by different business units
- The business plan is flexible, for example, CAPEX program can be scaled back or postponed
- Loss-making businesses are sold first in order to stop the drain on cash flow.

5.2.2.9 Valuation of distressed credits

The valuation of a distressed company should be done according to the following methods:

- Liquidation value
- Sales multiples and EBITDA multiples
- Discounted cash flow analysis.

In liquidation valuation, it is assumed that the underlying business is not viable and will be liquidated in parts. The analyst has to assign the most likely realizable values to accounts receivables, inventory and PP&E. Generally it happens through a haircut to the book value of those positions. The liquidation often takes a long time to execute and in many cases all cash positions as well as all debt obligations are not disclosed immediately. From the liquidation value we have to deduct all debt which ranks ahead of corporate bonds and then divide the remaining value by the total amount of outstanding bonds.

If one assumes that there is a chance of keeping the operative business going a valuation on the basis of sales multiples or EBITDA multiples is appropriate. In this case EBITDA is multiplied by an average market multiple and again all senior debt is subtracted before dividing the remaining value by the total amount of outstanding bonds.

The discounted cash flow analysis also assumes that the company is a going concern and the computed value serves as a starting point to estimate the value of outstanding bonds.

These three methods will result in three different company values and, hence, should be weighted according to the confidence in the information used in them. A ratio smaller than 1 implies that not all claims of bondholders can be served by the company if bankruptcy occurs at the time of evaluation.

5.3 FINANCIAL INSTITUTIONS

5.3.1 Banks

5.3.1.1 Introduction

While the focus of industrial and utility companies is primarily on the generation of revenues and cash flows, for financial institutions the management of assets is of paramount importance. Traditionally, banks' income statements and asset composition have been the primary focus of attention when assessing their credit strength. However, the high complexity of businesses and financial products has shifted the focus towards risk management. Off-balance sheet items and funding issues have become more important, therefore common metrics of credit risk are not able to reflect the complete risk profile of a bank. We would argue that the analysis of banks requires a completely different research process compared to industrial companies.

The importance of the banking sector results from the services it provides for the economy. In commercial banking, the main business is deposit taking and lending. According to Greenbaum and Thakor (1995) the role of commercial banks involves transformations with regard to duration, divisibility, risk, numeraire currency and liquidity. Additionally, they provide transaction and payment services as well as services related to securities accounts. Investment banks act as financial intermediaries in a broader sense, as they promote the efficiency of financial markets through underwriting, issuance and distribution of securities.

5.3.1.2 Regulation in the banking sector

Banks generally have to hold adequate capital against all risks that arise from their business. This capital is intended to provide a cushion for depositors and creditors, if the bank is confronted with unexpected losses. Thus, the probability that a bank is not able to repay its liabilities is minimized. Since 1988, the Basel Capital Accord defines the minimum capital requirements for all banks (Figure 5.27). The agreement was put forward by the Basel Committee on Banking Supervision, an organization founded

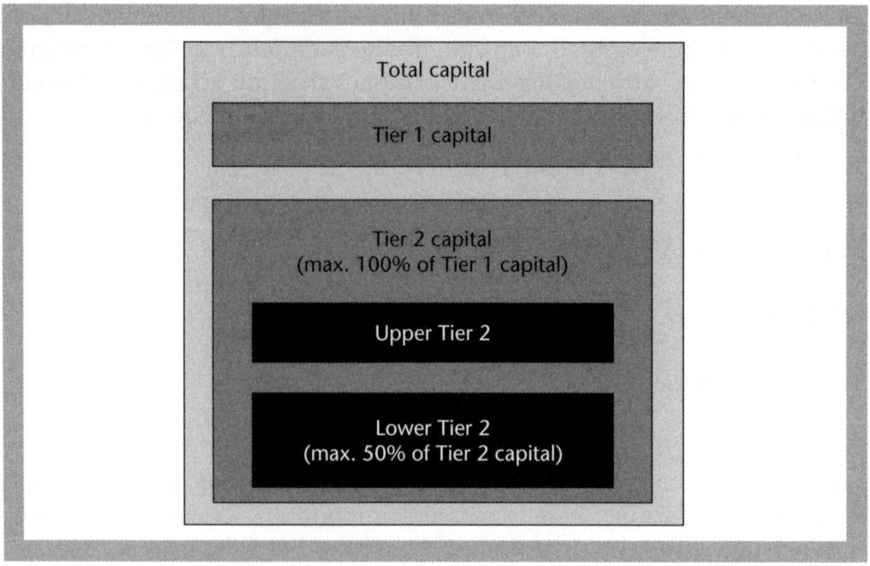

Figure 5.27 Regulatory capital of a bank according to the Basel Capital Accord

Source: DZ Bank

in 1974, following the severe crises of Bankhaus Herstatt in Germany and Franklin National Bank in the US to improve cooperation between bank supervisors. With the adoption of the Basel Capital Accord in a directive, the EU has created the basis to transform the guidelines into national law. Therefore, the capital requirements for banks are very similar across Europe. Essentially, they reflect the rules of the Basel Capital Accord, requiring banks to hold at least 4 percent of core capital and 8 percent of total capital against risk-weighted assets. In practice, however, most commercial banks target a Tier 1 ratio in the range of 8–9 percent. Still other banks carry even higher Tier 1 ratios, reflecting a steady earnings stream, hidden reserves, and a conservative dividend policy. Total capital consists of Tier 1 capital and Tier 2 capital, whereas the latter one is eligible only up to 100 percent of Tier 1 capital. Hence, the amount of Tier 1 capital determines the maximum total capital of a bank. Tier 2 capital consists of Upper Tier 2 and Lower Tier 2.

Banking crises generally lead to high losses for depositors. Since governments often feel obliged to cover part of these losses, there is a strong political interest to minimize the risk of bank failure through regulation. The basic idea is that regulatory authorities act on behalf of the depositors. But the goal of bank regulators is not only to protect depositors, but also to provide a stable environment for banks to operate in. In order to be allowed to take deposits, any authorized bank has to hold adequate capital. Generally, capital requirements depend on the size and type of risk associated with a bank's assets. In order to calculate the amount of capital that has to be held the bank's business has to be split up between its term lending and deposit-taking activities, classified as the "banking book," and its trading activities, or the "trading book." While the capital requirements for the banking book are laid out by the Basel Capital Accord, the Amendment to the Capital Accord sets out the guidelines for the trading book.

Trading book items comprise

- proprietary positions in equities, debt securities, money market instruments, financial futures, forward rate agreements, interest rate, currency and equity swaps, and call or put options on the above instruments as well as commodities and commodity derivatives held to benefit from short-term price or interest rate fluctuations;
- the above instruments held for hedging trading book items, repos and securities and commodities lending and reverse repos;
- exposures due to unsettled transactions, OTC derivatives, commission, fees, dividends, interest and margin on exchange-related derivatives.

Any instrument not named above, not held for trading purposes and any instrument used to hedge a banking book position is included in the banking book.

As pointed out before, regulators require banks to hold adequate capital against assets depending on the size and type of risk of the asset and in which book the risk arises in. Counterparty risk, currency risk and risk from positions in commodities, for example, are treated the same irrespective whether they arise in the banking or trading book. Items that are unique to the trading book like repos, require a special counterparty risk treatment. The amount of capital that has to be held also depends on netting opportunities and collateralization.

Assets in the banking book are risk-weighted according to their type. Generally, riskier assets require a higher amount of capital to be held. Table 5.14 illustrates the current risk-weighting scheme.

Besides counterparty risk, capital requirements that are due to trading book items depend on foreign exchange risk, commodity position risk, interest rate position risk and large exposures risk. It would be beyond the scope of this book to present a detailed description of how to determine capital requirements for each type of trading book asset. Interested readers may refer to the 200 pages of guidance notes issued by the FSA. Apart from the methodology laid out in this description, regulators allow banks to use authorized internal models to calculate their capital requirements.

The minimum requirement for the total capital ratio is 8 percent, but many banks use their own trigger ratios that are somewhat higher as an

Table 5.14 Risk-weighting scheme for banking book items

Risk weighting (%)	Asset type
0	Cash, gold, claims on and claims generated by OECD central governments
0, 10, 20 or 50 (according to national regulation)	Claims on loans guaranteed by domestic public sector entities
20	Claims on multilateral development banks, claims on banks incorporated in the OECD and claims on non-OECD banks with residual maturity up to 1 year
50	Residential mortgages
100	Claims on private sector, claims on non-OECD banks over 1 year, claims on non-OECD central governments, premises, other fixed assets, real estate and all other assets

Source: Basel Capital Accord

early warning signal. Each bank has to meet this requirement on an ongoing basis. A breach of the trigger ratio and of the target ratio that is defined 0.5 percent above the trigger ratio, has to be reported immediately and leads to intervention by the regulator. Trigger ratios and target ratios are set separately for the trading and banking book. The methodology of calculating capital requirements differentiates both books. While capital requirements in the banking book are set as a ratio of capital to risk-weighted assets, trading book requirements are set as an absolute level of capital "haircut" that has to be multiplied by 12.5 to bring it on the same basis as the banking book. A bank must always fulfil its capital requirements. In other words, a bank's supervisory capital position has to exceed 100 percent at any time.

The calculation of the trading book capital requirements follows the scheme displayed in Table 5.15. If the trading book trigger is X percent, trading book capital requirements are calculated in the described manner. Assuming a trigger ratio of Y percent the banking book requirement is shown in Table 5.16.

Yet, capital adequacy requires not only a certain amount of capital, but certain types of capital in relationship to the bank's assets. The different layers of capital are called "tiers". Tier 1 capital is the strongest form in that it offers depositors the highest degree of protection. It is followed by Upper Tier 2, then Lower Tier 2 and finally Tier 3 capital. Different types of subordinated debt represent only a part of bank capital. Besides perpetual noncumulative preferred securities, for example, Tier 1 capital is made up of common equity and retained earnings. In the following paragraphs we refer primarily to the debt components of capital.

Table 5.15 Trading book capital requirements

Risk type	Capital haircut	Notional risk-weighted assets	Capital required
FX position risk	A	12.5 × A	*X*% of (12.5 × A)
Equity position risk	B	12.5 × B	*X*% of (12.5 × B)
Interest rate position risk	C	12.5 × C	*X*% of (12.5 × C)
Large exposures incremental capital	D	12.5 × D	*X*% of (12.5 × D)
Trading book counterparty and settlement risk	E	12.5 × E	*X*% of (12.5 × E)
Commodity position risk	F	12.5 × F	*X*% of (12.5 × F)
Activities subject to internal models	G	12.5 × G	*X*% of (12.5 × G)

Source: FSA's Banking Supervisory Policy

Table 5.16 Banking book capital requirements

Risk	Risk-weighted assets	Capital required
Credit risk	H	*Y*% of H

Source: FSA's Banking Supervisory Policy

Tier 1 capital is also known as "core" capital. It is characterized by the following features.

- The issuer holds an option to defer dividend or coupon payments. If capital adequacy is threatened this option is transferred to the regulator. The cancellation of coupons is not considered a default.
- Coupons are noncumulative, that is, interest or dividends are not repaid at a later date, even if the bank would be able to repay deferred coupons without falling below regulatory capital requirements.
- Tier 1 capital is designed to absorb losses. Since it is subordinated to all other debt and senior only to common equity, it is able to absorb losses before or instead of creditors. In order to remain solvent, principal and interest may be written down.
- Tier 1 preferred issues are perpetual. Yet, the regulator allows a limited step-up associated with a call after the tenth anniversary of the issue. The call option may only be exercised if there is sufficient capital to fullfil regulatory requirements, and if the regulator explicitly allows the bank to call the issue.

- Since 1998, Lower Tier 1 issues are accepted as core capital by the Basel Committee for Banking Supervision and the national authorities of Germany and Luxemburg. These dated, noncumulative structures, however, are included in the calculation of core capital only up to a maximum of 15 percent.
- Tier 1 issues may include an equity settlement option at the call date. If the bond is not called, the investor has the right to redeem his Tier 1 bonds via a put option, and in turn receives stocks of the bank. Like a step up, equity settlement features are used to make sure that the bank calls its Tier 1 debt at the first opportunity, thus avoiding to have to increase its equity.

Besides Tier 1 preferred stock, there are some further components that belong to core capital. Equity is considered the strongest form of capital, as shareholders are last to be paid in the event of liquidation. Retained earnings, certain types of reserves and minority interest are also core capital. To avoid regulatory pitfalls such as double-counting of capital or connected lending, banks deduct holdings of own shares, own Tier 1 paper, current year's unpublished losses, goodwill and interim published net losses from Tier 1 capital. Further deductions have to be made from the sum of Tier 1 and Tier 2 capital, for example, in relation to investments in

- unconsolidated subsidiaries and associates;
- connected lending of a capital nature, including guarantees;
- holdings of another bank's capital over a maximum of the equivalent of 10 percent of a bank's eligible Tier 1 and Tier 2 capital base;
- investments in life assurance companies.

Upper Tier 2 debt securities differ from Tier 1 preferred in that they are not necessarily perpetual, but the repayment rather requires prior consent of the regulator. In response to the limited demand for straight perpetuals, most regulators allow issuers to include coupon step-ups as a signal that there is an economic incentive for the issuer to refinance. If the step-up is large enough, Upper Tier 2 issues can be compared to dated subordinated bonds. However, since the underlying is still a perpetual instrument and retains interest deferral and loss absorption features, a spread premium versus less subordinated bank securities is required. While coupon payments are also deferrable, they are cumulative. In other words, the issuer has to pay deferred coupons at a later date. As with Tier 1 principal and interest may be written down to enable the bank to remain solvent. As mentioned above, Upper Tier 2 is senior only to Tier 1 preferred and common equity. Besides qualifying debt instruments, general provisions and revaluation reserves in relation to fixed assets and fixed investments also belong to Upper Tier 2.

Dated subordinated debt with a minimum maturity of 5 years and perpetual debt with no loss absorbency or interest deferral features make up Lower Tier 2. Generally, Lower Tier 2 capital is regarded as offering a lower degree of protection, because it is only able to absorb losses in the event of insolvency. Furthermore, deferral of coupons or write-downs of principal are considered an event of default. Consequently, Lower Tier 2 is subordinated only to senior debt. Regulation requires that Lower Tier 2 is amortized on a linear basis during the last 5 years to maturity. To avoid this, various banks have issued Lower Tier 2 debt instruments with a step-up and call 5 years before its maturity.

Tier 3 debt can exclusively support market risk in the trading book. It ranks *pari passu* with Lower Tier 2 and is dated with a minimum maturity of 2 years. There are generally no write-downs or loss absorbency features. The specialty of Tier 3 capital is the "lock-in" clause. At the order of the regulator, interest and principal payments can be deferred if payment would cause capital to fall below minimum capital adequacy requirements. Yet, in this case coupons and principal have to be paid at a later date. Because of its short maturity and limited use Tier 3 capital is regarded as a weak form of capital by most regulators. The Amendment to the Basel Capital Accord recommends limiting the use of Tier 3 to the extent that the sum of Tier 2 plus Tier 3 should not exceed Tier 1 capital.

5.3.1.3 Risks associated with bank debt

Table 5.17 summarizes the major characteristics of the different layers of bank capital with an emphasis on the risks for investors. Please note that senior debt is no bank capital but is included here for reasons of completeness.

The three major rating agencies S&P, Moody's and FitchIBCA apply slightly differing approaches to account for the risks associated with the different layers of bank capital. The senior debt rating essentially reflects a rating agency's assessment of the fundamental creditworthiness of the bank. The ratings for subordinated bank debt clearly have to consider the probability of default and the loss severity given default. Subordinated debt and Tier 1 preferred are accordingly rated below senior debt. Table 5.18 shows the general notching methodology of the major rating agencies. Yet, it should be noted that the degree to which a specific issue is notched below senior debt also depends on a bank's overall ability to meet its financial obligations.

Unlike Moody's and FitchIBCA, S&P includes only part of Tier 1 preferred in its calculation of certain measures of capital strength. As the rating agency considers Tier 1 preferred a weaker form of capital than common

Table 5.17 Risks of bank capital to investors

Type of debt	Subordination	Interest deferral	Principal repayment	Principal write-down
Senior (no bank capital)	None	None	Failure is event of default	No
Lower Tier 2	Subordinated	None	Failure is event of default	No
Upper Tier 2	Junior subordinated	At the option of the bank, based on a test. Cumulative.	Early usually requires authorization of regulator.	Only after Tier 1 capital is fully written off
Tier 3	Subordinated	If the bank falls below its regulatory requirements. Generally cumulative.	Only if the bank complies with its regulatory capital requirements.	Only in liquidation
Tier 1 preferred	Ahead of common stock. Subordinated to everything else.	Payment of dividends is discretionary. Non-Cumulative.	Requires Non-authorization of regulator.	Mechanism varies. Usually only after common stock is written off.

Source: Morgan Stanley

Table 5.18 Notching methodology of the three major rating agencies for bank capital

Senior rating	Lower Tier 2	Upper Tier 2	Tier 1	Tier 3
S&P (Senior debt above BBB-)	+ 1 notch	+ 2 notches	+ 2 notches	+ 3 notches
Moody's Financial Strength Rating C and above	+ 1 notch	+ 1 notch	+ 2 notches*	+ 2 notches
FitchIBCA Senior Debt above A-	+ 1 notch	+ 1 notch	+ 1 notch	+ 1–2 notches
Senior Debt between BBB+ and BBB-	+ 1 notch	+ 2 notches	+ 2 notches	+ 2 notches

Note: * for issuers with senior debt ratings of Ba2 or higher

Source: Morgan Stanley

equity it accepts innovative Tier 1 preferred only up to 10 percent of a bank's tangible total equity. Straight preference shares and noninnovative Tier 1 are included up to 25 percent in the calculation of "adjusted tangible equity." Yet it is not taken into account in S&P's calculation of "adjusted common equity," or core capital. S&P's methodology comprises several different definitions, ranging from "total tangible equity" which includes Tier 1 preferred completely to "adjusted common equity," the narrowest definition which gives no equity credit to Tier 1 preferred. An example may help to understand the methodology. A bank has 120 million Euro of Tier 1 capital, consisting of 60 million Euro common equity and 60 million Euro Tier 1 preferred. Assuming that the bank has only banking book risk-weighted assets of 1 billion Euro, its regulatory Tier 1 ratio would be 12 percent. S&P would only include Tier 1 preferred up to a maximum of 10 percent of overall Tier 1 capital in its calculation, that is 12 million Euro. S&P would thus get a Tier 1 ratio of 7.2 percent. If the bank's Tier 1 capital exclusively consists of common equity, the Tier 1 ratio would again equal 12 percent, reflecting S&P's view that common equity is a stronger form of capital than Tier 1 preferred. Changes in the structure of Tier 1 capital rather than the structure itself are the relevant issue for investors in bank capital, because they may trigger actions by the rating agencies.

Although offering the highest spread of all bank debt instruments, investments in Tier 1 preferred are clearly most risky. The key question is how much worse off would a creditor be in a liquidation scenario by holding a bank's Tier 1 debt rather than its higher ranking subordinated bonds. From past experience, the answer is: not very much. Holders of subordinated debt have generally fared well when the viability of European banks has been in question, often because of protective government intervention or even bailouts. Therefore, the more relevant risk is probably the deferral of the coupon. However, throughout the history of the Tier 1 market, there has been no case in which a bank deferred its coupon payments or even declared bankruptcy, leaving investors with massive capital losses. Nevertheless, Tier 1 investors experienced significant mark-to-market losses during periods of high risk aversion, for example, after the Asian crisis, Russia's default and the collapse of Long-Term Capital Management in 1998, or in bank-specific cases that undermined the credit quality of the issuer.

After the introduction of the Euro the Tier 1 market has become a fairly large and liquid market with an established investor base. Between 1998 and 2003, the volume of the Tier 1 universe has increased from 1.5 billion Euro to more than 60 billion Euro. European investor demand for Tier 1 product has been supported by a diminished ability to generate outperformance by playing the differences in interest rates and currencies after the introduction of the Euro, falling government bond yields, and a recognition that credit will be the primary means by which to add value in fixed income portfolios. The inclusion of bank capital in major European credit indices in

2002 also contributed to broadening the investor base. Figure 5.28 depicts an overview of the most liquid Euro Tier 1 issues.

Confidence in structures and regulatory supervision as well as in the financial strength of the issuers have contributed to a remarkably resilient Tier 1 market. External shocks like September 11 nevertheless will impact the spreads of Tier 1 issues more than other types of bank debt. So far the market has benefited substantially from the discipline of the issuers. No Tier 1 issuer has ever knowingly allowed a Tier 1 preferred to step-up. While from the perspective of the issuer the risk of letting an issue step-up is rather reputational, we believe that it could impact the confidence of investors in the overall ability of issuers to pay coupons significantly. With respect to the overall sentiment for the market segment it will be important to monitor the ability and willingness of bank issuers to call not only their Tier 1 preferred issues, but also Upper and Lower Tier 2 instruments at the first opportunity. Especially, the Lower Tier 2 market is considered a fairly attractive and liquid market segment by many European investors. Figure 5.29 shows that there is sufficient market breadth and depth to implement relative value trades and to generate a variety of risk/return profiles.

As mentioned above, no coupons on Tier 1 preferred have ever been canceled, and no bank with Tier 1 issues outstanding has ever gone bankrupt. However, some issuers have experienced significant problems that questioned their ability to pay coupons. There are two major reasons why there has been no default on payments of interest or principal so far:

- Access to capital markets is vital for any bank. Therefore, it would do anything possible to avoid coupon deferrals or default.
- Governments tend to support major banking groups when financial resources are exhausted. Prominent examples for government support are Banesto and Crédit Lyonnais in 1993/94.

With that in mind, the primary risk does not seem to be coupon deferral, that the issue is not called at the first opportunity or even that the issuer defaults, it is rather the possibility of incurring substantial mark-to-market losses because of issuer-specific or economy-wide problems. Consequently, the risk budget and the degree of risk aversion of the portfolio manager essentially determine his ability and willingness to invest in Tier 1 preferred, and to hold onto these investments even in phases of high volatility and severe spread widening. Investors concerned with short-term mark-to-market losses may tend to prefer Lower Tier 2 issues (Figure 5.30).

To gauge the effect of severe exogenous shocks it is helpful to look at historical spread levels (Figure 5.31). The most recent events that might have had a large impact on Tier 1 spreads were September 11, 2001, and the Worldcom collapse at the end of June 2002. Both events caused corporate spreads across all sectors to widen, but being one of the most volatile

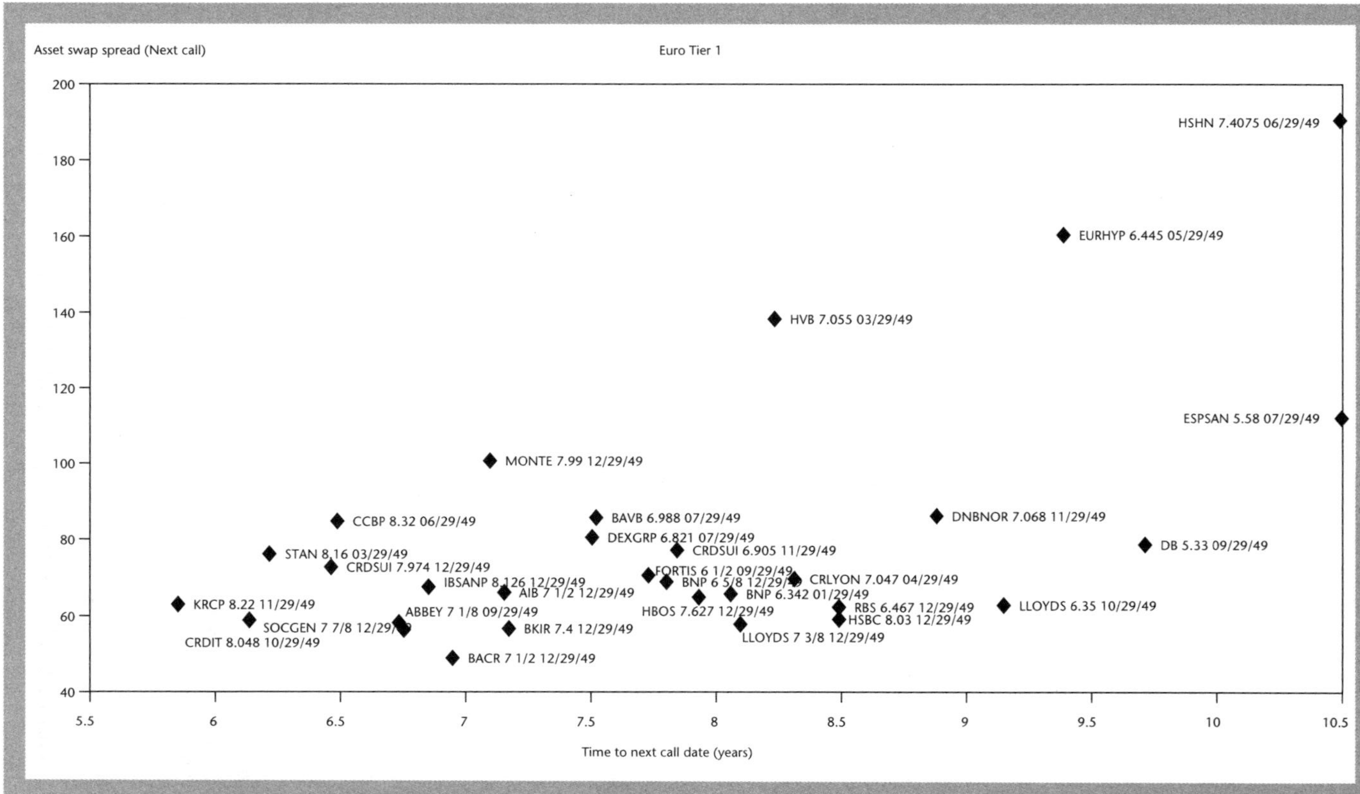

Figure 5.28 Asset swap spreads of Euro Tier 1 issues as of Jan. 2004

Source: Union Investment

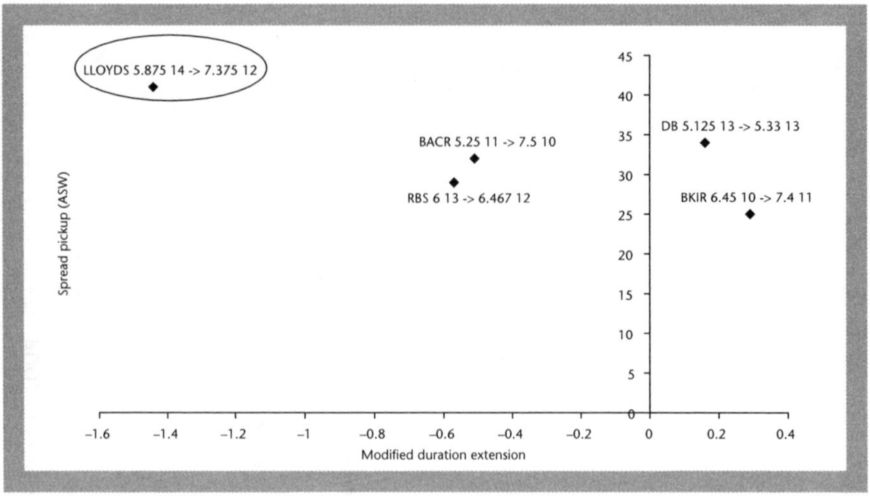

Figure 5.29 Asset swap spreads of Euro Lower Tier 2 issues as of Jan. 2004

Source: Union Investment

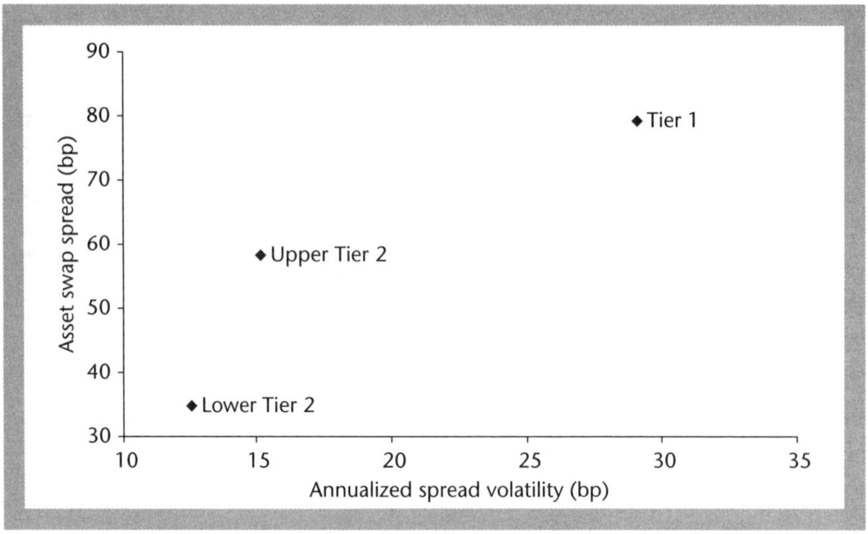

Figure 5.30 Risk-reward profile of different types of bank capital as of Dec. 2003

Source: Union Investment

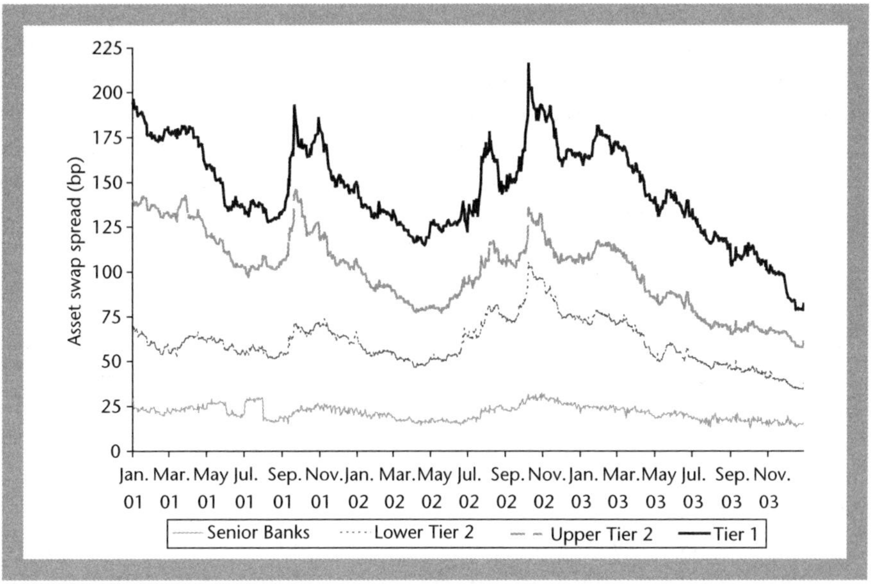

Figure 5.31 Asset swap spreads of Euro denominated bank issues

Source: J.P. Morgan

market segments Tier 1 spreads suffered far more than other sectors. After September 11, Tier 1 spreads widened about 70 bp on average, while Lower Tier 2 spreads widened a scant 20 bp. Although there was virtually no trading going on for two weeks, traders marked their books wider. When trading resumed, Euro Tier 1 spreads quickly retraced half of their widening. Thus the liquidity crisis was short-lived, which was a sign of the high confidence of investors in the strength of the issuers. A quick glance at the Euro subordination chart clearly shows how much spread compression Tier 1 and Upper Tier 2 bonds have experienced during 2003.

When WorldCom announced at the end of February 2002 that it had to restate financial statements for 2001 and first quarter of 2002, Tier 1 spreads widened by 50 bp on average. The moderate recovery until end of September 2002 was stopped abruptly by further corporate failures, a series of profit warnings from the European banking sector, and speculations about possible solvency or liquidity problems at Commerzbank, Hypovereinsbank and Credit Suisse. After the initial widening that followed these events the Tier 1 market has kept tightening, rewarding patient investors handsomely.

5.3.1.4 The subordination premium

Different degrees of subordination, not only in relation to the position in the capital structure but also to the structure of a banking group, of course, have a substantial impact on spread levels. At the same credit spread, we would prefer to own debt from the operating company rather than from the holding company. When it comes to the different types of subordinated bank debt, one may try to estimate fair spread differentials between Lower Tier 2, Upper Tier 2 and Tier 1 preferred. Yet, this proves extremely difficult. Since the data on defaults in the banking sector is scarce, the only way to estimate the fair spread differential for two bonds of a certain issuer is to impose assumptions with respect to default probability and loss given default to value the embedded options of extension, step-up, coupon deferral and cancellation of coupons. While sophisticated models may come up with an estimate of fair value spread differentials, liquidity as well as supply and demand can lead to substantial deviations of the actual spread differential from fair value, even in the longer term.

Generally, we believe that the spread difference between Lower Tier 2 and Tier 1 bonds of the same issuer should primarily reflect the maturity – or rather call date – extension associated with switching out of a Lower Tier 2 into a Tier 1 bond of the same issuer, and the risk premium required to move down the capital structure. As a proxy for the risk premium we use the implied equity volatility of the bank's common stock. A switch from a Lower Tier 2 to Tier 1 may involve issues with different maturity and call dates, respectively. Hence, the subordination premium should be greater between securities of different tenors. Since investors are usually more comfortable holding Tier 1 debt of highly rated banks which normally have a stable equity base, the subordination premiums tend to vary by the issuer's rating and the issuer's implied equity volatility. Typically, the more highly rated an institution, the lower one would expect the subordination premium to be, and vice versa. This relative value analysis is therefore most effective for comparisons of similarly rated banks.

In 2002 and 2003, the spread differential between Tier 1 preferred and Upper Tier 2 has exceeded the spread differential between Upper Tier 2 and Lower Tier 2 in the Euro market for most of the time, as Figure 5.32 shows. This observation does not correspond with S&P's methodology for rating bank capital. Investors seem to disagree with the rating agency that the step from dated to perpetuity justifies a larger increase of the risk premium than the step from cumulative to noncumulative. Figure 5.32 also highlights that the spread differentials between Upper Tier 2 versus Lower Tier 2 and Tier 1 versus Upper Tier 2 do not necessarily move in tandem. However, these observations should be interpreted with caution, because the indices that we have used to construct the time series are based on differing issuer universes.

From historical experience we can see again that the real risk for bank capital investors is not coupon deferral or liquidation, but a temporary liquidity crisis that leads to spread widening and mark-to-market losses. Of course, Tier 1 and Upper Tier 2 issues are more likely to suffer a massive spread widening than less subordinated Lower Tier 2 bonds. The examples above

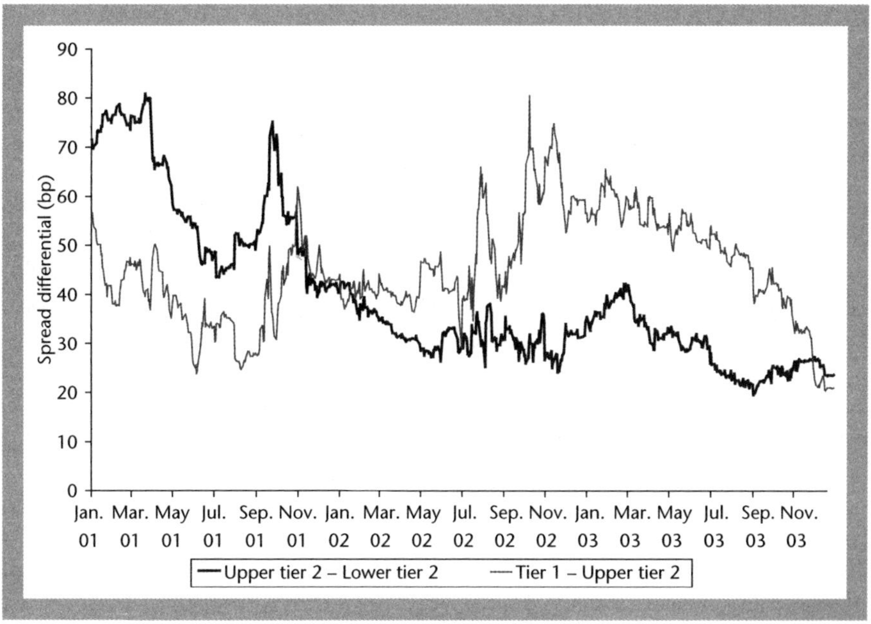

Figure 5.32 Spread differentials between different types of Euro denominated subordinated bank issues

Sources: J.P. Morgan, Union Investment

show that in crises prices are driven by traders, not by investors. Therefore, in the short term, fundamental arguments do not play any role. The immediate target for a spread widening is set by historic experiences. Hence, stress testing based on historic data does make sense to create worst-case scenarios and estimate the possible loss that is not exceeded with a high probability.

The European Tier 1 market is dominated by issues from highly rated and rather large banks. While one can imagine one of these banks getting into trouble over the longer term, a sudden credit crisis seems unlikely. Bearing in mind the series of various cases of fraud of corporate issuers, a similar event in the European banking sector could be a real stress test for the Tier 1 market. It is realistic to assume that in this case investors would not only face a repricing of the market, but also that there may be a period without a bid for the issues. With regard to the different structures of Tier 1 issues we believe that bonds with equity settlement features are most likely to be called, even if the issuer is in serious financial problems at the call date. Therefore, one can ask why banks do not issue common equity instead of Tier 1. The simple answer is that it is cheaper for them.

To compare the cost of equity and the cost of Tier 1 preferred from the perspective of the issuing bank, we apply the Capital Asset Pricing Model (CAPM). Accordingly, to invest in and hold a certain stock i investors require a return r_i that is defined as

$$r_i = r_f + \beta_i r_m$$

where r_f denotes the risk-free rate of return, β_i the beta of stock *i* with respect to the equity market, and r_m the risk premium of the equity market. Assuming that Tier 1 issues are called at the first opportunity, the cost of Tier 1 preferred is given by the spread to first call at the the time of issuance versus a duration-matched government bond plus the yield on that government bond. Several examples show that it is usually more efficient for banks to issue Tier 1 preferred than common equity, especially when taking into account the tax deductibility of Tier 1 (Table 5.19). Furthermore, issuing Tier 1 qualifying debt is a good possibility to balance the often divergent interests of banking industry regulators, whose objective is to preserve or strengthen the integrity of a bank's balance sheets, and shareholders, who demand high returns on their investment.

With respect to funding costs and ratings, European banks have tended to focus more on regulatory requirements than on economic capital. If a bank wants to increase its regulatory core capital ratio, it has a variety of options. Basically it can increase its Tier 1 capital or reduce its risk-weighted assets. As stated above, issuing Tier 1 preferred or common equity are the simplest ways to increase core capital, but from a longer term perspective the enhancement of profitability and thus retained earnings also helps to improve the Tier 1 ratio. Pressure from shareholders and the lower cost of capital lead many banks to consider the issuance of Tier 1 preferred as a particularly attractive way to improve the core capital ratio. However, the upper limit for innovative hybrid Tier 1 preferred of 10 percent of a bank's total tangible equity constrains the degrees of freedom. Overall, when a bank requires funding, raising Tier 1 or Tier 2 in the capital markets is the most compelling alternative. However, when no fresh capital is required there may be more efficient alternatives. Reducing risk-weighted assets also serves to accomplish better regulatory capital ratios. This can be done in two ways. Either through a reduction of risky assets, that is direct sales of some assets such as equity holdings or securitization of assets, or through a

Table 5.19 Comparison between the cost of common equity and the cost of Tier 1 preferred

Issuer	Cost of equity (%)	Cost of Tier 1 preferred	Cost of Tier 1 preferred (incl. tax deductibility)(%)
Sociéte Generale	8.35 ($\beta = 1.260$)	5.34 (7.875 2010)	3.58
Hypovereinsbank	7.91 ($\beta = 1.035$)	9.19 (7.055% 2012)	5.97
Barclays	9.52 ($\beta = 1.444$)	5.15 (7.500% 2010)	3.61

Source: Morgan Stanley

reduction of risk-weightings. Buying default swaps on risky assets or synthetic securitization are typical actions that help to reduce risk-weightings. Generally, when no funding is required securitization may be the cheapest way to achieve a better regulatory Tier 1 ratio. Investors should bear that in mind when forecasting issuance activity in the banking sector.

5.3.1.5 Identifying relative value in bank debt

Although we have spent some time on the specifics of bank debt, it is worth remembering that liquidity as well as supply and demand dynamics affect bank spreads in the same way as industrial or utility spreads. Liquidity typically depends not only on the size of a bond, but also on the time since it has been issued. While investors usually demand a premium to invest in less liquid bonds, strong retail demand can hold spreads tight, even if fundamentals are deteriorating or there is new issuance. Recent experience shows that the latest issue tends to become the new benchmark bond of an issuer, enjoying strong demand and therefore often trading relatively rich compared to previously outstanding bonds of the same issuer. During the last couple of years supply in the banking sector was driven to a large part by changes of the strategy of a bank. An example is the shift of the European banking sector away from retail banking towards investment banking in the late 1990s. M&A activity, reorganization of banking groups and recapitalization of insurance subsidiaries are further items to watch carefully.

Many large banks have experienced significant change in their business. Retail deposits are no longer sufficient to fund loan portfolio growth. Since banks increasingly use senior, secured and covered bonds to fund their business, liquidity and interest margin profiles have changed and become a critical factor in the financial performance and strategic success of a bank. Usually, a bank's liability profile adjusts slowly to the relative cost of funds from various sources. However, if the viability of a financial institution's business model depends on the availability, cost or pricing structure of funds the balance between funding cost and the business model can necessitate a change of the strategy. An in-depth analysis is therefore recommended if the relative importance of various funding sources changes significantly.

When trying to assess the risk profile of a bank, investors usually start with the information reported by the company itself. However, the aggregation undertaken by banks in their public reporting as well as the extremely heterogeneous disclosure from banks, make it a challenging task to fully perceive a bank's risk profile. Special attention should be paid to the relationship between on- and off-balance sheet risks. This is particularly true for changing business models. In such cases, potential divergences between loans on the balance sheet, regulatory capital requirements and profitability may arise. Another point to consider are contingent risks. They are particularly hard to identify, as examples like Ahold and Parmalat have shown. Capitalia's decision to compensate retail investors for the losses incurred by the purchase of Parmalat bonds is a typical example of a contingent liability. It highlights the extent to which reputation can influence the actions of financial institutions in certain situations.

Therefore, rating agencies tend to base their assessment of capital adequacy not only on balance sheet assets but also in relation to managed assets. In this context, managed assets additionally include assets previously originated by the bank and subsequently securitized. Typically, this relates to the securitization of credit cards and mortgages where the originator remains the servicer of the portfolio. Even though the assets are legally sold, the rating agencies frequently assume an enduring responsibility of the originator for the transaction. In the event that such a liability materializes, the financial and reputational consequences for the bank can be significant.

While the above-mentioned liabilites are contingent in nature, trading risks arise from the daily business of a bank, and as such, are rather transitory. In the meantime many of the trading risks of a bank are related to the use of derivatives. Banks now use derivatives to manage equity, FX, credit and interest rate risks and to construct products for customers. But the detail information provided on derivatives is usually rather limited, and infrequent, comparability between VaR measures low, and it is often difficult to determine exactly what constitutes trading risks and earnings. Nevertheless, it is essential to monitor these elements so that, over time, a broad picture of the risk profile evolves.

Generally, there are two problems with the estimation of potential losses from trading risks. Value at Risk (VaR) is an estimate of the loss that is not exceeded with a given high probability over a certain time horizon. It is derived from a bank's own risk model. Not only do these risk models vary between banks, but they also use different parameters and sensitivities. Hence, the same trading book positions may produce different estimates of risk. While many reported VaR measures are at the 99 percent confidence level for losses on positions held for a single day, others use different confidence levels, for example, 95 percent confidence levels and covering holding periods up to ten days. The choice of parameters feeds directly into the resulting VaR. Models will also change over time as they are updated in line with technological and business development. Consequently, even a single bank's VaR numbers are likely to be inconsistent over time. In particular, the extent to which models account for hedging, basis risks and correlations is likely to influence the reported VaR. While there are substantial difficulties in comparing reported VaR levels, they may be helpful to give a clue as to whether a certain financial institution has a higher level of market risk than others. In particular, it may reveal whether further analysis is required. Special attention should be paid, when the losses incurred frequently are greater than those predicted by the model. This is an indicator that the level of market risk is rising or the model does not accurately reflect the risks taken.

CHAPTER 6

High-Yield Investing

6.1 INTRODUCTION

This chapter describes an investment approach for credits rated below BBB at S&P and Baa3 at Moody's. After a short introduction to the asset class we will focus on the macroeconomic environment, credit fundamentals, technicals and valuation as the main factors driving the high-yield market. Generally, the main task for high-yield managers is to deal with the inherent credit risk. The importance of idiosyncratic risk relative to systematic risk tends to increase for lower rated credits. Issuer-specific risk is in fact dominant in high yield. Even in a well-diversified portfolio the effects of a credit blow-up can be substantial, therefore appropriate risk-management tools have to be in place. The access to new capital is a central point in the assessment of the condition of the high-yield market. If refinancing is available to companies the rating environment will improve and default rates will decrease. More investors will dedicate their investable assets to high yield and hence spreads will tighten in the high-yield market.

Depending on market conditions high-yield companies will have a varying access to new capital and this will have a direct effect on rating trends and default rates in the high-yield market. Another important factor similar to investment grade credits is the earnings outlook of high-yield companies which is closely related to GDP growth. Before deciding to invest in high yield the following points should be examined:

- GDP Growth
- Default Rates and Rating Cycle
- Distress Ratio
- Commercial and Industrial Lending Standards

- ISM Index
- Capacity Utilization and Industrial Production
- Credit Fundamentals
- Mutual Fund Flows
- Equity Markets
- Implied Equity Market Volatility
- Relative Value to other asset classes.

The text will also focus on the interest rate sensitivity of high yield and an indepth analyses will be provided for Fallen Angels and Crossover credits.

6.2 DESCRIPTION OF THE HIGH-YIELD MARKET

6.2.1 Definition of high-yield ratings

In Table 6.1 we present the definitions of Moody's Investor Service for corporate bond ratings. The wording for A and BBB-rated companies is included as well for the purpose of showing the increasing riskiness with lower ratings. Fixed income investors want to protect their principal and earn interest over a specified period of time. For high-yield investors the preservation of principal and interest is by no means guaranteed and high-yield portfolios have to be managed accordingly. An appropriate management approach will be presented in this chapter.

6.2.2 High-yield market growth

The high-yield market grows continuously and makes up around 20 percent of the high grade market. The influencing factors for its size are the volume of "Fallen Angels" (companies being downgraded to high-yield), "Rising Stars" (companies being upgraded to investment grade), redemptions and the new issue volume which is driven by demand (fund flows) and the willingness of companies to enter the high-yield market as a source of alternative financing. Particularly in Europe many companies used to depend heavily on bank loans. As banks are not willing to take more company risk a lot of companies are forced to the capital markets. High yield is an interesting alternative financing source especially for small- and medium-sized companies. High yield will also be the financing choice for many Leveraged Buy Outs (LBOs). Figure 6.1 shows high-yield market bonds as a percentage of outstanding corporate bonds by principal amount.

Table 6.1 Definitions of Moody's corporate bond ratings

A	Bonds and preferred stock rated A possess many favorable investment attributes and are to be considered as upper-medium-grade obligations. The factors that give security to principal and interest are considered adequate, but elements may be present that suggest a susceptibility to impairment some time in the future.
Baa	Bonds and preferred stock rated Baa are considered to be medium-grade obligations (i.e., they are neither highly protected nor poorly secured). Interest payments and principal security appear adequate for the present, but certain protective elements may be lacking or maybe characteristically unreliable over a great length of time. Such bonds lack outstanding investment characteristics and, in fact, possess speculative characteristics as well.
Ba	Bonds and preferred stocks rated Ba are judged to have speculative elements; their future can not be considered as being well assured. Often the protection of interest and principal payments may be very moderate, and thereby not well safeguarded during both good and bad times over the future. Uncertainty of position characterizes bonds in this class.
B	Bonds and preferred stock rated B generally lack characteristics of the desirable investment. Assurance of interest and principal payment or of maintenance of other terms of the contract over any long period of time may be small.
Caa	Bonds and preferred stock rated Caa are of poor standing. Such issues may be in default, or there may be present elements of danger with respect to principal or interest.
Ca	Bonds and preferred stock rated Ca represent obligations that are speculative in a high degree. Such issues are often in default or have other marked shortcomings.
C	Bonds and preferred stock rated C are the lowest rated class of bonds. Issues so rated can be regarded as having extremely poor prospects of ever attaining any real investment standing.

Source: Moody's Investor Service

6.2.3 Characteristics of high-yield market

High yield should be viewed as a separate asset class. Some of its advantages and disadvantages are listed below.

Advantages:

- High diversification potential because of a low correlation with other asset classes.
- Low interest rate sensitivity.
- Lower return volatility than equities because of the fixed coupon.

Disadvantages:

- Large sentiment shifts occur very fast.
- Large bid-offer spreads persist due to lack of liquidity.

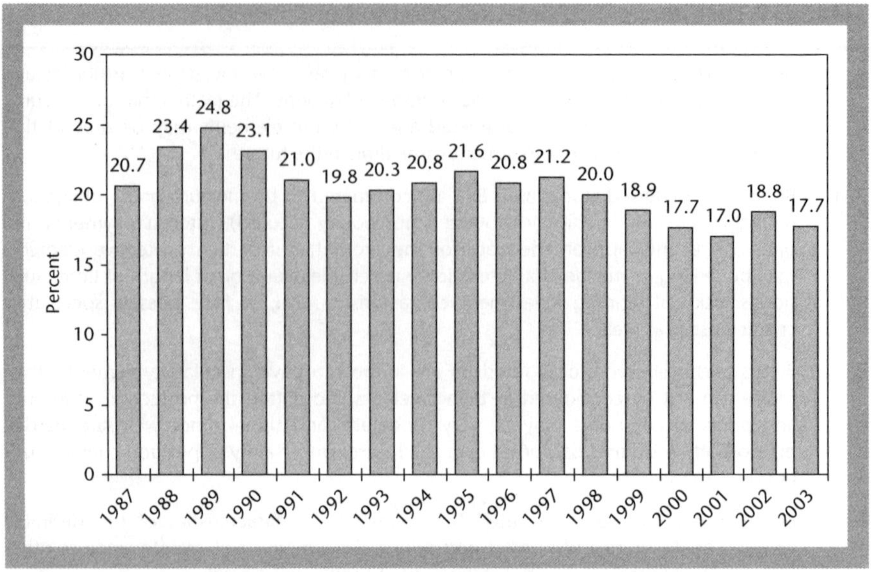

Figure 6.1 High-yield bonds as a percentage of outstanding corporate bonds by principal amount

Source: Moody's and Merrill Lynch

6.2.4 High-yield spread

Figure 6.2 shows historical spread levels for high-yield rating classes. Spread ranges can be observed for BBs (250 bp–550 bp), Bs (400 bp–700 bp) and CCC and lower (700 bp–2000 bp) depending on the market phase.

The high-yield spread can be described by the following formula:

Spread value = Annual default rate * (1 − Recovery rate)
Assumptions:
Recovery rate = 30 percent
Default rate = 8 percent
The spread value is computed as follows:
Spread value = 8 percent * (1 – 30 percent) = 560 bp

If the actual spread in the high-yield market is above 560 bp then we can conclude that there is value in the current spread dependent on our assumptions. A part of the difference between observed spreads and the calculated spread value, however, is due to migration and liquidity risk.

6.2.5 Correlation between rating and asset classes

The correlation matrix in Table 6.2 shows that high yield has a low correlation with other asset classes. The highest relationship exists with small stocks like the Russell 2000 Index. The weakest correlation was measured for Treasuries.

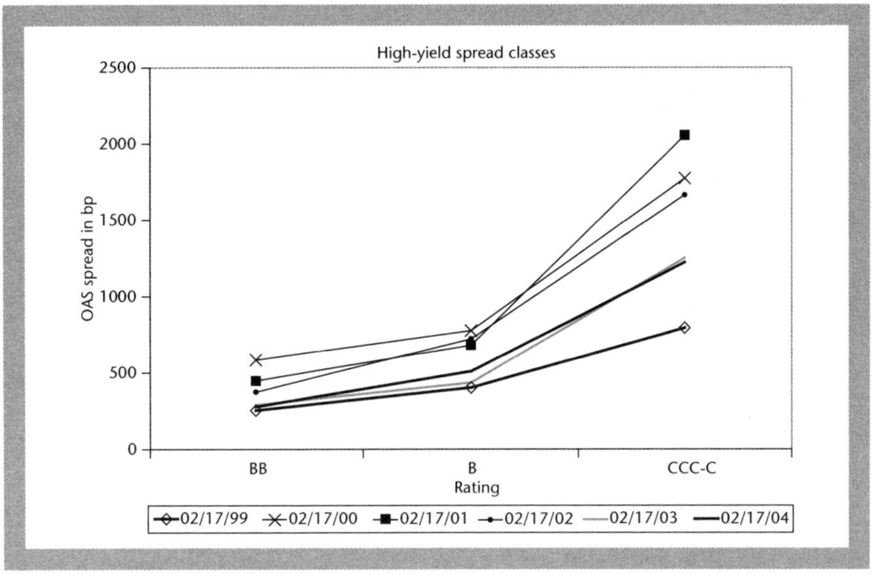

Figure 6.2 High-yield spread classes 02/99–02/2004

Source: Union Investment

It is of interest that the correlation with High Grade shows only a reading of 0.47 which is not very strong indeed. We will show later in this chapter that those relationships measured over a long period (here: Jul. 83–Dec. 03) can vary considerably during various economic and credit cycles.

Table 6.3 summarizes the correlation of monthly returns for the various rating classes. BB rated credits have the highest correlation with Bs even though there is also a strong relationship with BBBs. Bs have the highest correlation with C-rated paper. The relationship with BBBs is at 0.43 quite low. C-rated bonds behave almost completely independent from investment grade paper. Again we have to point out that the correlations will vary at different periods in the economic and credit cycle.

6.2.5.1 Rating migration

Corporate bond ratings are not static but rather tend to move over time. The lower the rating class the more likely a rating change over a 1-year period (Table 6.4). Corporate ratings will usually be assigned an outlook (credit watch positive, positive outlook, stable outlook, developing, negative outlook or credit watch negative). It is important to notice that the rating agencies Moody's and S&P may change the rating of a corporate issuer with a stable outlook immediately when an event occurs which justifies the rating action. The rating migration between lower investment grade (Baa3) and noninvestment grade (Ba1) is very important for the quality of the whole credit market. In times of deteriorating quality in the credit market

Table 6.2 Monthly total return correlation between various asset classes Jul. 83–1 Dec. 2003

	High Yield	Ba	B	Caa	Ca–D	Crossover	Emerging markets	US credit	S&P 500	Russell 2000	Government	10-yr Treasury
High Yield	1.000											
Ba	0.905	1.000										
B	0.980	0.854	1.000									
Caa	0.875	0.701	0.838	1.000								
Ca–D	0.644	0.439	0.593	0.660	1.000							
Crossover	0.855	0.970	0.752	0.644	0.414	1.000						
Emerging markets	0.505	0.466	0.493	0.391	0.286	0.446	1.000					
US credit	0.471	0.614	0.437	0.244	0.159	0.595	0.274	1.000				
S&P 500	0.503	0.512	0.502	0.395	0.203	0.512	0.535	0.340	1.000			
Russell 2000	0.530	0.502	0.526	0.457	0.275	0.471	0.507	0.133	0.732	1.000		
Government	0.240	0.393	0.209	0.034	−0.031	0.297	0.066	0.906	0.198	−0.061	1.000	
10-yr Treasury	0.217	0.376	0.185	0.014	−0.061	0.270	0.041	0.905	0.183	−0.062	0.980	1.000

Source: Lehman Brothers

Table 6.3 Correlation of monthly returns of corporate bonds by rating classes 1989–2003

	Ten-year Treasuries	AAA	AA	A	BBB	BB	B	CCC/CC/C
Ten-year Treasuries	1.000							
AAA	0.961	1.000						
AA	0.947	0.986	1.000					
A	0.926	0.979	0.985	1.000				
BBB	0.828	0.915	0.921	0.952	1.000			
BB	0.299	0.442	0.470	0.532	0.681	1.000		
B	0.018	0.181	0.194	0.271	0.433	0.781	1.000	
CCC/CC/C	−0.110	0.012	0.035	0.166	0.264	0.667	0.842	1.000

Source: Merrill Lynch

Table 6.4 Corporate average rating transition matrix in percent, 1985–2002

Rating from	Rating to								
	Aaa	Aa	A	Baa	Ba	B	Caa–C	Default	WR
Aaa	87.80	7.90	0.30	0.00	0.00	0.00	0.00	0.00	4.10
Aa	0.80	86.10	8.60	0.30	0.10	0.00	0.00	0.00	4.10
A	0.00	2.30	87.00	5.60	0.70	0.20	0.00	0.00	4.30
Baa	0.10	0.30	5.20	82.90	4.80	1.10	0.10	0.20	5.30
Ba	0.00	0.00	0.50	5.10	75.10	8.30	0.60	1.40	8.80
B	0.00	0.10	0.20	0.60	5.10	74.10	4.20	6.80	8.80
Caa–C	0.00	0.00	0.00	1.00	1.60	6.00	59.70	21.50	10.20

Source: Moody's

the number of "Fallen Angels" (companies which lost their investment grade status) will outweigh the number of "Rising Stars" (companies which were upgraded to investment grade status). In periods of improving credit quality and increased economic growth this trend will reverse and "Rising Stars" will outnumber "Fallen Angels."

6.2.6 Ratings cycle (Downgrade/Upgrade ratio)

The trend in the Downgrade/Upgrade ratio is another indicator for the direction of the high-yield market (Table 6.5). In a weak economic cycle this ratio will deteriorate. A reversal of this trend will occur when the economy

Table 6.5 Rating transitions for high-yield corporates 1997–2003

	Moody's							Standard & Poor's						
	1997	**1998**	**1999**	**2000**	**2001**	**2002**	**2003**	**1997**	**1998**	**1999**	**2000**	**2001**	**2002**	**2003**
Number of issuers														
Downgrades	116	227	317	325	409	370	289	97	212	353	394	595	514	365
Upgrades	168	153	137	99	115	92	157	149	136	93	96	93	121	134
Ratio	0.69×	1.48×	2.31×	3.28×	3.56×	4.02 ×	1.84 ×	0.65×	1.56×	3.80×	4.10×	6.40×	4.25×	2.72×
Principal amount ($ billions)														
Downgrades	$44.9	$62.2	$89.8	$182.8	$360.9	$414.4	$241.2	$31.5	$58.7	$111.5	$155.6	$502.4	$786.4	$395.0
Upgrades	$64.0	$159.9	$96.4	$55.7	$75.0	$33.5	$100.3	$83.9	$117.0	$54.4	$55.3	$60.3	$85.2	$126.9
Ratio	0.70×	0.39×	0.93×	3.28×	4.81×	12.36×	2.41×	0.38×	0.50×	2.05×	2.82×	8.33×	9.23×	3.11×

Moody's figures include convertibles-only issuers. Standard & Poor's figures are US industrial, financial, telecommunications and utility issuers

Source: Moody's, S&P and Merrill Lynch

gains on strength resulting in higher company profits. As a result, the credit quality of companies will improve and hence the Downgrade/Upgrade ratio. If this ratio is computed on the basis of the nominal amount of debt outstanding one will observe a sharp increase in 2002. The large amount of Fallen Angels is responsible for this spike.

It has to be mentioned that this ratio has a lagging character concerning the future direction of high-yield spreads because rating agencies will usually react to a change in the credit quality of companies and the whole market only with a lag of a couple of months. Nevertheless, this ratio appears to be useful for describing the current state of the credit market. Hereby the absolute number is less important than the trend, for example, in 2003 we have seen a clear deleveraging effort in the credit market even though downgrades outnumbered upgrades. The important message was that the negative trend from 2001 to 2002 was stopped.

High-yield issuers have less room for rating downgrades (average rating B). They can experience a severe deterioration in credit quality during short periods of time (Figure 6.3). At this point, it has to be mentioned that investment grade companies, too, can default within a short period of time if, for example, fraud is detected like in the case of Enron, WorldCom and Parmalat.

6.2.7 Migration of corporate bond prices

Another way of showing the predominant risks in lower rated (BBB-B) corporate bonds is to observe the price migration over a 1-year horizon after

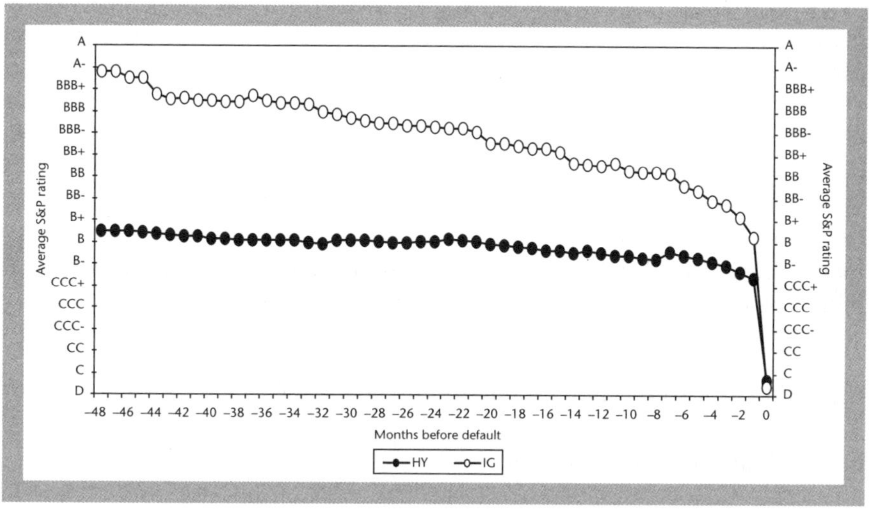

Figure 6.3 Investment grade and high-yield average path to default, Aug. 2001

Source: Salomon Smith Barney

Table 6.6 The change in bond prices over a 12-month horizon

Percent of Par 1 year later	Percent of par after the price dropped the first time below 90 percent				
	90–80 percent	80–70 percent	70–60 percent	60–50 percent	50 percent
100+ percent	12.83	3.47	2.78	0.00	8.30
90–100 percent	28.38	13.19	11.11	6.67	0.00
80–90 percent	22.22	24.31	27.78	20.00	8.30
70–80 percent	13.13	18.06	2.78	6.67	0.00
60–70 percent	7.58	11.81	22.22	26.67	8.30
50–60 percent	5.45	9.72	8.33	13.33	0.00
50 percent	10.40	19.44	25.00	26.67	75.00
Defaults in percent	8.48	20.83	27.78	26.67	58.33
Number of issues	1 247				

Source: CSFB

the bond price fell below 90 percent of par for the first time. Table 6.6 shows a study conducted by CSFB for 1247 corporate bonds between 1993 and 2000.

Table 6.6 shows the downside risk faced by every bond investor. In fact, there is a high probability for a bond price to decline further once it has fallen below a certain threshold (e.g. 80 percent of par). This probability increases in a very volatile environment when the risk appetite for credit products is declining.

An important measure for the current state of the high-yield market is also the outstanding total amount split up by price buckets, for example, percentage trading at or above par, between par and 90, 90 and 80, and so on. This is helpful for projections about expected total returns since the two components of total returns are capital appreciation and coupon payments. Low-priced debt has a more symmetric total return potential but will experience greater standard deviation of total returns.

6.3 DRIVERS OF THE HIGH-YIELD MARKET

6.3.1 Macroeconomic factors

The most important macroeconomic variables which have an effect on high-yield spreads are highlighted as we proceed.

6.3.1.1 GDP growth

The economic cycle has a large impact on the performance of high-yield bonds. High-yield companies have usually either a tight liquidity plan or operate with a high business risk. Small changes to their profit outlook will immediately have an effect on their credit profile. During periods of weak economic growth, spreads in the high-yield market tend to widen.

There is a correlation between the ratings cycle and GDP growth. In strong growth periods the majority of companies will use part of their free cash flows to pay down debt and hence will improve their credit profile. This translates into better credit ratings. In an environment of slow economic growth companies with a weak credit profile will find it difficult servicing their debt and a fast deterioration of their credit profile can occur. We could find a correlation of 56 percent between GDP growth and high-yield spreads which is statistically significant (Figure 6.4). The relationship is not stronger because high yield has a strong component of nonsystematic risk (credit specific risk) rather than systematic risk.

6.3.1.2 Default rates

The following paragraph will deal with default rates because they are of central importance for high-yield investors. Figure 6.5 compares the three major default peaks since 1920.

Default rates have to be distinguished between "issuer-weighted" and "dollar-weighted" (Figure 6.6). The increasing amount of Fallen Angels in 2002 resulted in a sharp increase of the "dollar-weighted" default rate. High-yield spreads tend to lead default rates, which means that a tightening will occur prior to a fall in the default rate because market participants will already anticipate the future development of the default rate. This relationship broke down in 2002 for a couple of months due to the large divergence of the "dollar-weighted" from the "issuer-weighted" default rate.

As we can see in Table 6.7 cumulative default rates tend to increase progressively with a decreasing rating class.

A strong negative correlation between default rates and economic growth could always be expected, but during the economic crisis in the United States in the 1970s and 1980s a sharp increase of the default rates could not be observed. It was the economic slowdown in 1990, which was accompanied by extremely increasing default rates. The same acceleration of default rates occurred in 2001 due to a prolonged downturn of the economy, high political uncertainty after September 11, 2001, company accounting scandals, and aggregate weak credit fundamentals. Structural changes in the credit markets can explain the weaker than assumed relationship between the default rates and the economic cycle. This leads to the conclusion

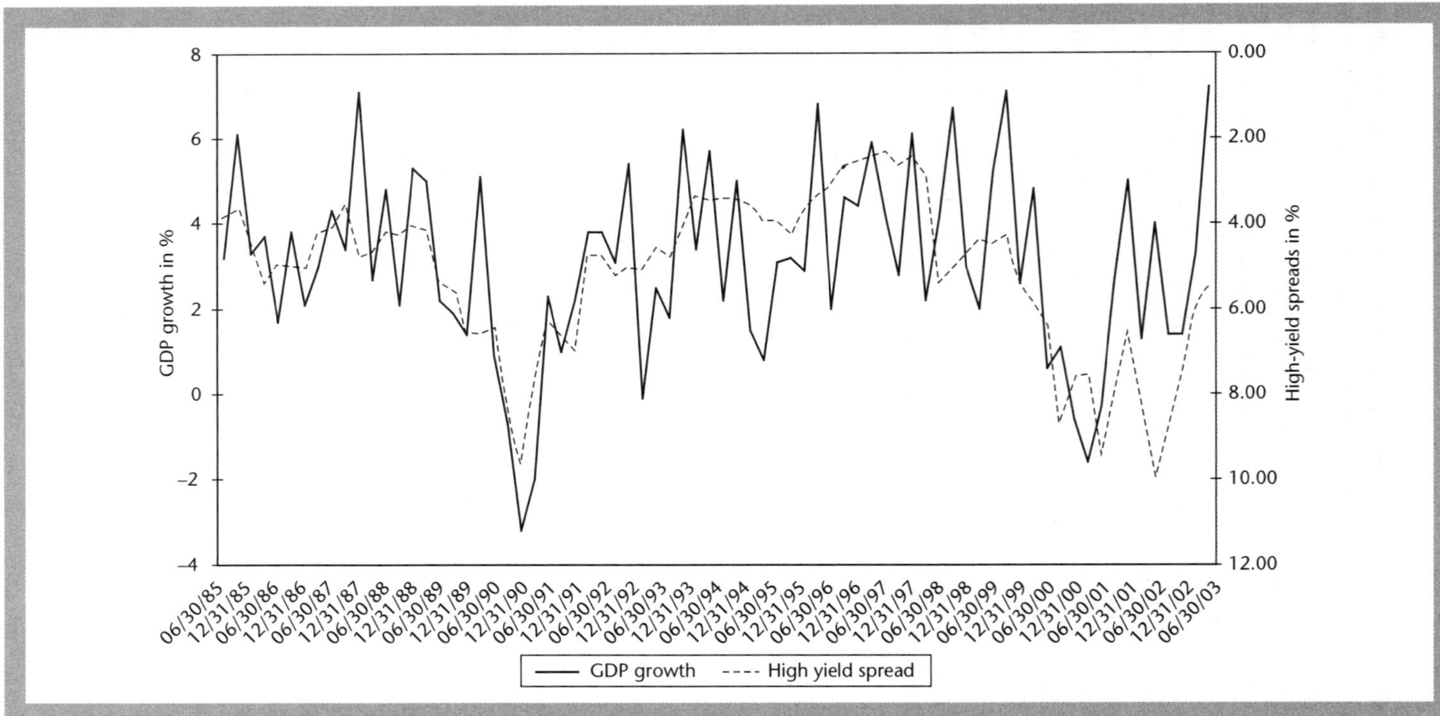

Figure 6.4 Relationship between GDP growth and US high-yield spreads Jun. 85–Sep. 2003

Source: Union Investment

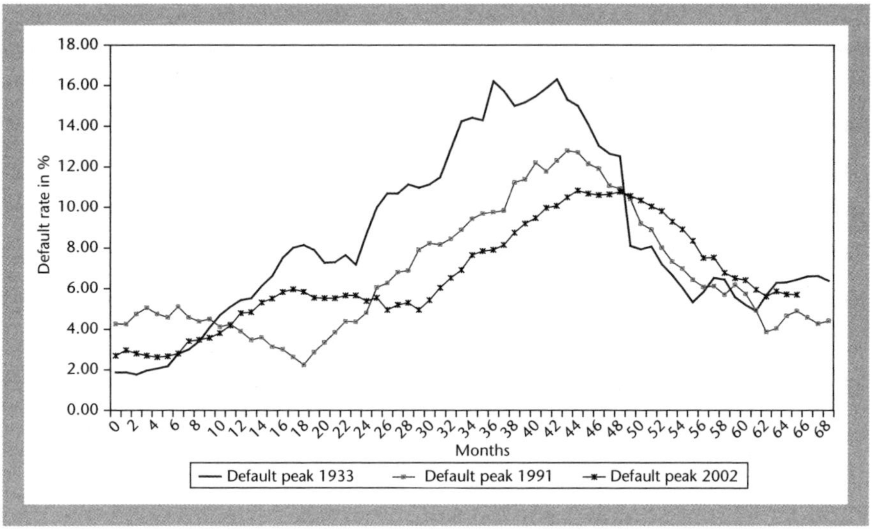

Figure 6.5 Default rate peaks between 1920 and 2003

Source: Moody's

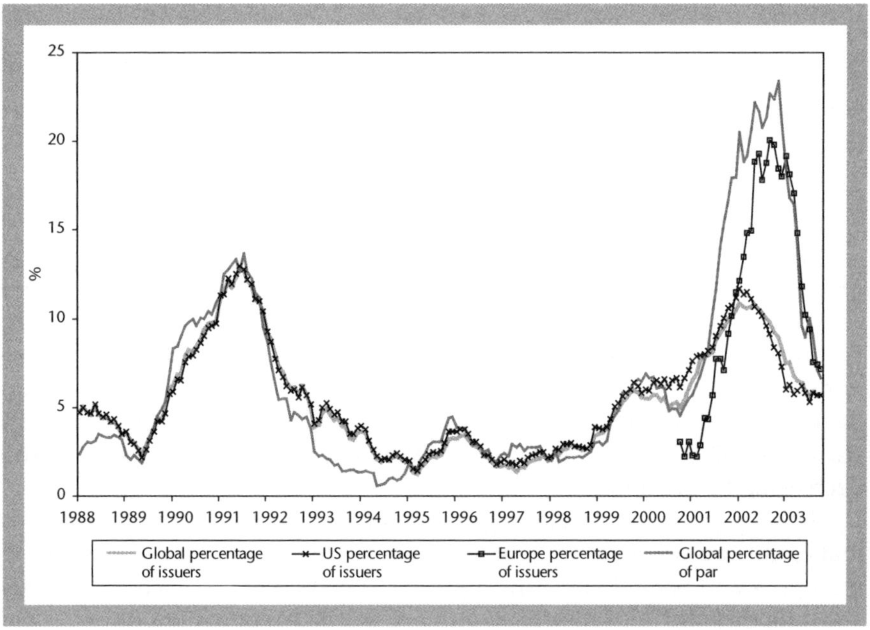

Figure 6.6 Default rates cycle by issuers and the amount outstanding 1988–2003

Source: Merrill Lynch

Table 6.7 Cumulative average default rates 1983–2002

	1	2	3	4	5	6	7	8	9	10
Aaa	0.00	0.00	0.00	0.05	0.17	0.24	0.31	0.40	0.40	0.40
Aa1	0.00	0.00	0.00	0.17	0.17	0.28	0.28	0.28	0.28	0.28
Aa2	0.00	0.00	0.05	0.15	0.33	0.40	0.48	0.57	0.68	0.81
Aa3	0.05	0.07	0.13	0.21	0.29	0.38	0.38	0.38	0.38	0.48
A1	0.00	0.02	0.24	0.37	0.47	0.57	0.62	0.72	0.78	0.93
A2	0.03	0.09	0.24	0.48	0.68	0.89	1.04	1.41	1.73	1.86
A3	0.04	0.21	0.34	0.47	0.62	0.84	1.15	1.34	1.57	1.75
Baa1	0.21	0.60	1.02	1.40	1.80	2.10	2.39	2.56	2.77	2.90
Baa2	0.15	0.46	0.84	1.56	2.24	2.89	3.47	3.99	4.61	5.50
Baa3	0.50	1.27	2.05	3.15	4.23	5.40	6.52	7.55	8.25	8.97
Ba1	0.70	2.11	3.76	5.82	7.61	9.64	10.93	12.23	13.01	13.96
Ba2	0.65	2.34	4.72	7.30	9.42	11.01	13.00	14.44	15.61	15.92
Ba3	2.38	6.60	11.49	16.22	20.70	24.98	28.59	32.32	36.05	39.29
B1	3.33	9.73	16.14	22.05	27.56	32.77	38.42	42.50	46.26	49.97
B2	7.14	15.99	23.43	29.57	34.49	37.94	40.40	42.57	44.96	47.37
B3	11.97	21.97	30.41	37.92	44.40	49.26	53.64	58.21	61.39	62.60
Caa–C	23.65	36.95	47.47	55.61	60.99	66.16	69.72	74.94	78.07	81.73
Investment grade	0.09	0.26	0.48	0.77	1.05	1.31	1.55	1.79	2.00	2.21
High Yield	5.48	11.25	16.59	21.34	25.38	28.90	32.03	34.77	37.08	38.99
All corporates	1.86	3.80	5.57	7.12	8.37	9.42	10.30	11.06	11.68	12.20

Source: Moody's

that the relationship between default rates and the spread level in the corporate bond market is a very complex one and that a good performance in the corporate bond market (tightening of credit spreads) can be consistent with increasing default rates at times where the market anticipates future decreasing default rates.

The change in default rates lags the change in credit spreads. This means that credit spreads begin to tighten some time before the default rates reach their peak and begin to fall. The highest correlation between credit spreads and Moody's default rate exists with a lag of 2–4 months (Figure 6.7). For the period Mar. 1985–Nov. 2003 it was 85 percent. A high correlation of 87 percent between the default rate and high-yield spreads could be observed for the period Dec. 96–Oct. 03.

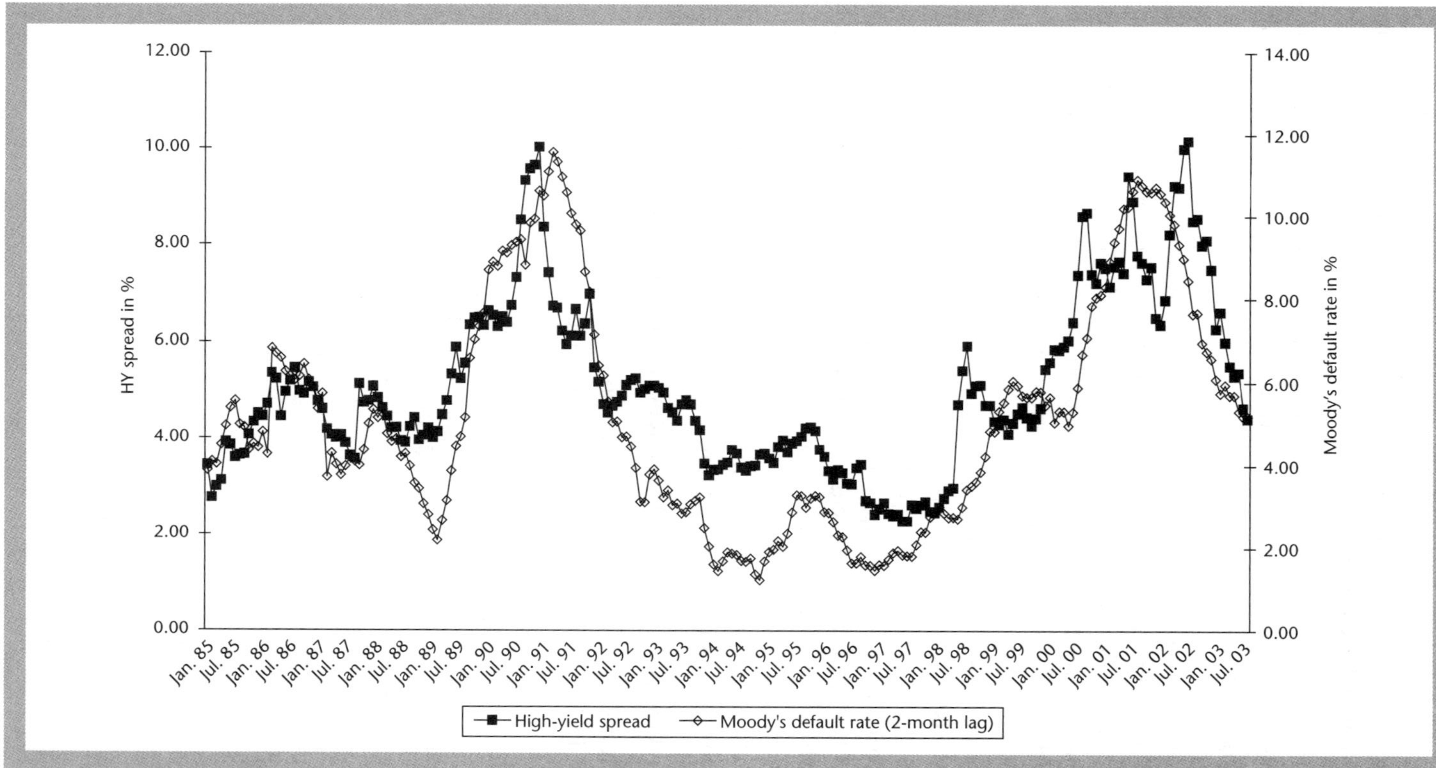

Figure 6.7 Correlation between high-yield spreads and Moody's default rate Jan. 1985–Jan. 2004
Source: Union Investment

Two arguments can explain this time lag:

- The decrease of short-term interest rates has a lagged effect on economic growth, which determines the trend in default rates.
- In a low interest rate environment the demand for lower rated credit is spurred. The companies benefit from this situation through better refinancing conditions.

The recovery rate is another important figure when evaluating corporate bonds. This is the amount that the bondholders will get after a company defaults and all debt obligations are restructured. Depending on the ranking in the capital structure (senior secured, senior unsecured, junior) and the industry and economic cycle, the recovery rate can vary substantially as shown in Table 6.8.

Recovery rates and default rates tend to be inversely correlated. Moody's finds a statistically significant relationship for high-yield default rates and recovery rates between 1983 and 2002. About 56 percent (R^2) of the variance in recovery rates can be explained by default rates. If two outliers are removed the R^2 statistics increases to 88 percent. This finding is consistent with the hypothesis that a higher volume of distressed bonds leads to lower recovery rates and vice versa.

The actual Credit Loss Rate is important for a high-yield bond portfolio. We can compute this figure as follows:

Credit Loss Rate = (Default Frequency) $*$ (1 − Recovery Rate)

The credit loss is the loss in total return of a fixed income portfolio due to defaults. In Figure 6.8 Moody's finds the following average annual credit

Table 6.8 Recovery rates by security and priority in Europe and the United States (in percent) (1982–2002)

Priority in capital structure	Europe	US
Secured bank loans	47.60	61.70
Senior secured	48.30	55.20
Senior unsecured	18.20	41.10
Senior subordinated	24.30	31.90
Subordinated	7.80	31.00
Junior subordinated	NA	23.60
All bonds	20.30	38.00

Source: Moody's

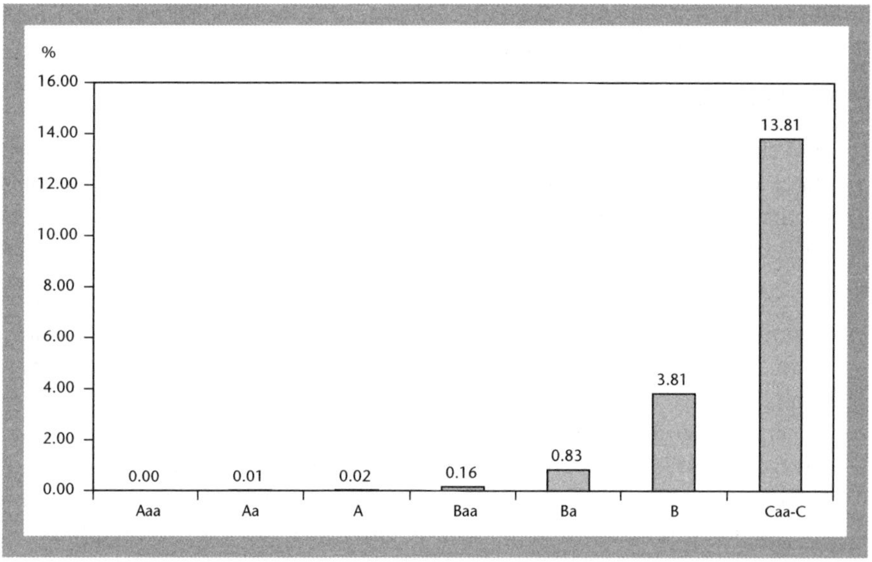

Figure 6.8 Average 1-year credit loss rates 1982–2002 (in percent)
Source: Moody's

losses for portfolios constructed primarily on the basis of Moody's ratings for the 1982–2002 period.

The level of default rates is a good indicator for the state of the credit market. The default risk premium should rise or fall in accordance with the prevailing probability of default. More importantly, the expected default rates set the tone for the future development of the credit market. The expectations about future default rates depend on several factors:

- GDP growth, because slower economic growth is accompanied by lower corporate earnings expectations and hence less companies will generate necessary cash flows to serve their debt obligations. Default rates move inversely with economic strength. Periods of high GDP growth go along with declining default rates.
- The distribution of all outstanding issues on the rating spectrum. The default probability increases with proportionally more lower rated (B– and worse) issues than better rated issues in the corporate bond market.
- Distressed debt totals.
- Financing alternatives during an economic downturn can have severe implications on the credit market. Deteriorating credit statistics in the credit market will force the banks to tighten their lending policies (more security + higher risk premiums) resulting in less available liquidity for the corporate sector. The lower rated companies (e.g. B- and C-rated) are

the first to be impacted. Lending policies of commercial banks can be an indicator for future default rates in the corporate sector.

- Fed Fund Policy.
- *Direction of equity markets*. The current state of the equity market has an effect on default rates because it determines asset values, investor's sentiment towards risky assets and the accessibility of capital markets for companies.
- *Age effect of bonds*. The likelihood of payment default by a bond issuer can change with decreasing time to maturity. At the time of issuance, the new issuer has abundant cash and payment default is easily avoided. In addition it is quite common to put some restricted cash from the issuance into an account to cover the first 3–4 coupon payments. Over time the "hazard rate" grows as cash reserves gained through the bond issue are used. The critical period is reached when the success of the firm is least certain and the hazard rate is at a maximum. However, after corporate plans are successfully implemented and sufficient profit has been generated to offset debt, the critical phase is past and the likelihood of payment default declines rapidly. Several empirical studies show that the critical time after first issues is approximately 3 years after issuance for B-rated bonds and climbs to approximately 4 years for BB-rated bonds. Table 6.9 shows that the amount of defaults drops significantly after the critical period of the first 3–4 years is survived by the issuer.
- *Quality of new issue volume*. An important measure for the quality of the high-yield market is the percentage amount of new issuance being used to refinance debt. During periods of balance sheet repair (1990–93 and 2001–03) the percentage of total new issue volume will reach high levels as shown in Figure 6.9.

The refinancing sensitivity increases with a decreasing credit quality. This means that weak B- and C-rated companies are the most refinancing sensitive. There is a close relationship between the ratings cycle and the Fed fund cycle. A tight Fed policy goes hand in hand with a lower amount outstanding of CCC paper. If the Fed switches to an easing mode the proportion of CCC-rated bonds will increase in the credit market. A Fed tightening policy goes along with credit rating upgrades whereas an easing policy cycle is usually associated with credit rating downgrades. This is because the effects of the Fed policy will have an impact on the credit markets with a time lag of several months.

A steepening of the treasury curve – driven by declining short-term rates will provide the credit market with liquidity, which in turn helps to lower default rates. In this scenario, companies will have easier access to liquidity (e.g. bank loans, debt and equity markets).

Table 6.9 Distribution of years to default from original issue date 1989–Sep. 2003

Years to default	1989	1990	1991	1992	1993/ 1994	1995	1996	1997	1998	1999	2000	2001	2002	2003	1989–2003
1	4	3	0	0	3	1	2	5	2	32	19	40	29	16	159
2	12	25	18	0	6	9	3	4	5	37	51	69	51	30	322
3	15	23	26	7	5	7	3	4	10	15	56	87	61	25	341
4	13	18	29	10	2	3	8	9	3	14	14	65	56	18	263
5	1	23	35	8	4	1	1	3	10	7	13	27	45	37	215
6	7	5	10	12	8	2	5	0	2	8	5	14	21	15	115
7	7	5	4	5	7	2	0	0	1	10	12	21	8	25	109
8	2	4	10	4	0	2	0	0	0	2	4	5	7	2	42
9	1	1	3	0	0	4	0	0	0	0	3	4	12	4	34
10	3	1	2	8	2	1	0	0	0	0	6	3	54	14	97
Total	65	108	137	54	37	32	24	25	33	125	183	335	344	186	1697

Source: Salomon Smith Barney

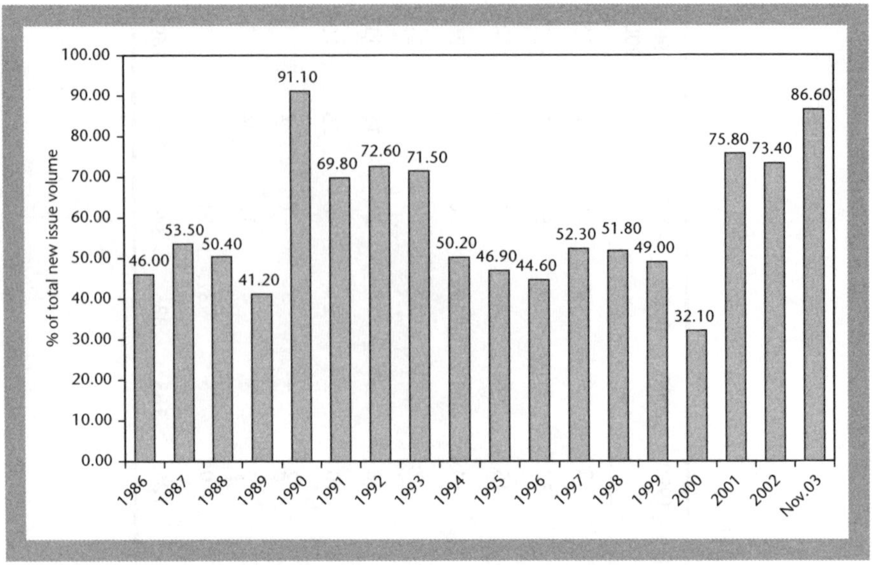

Figure 6.9 New issuance being used to refinance 1986–Nov. 2003 (in percent)

Source: J.P. Morgan

6.3.1.3 *Distress ratio*

The distress ratio is an indicator for the current state of the high-yield market. It can be defined as the percentage amount of all outstanding high-yield bonds trading at a spread of at least 1,000 bp over a comparable government bond (Figure 6.10). The lower the distress ratio the better the shape of the high-yield market.

There is a lag of around four months between the distress ratio and Moody's default rate observable for the US high-yield market (Figure 6.11). At a correlation of 0.89 we can conclude that the current levels of the distress ratio allow to make a reasonable forecast for future default rates. A falling distress ratio implies falling default rates in future.

6.3.1.4 *Capacity utilization/industrial production*

Capacity utilization (CAPU) emerges as an important factor for high-yield investments because it is a good indicator for the direction of high-yield spreads. The strongest correlation (−0.76) is found by lagging CAPU rates by about six months (Figure 6.12). Low CAPU rates are not sustainable in the long term. Companies have to adjust their business models in order to address the overcapacity. A strong correlation can be found between CAPU rates and Commercial and Industrial lending. The year-on-year change in

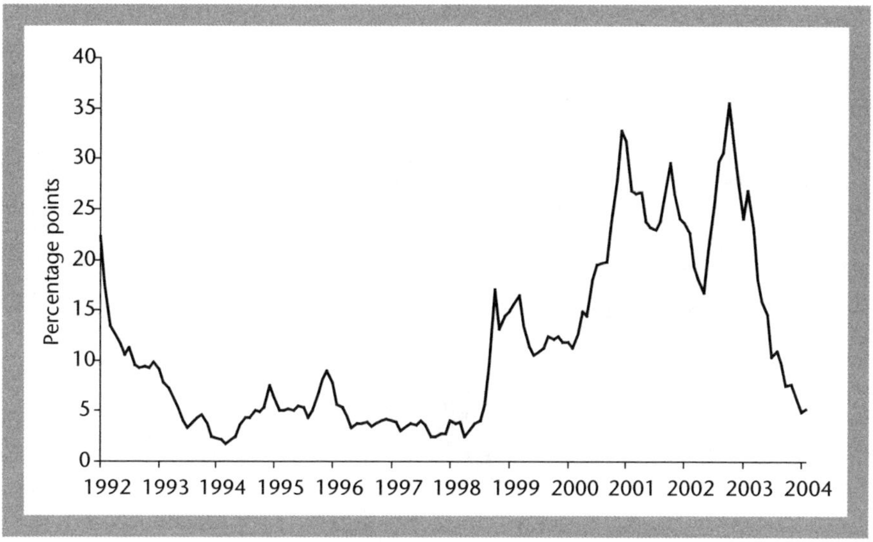

Figure 6.10 Distress ratio 1992–Feb. 2004

Source: Merrill Lynch

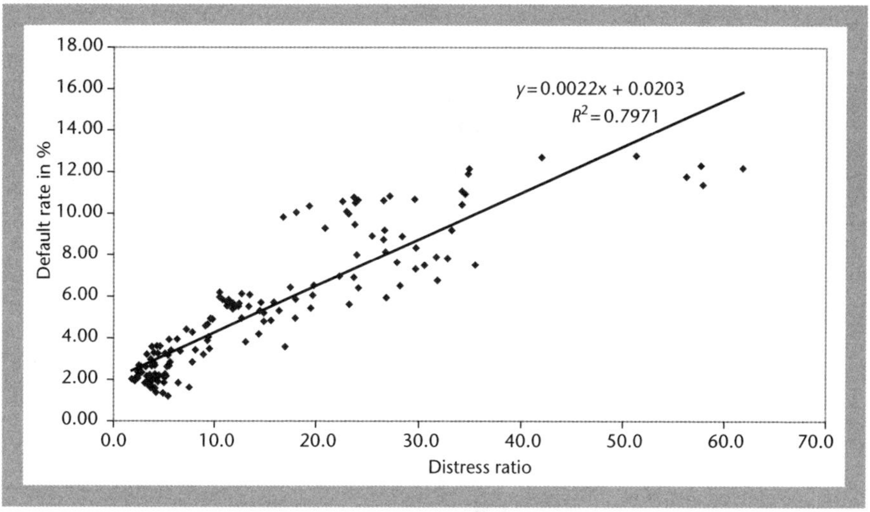

Figure 6.11 Moody's default rate and the distress ratio 1990–2003 (in percent)

Source: Union Investment

Commercial and Industrial lending will fall with falling CAPU rates and vice versa.

Sectors with high utilization rates will experience greater manufacturing demand and will probably benefit from a better pricing power. On the other hand, sectors with low CAPU rates are more likely to have little or no

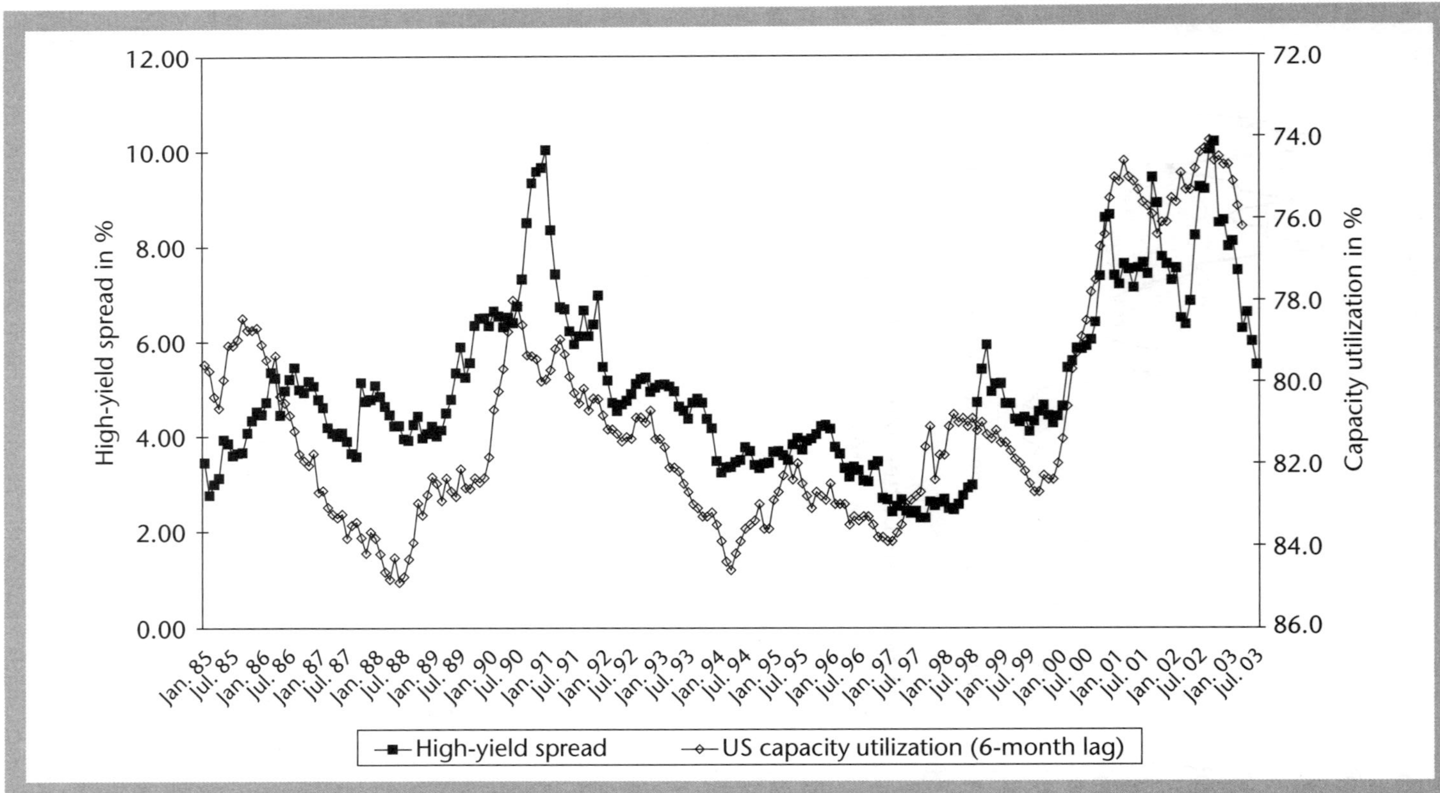

Figure 6.12 Correlation between US capacity utilization and high-yield spreads Jan. 1985–Jan. 2004

Source: Union Investment

pricing power and are forced to shrink the available capacity. This implies that sectors with improved CAPU rates on a year-on-year basis should experience tighter spreads than sectors with worsening CAPU rates where spreads should tend to widen.

Industrial production (IP) is another lagging indicator. A robust relationship between high-yield spreads and industrial production is found at −0.76 with a 5–6 month lag. This means that a spread tightening in the high-yield market will induce an improvement in industrial production in a couple of months and give high-yield investors some comfort that spreads will be supported further in the future by better macroeconomic data like industrial production.

In Figure 6.13 industrial production is compared with default rates. A better IP is associated with increased profitability and cash flow situation of companies. This implies a better access to the capital markets and therefore lowers liquidity risk. As a result default rates will fall when IP rises and this translates directly into tighter spreads.

A robust negative correlation of around −0.75 exists between Moody's trailing 12-month issuer-based default rate and the US year-over-year production for the period 1988–2003.

6.3.1.5 ISM Index

The level of the ISM Index is another indicator for high-yield spreads. A reading above 50 signals economic expansion and a weak economic activity is associated with values below 50. A lower ISM Index is accompanied by wider credit spreads and vice versa. This relationship holds well since 1985 (Figure 6.14). There is almost no time lag between the two series with a correlation of −0.54. This correlation improves marginally when the ISM Index is lagged by 1 month.

6.3.1.6 Commercial and industrial lending

Easier lending standards signal lower default rates in future. Banks will usually ease their lending standards only when an upturn in the economy is in sight and companies have greater prospects for profits. During an economic slowdown the net percentage of banks tightening their standards will rise. This could be observed in 1990/91, and then during 1998 with the Asian crisis and LTCM. The last period of tight lending standards was seen between August 2000 and November 2001 when the US economy went through a recession. Since then, with improving macroeconomic data, banks started to ease their lending standards and companies' demand for loans started to increase at the same time (Figure 6.15). A high correlation of

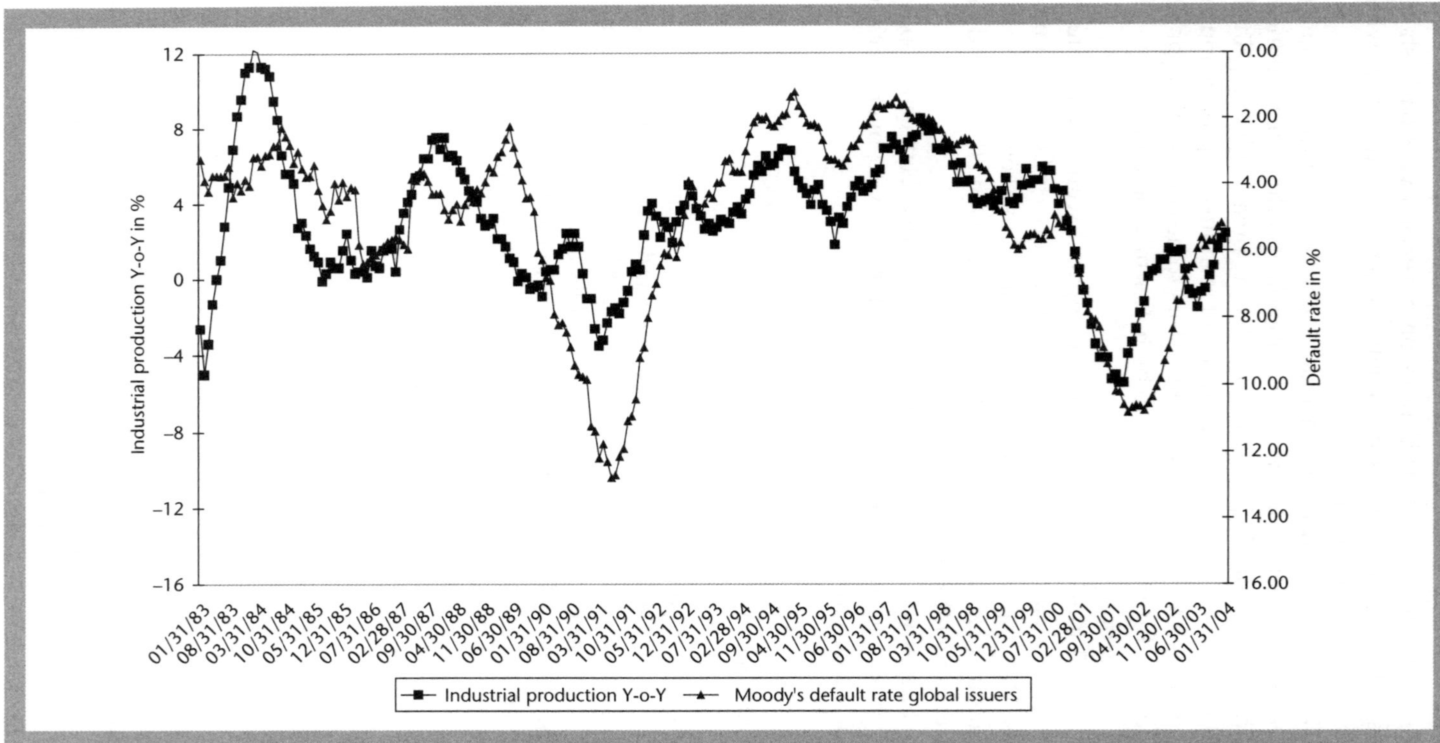

Figure 6.13 Relationship between IP and default rates 1983–2004

Source: Union Investment

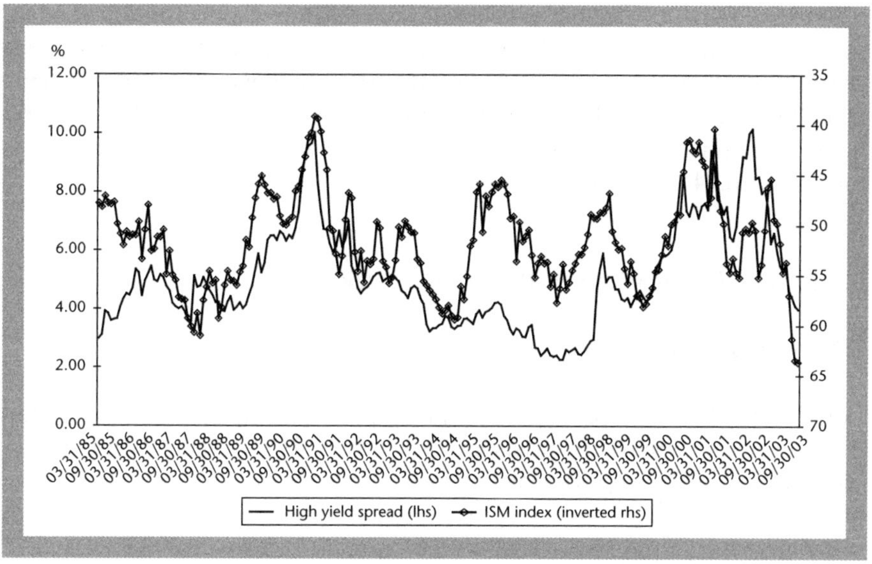

Figure 6.14 Relationship between high-yield spreads and ISM index 1985–2003

Source: Union Investment

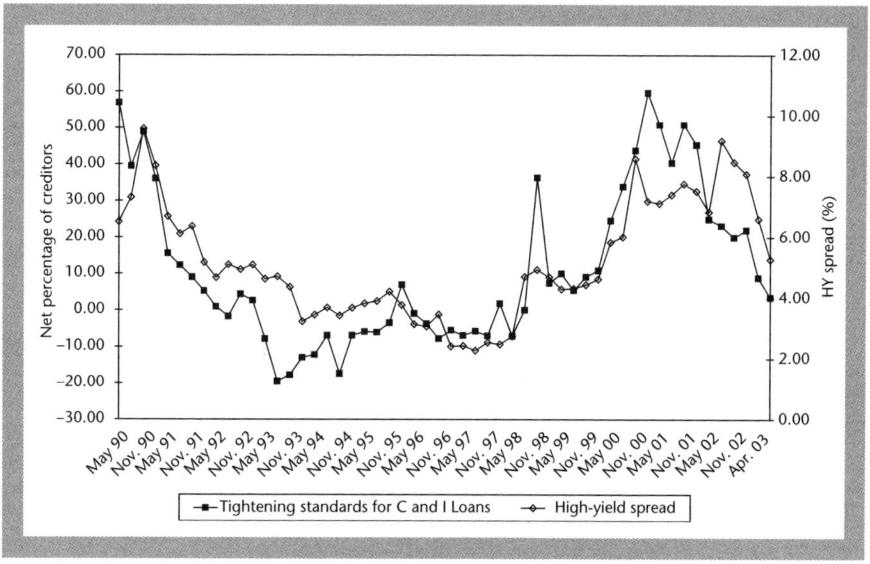

Figure 6.15 Correlation between high-yield spreads and the tightening standards for commercial and industrial loans 1990–2003

Source: Merrill Lynch

0.79 exists between the net percentage of creditors reporting tighter standards for Commercial and Industrial loans and high-yield spreads for the period May 1990–August 2003. For the period November 1991–August 2003 the correlation between high-yield spreads and the reported demand for Commercial and Industrial loans by large and medium-sized companies is at −0.84 (Figure 6.16).

6.3.2 The implications of the equity market

6.3.2.1 High yield and equity market

Lower rated bonds or bonds with higher spreads behave more like equities in falling equity markets (crisis scenario). For high-yielding bonds (high-yield debt), the strike price (the value of indebtedness) is normally closer to at-the-money than in the case of investment grade bonds.

In Figure 6.17 the high-yield market spread is correlated with the S&P 500 as a proxy for the equity market. A significant correlation between the S&P 500 and high yield market spreads was measured between March 2000 and December 2003. Prior to this period the relationship was not very significant. Equity markets experienced a boom phase during the late 1990s but credit fundamentals played a greater role for the performance of high yield. With the sell-off in the equity markets the correlation with high yield rose significantly to an average of over −0.80 until December 2003. For the

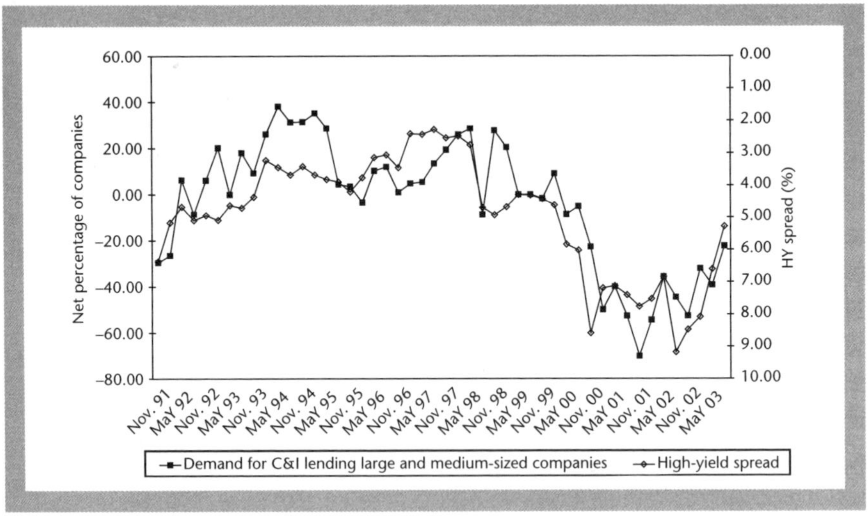

Figure 6.16 Relationship between high-yield spreads and the demand for Commercial and Industrial Loans 1991–2003

Source: Merrill Lynch

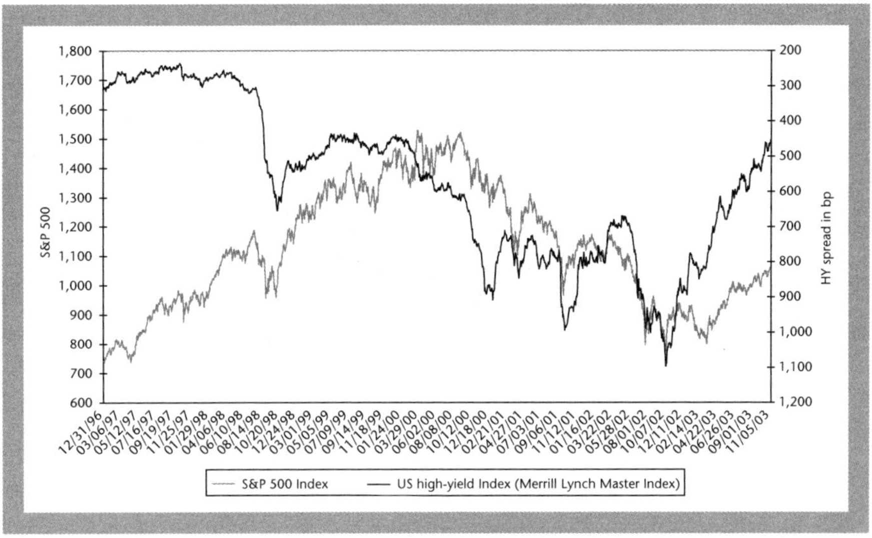

Figure 6.17 Relationship between equity (here: S&P 500) and high-yield markets Dec. 96–Nov. 2003

Source: Union Investment

period Jan. 2002–Oct. 2002 the correlation was strongest with −0.90 and stayed at respectable −0.82 between Oct. 2002 and Nov. 2003.

6.3.2.2 High yield and implied equity market volatility

The VIX Index reflects the equity and options markets' expectation of earnings volatility. Companies with deteriorating credit statistics are more likely to experience high equity price volatility than companies with a stable credit trend. As financial profiles of companies improve and the uncertainty about their future earnings declines the hedging costs to invest in those companies will come down and the VIX Index will decline.

High-yield market sensitivity to changes in VIX varies over time and it does not vary simply by ratings. The correlation will always increase when an increased leverage in the whole credit market can be observed. This is usually the case when CCC-rated companies have a high share of the credit market. So it can be stated that the CCC portion of the market drives the sensitivity between high yield and the VIX Index. A decline in implied equity market volatility results in lower risk premiums in the high-yield market.

The correlation between the VIX Index and high-yield spreads was only moderate at 0.45 during the period Dec. 1996–Nov. 2003. A high correlation of 0.83 can be measured for the period Aug. 2000–Nov. 2003 (Figure 6.18).

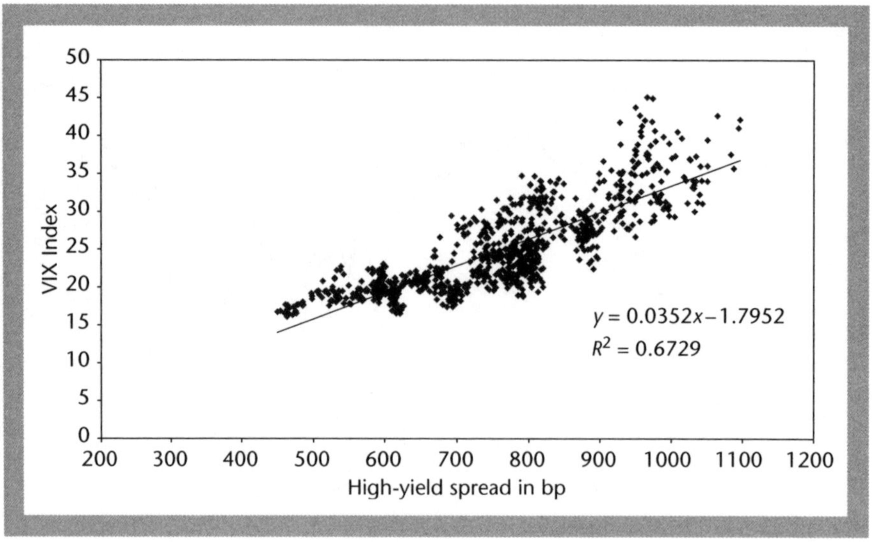

Figure 6.18 Correlation between high-yield spreads and equity market volatility Jan. 2000–Dec. 2003

Source: Union Investment

6.3.3 Mutual fund flows

Fund flows measure the amount of money that comes into or leaves the open-ended mutual funds during a given period. Coupon payments are not included. The flows of pension funds, hedge funds and insurance companies are not tracked in this number. Nevertheless, there is a high correlation between high-yield market total returns and mutual fund flows. The reason is that mutual funds account for a big part of secondary trading.

During a period of high market uncertainty and increasing negative event risks the correlation with equity markets tends to rise. Fund flows in the high-yield market are directly related to the developments in the equity market (Figure 6.19).

Fund Flows are a function of:

- Expected risk
- Interest rates
- Inflation
- Default rates
- Economic outlook
- Event risk

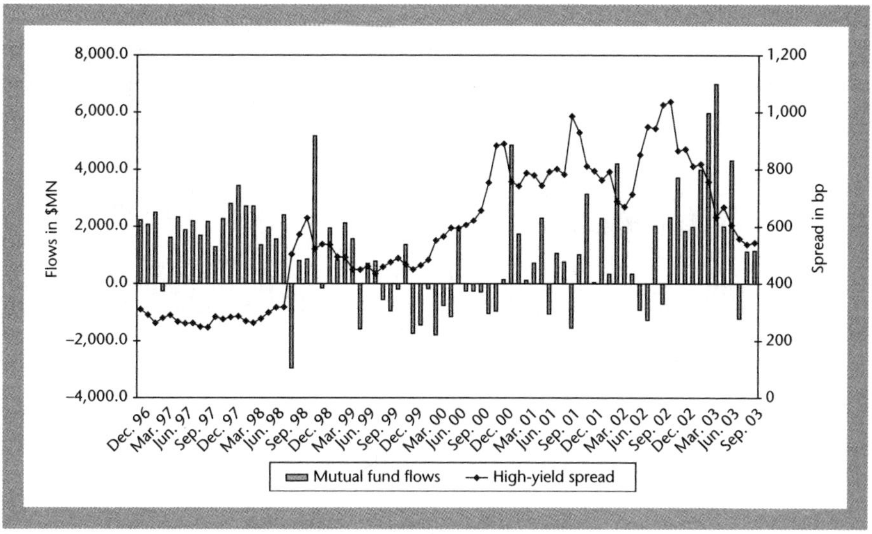

Figure 6.19 Relationship between mutual fund flows and high-yield spreads

Source: Merrill Lynch

- Expected excess return over government bonds and equities
- Opportunity costs (risk-adjusted returns of other asset classes).

The sensitivity of high-yield total returns to fund flows is higher when the average market price is low. It decreases with an increasing market price (e.g. above par markets). The correlation between mutual fund flows and the total return in the high-yield market for the period Oct. 1996–Dec. 2003 was quite high at 0.78 (Figure 6.20).

There is another important ratio to look at in connection with the fund flows. The Liquidity ratio of mutual funds is computed as follows:

$$\text{Liquidity ratio} = (\text{Government Securities} + \text{Municipal Bonds} + \text{Cash} + \text{Receivables} - \text{Liabilities}) / \text{Total Assets}$$

This ratio fluctuates over time and will be the highest when default rates are high because fund managers are reluctant to hold low quality names and cannot add to their high quality paper at the same time because they are overweight already (Figure 6.21).

6.3.4 Credit fundamentals

Aggregate financial ratios give a reliable picture of the state of the high-yield market and should not be neglected irrespective of technical factors.

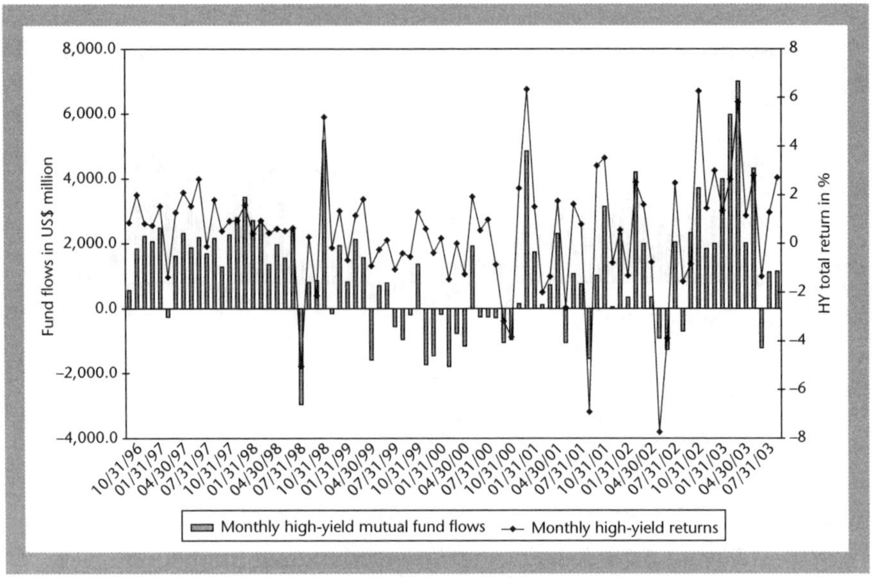

Figure 6.20 Relationship between mutual fund flows and high-yield total returns
Source: Deutsche Bank

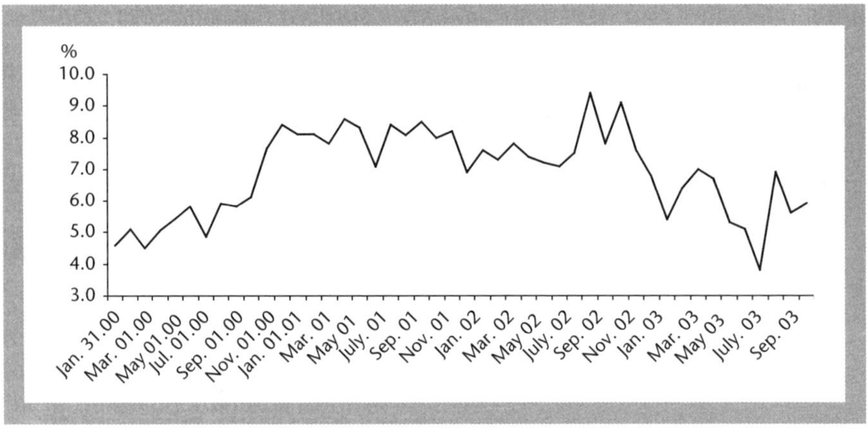

Figure 6.21 High-yield mutual fund liquidity ratio Jan. 2000–Oct. 2003
Source: Deutsche Bank and Investment Company Institute

Technical factors driving the high-yield market can change fairly quickly but credit status will persist as hard evidence and change only slowly over time. The most important fundamental measures are:

- Free cash flow generation
- Refinancing calendar

- Access to capital markets (bank lending standards)
- Reported earnings and earnings outlook
- Equity performance
- Growth prospects
- CAPEX needs
- Leverage trend
- Coverage trend.

Leverage and coverage ratios are particularly important for the analysis of high-yield issuers. We find significant correlations between the spread levels of selected high-yield issuers and their coverage ratios (Figure 6.22) and their leverage ratios (Figures 6.23 and 6.24).

6.3.5 Interest rate environment and high yield

A correlation between total returns of high yield and treasury bonds shows that interest rate risk can certainly not be neglected by high-yield investors (Figure 6.25). The mid-1990s serve as a good example. High yield and

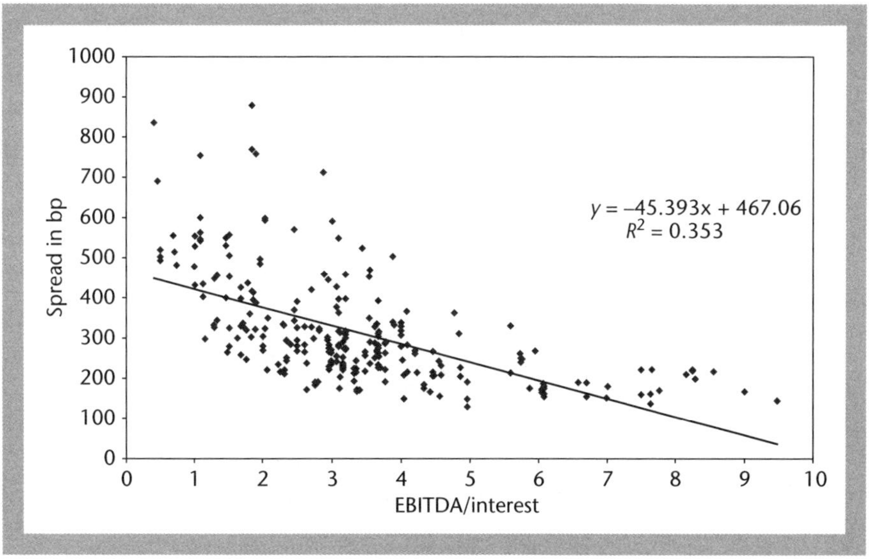

Figure 6.22 Coverage (EBITDA/Interest) and spread levels for selected high-yield companies (Merrill Lynch BBs and Bs in Euro and US$, Nov. 2003)

Source: Union Investment and Bloomberg

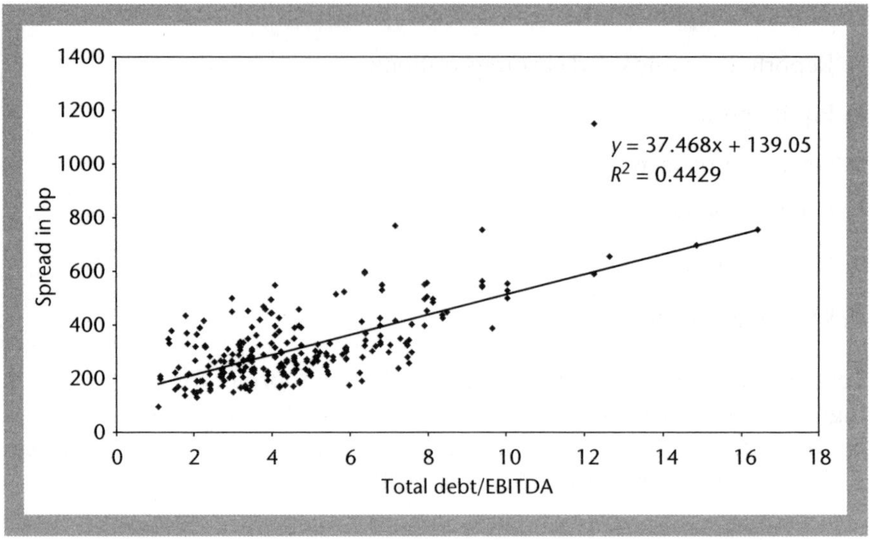

Figure 6.23 Leverage (Total Debt/EBITDA) and spread levels for selected high-yield companies (Merrill Lynch BBs and Bs in Euro and US$, Nov. 2003)

Source: Union Investment and Bloomberg

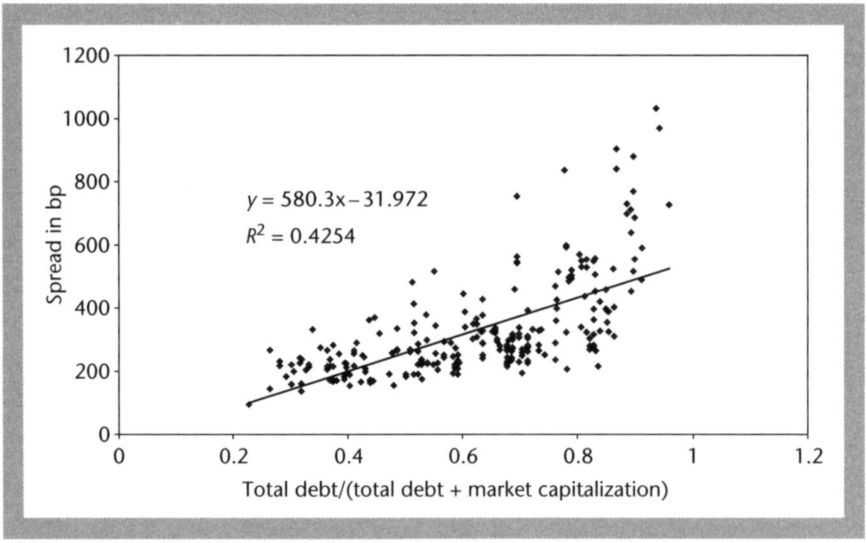

Figure 6.24 Leverage (Total Debt/(Total Debt + MarketCap) and spread levels for selected high-yield companies (Merrill Lynch BBs and Bs in Euro and US$, Nov. 2003)

Source: Union Investment and Bloomberg

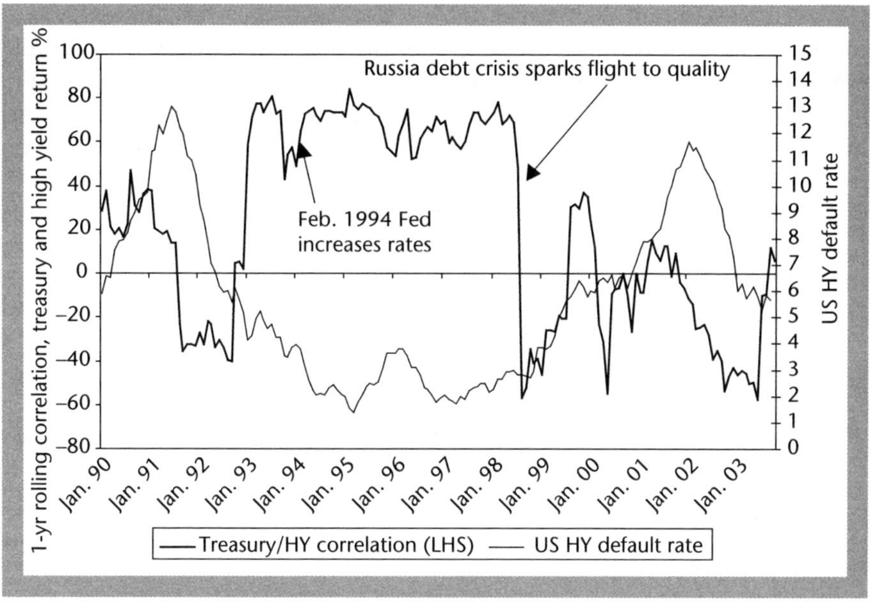

Figure 6.25 Correlation between treasury returns and high-yield market returns 1990–2003

Source: Bank of America

treasury returns had a quite high correlation in an environment of low default rates and tight credit spreads. In 2003 an increased correlation could be observed again when spreads were approaching historical lows and default rates were falling.

High-yield sensitivity to interest rates is a function of credit risk. This means that the high-yield upper tier (BB+/BB) segment's correlation to 10-year treasuries is higher than for lower tier credit (B− and below).

Duration management in high-yield portfolios will have a positive performance contribution. Particularly crossover credits and BB's total returns will be also determined by the movements of interest rates.

During times of low default rates, historically tight spreads and low interest rates it is worthwhile to analyze the duration contribution of various sectors to the high-yield index. In a scenario of rising interest rates, sectors with tight spreads and a high average duration should be watched closely due to a high underperformance potential.

6.4 CROSSOVER CREDITS/FALLEN ANGELS

The following paragraphs are devoted to crossover credits/Fallen Angels because of their importance for the high-yield market.

Fallen Angels are companies which have lost their investment grade rating in the past due to a downgrade into high yield. Crossover credits have an investment grade rating from at least one rating agency but tend to trade on high-yield levels. Their significant spread volatility bears investment opportunities as well as risks. Fallen Angels have a large impact on the high-yield market because of the high nominal volume of bonds.

Fallen Angels and crossover credits are often targeted by alternative investor groups like hedge funds and risk arbitrageurs who speculate on the mispricing between the various financing instruments of a company.

Characteristics of Fallen Angels:

- High leverage in respect to operating cash flows
- Weak industry trends lead to low and unpredictable operating cash flows
- A further deterioration of the operating performance is not sustainable with the financial profile
- Loss of market share
- Not enough liquidity to support the ongoing business
- Decreasing asset quality
- Management is unable to identify profitable business units
- Weak and complex debt structure
- Unfavorable regulatory environment and lack of support by the government (mainly for European companies)

A downgrade into high yield may have the following effects:

- Forced selling activities from investment grade accounts
- Direct effect on the financial flexibility of a company (CP program, bank covenants triggered), may result in "financial distress" in a worst-case scenario

The spread behavior prior and after a downgrade into high yield or an upgrade into investment grade is of particular interest. Figure 6.26 shows the average spread for 15 companies' 200 trading days before and after a downgrade into high yield. Day "0" is set as the day where the first downgrade from investment grade into high yield occurred either by Moody's or S&P. The bonds we chose for this analysis were downgraded between 2002 and 2003 and are presented in Table 6.10.

It is noteworthy that a significant deterioration in spreads occurs long before the actual rating action takes place (Figure 6.26). At the day "0"

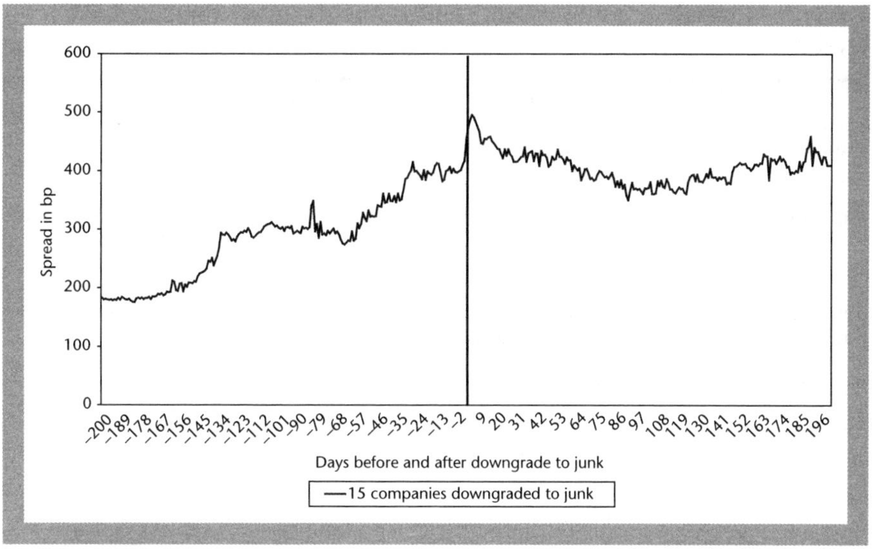

Figure 6.26 Average spread for selected companies 200 days before and after being downgraded to high yield by either Moody's or S&P during 2002–2003, The vertical line marks day "0"

Source: Union Investment

Table 6.10 15 bonds from companies which were downgraded from investment grade into high yield by either Moody's or S&P during 2002–2003

EMI 8.25% 05/20/08	TYCO 6.75% 02/15/11	Ericsson 6.5% 05/20/09
British Airways 7.25% 08/23/16	Invensys 5.5% 04/01/05	Arvin Meritor 8.75% 03/11/12
Fiat 6.75% 05/25/11	Tenet Healthcare 6.5% 06/11/12	Bowater 7.95% 11/15/11
Thyssen Krupp 7% 03/19/09	Park Place Entertainment 8.875% 09/15/08	Teco Energy 6.125% 05/01/07
El Paso 7% 05/15/11	RJ Reynolds 7.25% 06/01/12	Heidelberger Zement 4.75% 04/09/09

We have excluded bonds of issuers who defaulted shortly after being downgraded into high yield

Source: Union Investment

obviously in most cases further spread widening/price fall takes place but this can be explained by technical factors. Forced sellers will emerge and in an illiquid market bid-offer spreads can be as wide as 3–4 price points and prices can deteriorate quickly if no buyers arise.

Almost all bonds of companies being upgraded into investment grade show a significant spread tightening long before the actual rating action.

Table 6.11 Analysis approach for "Fallen Angels" and other troubled credits

	Stressed	**Distressed**
Liquidity	Adequate, Bank lines are in place	Immediate liquidity crisis, no access to capital markets
Capital structure	High leverage, is under control	Unmanageable capital structure with a heavy dependence on banks
Business fundamentals	Cyclical downswing, a recovery can be expected	Heavy downturn with no recovery in sight
Business model	Sound	Questionable
Management	Communicates with high-yield investors	Miscommunication, poor disclosure
Valuation method	Compared with high-yield credits	Asset break-up value

Source: Citigroup

Of course at the time of the upgrade technical factors (new previously restricted buyers emerge) tighten the spreads further.

Table 6.11 is an effort to categorize the evaluation of Fallen Angels. Only the most important points are mentioned. In a first step, the analyst has to decide whether the company falls into the category stressed or distressed. The following points should help in the decision-making process. A distressed credit is very likely to default, and break-up value has to be determined. A stressed credit has a realistic chance for a turnaround and one has to estimate how likely this case is.

Companies that have a successful turnaround will show most of the following characteristics:

- Successful deleveraging and improvement of the liquidity situation is realistic.
- Asset Sales can be done in an adequate time and at acceptable levels.
- Debt maturity profile is improved by refinancing (new bank lines and bond issues).
- Additional rights issue is feasible.
- Capital structure option is exercised in favor of bondholders and the equity market rewards these steps as well.
- Corporate actions (reduction of CAPEX, postponement or cancellation of acquisitions, cost cutting, solid management of working capital).
- Change of management.

At this point it has to be noted that the asymmetric risk inherent in high-yield bonds decreases with increasing distressed levels. In fact, distressed debt is priced based on the recovery value. If an issuer is able to regain financial health the returns can be enormous.

6.5 RISK MANAGEMENT IN HIGH YIELD

The developments in credit markets since 2000 have shown that a disciplined approach to minimize risk is necessary (Figure 6.27). This includes the determination of stop-loss marks which have to be defined on a case-by-case basis. Important is the volatility of the particular bond and the risk profile of the portfolio. A portfolio with a high-yield benchmark will be able to take the highest volatility but a buy-and-hold strategy is also not compatible for such a portfolio if a specific bond has to suffer a huge price loss. The price mechanism of Fallen Angels and high-yield bonds requires disciplined stop loss marks. Fallen Angels tend to trade on very wide levels prior to a downgrade in high yield but a downgrade will usually induce another sell-off in the bonds so that a significant price fall will occur. Besides fundamental facts, technical factors play an important role and current risk appetite of investors determines basically a floor for the Fallen Angel. If new buyers arise upswings in price can be significant, supported through positive credit news.

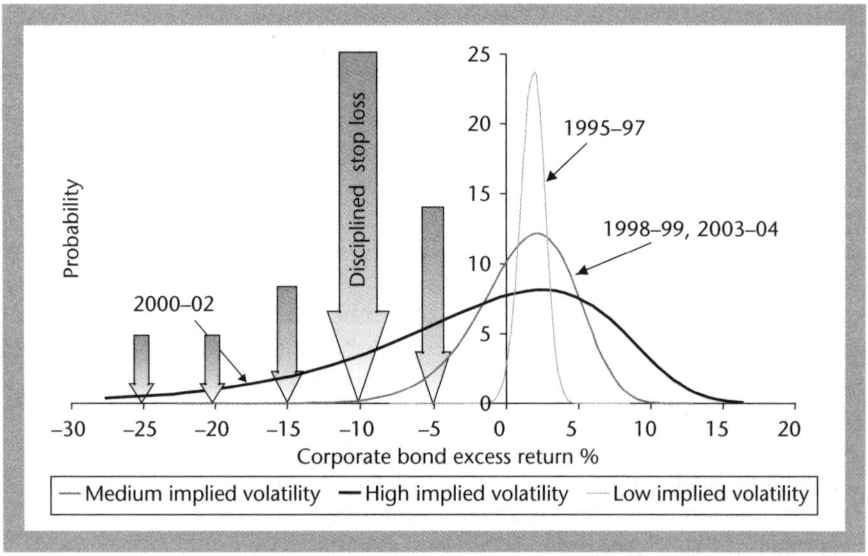

Figure 6.27 Disciplined stop loss marks for a high-yield portfolio, in percent

Source: CSFB and Union Investment

Table 6.12 Categories of troubled companies (December 2003)

	Categories of troubled companies			
	Accounting fraud		**Weak fundamentals**	**Litigation**
Liquidity (short term)	NO	YES	YES	YES
Liquidity (long term)	NO	Uncertain	Uncertain	Uncertain
	Enron	Tyco	Alcatel	ABB
Examples	WorldCom	Ahold	Ericsson	
	TXU Europe		Fiat	

Source: Union Investment

Table 6.12 categorizes troubled companies. A simple approach is to differentiate between short-term and long-term liquidity constraints and the reasons leading to the constraints. If deteriorating fundamentals are the driving force, an indepth credit analysis should specify the point in time when a company will run out of cash. The thing an investor has to decide is whether current trading levels compensate sufficiently for the uncertainty of improving fundamentals and hence the ability to preserve enough liquidity in the long term.

If litigation (e.g. asbestos, tobacco) forces a company to trade at distressed levels, usually short-term liquidity is in place so that the risk of an imminent default is low. If a company cannot resolve its litigation issues in the long term, bankruptcy is then a probable scenario.

Accounting fraud is accompanied by the most severe price movements. The analysis of sources and uses of cash will help to determine the recovery value. Of course, it is in such cases almost impossible to find a reliable fair value of the company's debt so that enormous price swings in the bond prices can be expected on a daily basis. Equity value will converge towards zero within a short period of time.

Figure 6.28 shows the bonds of Ericsson, Tyco and ABB. All three companies had credit-specific issues in the past and seemed to have overcome those at the time of writing (December, 2003). Their lowest prices were quoted almost at the same time (October, 2002) where risk tolerance reached the lowest level in a decade (measured by VIX). The important point to illustrate is that nonsystematic risks induced the first price falls in all three companies at different points in time. Idiosyncratic risks were responsible for the first massive downward price movement. In this situation, an assessment of the credit should not be based only on credit fundamentals but every credit portfolio manager has to evaluate what volatility his portfolio can sustain because the main task for a high-yield portfolio manager is to manage risk. Technical factors have to be considered because it is likely that market liquidity for a troubled bond will disappear quickly

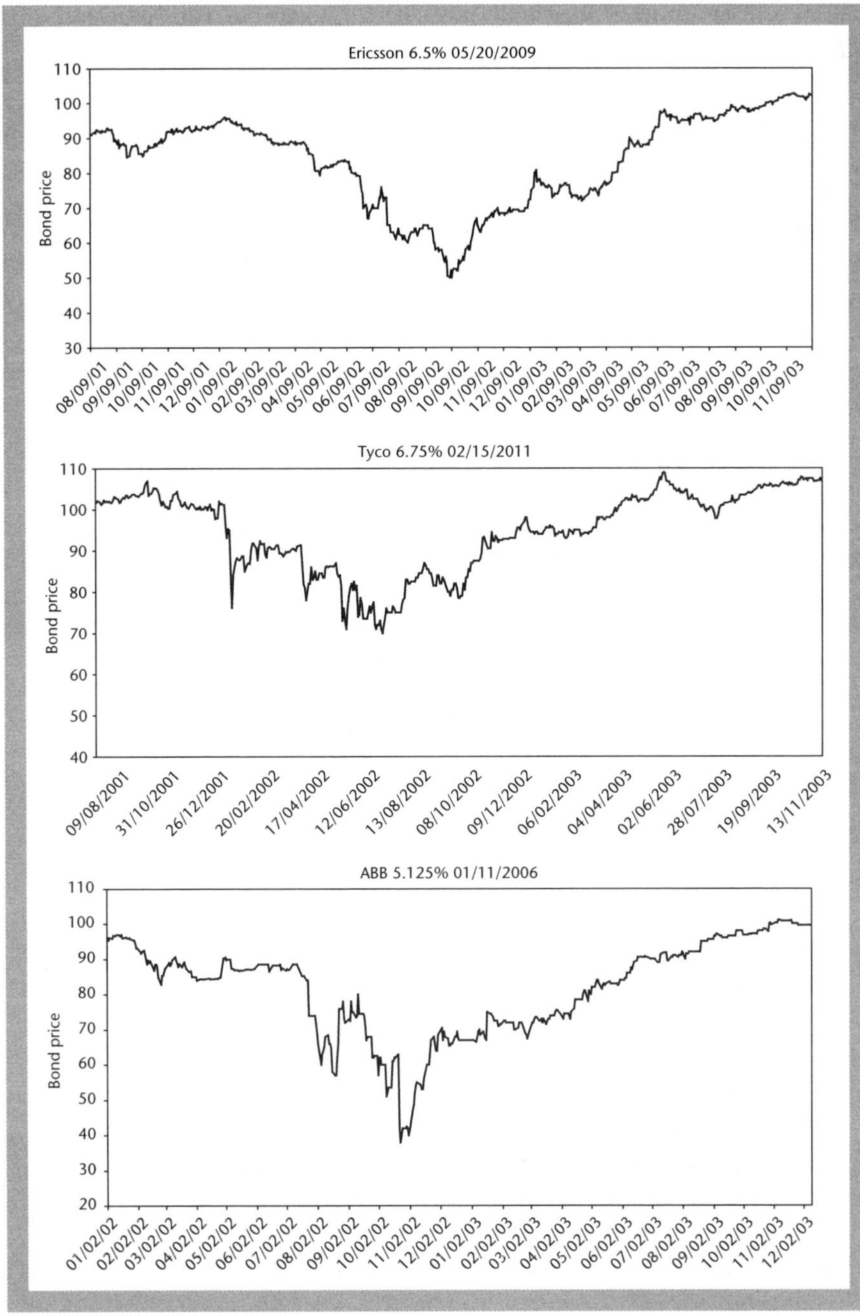

Figure 6.28 The evolution of bond prices for Ericsson, Tyco and ABB during phases of distress

Source: Union Investment and Bloomberg

which will result in a "free fall" in price. An example shall illustrate this effect further:

Benchmark weight of a bond: 0.5 percent
Weight of bond in portfolio: 1.0 percent
Bond price falls 10 price points (e.g. from 100 to 90)
Underperformance versus benchmark: $(10/100) \cdot (1.0 - 0.5 \text{ percent})$
$= 0.1 \cdot 50 \text{ bp}$
$= 5 \text{ bp}$

For an absolute return investor (no benchmark) the loss is computed as follows:

$(10/100) \cdot 1 \text{ percent} = 0.1 \cdot 100 \text{ bp} = 10 \text{ bp}$

According to the credit-spread term-structure model, highly leveraged firms or firms with fast deteriorating credit fundamentals will experience an inverted credit curve. The bonds begin to trade on a price basis. If default is a very likely scenario, bonds of the same seniority trade with the same price, irrespective of their maturity and coupon. This has the effect of elevating short-maturity spreads and inverting the credit curve. Depending on the investment objective the following investment strategy should be pursued:

1. Uncertainty about medium-term prospects prevails and a further deterioration is most likely: shorter duration, long-dated paper will underperform.
2. Uncertainty about medium-term outlook is present but the price move in the bonds seems to be overdone (e.g. due to technical factors). A turnaround appears to be a likely scenario: buy the cheapest bonds (long-dated paper). If the situation stabilizes then this strategy will result in the highest capital gains.
3. Same scenario like Scenario 1 but the uncertainty about the short-term outlook of the company increases. Default is a distinct possibility. In this case investors should sell their short-dated paper first. Those bonds have the highest price and will underperform as all maturities will converge towards the estimated recovery value (prices of short-dated paper will collapse).

Parmalat is an example where fraud and the apparent short-term illiquidity resulted in a severe sell-off in the bonds across all maturities. They lost within several days almost 80 percent of their value (Figure 6.29).

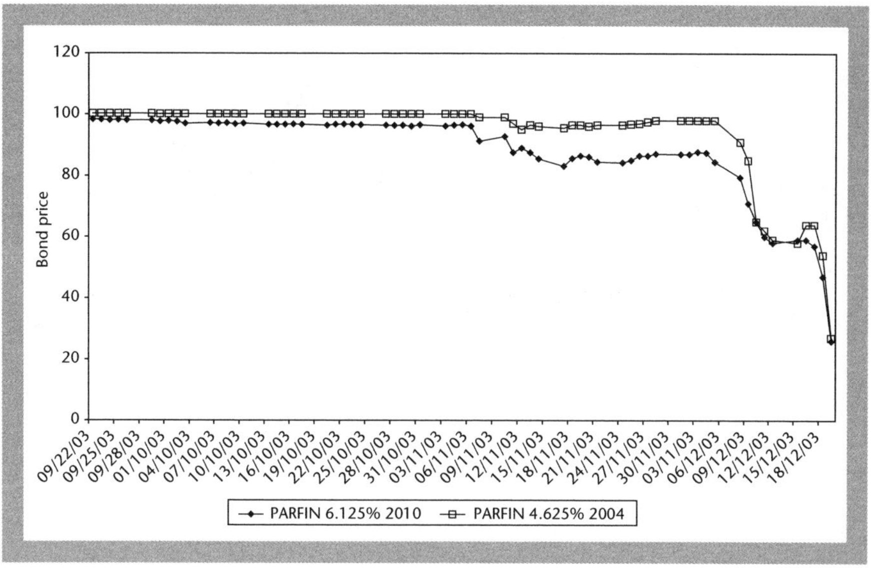

Figure 6.29 Parmalat bond prices Sep. 03–Dec. 03

Source: Union Investment and Bloomberg

6.6 RELATIVE VALUE

6.6.1 High yield in investment grade portfolios

High yield is an attractive asset class particularly at the beginning of an upturn in the credit cycle. Figure 6.30 shows that high-yield bonds can have a significant contribution to investment grade portfolios returns. Several factors have to be in place to achieve a positive effect:

- Improving overall credit quality (default rate peak)
- Low interest rate environment (hedge against rising interest rates)
- Long period of positive mutual fund flows (liquidity in high-yield market)

Another good way of looking at valuations between investment grade and high yield is the spread differential between BB and BBB spreads (Figure 6.31). During times of high uncertainty and deteriorating credit fundamentals the spread differential will approach its widest levels. It will tighten with improving credit fundamentals.

In the following section, we define three different scenarios for high yield in order to answer the question when high yield is appropriate as a mix for investment grade portfolios.

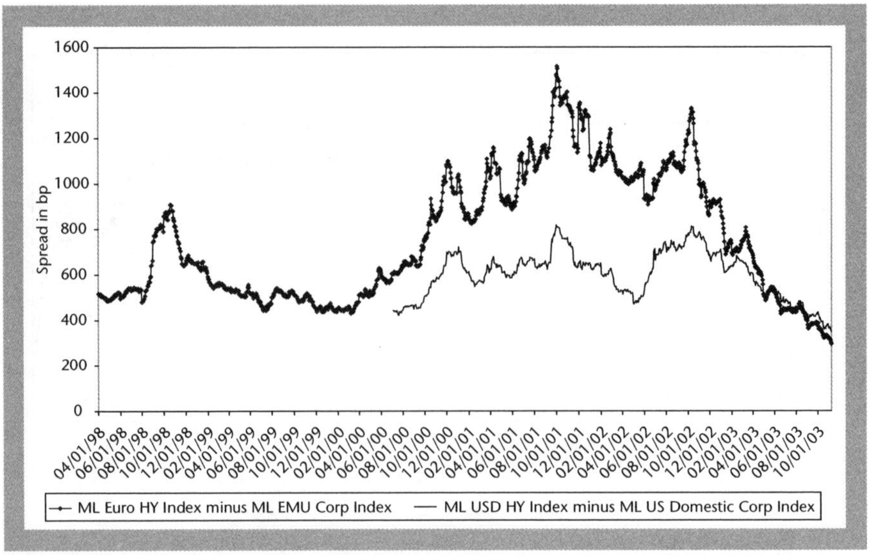

Figure 6.30 Spread differential between investment grade and high-yield indices in Euro and US$ Apr. 1998–Nov. 2003

Source: Union Investment and Bloomberg

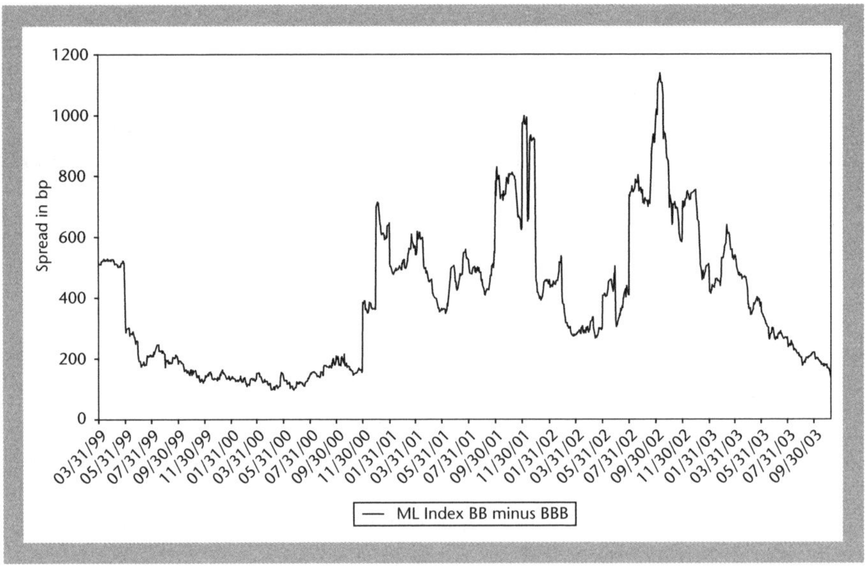

Figure 6.31 Spread differential between BBB and BB spread in Euro Mar. 1999–Nov. 2003

Source: Union Investment and Bloomberg

In Scenario 1 we assume that the economy is going through a recession:

- Companies miss their profit forecasts.
- Refinancing is difficult to obtain for companies with weak credit profiles.
- Equity markets sell-off.
- Risk aversion is high (flight to quality).
- The correlation between equity and high yield increases. Implied equity-market volatility is a good explanatory variable for high-yield spreads.
- Spreads between BB credits and B credits tend to widen as well as spreads between cyclical and noncyclical sectors.
- Event risks clearly dominate the high-yield landscape.
- Default rates increase.
- The required risk premiums from high-yield investors rise.
- Deleveraging takes place but at a slow pace.
- High yield will underperform other fixed income asset classes.

In Scenario 2 we assume an economic recovery:

- The correlation with equity markets is less strong than it was during recession.
- Implied equity-market volatility decreases and stops to be a good explanatory variable for high-yield spreads.
- The fixed income characteristics of high-yield bonds become an important factor.
- As risk aversion disappears out of the market credit fundamentals (credit selection) start to be more important for the direction of high-yield spreads.
- Spread compression takes place and the most risky investments will outperform.
- Single company credit stories are recognized as isolated cases and have a lesser effect on the whole market.
- Positive event risk support a good investor sentiment.
- Credit fundamentals improve – default rates fall.
- Especially in a low-yield environment high yield is a good hedge against interest rate risk.

In this environment an increasing number of investors will turn its focus towards high yield.

Scenario 3:

- The economic recovery gains momentum. A clear improvement in macroeconomic data can be observed and is sustainable.
- Rising interest rates become a threat to high yield, especially if rates and spreads are at historic tight levels.
- Balance sheet discipline is not first priority for management.
- Relative attractiveness of high yield diminishes.
- Fund outflows into the equity markets could hurt the valuation of high yield.
- Increasing volatility and inflation threaten total returns in high yield.

Clearly in Scenario 2 it makes sense to mix high yield into corporate bond portfolios while in Scenario 3 high yield continues to offer value but downside risks are increasing. In Scenario 1 high yield has to be avoided.

6.6.2 Selection within the high-yield rating classes

The spread differential between B and BB corporates is a useful tool for the allocation decision between high beta and low beta investments in the high-yield universe (assuming BBs as "save" and Bs as "risky") (Figure 6.32). During times of high-risk aversion the spread between those two will widen significantly. Periods of positive total returns in the high-yield market go along with an outperformance of Bs versus BBs. During periods of increased market uncertainty and rising default rates BBs will outperform B credits as the Flight-to-Quality occurs and more funds are allocated to BBs who represent the safest investments in the high-yield universe.

Figure 6.33 offers a possible way to evaluate the relative value of various rating classes. Spreads (here: C-rated paper) are plotted on the *y*-axis and Moody's default rate on the *x*-axis. C-rated paper appeared to be overvalued at the time of the analysis (Dec. 2003) (too tight for the prevailing Moody's default rate). Going forward it could be expected that either the spreads will widen to historical averages or Moody's default rate will come down to historical levels given the actual spread levels.

The average rating for all high-yield sectors will vary between Ba1 and Caa1. Table 6.13 is an example for selected US high-yield sectors. Depending on market conditions investors will allocate their funds to "safe" sectors with a higher rating during a recession and increase their risk profile during growth periods.

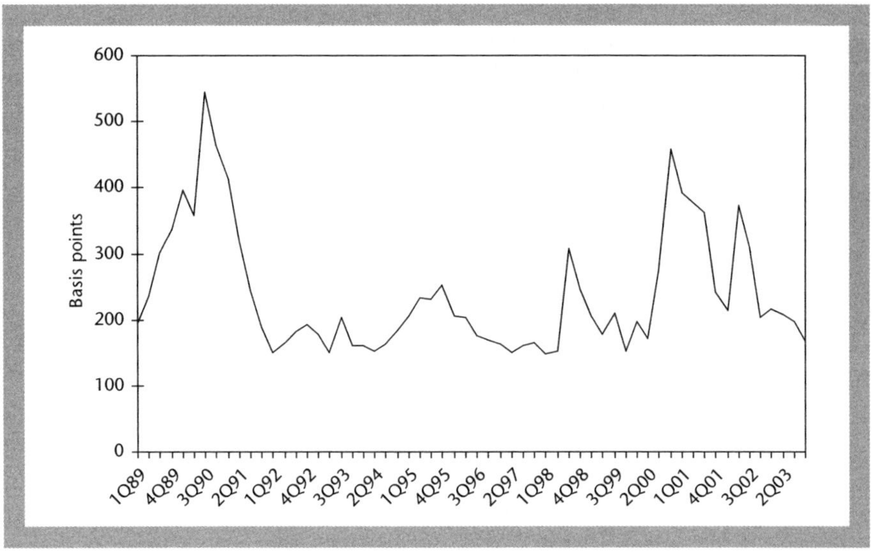

Figure 6.32 Spread diferential between BBs and B, US issuers 1989–2003
Source: Merrill Lynch

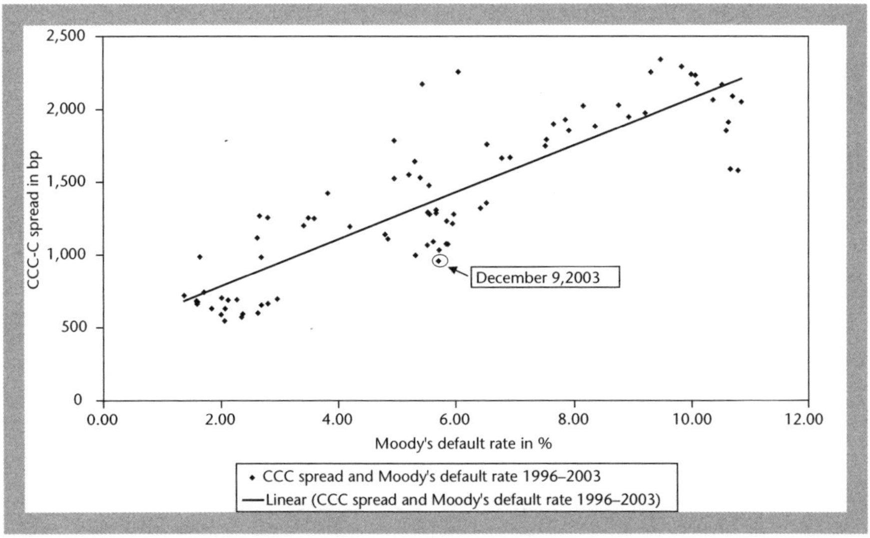

Figure 6.33 Relative value of CCC-C rated bonds
Source: Union Investment

6.6.3 US versus Euro high yield

The European high-yield market has only a limited history. Reliable data is available since 1997–98. Figure 6.34 shows that the two markets tend to move together. The European high-yield market commanded a premium

Table 6.13 Average ratings for selected US high-yield industries in Feb. 2004

Sector	Average rating
Capital goods	Ba3
Homebuilders	Ba3
Gaming	B1
Media	B1
Technology	B1
Utilities	B1
Leisure	B2
Broadcasting	B3
Cable TV/satellites	B3
Telecommunications	Caa1

Source: Merrill Lynch and Bloomberg

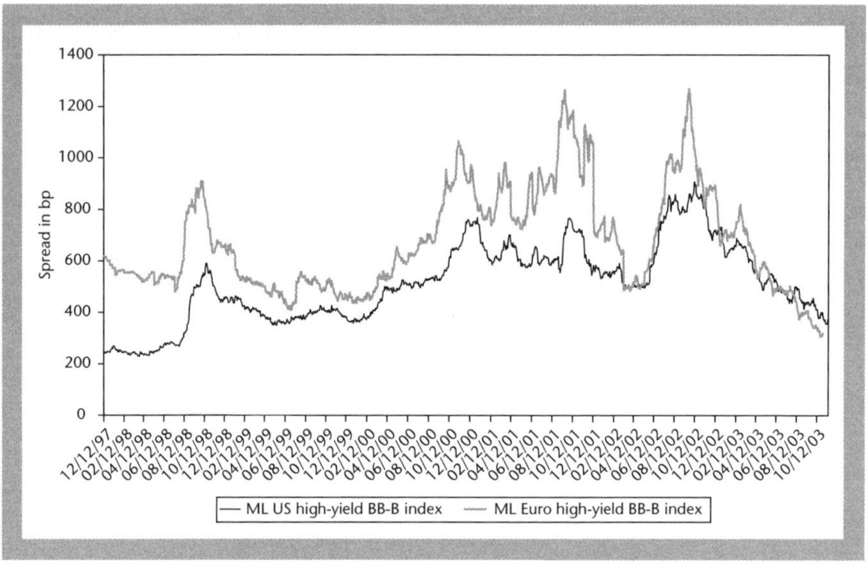

Figure 6.34 Spread differential between US and Euro high-yield markets Dec. 97–Nov. 2003

Source: Union Investment

over the US high-yield market because of greater illiquidity and lack of diversity. Furthermore, Fallen Angels had a negative impact on the European high-yield market because of its small size. In 1Q03 default rates for the European high-yield market fell below those observable in the US high-yield market which explains the reversed risk premium between those two markets. The notional amount outstanding for the US high-yield market was $565 billion and the European high-yield market had a notional amount outstanding of Euro 75 billion (December 2003).

6.6.4 Relative value and other asset classes

According to our correlation matrix high yield is best comparable with equities. Figure 6.35 shows the value of $100 invested in January 1987 in high yield and the S&P 500 Index. It can be said that investors realized similar returns over the period Jan. 1987–Dec. 2003.

Figure 6.36 brings more clarity into the relationship between high yield and equity markets. Obviously both markets are affected by similar macroeconomic factors, so that they show parallel fluctuations in risk. But it is important to note that high yield experienced less risk over this period, meaning that high yield returns experience less volatility than that observed with equities.

Figure 6.37 shows historical yields in the high-yield market versus 10-year Treasuries and BBBs. The spread differential varies significantly depending on the phase of the credit cycle.

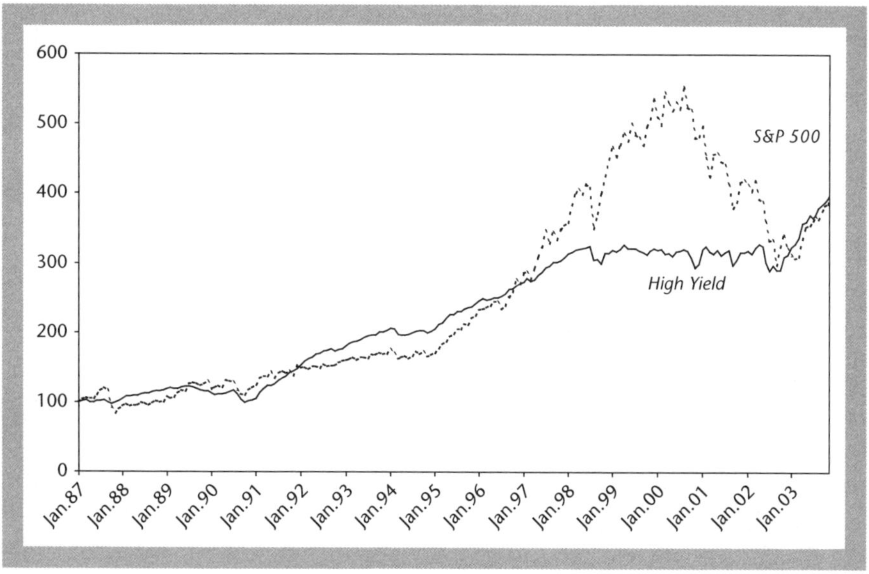

Figure 6.35 Value of $100 invested in high yield and S&P 500 Jan. 1987–Dec. 2003

Source: Deutsche Bank and Bloomberg

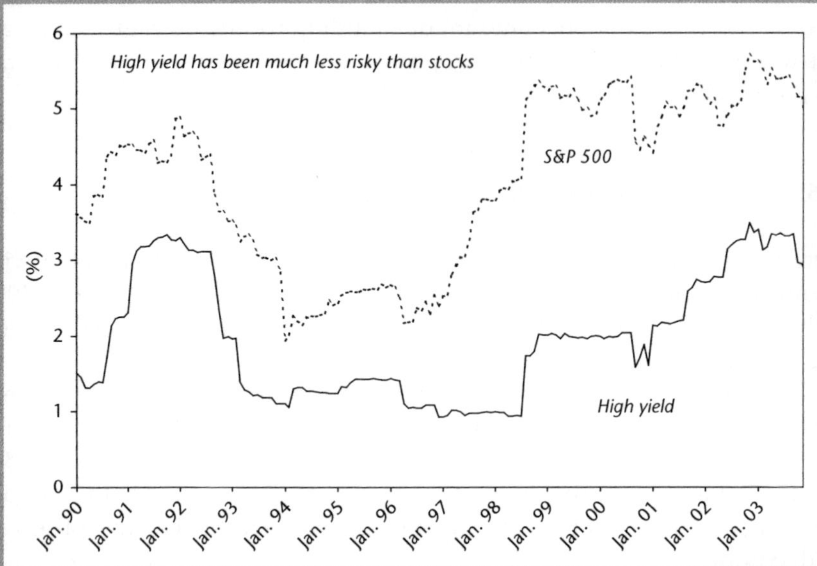

Figure 6.36 Two-year rolling volatilities of returns for high yield and equities, Jan. 1990–Dec. 2003

Source: Deutsche Bank and Bloomberg

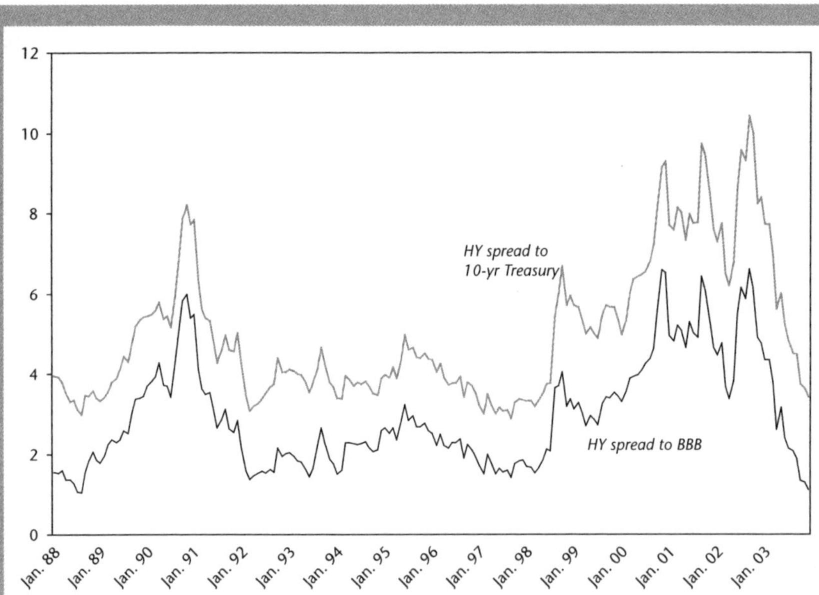

Figure 6.37 Yields in high-yield market to BBBs and the 10-year Treasury Jan. 88–Dec. 2003

Source: Deutsche Bank and Bloomberg

CHAPTER 7

Credit Derivatives

7.1 INTRODUCTION

Credit derivatives are probably the most important new mechanism for transferring credit risk. They are over-the-counter products and can therefore be tailored to individual requirements.

Single-name credit default swaps (CDS) remain the most widely used instruments in the credit derivatives market.

The growth in CDS has been driven by hedging demand generated by synthetic CDO (collateralized debt obligations) positions and the loan books of the major banks. Hedge funds and insurance companies have been users of CDS as well. Especially hedge funds are using credit derivatives as a way to exploit capital structure/convertible bond arbitrage and to go outright short/long the credit markets.

7.2 CREDIT DEFAULT SWAPS

CDS are used to transfer the credit risk of a reference entity from one party to another. One party (the protection buyer) pays a periodic, fixed premium to another (the protection seller) for protection related to credit events on the reference obligation. If there is no credit event, such as default during the life of the swap, these premiums are the only cash flows (Figure 7.1). If a credit event occurs the protection seller is obliged to make a payment to the protection buyer. For physically settled contracts, following a credit event, the protection buyer delivers the defaulted reference obligation (Figure 7.2, any bond of the company but appropriate seniority).

Cash settlement (par minus market value) is the alternative to physical settlement and is used less frequently in standard CDS but overwhelmingly in tranched CDOs. The 2003 ISDA definitions further clarify the three types

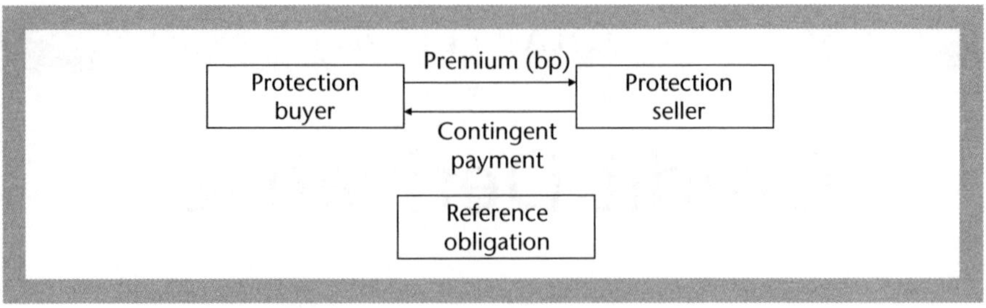

Figure 7.1 A typical credit default swap
Source: Union Investment

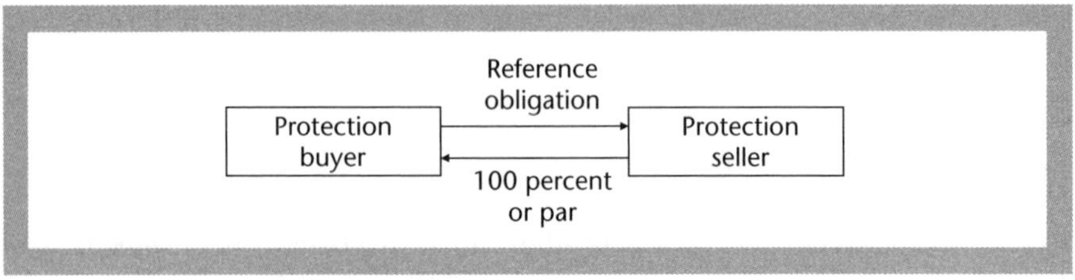

Figure 7.2 Physical settlement (credit event)
Source: Union Investment

of credit events:

- Bankruptcy
- Failure to pay
- Restructuring.

Just like cash bonds or loans, CDS transfer credit risk (see Figure 7.3). To remove the interest rate component of a cash bond, a synthetic floating-rate note can be created via an asset swap which eliminates the duration and convexity exposure of the cash bond. An unfunded position in the bond would have to be financed in the repo market. A CDS is equivalent to a financed purchase of a bond with an interest rate hedge (selling protection through a CDS or buying a corporate bond, asset swapping the coupon to floating and financing the holding in the repo market).

Net payment flow on the default swap:
premium in basis points = default swap rate

Net payment flow on a financed floater investment:
Spread + Libor − Repo

Other payments are similar, therefore:
default swap rate = Spread + Libor − Repo

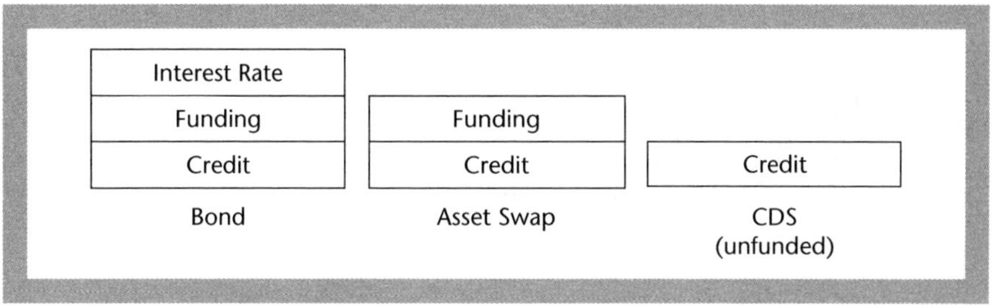

Figure 7.3 CDS isolate the credit risk component
Source: Union Investment

The annual default probability can be determined (approximated) using:

$$\text{Annual Default Probability} = \frac{\text{Default Swap Spread}}{(1 - \text{Recovery Rate})}$$

Assuming, for example, a spread of 75 bp and a recovery rate of 25 percent, the default probability q and the 1-year survival probability p are the following :

$$q = \frac{0.0075}{1 - 0.25} = 0.01 \text{ or } 1 \text{ percent p.a.}$$

$$p = 1 - q = 0.99 \text{ or } 99 \text{ percent p.a.}$$

The cumulative default probability P in a flat/slightly upward sloping CDS spread curve in 3 years can be calculated using the following equation (CDS 3 years, recovery rate of 40 percent):

$$P = \frac{1 - \left(\frac{1}{(1 + 0.0075)}\right)^3}{(1 - 0.4)} = 0.0369$$

$$= 3.69 \text{ percent.}$$

7.2.1 CDS basis

The difference between asset swapped bond spreads (par floater spread) and CDS spreads is known as the default swap basis, defined as

CDS basis = CDS premium − asset swap spread.

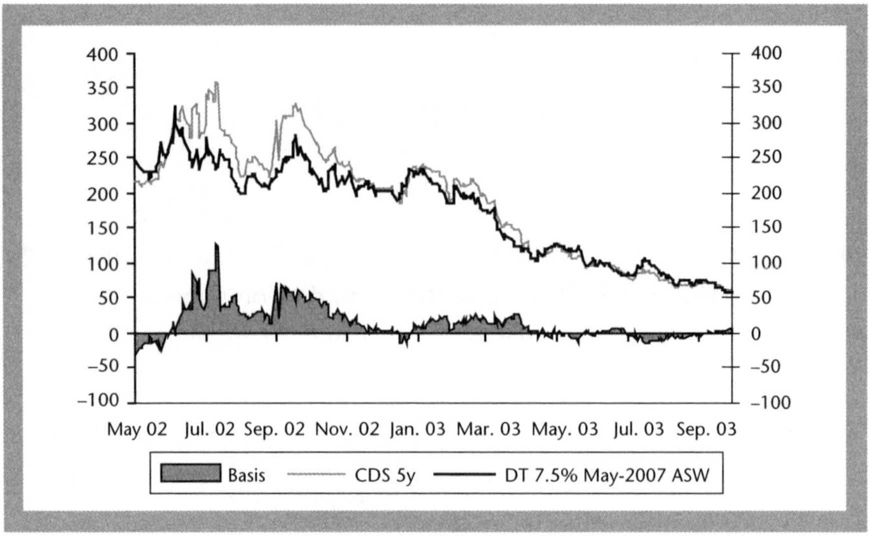

Figure 7.4 Deutsche Telecom CDS basis
Source: Merrill Lynch

If the CDS premium is higher than the asset swap yield, the basis is positive and negative if the CDS trades through the asset swap. Figure 7.4 illustrates how the asset swap and protection levels can diverge for the European telecom sector.

7.2.2 Drivers of the basis

The factors that drive the widening and the tightening of the basis are explained below:

Factors that pull protection tighter (negative basis):

- Strong demand from protection sellers because of the unfunded nature of CDS and a lack of desired exposure/liquidity in the debt market.
- Synthetic CDOs can drive default swap spreads tighter because the manager needs to sell protection in order to buy synthetic credit risk into these structures.
- The existence of a default swap curve in 1, 3, 5 and 10 years can offer investors a broader range of maturities to construct a better portfolio.
- Assets trading above par, that is, the protection seller is exposed to a lower amount than the cash investor.
- Improving credit quality and decreasing spreads/basis volatility (CDS = high beta instrument).

As the basis becomes more negative, investors with a low funding cost would be better buyers of the bond and buyers of protection to maturity to lock in the positive carry.

Factors that widen the basis (positive basis):

- Strong demand from protection buyers such as banks or hedge funds
- Bonds can usually be funded in the repo market at or around Libor. If the bond becomes special the investor holds a repo market option that makes the bond more attractive than the CDS and tends to widen the basis (short positions in bonds cannot be locked in for years because of a nonexisting repo market).
- Deteriorating credit quality and increasing spreads/basis volatility or equity volatility (CDS = high beta instrument).
- Assets trading below par, that is an investor who pays $80 for $100 face value has less credit exposure than a protection seller at par. Therefore, the protection seller would demand a higher premium (spread) than the bond.
- Convertible bond issuance may lead to hedging credit risk to unlock "cheap" equity volatility.
- The cheapest to deliver option is a structural factor, which tends to widen the basis (protection buyer is able to deliver any qualifying loan/bond).

The default basis can also be viewed as a risk indicator. In general, the sale of default protection should be more attractive than purchasing a bond when the basis is high relative to the equity volatility of the firm and vice versa.

7.2.3 Relative value trades using CDS

Directional trades: This refers to a situation where the CDS market can be used to take a low-cost bearish view because of a negative basis. If the basis is positive and has widenend for "technical" reasons, it possibly represents an opportunity from a hedging-driven market dislocation. Figure 7.5 provides an example for Siemens.

Spread trades: Investors who are positive about France Telecom relative to Vodafone can express this outperformance view via selling protection in France Telecom versus buying protection in Vodafone. Depending on the chosen credits this could result in high positive carry trades (Figure 7.6).

Curve trades/Forward trades: As an issuer's credit quality deteriorates, the spread curve of the issuer moves from being upward-sloping to inverted.

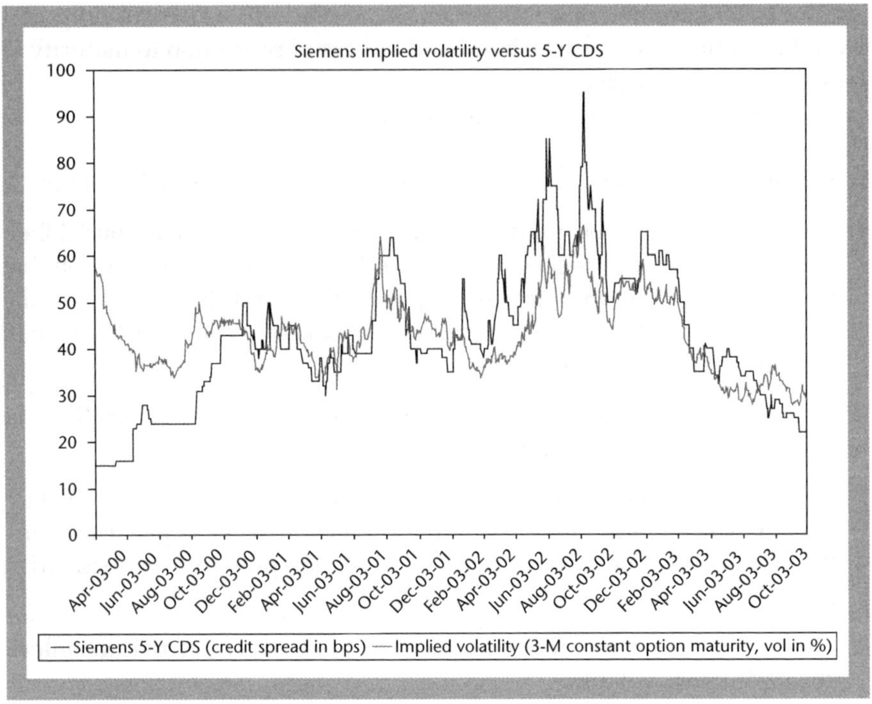

Figure 7.5 CDS spread is highly correlated to implied equity volatility

Source: J.P. Morgan

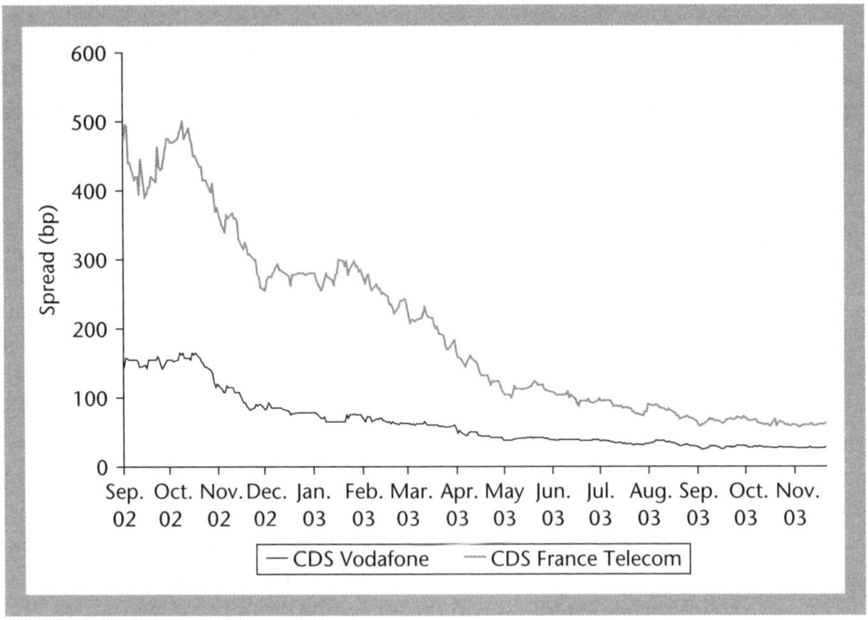

Figure 7.6 Spread trade: Vodafone CDS versus France Telecom CDS

Source: Union Investment

Default curve inversion may present an opportunity to shorten maturity and enhance yield. Curve inversion in the default market also allows investors to purchase forward protection at lower levels. This can be achieved by buying longer dated protection and selling shorter dated protection.

On the other hand, if one has a negative short-term view on a credit but believes it to survive for the next 5 years, its credit quality will improve significantly. This view can be expressed via buying a long-dated 30-year par asset swap and buying 5-year protection on the single name thereby creating a long forward spread position (or buying short-dated default protection and selling longer dated default protection). This position would benefit from a flattening of the credit curve.

A steep credit curve implies a steep forward credit curve.

A forward default swap is buying or selling protection for the given maturity at a given point in the future at the forward CDS spread. For example, Munich Re senior 2-year protection is at 21 bp and the 7-year protection trades at 34 bp. Selling 2-year protection and buying 7-year protection results in a 5-year CDS two years forward (2 × 5 spread) at a level of 40 bp.

$$S_{\text{forward}} = \frac{S_{\text{long}} - (\text{PV01}_{\text{short}} / \text{PV01}_{\text{long}}) \times S_{\text{short}}}{1 - (\text{PV01}_{\text{short}} / \text{PV01}_{\text{long}})}.$$

Selling short-term and buying long-dated protection leaves a forward short position, which would benefit from a steepening in the credit curve and vice versa.

Senior versus subordinated CDS strategies: The senior-to-sub spread differential in CDS is driven fundamentally by expected recovery values. If senior spreads are half those of subordinated, then the expected senior loss following default is half that of sub. A 50 percent senior recovery (50 percent loss) would imply a 0 percent subordinated recovery (100 percent loss) (see Figure 7.7).

Example:

Allianz 5 year senior CDS spread = 40 bp per year

Allianz 5 year subordinated CDS spread = 80 bp per year

If $R_{\text{sub}} = 0\%$, $R_{\text{senior}} = 1 - (40/80) \times (100\% - 0\%) = 50\%$

A potential strategy is to sell subordinated protection and to buy senior protection (weighted). It offers the chance to unwind at a profit if the senior-to-sub ratio mean reverts to historical averages (positive carry trade). If a credit event occurs, the payoffs will reflect the actual relative recoveries in sub and senior debt.

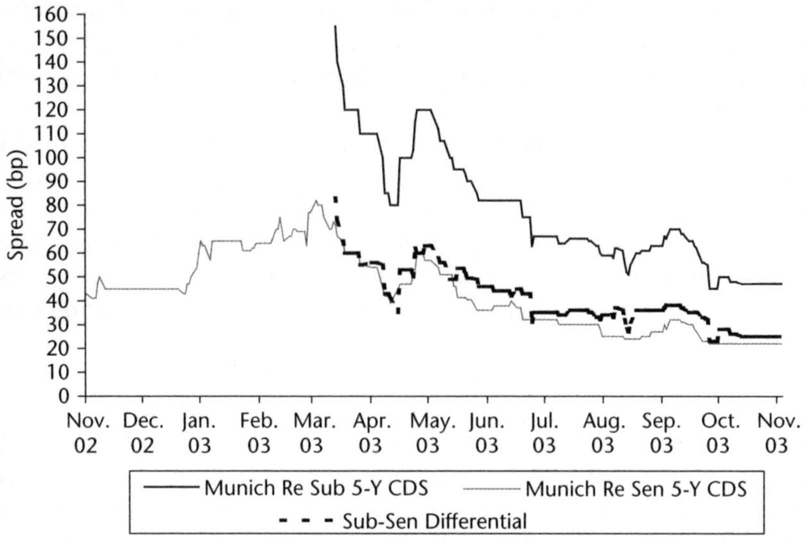

Figure 7.7 Munich Re senior versus subordinated CDS spreads

Source: J.P. Morgan

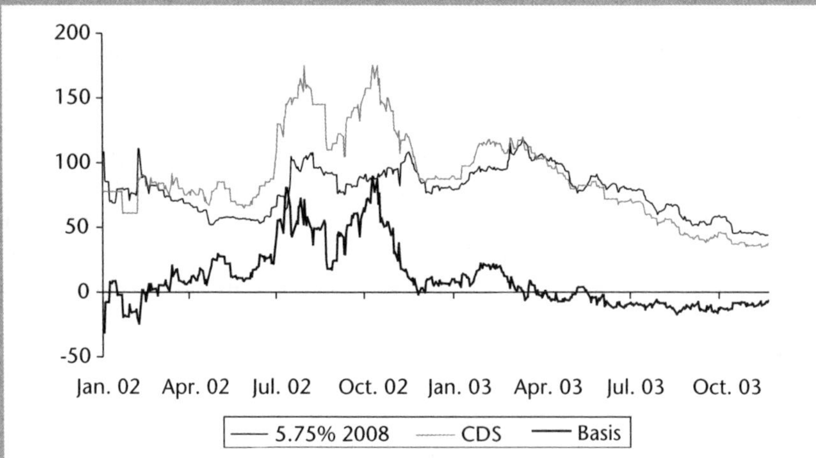

Figure 7.8 CDS basis for PHILIPS ELECTRONICS

Source: Barclay's

Basis trades/Convertible bond hedging: As an example the basis for Fiat widened massively following issuance of a 2.2 billion convertible and deteriorating credit sentiment at the end of 2001 (Figure 7.9). It is worth mentioning that the negative basis trade (long cash, long protection) is not entirely risk-free. If the bond is actually restructured at the time of default

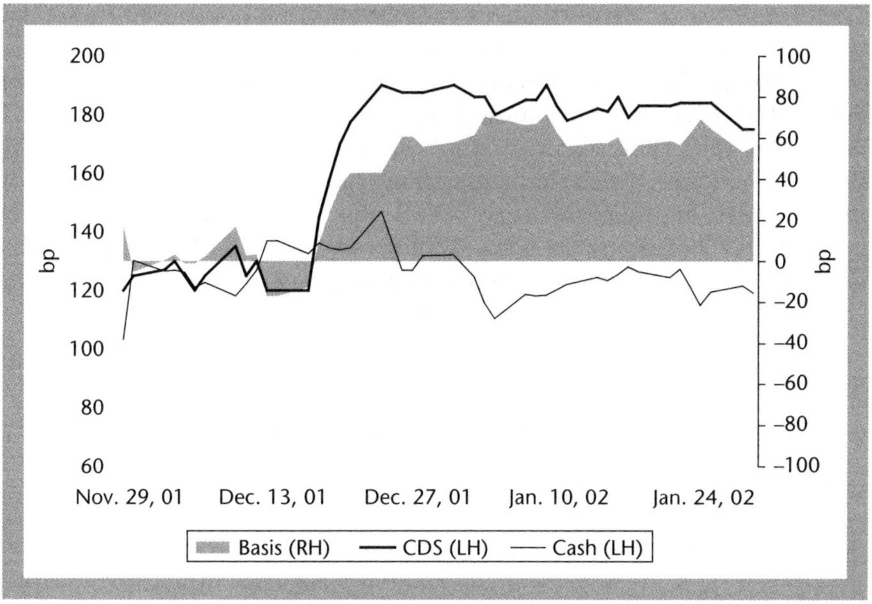

Figure 7.9 Widening in the Fiat basis because of convertible bond issuance (hedging)

Source: Morgan Stanley

it is no longer deliverable. The risk-free positive basis trade cannot be set up till maturity because one is not able to lock in the repo rate of the bond (short cash, short protection).

Capital structure arbitrage: These might be strategies where investors take a position in a default swap versus an equity put option. If equity is undervalued, CDS levels are tight and debt is rich the following strategy appears to be appropriate. For example, selling out-of-the-money puts versus buying protection allows to position for a rally in the stock/declining equity volatility and to "hedge" this opinion against the risk of the widening of spreads on the company's debt. The option premium earned is used to fund the CDS, with positive or negative carry. It is important to realize that this is not a pure arbitrage or risk-free trade.

7.3 COLLATERALIZED DEBT OBLIGATIONS

7.3.1 Definition of CDOs

The idea in a CDO transaction is to securitize debt collateral to make it more attractive to different classes of investors. In the earlier days, CDOs purchased high yield/emerging market debt through a special purpose vehicle (SPV) and raised funds by issuing securities ranging from AAA to BB/B.

The overall risk of the portfolio of various collateral is tranched from relatively safe to speculative to satisfy different degrees of risk appetite.

Beginning with the most senior class, the cash flows from the collateral are used to service the outstanding notes sequentially. Losses are allocated on the basis of reverse seniority. This basic structure is also known as a cash flow CDO because the collateral cash flows are used to sevice the outstanding securities (Figure 7.10). Every CDO has an asset side, generating its revenue, and a liability side, whose obligations need to be satisfied. The difference between them is termed the funding gap.

The following types of CDOs are rather common:

- Investment grade CDOs (synthetic)
- Collateralized loan obligations/Synthetic balance sheet CLOs
- High-yield CBOs/Emerging market CBOs

A typical feature of collateralized loan obligations (CLOs) is that all loan collateral is typically in a senior and secured position in the borrower's capital structure. Various covenants also serve to enhance the secured nature of loans. Loans are typically issued as floating rate instruments and have shorter average lives than high-yield CBOs. The single most important differentiating factor between loans and high-yield bonds is the senior secured nature of the loans (much higher recoveries and actually lower default probability). Figure 7.11 shows the leveraged loan spreads.

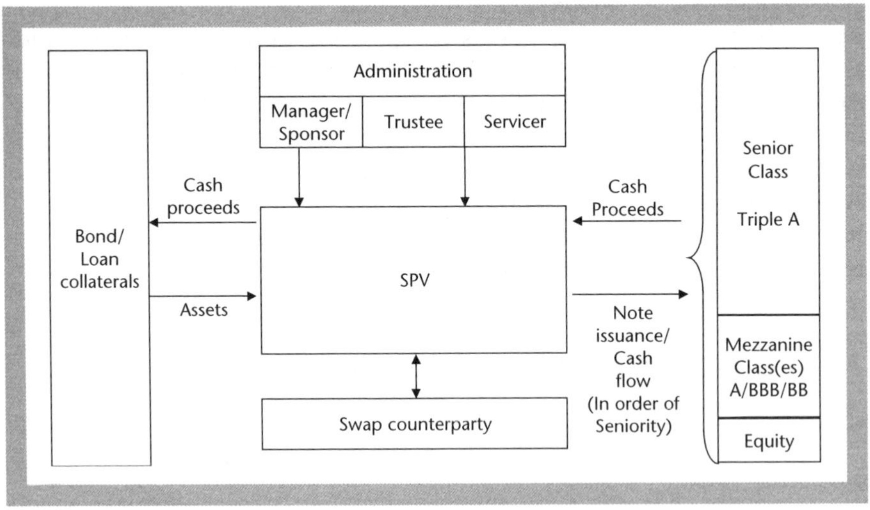

Figure 7.10 Funded cash flow CDO
Source: Union Investment

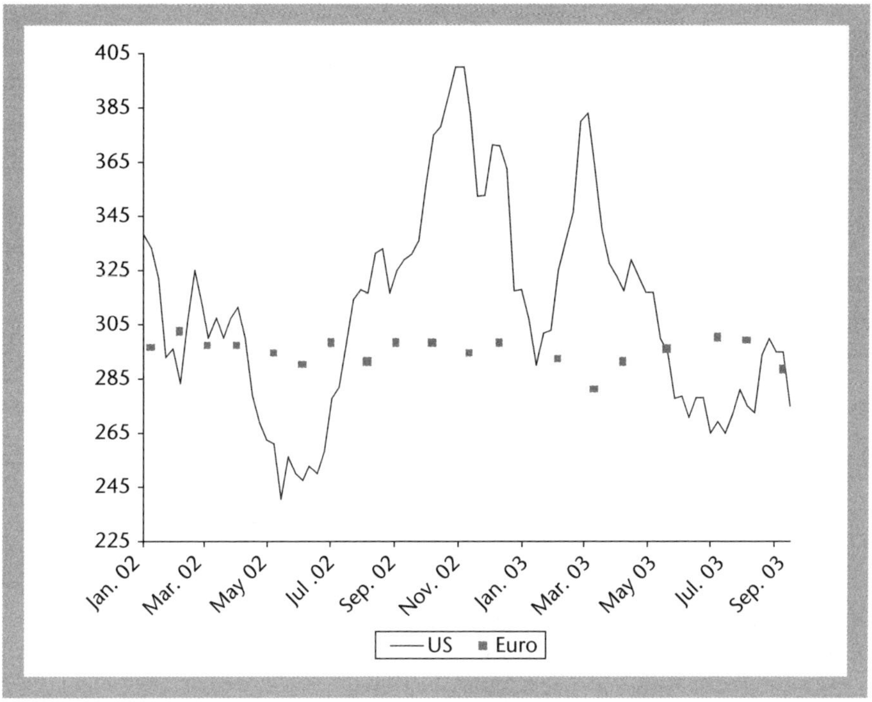

Figure 7.11 BB/BBB-Leveraged loan spreads
Source: J.P. Morgan

Adjusting CDS spreads and loans in the investment grade universe for risk (default and recovery rate) and reward (loan pricing) shows that the CDS loan basis should be rather positive.

7.3.2 Synthetic CDOs

A synthetic CDO is an investment in which the underlying collateral is a portfolio of CDS. The issuer does not own the underlying assets but retains the credit and economic risks. The recent CDOs make use of "unfunded" senior tranches. The super senior investor will enter into a CDS with the SPV. The super senior is typically unfunded, matching the unfunded nature of CDS. The super senior tranche provides second-loss credit protection. As in cash CDOs, the rated note and equity pieces are generally funded. Synthetic deals can have a final maturity of 5–7 years (Figure 7.12).

Example: Collateral pool
No of reference entities: 100
Notional amount of CDS: Euro 5 million
Total size: Euro 500 million

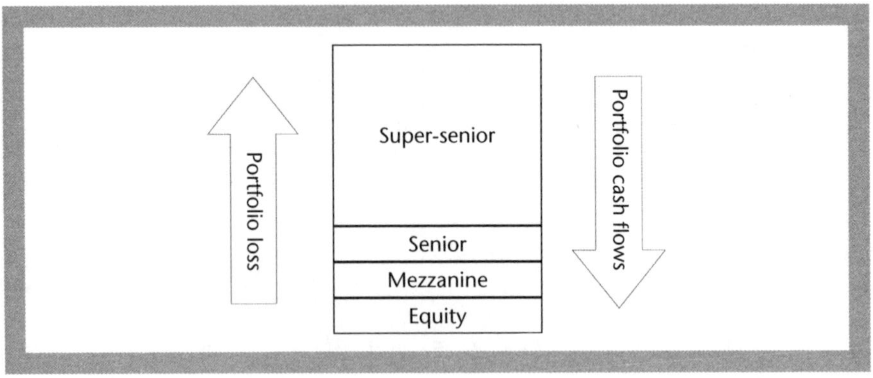

Figure 7.12 CDO Capital structure
Source: Union Investment

Tranche	Size (%)	Liability cost (%)
Equity	0–5	N/A
Mezzanine tranche	5–9.5	4.00
Senior tranche	9.5–13	0.60
Super senior tranche	13–100	0.08
		= 0.27

The example details a possible tranching of a 500 million portfolio into four tranches. Losses in the portfolio up to 5 percent (Euro 25 million of losses in total) would result in a complete write-down of the equity tranche. Further losses in the portfolio in excess of 5 percent and up to 9.5 percent (losses of Euro 47.5 million in total) would then result in a write-down of principal in the mezzanine tranche. If each credit had a 50 percent recovery rate, each default in the underlying portfolio would result in a loss of Euro 2.5 million. Therefore, it would take 10 defaults to write-down the equity tranche.

7.3.3 Synthetic versus cash high grade CDOs

Cash CDOs are collateralized by a portfolio of cash assets and the entire liability structure is used to fund the purchase of collateral. Synthetic CDOs transfer credit risk from the CDO issuer to CDO note holders through CDS. The synthetic CDO normally funds only a small portion of the notional value of the credit exposure. Therefore the weighted average cost of liabilities are much smaller for a synthetic CDO because of the unfunded super senior tranche (around 85–90 percent of the capital structure) which leads to a higher return on the equity tranche (Figure 7.13).

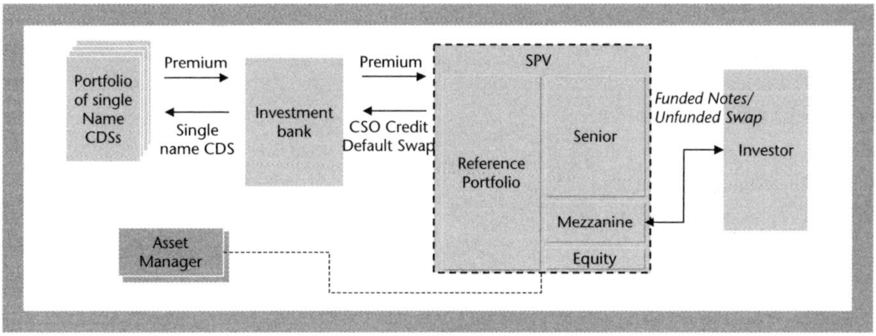

Figure 7.13 Synthetic CDO
Source: Barclay's

Other advantages of synthetic CDOs are as follows:

- diversify away from frequent issuers in the bond market
- no restrictions in terms of volume
- ability to tailor maturity.

A synthetic CDO referencing investment grade CDS can be structured with much higher leverage compared to a high-yield CBO. The equity in a synthetic deal normally ranges from 2 to 5 percent, which equates to 20–50 times leverage. Equity in a high-yield CBO is around 10 percent on average (10 times leverage).

7.3.4 Managed versus static synthetic pools

In a basic static transaction a sponsor selects a portfolio of about 100 or more investment grade names. Once a static synthetic CDO begins, the reference portfolio remains fixed until maturity. In a static pool delivered obligations usually must be liquidated within a preset timeframe.

Some typical trading activities in managed synthetic deals include:

- Terminating credit-improved CDS to generate cash into the CDO
- Terminating credit-deteriorated CDS to avoid/limit future losses
- Buying protection for a smaller amount
- Conducting limited discretionary trading, that is, 10–20 percent annual portfolio turnover.

Normally, managed pool risk offers lower expected loss and lower probability of large loss (Figure 7.14).

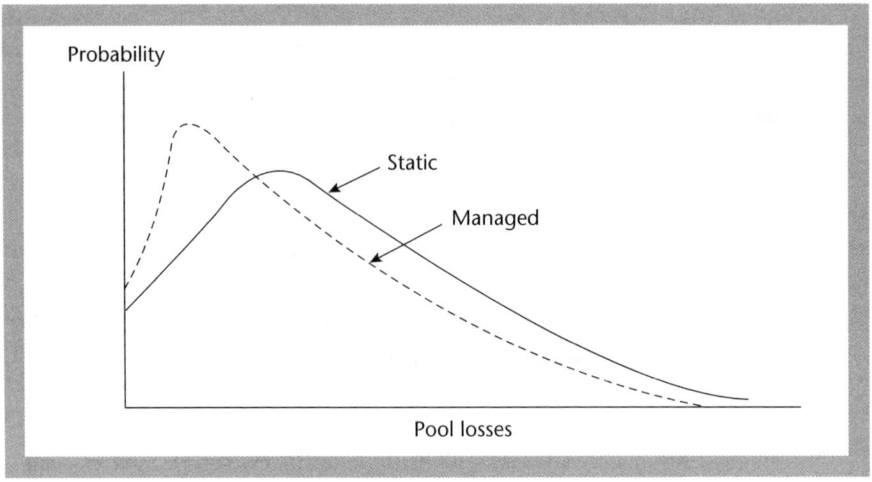

Figure 7.14 Static versus managed CDO

Source: Deutsche Bank

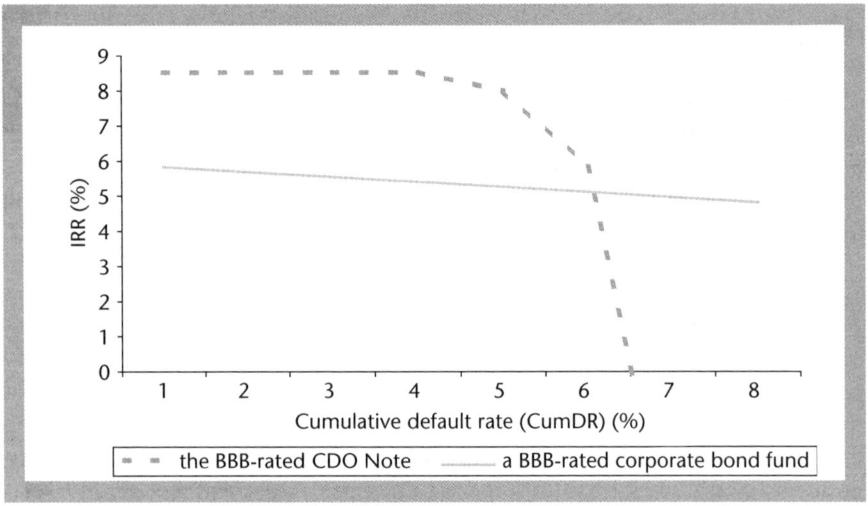

Figure 7.15 BBB–CDO note versus a BBB-corporate bond fund over 5 years

Source: CSFB

7.3.5 Corporate bond portfolios versus synthetic CDOs

To compare both asset classes and tranches one needs to construct a corporate bond fund invested in 100 equally weighted BBB corporate bonds (assuming that the bond fund pays a Libor + 100 bp and runs a maturity of 5 years).

The risk/return tradeoff between a corporate bond fund and a BBB–CDO note looks as shown in Figure 7.15.

The BBB note sustains a higher cumulative default rate before suffering any losses, as the equity absorbs the initial losses. But the corporate bond fund may outperform in severe default scenarios. This is largely because of the leverage in the CDO note. At one stage the mezzanine notes become the equity of the structure. The huge difference in IRR is explained by the extra risk between the cash bonds and the BBB-tranche as a total.

7.3.6 Senior and mezzanine classes of synthetic CDOs

The senior and mezzanine return profile has an option-like feature, like short puts out-of-the-money (BBB) and far-out-of-the money (AAA) in return terms. When investment grade default rates rise significantly above their long-term historical average, mezzanine notes become impaired. On the other hand, CDS portfolio deterioration causes in general mark-to-market losses and might result in rating downgrades with respect to the notes.

Assumption: The annualized 5-year cumulative BBB credit loss rate is 0.20 percent, assuming a recovery rate of 40 percent. The size of the first loss tranche equals 4 percent, the size of the BBB-note 2.5 percent and the AAA note 3 percent in the example with a portfolio of BBB rated CDS.

Hypothetical capital structure:	Equity 4 percent
	BBB 2.5 percent
	AAA 3 percent

Average spread of the collateral is around 100 bp.

The break-even in the IRR profile of the AAA tranche is a multiple of the annualized historical average loss for BBB-rated corporates (10x in this case). The BBB-class hits the IRR of the portfolio at around 0.9 percent which is 4.5 times the historical average loss. Static synthetic mezzanines normally exhibit a lower rating stability than mezzanine notes of managed synthetic CDOs, depending on the skill of the manager.

Assumption: The 5-year cumulative default rate for BBB is around 1.60 percent, assuming a 40 percent recovery rate. This equals an annualized 0.2 percent expected loss rate. The size of the mezzanine tranches affects the expected loss (probability of loss unaffected).

As the size of the mezzanine class decreases the expected loss tends to increase hyperbolically as seen in Figure 7.20 (binomial expansion technique with a diversity score of 55 was used).

The ratio of the expected tranche losses to the expected CDS portfolio losses would define the risk leverage. When the ratio is above 1 the mezzanine note has a greater expected percentage loss than the underlying portfolio. The percentage of the first loss class has a major impact on the

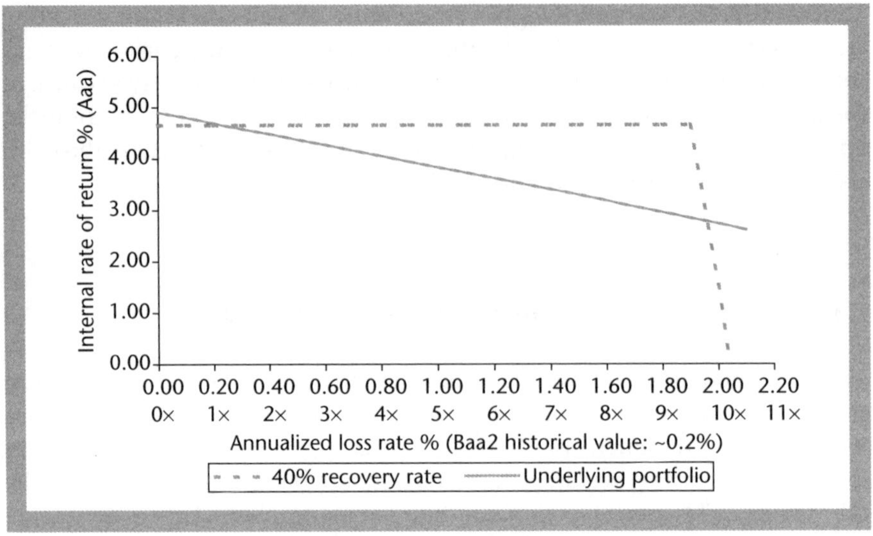

Figure 7.16 Inflection point of a AAA-note (annualized 5-year cumulative credit loss rates), around 10 × the historical multiple loss

Source: J.P. Morgan

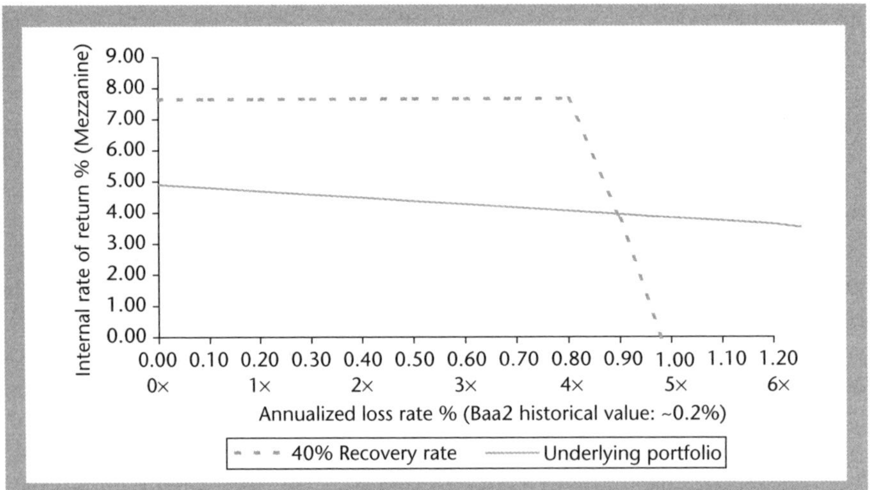

Figure 7.17 Inflection point of a BBB-note (annualized 5-year cumulative credit loss rates), around 4.5 times the historical multiple loss

Source: J.P. Morgan

leverage of the mezzanine class (assuming the same underlying exposure in size; see Figure 7.21).

Key parameters in the valuation of synthetic CDOs are default probability, default correlation and recovery rate. Various models exist for determining

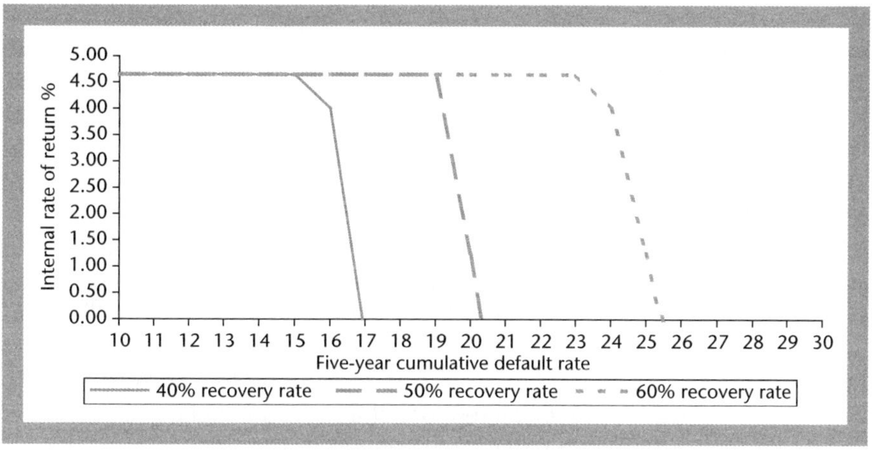

Figure 7.18 Inflection points assuming different recovery rates (5-year cumulative default rates) for AAA-notes

Source: J.P. Morgan

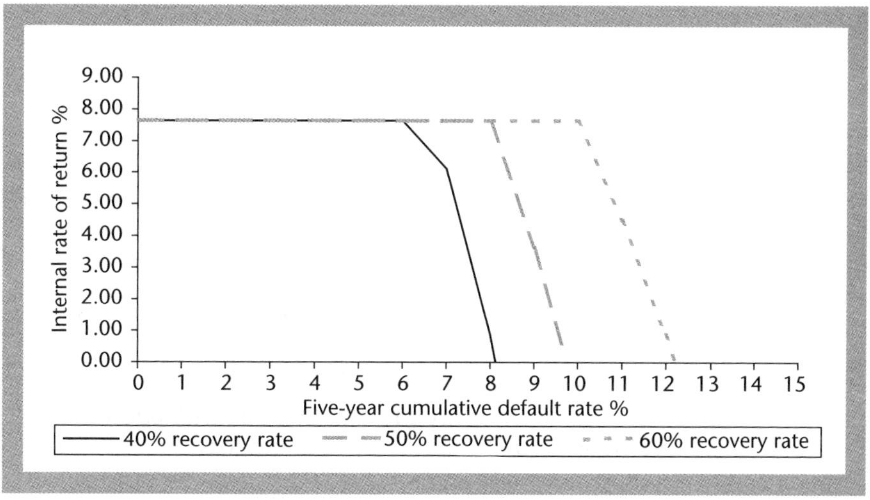

Figure 7.19 Inflection points assuming different recovery rates (5-year cumulative default rates) for BBB-notes

Source: J.P. Morgan

the default probability:

- Historical default rates based on the rating agencies
- Default rates implied by the spreads of CDS and
- Structural Merton-type models like KMV (based on asset value and asset volatility).

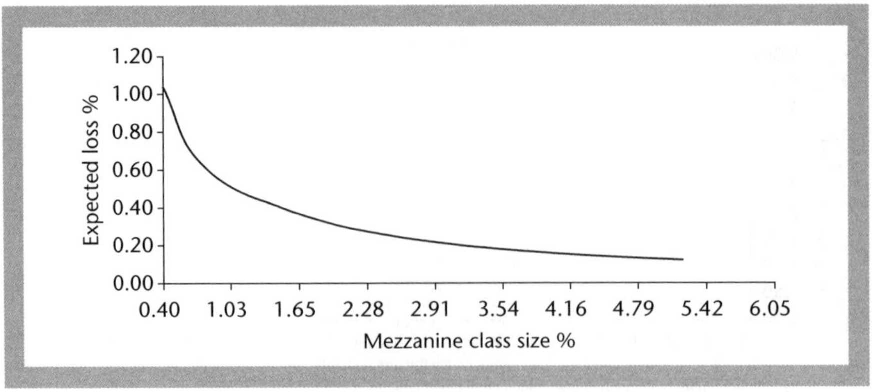

Figure 7.20 Expected loss of a mezzanine class (equity 4 percent) in relation to the size

Source: J.P. Morgan

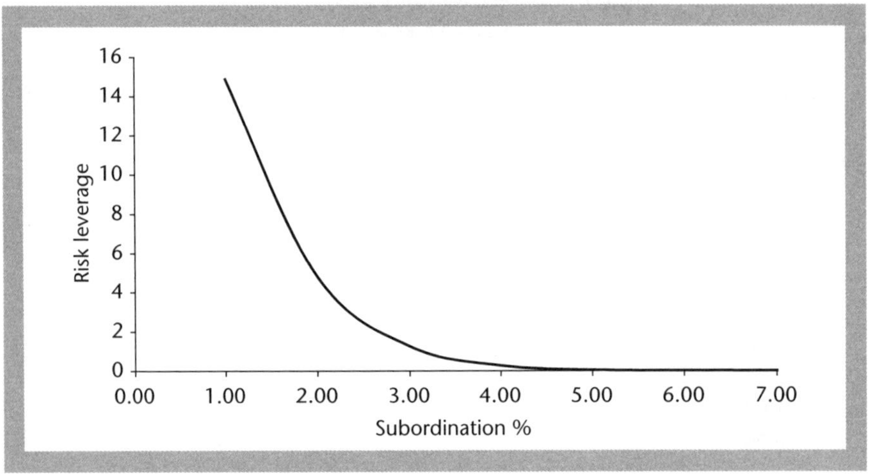

Figure 7.21 Risk leverage as a function of subordination compared to the portfolio expected loss

Source: J.P. Morgan

Figure 7.22 shows the comparison of the implied default risk premium for the assets in a synthetic CDO (similar to a portfolio with the same quality) versus the expected default losses by KMV and the trailing 12-month Moody's default rate. Default correlation measures the tendency of assets defaulting together. If the correlation is zero there is no link between their possible defaults.

The standard definition is as follows:

$$\text{Default Correlation (A, B)} = \frac{P_{\text{A and B}} - P_{\text{A}} \times P_{\text{B}}}{\sqrt{P_{\text{A}} \times (1 - P_{\text{A}}) \times P_{\text{B}} \times (1 - P_{\text{B}})}}$$

where P_{A} denotes the probability of asset A defaulting.

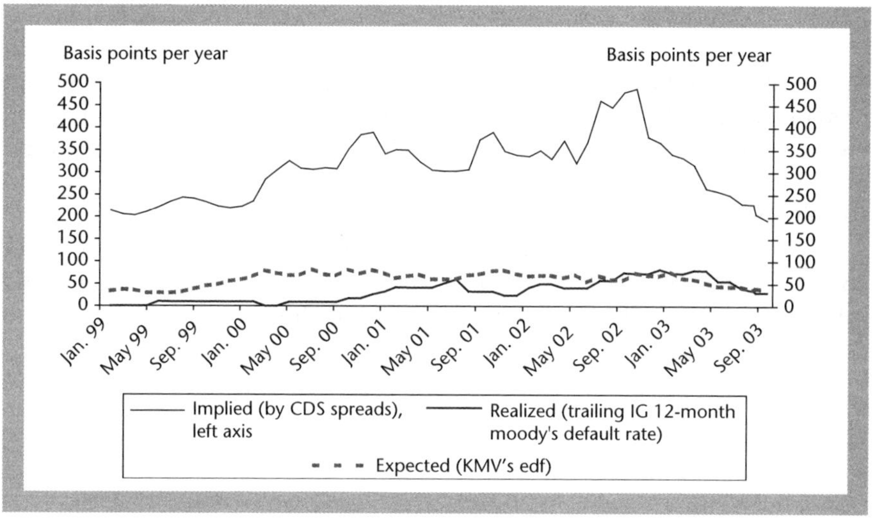

Figure 7.22 Different annualized default risk measurements

Source: Lehman Brothers

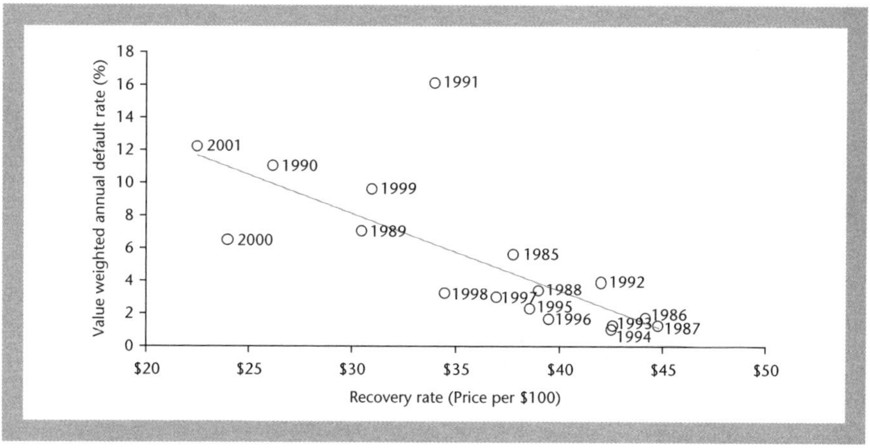

Figure 7.23 Default rates of speculative issuers regressed to their recovery rates

Source: Moody's

For lower recovery rates the IRR of the tranche remains constant just for a shorter period. In the case of the mezzanine tranches higher recovery rates mean that there is a slower exhaustion of subordination benefit.

There is a relationship between recovery rates and default rates of corporate bond issuers. They tend to be negatively correlated, meaning a decrease in default rates is generally associated with an increase in the average recovery rate (Figure 7.23 for speculative issuers).

7.3.7 CDO equity

The level of credit losses in the underlying portfolio is the main determinant of synthetic CDO's equity performance. At around 0.5 percent the two IRR cross at roughly 2.5 times the historical loss multiple. Again the historical average Moody's annualized cumulative Baa2 credit loss rate is 0.2 percent (see Figure 7.24).

One should expect managed vehicles to outperform unmanaged pools, so a skilled manager will be able to add value by making trading gains and minimizing losses. The right timing to dispose off Fallen Angels/distressed assets or to hold on/add on to them can maximize recovery rates.

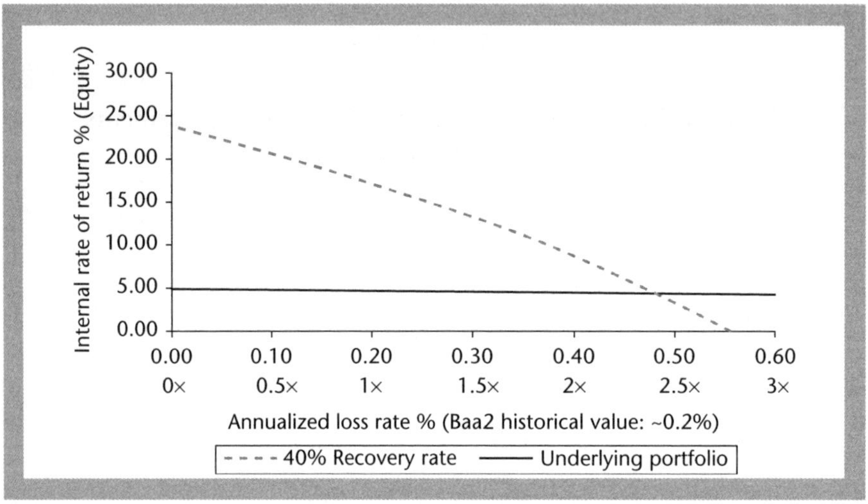

Figure 7.24 Breakeven point of an equity-note (annualized 5-year cumulative credit loss rates), 2.5 × the historical multiple loss

Source: J.P. Morgan

CHAPTER 8

Credit Indices

8.1 INDEX SELECTION

Having determined the long-term investment objectives, the right benchmark has to be chosen. Usually the portfolio manager is not involved in this process, because benchmark selection is carried out throughout product development. This is especially true when the portfolio is set up for an institutional client. Currently, there is a variety of indices that track the performance of the corporate bond markets, based on only slightly differing criteria. Index selection is important because it constitutes the basis for strategic asset allocation decisions, the measurement of actively and passively managed credit portfolios, for derivative contracts, as well as for financial modeling and other academic research. Over-the-counter derivatives, exchange-traded funds and the provision of more data to investors have opened up new business opportunities for brokerage houses as well as for exchanges.

With so much choice available to investors, selection of an index is becoming more problematic as the differences between providers become more technical. The European Federation of Financial Analyst Societies (EFFAS) proposed a set of rules for calculating bond indices that provide transparency and consistency across index providers. In addition, there are some best practices in index construction that define a good index. Among the highlighted features some are technical, and some softer. Yet no index family and no individual index carries all of these features. Some are commonly found; others are scarcer. The weighting of the different features depends on the characteristics of the portfolio that is managed against the index, and on the preferences of the investor.

Among the most important characteristics for index families are representativeness, transparency and reliability. Especially for institutional investors the observance of these criteria is relevant, because the benchmark not only defines the strategic investment goal, but also the investment universe and thus the neutral position. Every deviation from the index characteristics, be it with respect to duration, yield curve, industry or issuer weighting results in tracking error. The smaller the tracking error limit for an actively managed portfolio is defined, the more is the longer term risk/return profile of the portfolio determined by the selected index. Therefore, benchmark indices have to suffice several criteria, of which the most prominent are detailed in Table 8.1.

If the investment universe of a portfolio and the composition of the benchmark index diverge significantly, the portfolio manager faces an additional risk. This benchmark risk is unsystematic and causes performance differences between the portfolio and its benchmark that cannot be controlled by the manager. This point should be kept in mind during the process of product development as well as during index selection, because this unsystematic risk causes tracking error without giving the investor the opportunity to generate any systematic outperformance versus the benchmark.

To accommodate the needs of different types of investors, a variety of types of indices have been developed. Broadly, these can be grouped into four main categories:

- narrow indices used primarily as the basis for index futures contracts,
- large capitalization indices used by international investors,
- broad market indices used by local investors, and finally
- specialized indices (e.g. sector, style or market segment indices).

When using the criteria described above, it would be normal to compare indices within the broad groupings listed above rather than across those groupings.

A market capitalization-weighted index will be a prerequisite for the vast majority of investors. There is a move by index providers to refine pure market capitalization weightings to take into account common investment constraints. Examples for this are issuer-capped or -constrained indices. They tend to be useful in less diversified market segments like the Euro high-yield bond market. Yet investors have to keep in mind that the tracking of issuer-capped indices causes higher transaction costs than traditional market capitalization-weighted indices do.

Total return indices will be the performance benchmark for most investors. Usually, these are calculated on a daily basis. In addition, capital or price only indices are a useful portfolio management tool. Indices that track the average spread versus government bonds or swaps, dollar or modified duration, coupon and market value of the index universe should supplement an index family. From a portfolio manager's point of view these index characteristics must be accessible on a daily basis, whereas historical data enables comprehensive analyses.

Table 8.1 Criteria for the selection of benchmark indices

Performance	The index should represent the performance of the market segment adequately. Performance and price indices should be available.
Relevance	The benchmark index should be relevant for the investment goals and investment universe. General acceptance by investors increases the likelihood that the peer group portfolios are measured against the same benchmark and thus enhances comparability.
Representativeness	The index should provide an accurate picture of the market it claims to represent. Sector, maturity and rating buckets should be mirrored appropriately, and a market-weighting scheme applied. In less diversified markets issuer-capped indices should be provided as an alternative.
Breadth	To reflect the performance of the market segment adequately, the index must offer sufficient diversification. The performance of narrow, concentrated indices is vulnerable to idiosyncratic, that is issuer-specific risks.
History	Research and evaluation of portfolio management performance should be based on the same index. Hence, a long history for financial modeling and analyses is desirable.
Transparency	The criteria for index additions and deletions and the rules for index calculation must be published and outlaid clearly. Changes to the rules must be announced early enough to allow investors to adjust their portfolios appropriately.
Data availability	Index data must be of high quality and published on time, if possible realtime, on information systems like Reuters and Bloomberg and on a web page. Structural reports, subindices and customized indices should also be available, at least upon request.
Compliance with industry standards	The index has to comply with international standards and regulatory requirements. Independence of the index owner/compiler helps to promote the credibility of an index family.
Replicability	The index portfolio should be replicable to allow the portfolio manager a neutral positioning. Sufficient liquidity and tradeability of the index constituents should be warranted. This point is essential for passively managed portfolios.
Reliability	The pricing must be accurate and reliable. Trader prices are preferred to matrix pricing.
Stability	The rules for additions and deletions must not be changed too often to enable tracking of the index and to minimize transaction costs.
Existence of derivates	Index derivatives should be available as a tool for efficient hedging against adverse market movements.

Source: Union Investment

Institutional investors want their indices to represent the investable universe. Much of the theoretical justification for indexing as an investment strategy relies on the index fund being the "market portfolio." Broad coverage within a market will allow valid comparisons between different investment styles, including active and passive. Internationally, the Lehman family of fixed income indices and the Merrill Lynch fixed income index family are designed to give a comprehensive coverage.

Ideally an index will have a set of rules that are preset, unambiguous and publicly available. This is particularly important for constituent reviews and corporate actions. Establishing rules at the outset reduces the risk of "interested parties" influencing the list of constituents. The best indices in this regard will have a set of rules that allow someone with those rules, the necessary data on the investment universe and (most rarely) the inclination, to replicate the list of constituents themselves. The rapid development of the European corporate bond market has necessitated various adjustments to the index-inclusion criteria. At the foremost, index providers like Lehman Brothers and Merrill Lynch had to increase the minimum size of the corporate bond issues included to represent the more liquid and thus investible part of the universe.

Daily electronic data feeds of index levels, constituents, changes and prices are vital to the portfolio management process. This data needs to be of high quality with very low error and recalculation rates. Downloads via the internet and, more importantly, via information systems like Bloomberg facilitate the use of benchmark indices. Tools that help to split indices according to sectors, rating classes and maturity buckets are a good basis for a structured portfolio management.

Now we come to the softer criteria. Investors will want a benchmark that is well-known and widely used within their peer group. This will give them some comfort as to the ongoing integrity of the index and the ability to make peer group comparisons. This would also allow multinational companies to standardize approaches across their pension plans.

Histories of indices will be used by investors and their consultants to formulate strategic allocation policies. Asset allocators and academics also have an interest in long data histories when building allocation models. The asset–liability modeling exercises that many pension funds and insurance companies now undertake on a regular basis to review strategic benchmarks, all tend to use historical volatilities and covariances that are derived directly from index histories. There may be some advantage to investors in using the same index for the ongoing fund management benchmark as that used in the prior modeling exercise.

Conflicts of interest can only damage the standing of an index. Suspicion surrounding the motives of interested parties is almost as bad. The involvement of investment banks in index compilation tends to create such suspicions, particularly around constituent review time. Most bond indices are proprietary indices that use trader pricing. Thus they are susceptible to be biased by the positioning of the trader. For short positions, for example, the trader has an interest in pricing the bond on the lower end of the market. Even the absence of positions on the trading book can distort an index, because those bonds are not marked actively. Indicative prices are highly susceptile to be erroneous. Hence, indices that are owned by exchanges or rely on the pricing of more than one investment bank are more likely to be accepted as independent. Especially among institutional investors the iBoxx index family has attracted a lot of interest, because it relies on pricing information of seven investment houses.

More and more investors are beginning to focus on transaction costs, and in less liquid market segments also on market impact costs. Clearly, good liquidity is an important factor in reducing market impact. International investors in particular are increasingly looking for liquid benchmarks and securities. This is reflected in the large cap bias found in many of the newer indices and exchange traded funds that are often based on very focused indices like, for example, the iBoxx Euro Liquid Corporate Index.

Investors' benchmarks, strategies and horizons change. Indeed the pace of change has accelerated in recent years, be it moves from pure government benchmarks to aggregate indices, from broad market to large cap benchmarks, or to indices that include issuer constraints. In these circumstances, institutional investors are becoming more focused on transition costs as they change their benchmarks. Index series that encompass a wide range of benchmarks and styles with similar methodologies have an advantage here.

Derivative contracts, in particular credit-linked notes on corporate bond indices, have a variety of uses: to gain synthetic exposure, as an arbitrage tool, to effect overlay strategies and to invest cash balances efficiently. The growing popularity of JECI and Trac-X as well as the exchange traded funds on the iBoxx Euro Liquid Corporate Index and the Goldman Sachs USD InvesTop Corporate Bond Index demonstrate the rising sophistication of market participants in the credit markets. They have realized that using a benchmark index that also has a liquid derivative contract can be of great benefit to investors.

The index market is becoming increasingly competitive and commercial. With little differentiation in construction methodology, competition between index providers is focusing on brand. Nevertheless, investors have to keep in mind their intended usage, be that fund management, trading, advice or research.

8.2 EXCHANGE TRADED FUNDS

The importance of asset allocation, or deciding what percentage of a portfolio to devote to various asset classes, cannot be overstated. Especially equity and corporate bond investors spend enormous efforts on picking individual investments, while they spend relatively little time on deciding what types of stocks or bonds to buy into their funds. Numerous empirical studies have shown that a large part of money managers' performance can be explained by asset allocation, not by their selection of individual stocks. Therefore it should be just the opposite. Investors should spend most of their time on overall asset selection and ignore individual investments for the most part. When a stock performs well, invariably stocks from the same asset classes follow in parallel. The primary goal should be to pick the right asset classes in order to outperform. Asset allocation is not easy and requires completely different skills than the selection of individual investments, but it is less detailed, and it rewards skilled investors generously. Before 2001, credit played a minor role in the asset allocation of private as well as institutional investors. This is due to the fact that there was no easy and cost efficient way to replicate the performance of credit markets appropriately.

The first credit portfolio product that gained widespread attention was Morgan Stanley's Tradable Custodial Receipts (Tracers), launched in October 2001. Tracers contain 30–35 corporate bonds or 50 credit default swaps on corporate issuers selected by liquidity and diversity. In the meantime, Lehman Brothers offered a similar product, Targeted Return Index Securities (Trains). Tracers and Trains were welcome arrivals, but have drawbacks. Both require accrued interest calculations atypical of other bonds and thus represent a serious challenge to back-office accounting. Also, when bonds in Trains or Tracers fall below investment grade, they are kicked out of their trusts and are either liquidated or delivered to investors. Yet the structures allow relatively long redemption periods for downgraded bonds, for example ten days for Trains. If the downgrade was triggered by serious financial problems, it is likely that the bond price deteriorates significantly before the bonds are sold.

The most important concern investors have with credit portfolio products like Tracers and Trains is liquidity. It is crucial that dealers will be ready to offer tight markets on the products, even several years down the road. In 2003, daily trading volumes for cash Tracers averaged US $75 million and US $100 million for the synthetic products. The average bid-ask spread was 5 bp, with other dealers than Morgan Stanley having stepped up to make markets in Tracers: Credit Suisse First Boston in the cash product and Merrill Lynch and JP Morgan Chase in the synthetic versions.

Compared with their equity counterparts, bond ETFs are still rare. This can be explained by the problems inherent in passive bond investing. Many of these problems are related to the issue of pertinent indices in this investment universe. Characteristics that separate bond indices from their counterparts in the equity universe relate to pricing, turnover and liquidity. With regard to constructing a portfolio that tracks a bond index, the high turnover of index constituents due to new issuances and the maturation of debt securities leads to rebalancing costs that are a lot higher than in equity trackers, where index components remain relatively stable. Especially in the credit universe, the degree of liquidity of bond index constituents does not always allow frequent trading and thus restricts investability.

However, since July 2002 there are some exchange-traded funds that aim to offer a cost-efficient way of diversifying into corporate bonds. Passive products specialist Barclays Global Investors has launched mutual funds which replicate an index, based on strict rules, allowing the investors exposure to the major issuers of US and European corporate bonds. Underlying indices are the Goldman Sachs USD InvesTop Corporate Bond Index and the iBoxx Euro Liquid Corporates Index. A rules-based structure allows investors to have a high level of confidence about transparency, because the index is a fair reflection of the liquid part of the market at any time. While the US ETF contains 100 issuers, the European index tracker consists of only 40 issuers. These focused indices allow the ETFs to be priced competitively and at realtime. Investors can trade them instantaneously in the same way as a stock or bond. The total expense ratio is capped at 20 bp, compared with 60–100 bp for an actively traded corporate bond mutual fund, making corporate bond ETFs interesting products for the strategic and tactical asset allocation of institutional investors.

However, the high default rates in the last few years and blowups of large companies like Enron, WorldCom and Ahold should remind investors of two basic priciples of investing in corporate bonds: the importance of diversified portfolios and the need for a thorough fundamental analysis. Skilled analysts can add significant value to corporate bond portfolios through their overweight or underweight recommendations on individual issuers. One can argue that an active management approach cannot avoid becoming a victim of fraud and corporate malfeasance. When rating agencies are not able to uncover the signs of fraud, investors will not be able to detect it based on publicly available information either. With regard to ETFs, risk is concentrated in a scant 40–100 issuers. This raises two questions: How many issuers are needed in a portfolio to protect sufficiently from losses through credit events? Do passively managed portfolios that are based on liquid corporate indices adequately represent the performance of the corporate bond market?

As of December 2003, the iBoxx Euro Liquid Corporates Index offered a spread over duration-matched government bonds of 60 bp. Assuming stable spreads, an investor, who measures his performance against government bonds, would have expected to earn an excess return of 60 bp. Yet, this calculation ignores the risk of credit events. If one name blows up and the price of the bond falls to 70 until it is excluded from the index, the portfolio suffers a loss depending on the weight of the issuer. If the index weight of the issuer exceeds 2 percent, the loss on this one name wipes out the complete expected excess return. This example illustrates that insufficiently diversified portfolios are highly vulnerable to idiosyncratic risks. Even for an actively managed portfolio, the concentration on only 40 issuers would require an extremely high success rate of the analyst and portfolio manager in anticipating possible blowups. Clearly, it might be objected that most blowups have significantly smaller weightings and that focusing on "safe" names in actively managed portfolios reduces risk. Yet, especially for real money investors who are benchmarked against government bonds, the risk associated with investing in narrow corporate bond baskets is asymmetric, because they are not able to benefit from an underweight position on overall corporate bonds and particularly on single names.

Compared with credit portfolio products like Tracers and Trains, corporate bond ETFs seem to be the most promising products due to their flexibility of use and ease of shorting. Especially with hedge funds and retail investors they are very popular. Yet, institutional investors face additional investment constraints. Investment guidelines prevent many fixed income portfolio managers from holding corporate bond ETFs because they are considered as equity.

CHAPTER 9

The Role of Ratings

9.1 REDUCING INFORMATION ASYMMETRY

Agency ratings are a standard metric of credit quality. Yet the blowup of large corporations like WorldCom, Enron and Parmalat has raised questions about the timeliness of rating changes. Nevertheless, agency ratings are a convenient, widely used indicator for a borrower's ability to service its liabilities. In their mission statement Moody's, one of the world's leading rating agencies, argue that "Credit ratings and research help investors analyze the credit risks associated with fixed-income securities. Ratings also create efficiencies in fixed-income markets and similar obligations, such as insurance and derivatives, by providing reliable, credible, and independent assessments of credit risk. For issuers, Moody's services increase market liquidity and may reduce transaction costs." This statement stresses that rating agencies see themselves as the providers of independent assessments of the credit quality of an issuer. Thus their objective is to promote the efficiency of credit markets by reducing the information asymmetry between borrowers and lenders.

Clearly corporate borrowers have more detailed information about their businesses and credit profiles than do lenders, in particular when they access capital markets to finance their business. Commercial banks usually have a close contact with their clients, thus lending decisions are based on a profound understanding of the borrowers. Because relations between companies and banks tend to be long term, commercial banks are able to monitor the credit quality of a borrower constantly and use covenants to prevent potentially credit-detrimental activities. If necessary, banks can agree to restructure loans in order to recover funds before allowing the company to default.

When companies decide to access the capital markets the relationship between borrower and lender is rather impersonal in the sense that borrowers do not know nor control who lent them the money. Conversely, bond investors often are not able to meet the company management regularly and thus rely primarily on information published by the company itself. Because of this distance between borrowers and lenders, rating agencies' assessments of the credit quality of an issuer help investors to mitigate the information asymmetry.

Credit rating agencies try to provide investors with a reliable estimate of credit risk. While S&P's assessment of credit quality is based on the probability of default, Moody's uses the product of the probability of default and loss given default, or in other words loss severity, to arrive at a rating. The default probability tracks relative risk over time. When loss severity is estimated, rating agencies consider issue characteristics, the degree of seniority and sector differences. Furthermore, it has to be taken into account that recovery rates vary over time and across jurisdictions. Ultimately, the rating is expected to mirror the future expected loss over time, based on historical experience.

The rating process itself is based on three pillars:

- Evaluation of financial strength with respect to the quantifiable aspects of a particular company's business;
- Assessment of the management quality and its commitment and ability to maintain a certain credit profile;
- Analysis of the impact of various scenarios on the credit quality of an issuer.

In order to arrive at a rating, one crucial assumption is made: creditworthiness is a stable concept. This means that historical data may be used to transform the information obtained from a company into estimates for default probability and loss severity. Since fundamentals change gradually over time, multinotch rating changes are unlikely. Rating agencies therefore use Outlooks and Watch Lists as leading indicators for potential rating changes. They signal in which direction the next rating step will probably occur. If, for example, a negative outlook is assigned, the rating agency usually defines certain criteria that have to be met by the issuer over a certain period of time, otherwise a rating downgrade can be expected. An example would be that a company must achieve positive free cash flows within a predetermined time-horizon. The failure to do so will result in the loss of the current rating.

However, rating outlooks and watchlists tend to have a built-in lag, too. Moody's has an 18-month horizon for its outlooks and 90 days for its watchlist, whereas S&P targets 90 days for its credit watch listings, and a longer but unspecified time-horizon for outlooks. Hence, credit ratings appear to be serially correlated. This in turn creates the impression that rating actions tend to lag changes in credit quality and their perception by market participants, reflected in spreads, substantially.

Current research focuses on the rating outlook and its impact on corporate bond prices. Since the mid-1990s, European corporate bond investors on average have become much more professional. Consequently, changes in an issuer's credit quality are anticipated earlier than they were some years ago. In conjunction with the increased liquidity of the European corporate bond market this has led to the observation that bond prices adjust rapidly to the fundamental assessment of market participants and their expectations regarding a possible rating change. Therefore, changes of the rating outlook that lead actual rating changes are monitored closely by corporate bond investors.

Significant price changes are not only observed after changes of the rating, but also after changes of the rating outlook. In many cases technical factors represent a major reason for bond price changes after a negative rating action. In particular, large price movements can be observed when investment restrictions of institutional investors are triggered by a rating action. A good example is the downgrade of Fiat in June 2002. The downgrade from Baa2 to Baa3 induced a large sell-off because investors anticipated a further downgrade to high yield. But Figure 9.1 also shows that bond prices already fell significantly when Moody's put Fiat on review for downgrade.

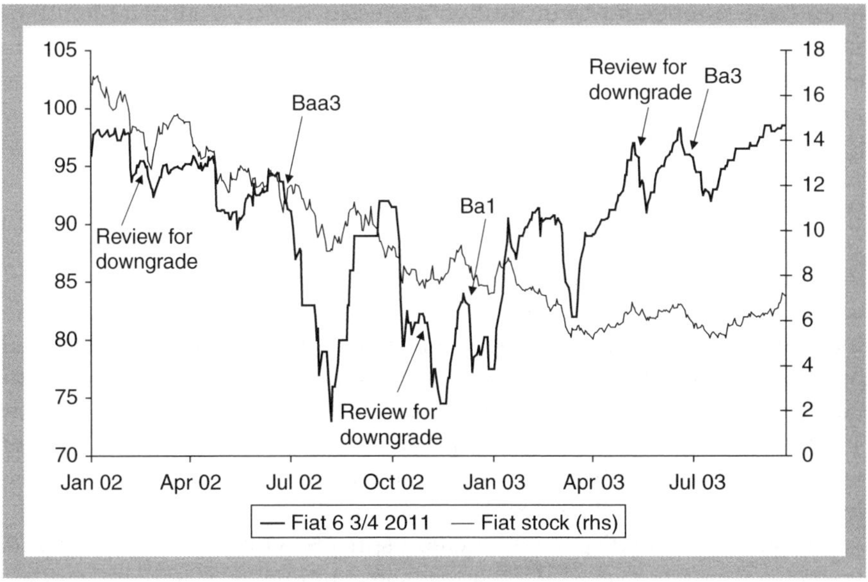

Figure 9.1 Reaction of Fiat bond and stock prices on rating actions

Sources: Bloomberg and Union Investment

Empirical studies by Weinstein (1977), Hand *et al.* (1992) and Kliger and Sarig (2000) highlight the following relationships between rating changes and a corporate issuer's bond and stock prices:

- Bond prices adjust to a new rating.
- Equity prices also react on rating changes, usually opposite to the bond price movements.
- Surprise upgrades tend to result in a reduced implied equity volatility.
- There is no indication that new rating information has an impact on firm value. According to the Asset Substitution Theory equity and bond prices react in opposite directions to rating changes, which ultimately leads to changes in the ratio of the market value of equity to debt.
- The higher the leverage of an issuer the stronger the bond price reaction to a rating change tends to be.

The majority of price movements that is caused by a rating action is explained by new information which is revealed at the time of the rating action. Typically companies reserve the right to hold back certain information from investors, clients, business partners and competitors. This can be long-term projections, business plans or internal analyses. Usually rating agencies have access to internal documents during their rating process. Therefore, the rating of a company reflects more information than available to the public and to institutional investors such as mutual funds or insurance companies. A rating change itself is therefore an information about a change of a company's credit quality because it incorporates non-public information.

9.2 RATINGS AND CREDIT SPREADS

Ratings are designed to reflect credit risk over time. Two bonds from different issuers that share the major characteristics, for example with respect to the degree of structural and legal subordination, coupon and embedded optionality, and additionally have the same rating, should trade approximately at the same level. Bond spreads of course also depend on maturity, yielding a term structure of credit spreads. The average spread of an issuer within a particular rating class furthermore depends on the liquidity of the individual bonds and its sector classification.

Despite the wide dispersion of credit spreads within the rating buckets the general link between credit spreads and ratings is clear, with average spread increasing as credit quality decreases. However, as Figure 9.2 illustrates there are large overlaps between individual rating distributions.

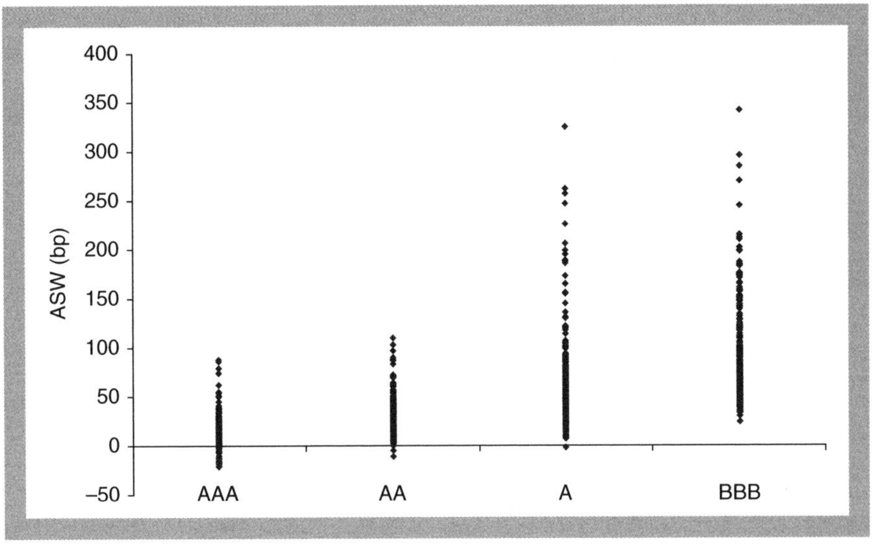

Figure 9.2 Spread dispersion of Euro investment grade corporate bonds by rating class as of February 27th, 2004

Source: Merrill Lynch

Myriad examples can be found to show that market participants often perceive the risk of one company in comparison to another to be completely different, even if both have the same rating. It should be noted that Figure 9.2 includes bonds with rather different maturities and coupons. Altman (1989) and Taylor and Perraudin (2001) have shown the presence of highly persistent inconsistencies between credit ratings and bond spreads, even after adjusting for liquidity and potential tax effects.

One example from the automotive sector is the large spread differential between Ford and Renault bonds with similar coupon and maturity. Although the rating agencies assign approximately the same credit risk to both issuers, investors view the risk that is related to owning Ford bonds as significantly higher. Figure 9.3 clearly outlines that Ford bonds have been much more volatile than Renault bonds between September 2003 and February 2004. When S&P put Ford on credit watch negative on October 21, 2003, spreads widened massively. Even if only very few investors feared a multiple notch downgrade of Ford from the then BBB rating, a 1 notch downgrade to BBB coupled with a negative outlook would have caused concerns about a later downgrade of Ford into high-yield. There were fears that the high-yield market would not be able to absorb the large volume of outstanding Ford bonds, and from a fundamental perspective that the company's financing costs would rise, thus limiting the company's financial flexibility massively. This example highlights that market technicals at least temporarily can be the dominant driver of credit spreads.

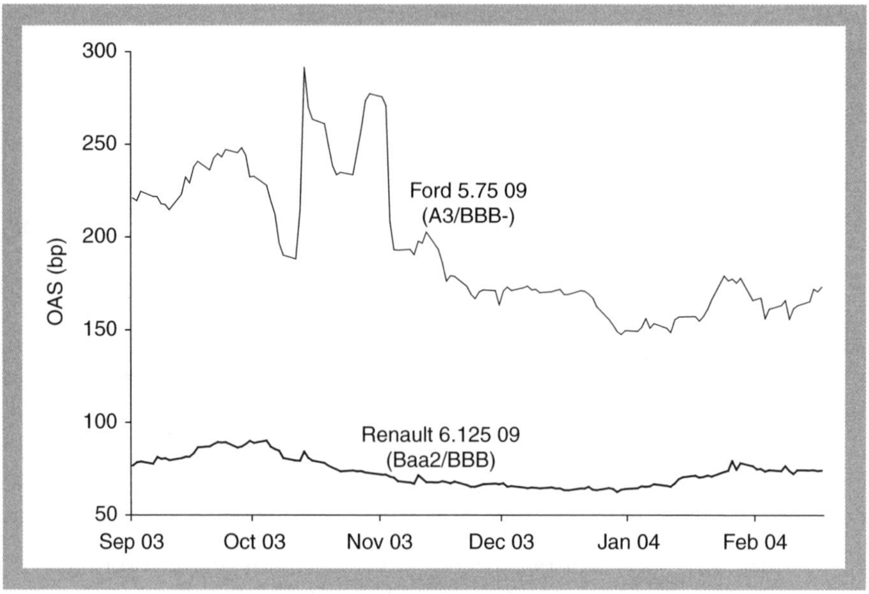

Figure 9.3 Spread history of Ford and Renault issues with similar characteristics

Source: Bloomberg

One typical reason for spread differentials between bonds of the same rating are liquidity considerations, particularly with respect to stress situations. Generally, bonds with a large issue size, issued recently and actively traded by several market makers tend to be the most liquid. Sometimes old bonds with a small issue size, too, trade at rather tight levels. This is often the case for typical "CDO (Collateralized debt obligations) names", that is bonds that are often included when CDOs are set up. Another reason for wide spread differentials between issuers with similar credit quality is that many market participants are concerned with potential mark-to-market losses. Therefore, rather illiquid and more volatile bonds require a higher spread, even if spread volatility is rather due to market technicals than uncertainty regarding company fundamentals. Consequently, it is natural that credit spreads differ even for bonds and issuers with the same rating. But more importantly, only a fraction of the actual credit spread is explained by credit risk, which in turn is reflected by the rating.

9.3 THE PERSPECTIVE OF BUY-AND-HOLD INVESTORS

Based on historical data on defaults we can derive the fraction of the spread over riskless bonds for different rating classes and maturities, that is solely due to the probability of default and loss given default. The expected loss rate is derived from these two factors. Market participants who have a buy-and-hold perspective must decide on whether the current spread of a corporate bond sufficiently compensates for default and migration risk. This is rather the perspective of a private than an institutional investor, because the latter in general has a short- to medium-term investment horizon and rarely holds a bond to maturity. In general, the institutional investor tries to achieve an excess return against a benchmark with a trading oriented management approach.

However, for the calculation of the required spread from a buy-and-hold perspective reliable default probabilities and recovery rates have to be used. If the issuer has an agency rating, Moody's historical database is a good starting point. This database compiles expected default probabilities on a historical basis which is updated annually and also average recovery rates depending on the seniority of a bond (Tables 9.1 and 9.2). Those values allow to calculate a "fair" spread that solely mirrors credit risk.

For a corporate bond investor who is willing to hold a corporate bond to maturity the credit spread has to compensate fully for the loss if the company defaults during the lifetime of the bond. The expected loss is given by

Table 9.1 Cumulative default probabilities of corporate bonds for the period 1970–2002

	2 years(%)	5 years(%)	10 years(%)	20 years
Aaa	0.00	0.12	0.64	1.65
Aa	0.03	0.26	0.73	2.96
A	0.22	0.51	1.56	5.17
Baa	0.61	2.25	5.26	12.73
Ba	3.51	11.36	21.29	39.15
B	14.16	32.31	50.01	61.35
Caa-C	37.12	60.09	78.54	80.92

Source: Moody's

Table 9.2 Recovery rates for defaulted US corporate bonds for the period 1982–2002

	Investment grade	Speculative grade
Secured bank loan	74.88	68.51
Senior secured	70.10	45.43
Senior unsecured	45.02	32.19
Subordinated	33.94	30.48

Source: Moody's

the product of the probability of default, p_D, and loss severity, which is defined as 100 percent minus the recovery rate, R. On the other hand, if the company does not default, the investor earns an excess return equivalent to the spread, S, times maturity of the bond, T. The effect of interest on interest is ignored in this calculation. Hence the minimum spread required by buy-and-hold investors for taking on credit risk can be derived from the following equation:

$$p_D \cdot (1-R) = (1-p_D) \cdot S \cdot T.$$

Consequently the fraction of the spread that is explained by default risk is given by

$$S = \frac{p_D \cdot (1 - R)}{(1 - p_D) \cdot T}.$$

Based on the Moody's data depicted above, Figure 9.4 provides an overview of the spreads that are required to compensate investors for default risk associated with holding corporate bonds of a certain rating class. Even if the general approach is buy-and-hold investment restrictions

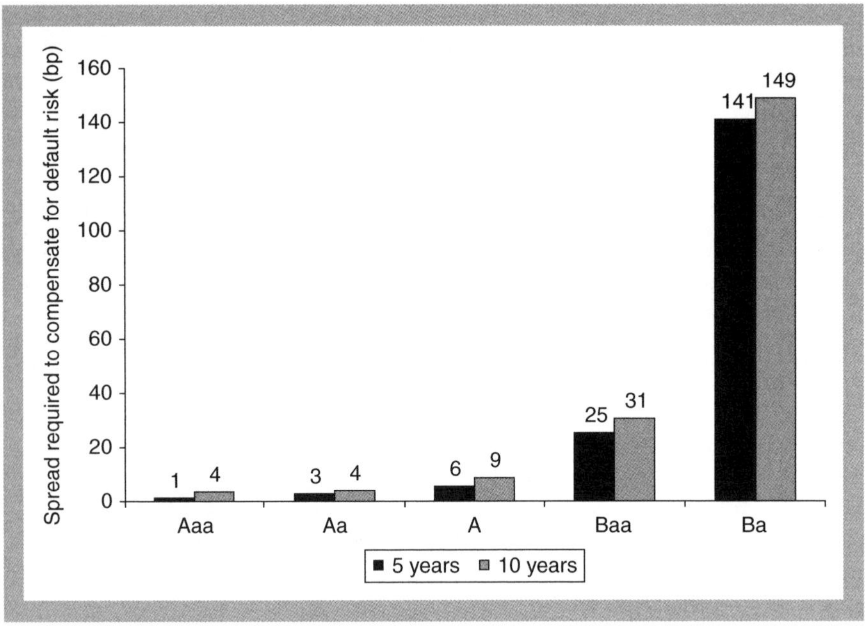

Figure 9.4 Spreads required to compensate investors for taking on default risk under the assumption that future default probabilities and recovery rates equal historical ones

Sources: Moody's and Union Investment

with respect to ratings may cause investors to be forced sellers when the bonds of an issuer are downgraded, for example, below investment grade. This effect is not considered in the computed spreads, because this is rather the perspective of an active investor, which is laid out below.

Figure 9.5 shows that a spread level of merely 25 bp was never achieved between 1989 and 2003 for Baa rated US corporate bonds. One reason is that from an economic perspective the default probabilities and recovery rates that were assumed to calculate the required spreads were too optimistic for this period. Especially between 1997 and 2002 the fundamental environment for corporate bonds was unfavorable. New technologies, company takeovers and equity buyback programs were primarily financed by the issuance of corporate bonds, resulting in an increased level of leverage in the corporate sector. Investors consequently required higher risk premia to invest in corporate bonds. One way to obtain more adequate estimates of required spreads is to use default probabilities and recovery rates that are typical for the current stage of the business cycle. Modern models for credit risk management and the pricing of credit derivatives account for the current economic environment. In particular, they differentiate between periods of expansion and contraction, because historically default rates increased and recovery rates fell during economic downturns, thus leading to a higher risk for credit investors. Additionally, a worst-case-scenario can be constructed assuming a zero per cent recovery value. A fair spread of

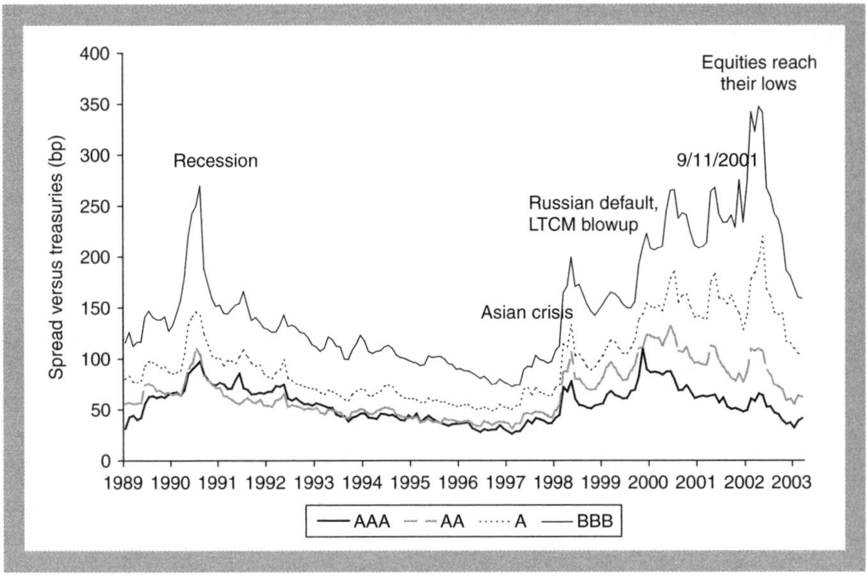

Figure 9.5 Spread history of US corporate bonds by rating class

Sources: Lehman Brothers

0.46 percent will be computed for Baa rated corporate bonds with a maturity of 5 years which is again a lot lower than the actually observed spreads.

9.4 THE PERSPECTIVE OF AN ACTIVE MANAGER

As mentioned before, from an active portfolio manager's perspective a major concern is migration risk. Investors who do not hold a bond until maturity have to be compensated for a possible deterioration in credit quality, a potentially resulting downgrade and increased volatility. This becomes even more important if the downgrade triggers investment restrictions. For a specific corporate bond the expected excess return over duration-matched government bonds can be estimated in three steps:

- The probability of rating changes are derived from a rating transition matrix;
- Spread and price changes for up- and downgraded bonds have to be estimated.
- Expected return is computed as the weighted sum of the price changes.

Consider a portfolio of 5-year A-rated US corporate bonds. Between 1989 and 2003 they traded on average at a premium of about 100 bp over duration-matched government bonds which is roughly the level that was reached in August 2003. Table 9.3 shows that 91.20 percent of these bonds maintain their rating and hence can be expected to earn an excess return of 100 bp over a 1-year time-horizon. Of the bonds rated A at the beginning of the year 2.66 percent can be expected to receive an upgrade in the course of the year. Investors would expect to benefit from a subsequent spread tightening to an average of 55 bp if upgraded to Aaa or 70 bp if the bonds are upgraded to Aa.

Table 9.3 One-year rating migration probabilities for US investment grade corporate bonds

Rating at the start of the year	Rating at the end of the year						
	Aaa%	Aa%	A%	Baa%	Ba%	B%	C or D%
Aaa	91.90	7.38	0.72	0.00	0.00	0.00	0.00
Aa	1.13	91.26	7.09	0.31	0.21	0.00	0.00
A	0.10	2.56	91.20	5.33	0.61	0.20	0.00
Baa	0.00	0.21	5.36	87.94	5.46	0.82	0.21

Source: Moody's

Table 9.4 Example for the calculation of expected excess return for a 1-year investment horizon

Rating at the end of the year	Expected spread at the end of the year (bp)	Expected return over treasury bonds (bp)	Migration probability (%)	Contribution to expected excess return (bp)
Aaa	55	258	0.10	0.26
Aa	70	205	2.56	5.25
A	100	100	91.20	91.20
Baa	150	−75	5.33	−4.00
Ba	250	−425	0.61	−2.59
B	400	−950	0.20	−1.90

Source: Union Investment

Conversely, downgrades below A would result in widening credit spreads and consequently negative excess returns versus duration-matched government bonds. Differences in accrued interest between corporate bonds and government bonds can be considered at this stage.

If the issuer does not default, which is, measured by historical standards, extremely unlikely for an A-rated company, an investor earns an incremental coupon income of 100 bp over a 1-year horizon. Conditional on the fact that the bond receives a downgrade to Baa during the course of the year, a price depreciation of 50 bp times the duration of the bond at the end of the year, that is approximately 3.5, would have to be expected. Since Baa-rated US corporate bonds on average traded at 150 bp over treasuries, 50 bp represents the spread widening that has to be expected as a consequence of the downgrade. Consequently the investor expects a negative excess return of $100 - 3.5 \times 50 = -75$ bp, if the rating is downgraded from A to Baa. Table 9.4 details the same computation for the other potential rating changes.

The addition of the individual contributions to expected excess return in Table 9.4 yields an expected 1-year excess return of 88.2 bp for A-rated corporate bonds with a maturity of 5-years. This is significantly below the initial spread of 100 bps. The difference reflects the fact that a downgrade is more probable for A-rated corporate bonds than an upgrade, and that the associated spread changes are not symmetric. The magnitude of spread widenings due to downgrades is usually much higher than the spread tightening after rating upgrades. It is interesting to note that among investment grade bonds the ratio of upgrades to downgrades is most favorable for Baa-rated bonds. However, in the case of a downgrade these bonds often suffer massive price declines, because they fall below investment grade levels.

9.5 RATINGS AND RISK MANAGEMENT

For purposes of risk management bonds are often grouped according to agency ratings based on the assumption that bonds with similar ratings tend to show a high degree of comovement. Breger *et al.* (2003) examine whether the correlation between individual bonds increases if they are grouped by implied ratings, that is by spread classes rather than by agency ratings. The rationale for this would be that market valuations are a better indicator for the drivers of credit spread changes, namely perceived credit quality and risk exposure, than are agency ratings. In their empirical study they find that bonds of the same spread class are more similar than bonds with the same rating from a risk/return perspective. Breger *et al.* (2003) conclude that the classification of bonds based on market data provides a more reliable basis for modeling return relationships than does a classification by agency ratings. However, one has to note that the motivation behind this study differs significantly from the rating agencies' approach. The objective is not to predict default risk, but rather to improve the classification of corporate borrowers and provide a basis for reliable spread risk forecasts.

The rating agencies have been criticized for being too slow to react to changes in the credit quality of an issuer, leading to serially correlated rating patterns and limiting the value of ratings as a risk management tool. As a reaction, Moody's decided to put its rating process under review, and acquired KMV to be able to provide investors with additional, market-based assessments of an issuer's credit quality. The feedback from market participants was surprising. Since investors themselves tend to use spreads and spread volatility as indicators for credit risk, the vast majority does not want Moody's or the other rating agencies to switch to a more market-based approach when assessing the credit quality of an issuer. There is really a need for, according to the feedback, more transparency with regard to the rating process. This would allow investors to use rating agency information in their risk management most efficiently.

CHAPTER 10

Portfolio Construction

10.1 INTRODUCTION

So far we have described a rather intuitive way of combining individual views in a portfolio. Top-down and bottom-up analyses have determined the overall strategy for the portfolio, spread class and sector selection and finally issuer weightings. This qualitative methodology does not require estimates of returns, risks and correlations between the investments, and therefore is easy to implement. Yet, it is not able to capture the full benefits of diversification and to tailor the expected risk/return profile of the portfolio to the preferences of the investor. Since the seminal work of Markowitz (1952), diversification is a central tenet of modern investment theory. In the context of credit portfolios it plays a crucial role, because it helps to control downside risk arising from single issuer credit events. Since the mid-1990s debt-financed M&A activities, share buybacks, and the introduction of new technologies have fueled the new issue pipeline and broadened the corporate bond universe. Meanwhile, the European corporate bond market offers sufficient market breadth and depth for institutional investors to construct thoroughly diversified portfolios. If the portfolio manager is capable of quantifying the risk and return characteristics of his investment alternatives, portfolio optimization approaches present a formalized and thus objective way of deriving investment recommendations. This applies irrespective of the performance target of the investor. Portfolio optimization can be used with respect to portfolios that are managed in absolute risk/return terms as well as portfolios that are managed relative to a benchmark index (Figure 10.1). Various constraints can be included, for example a short

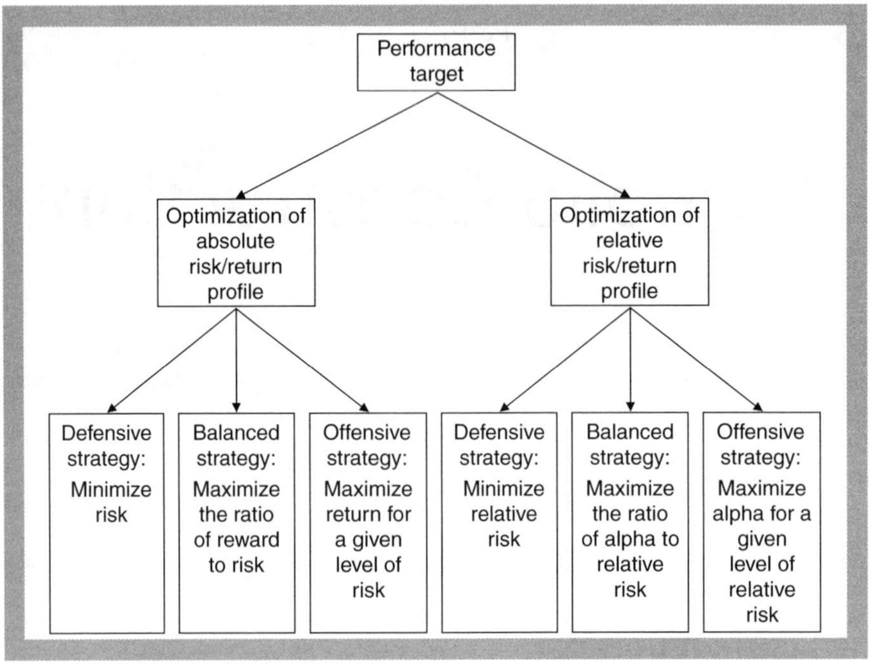

Figure 10.1 Portfolio optimization objectives

Source: Union Investment

sales restriction for real money investors, maximum concentration limits or desired duration ranges.

Clearly investors willing to allocate a part of their budget to corporate bonds are facing two questions. First, they have to decide how much of their budget they want to invest in corporate bonds. In this context we will focus on a pure fixed income portfolio. Usually private as well as institutional investors define their long-term asset allocation with respect to the asset classes such as stocks, bonds and real estate in a preliminary process. The second decision concerns the sector allocation of the portfolio which is part of the tactical asset allocation. As noted before, the sector allocation of a corporate bond portfolio essentially determines its risk/return profile and portfolio beta.

In this chapter, we will take the view of an investor who evaluates portfolio performance by the excess return over treasury bills and risk either by the dispersion of returns or a downside risk measure. That said, the described process is well suited for total return investors, whereby total return investing is understood as the target of achieving above-average returns in the medium- and long term. It must not be confused with absolute return concepts that focus on avoiding below target returns over a clearly defined period of time. In most cases, the ultimate goal is to avoid negative returns under all circumstances. It is worth mentioning that all of the portfolio construction frameworks can be tailored to the needs of active, but nevertheless benchmark-oriented managers.

Mean–variance analysis, made popular by Markowitz and Sharpe, has been the basis for the process of portfolio optimization since the 1990s. Yet, the method itself suffers from various pitfalls. Among others it ignores deviations of the return distributions from normality. The asymmetric risk profile of corporate bonds and the illiquidity of certain segments of the international corporate bond markets make great demand on the process of portfolio construction. Merton (1974) clarified that corporate bonds can be replicated by the combination of a riskless bond and a short put on the assets of the company. This shows that the return potential of corporate bonds is somewhat constrained whereas the possible loss in the event of default is only limited by the recovery. Between 2000 and 2002, spectacular defaults like Enron and WorldCom heightened the sensitivity of investors to the risks associated with credits. In general the following relation holds: the higher the leverage of an issuer, the higher the credit risk. Remember that the short-put option on the assets of a highly leveraged issuer is much closer at-the-money than that of a conservatively financed company. And the closer the short put option is at-the-money the more asymmetric becomes the risk profile of a corporate bond. For those issuers small changes in credit quality such as, for example, due to increased dividend payments, can lead to significant volatility of spreads and corporate bond prices.

A special situation occurs in the high-yield sector. The illiquidity in large parts of the universe causes price lags meaning that the aforementioned small changes in credit quality are not immediately reflected in bond prices. In the economic literature, this effect is known as non-trading. With respect to high-yield indices non-trading and non-synchronous trading of index bonds can lead to autocorrelation of returns. Therefore, estimates of the index volatility for illiquid asset classes can be distorted. Usually the true volatility of illiquid asset classes is underestimated. In a portfolio context too large portfolio weights are the consequence. Especially portfolios constructed in the classical mean–variance framework suffer from that problem.

In this chapter, two alternative approaches to portfolio optimization are introduced. Like the mean–variance framework they are consistent with the assumption of risk-averse investors. But additionally the methodologies proposed are able to cope with skewness and leptokurtosis (fat tails) in the distribution of returns. Particular attention is paid to autocorrelation in index returns due to the illiquidity of certain market segments. A technique for the adjustment of index returns is presented. The empirical analysis in this chapter relies on the US bond market because of its longer history and more reliable data compared to the European bond markets. It focuses on the effects of autocorrelation, skewness and kurtosis in index returns on the process of portfolio construction and on the composition and risk/return profile of the optimized portfolios.

10.2 STATISTICAL PROPERTIES OF BOND RETURNS

The asymmetric distribution of corporate bond returns is easily explained by the Merton model introduced in Chapter 2. Numerous studies substantiate that even the return distributions of less risky and more liquid asset classes like government bonds are skewed and leptokurtic. Moreover, index returns exhibit significant autocorrelation that can be explained partially by a permanent component. Basically, bond returns are a result of price movements, interest accrual, pull to par, and roll down of the yield-curve effects. While the first component is highly variable the other three components are rather stable over time.

Because of their long history and good data reliability the empirical study is based on Merrill Lynch indices for the period January 1987 to September 2003. So the sample period comprises 201 months, spanning more than two business cycles. It contains the 1989/90 US recession, two periods of dramatic Fed tightening, the Tequila crisis in 1994, the Asian crisis in 1997, and Russia's default in 1998. Driven by a secular trend of disinflation the yield of 10-year treasury notes declined from 7.2 to 3.9 percent in this period. With regard to future return expectations this should be kept in mind.

Table 10.1 demonstrates that all of the examined bond indices exhibit negative skewness and excess kurtosis, both of which increase the probability of

Table 10.1 Descriptive statistics of Merrill Lynch US bond indices during the sample period Jan. 1987–Sep. 2003

	Government	Agency	MBS	Corporate	High yield
Mean	0.642	0.651	0.663	0.711	0.728
Median	0.619	0.750	0.707	0.775	0.955
Standard Deviation	1.369	1.113	1.082	1.413	2.025
Skewness	−0.259	−0.336	−0.162	−0.289	−0.498
Kurtosis	3.284	3.302	4.189	3.383	6.429
Jarque–Bera statistic	2.919	4.545	12.726*	4.032	106.799*
1st Order serial correlation	0.136	0.188*	0.162*	0.152*	0.264*

Notes: All numbers are based on monthly percentage returns. * denotes significant statistics at a confidence level of 5 percent. Critical levels for the Jarque–Bera statistics and the autocorrelation coefficients are 5.991 respective 0.138

Source: Union Investment

extreme negative returns. For all asset classes except for the most liquid sector, government bonds, significant autocorrelation is identified in monthly index returns. Therefore, sample estimators of standard deviation, skewness and kurtosis are biased. Hence, the results of common tests for normality of returns should be interpreted carefully. For reason of completeness the results of one test of normality are provided. The Jarque–Bera (1987) test for the normality of observations can only be rejected for the mortgage-backed securities and high-yield sector. However, it should be noted that the distribution of returns of single corporate bond issuers is highly skewed. But the broad diversification on the index level mitigates this effect.

10.3 PORTFOLIO OPTIMIZATION WITH SKEWNESS AND KURTOSIS

The statistical properties of bond returns do not correspond with one of the basic assumptions of modern portfolio theory. As indicated by the descriptive statistics the empirical distributions of bond returns significantly deviate from a normal distribution. Keeping in mind this deficiency we nevertheless provide the results of the classical mean–variance framework as a benchmark in the empirical part of this chapter. As an alternative, two techniques are introduced that explicitly take account of skewness and kurtosis during the process of portfolio construction.

Downside risk measures apply to the intuitive understanding of risk of most investors. They associate risk with below-target returns. Typical targets are "preservation of nominal or real capital invested". By utilizing below-target returns, lower partial moments are measuring the amount of negative skewness of an empirical distribution. The lower partial moment of order n, a downside risk measure proposed by Fishburn (1977), is defined as

$$\mathrm{LPM}_{\tau}^{n} = E[\max(\tau - R, 0)^{n}].$$

The random variable R denotes asset returns, τ is the (stochastic or deterministic) target level. Special attention is due to the lower partial moments of order 0 to 2. LPM_0 denotes shortfall probability, LPM_1 shortfall mean and LPM_2 shortfall variance. As Bawa (1975) shows, the lower partial moment of a particular order n corresponds to a certain type of utility function. We will focus on the lower partial moment of first order because it is consistent with the utility function of a risk-neutral investor. Moreover, second-order stochastic dominance algorithms allow to test the efficiency of the optimized portfolios.

Harlow (1991) proposes an algorithm for portfolio optimization in a mean–shortfall risk framework. According to this methodology the minimum risk portfolio is obtained by minimizing the expression

$$\frac{1}{T}\sum_{t=1}^{T} \max(\tau - \omega_P' R_t, 0)$$

subject to the constraints $\omega_P'1 = 1$ and $\omega_P \geq 0$, where ω_P denotes the vector of portfolio weights. The latter constraint excludes short sales and can be relaxed in a hedge fund context. The target level τ could be chosen to be the risk-free rate, but for benchmark-oriented managers it is also possible to use bond index returns as a performance target. Bawa and Lindenberg (1977) and Nawrocki (1991) present an alternative methodology for estimating the lower partial moment of order n for a portfolio which relies on the correlation matrix of asset returns. Since correlation primarily reflects dependency in the middle of the return distribution, that is, in normal times, we prefer to follow the Harlow methodology.

Negative skewness and leptokurtosis increase the risk of extreme negative returns. Therefore, our second alternative risk measure explicitly captures the third and fourth moment of the probability distribution. The Cornish–Fisher (1937) expansion provides an extension of the widely used value at risk (VaR) concept. Although the VaR concept is by definition designed to capture the risk of extreme losses, the Cornish–Fisher expansion specifies this concept with respect to skewness and kurtosis. According to the Cornish–Fisher expansion the adjusted value at risk is defined as

$$\mathrm{VaR}_{\mathrm{CF}} = m + \sigma\left[z_c + \frac{1}{6}\left(z_c^2 - 1\right)\chi + \frac{1}{24}\left(z_c^3 - 3z_c\right)\kappa - \frac{1}{36}\left(2z_c^3 - 5z_c\right)\chi^2\right],$$

where χ denotes skewness, κ excess kurtosis and z_c the quantile of the normal distribution for a given confidence level c. Setting the confidence level c to 99 percent and ignoring the drift m renders

$$\mathrm{VaR}_{\mathrm{CF}}^{0.99} = \sigma(2.33 - 0.738\chi + 0.236\kappa + 0.379\chi^2).$$

From this expression it can be seen easily that $\mathrm{VaR}_{\mathrm{CF}}$ increases when

- volatility increases,
- skewness decreases (becomes more negative),
- kurtosis increases,
- the absolute level of skewness increases.

Altogether, the adjusted VaR has the desired properties to cope with non-normal return distributions. Moreover, in conjunction with the correlation matrix of asset returns it allows to calculate the optimal portfolios with an algorithm similar to the quadratic programming algorithm used in the mean–variance framework. For the description of further transformations interested readers may refer to Mina and Ulmer (1999) and Li (2000).

Despite the obvious advantages of the VaR concept, investors should be careful when applying this approach for portfolio optimization. Although VaR fulfils our requirements with respect to reflecting downside risk, Artzner *et al.* (1997) have shown that it does not comply with one of the basic requirements of a satisfactory risk measure. In mathematical terms, it is not necessarily coherent, meaning that the condition of sub-additiveness is hurt. In other words, under certain circumstances the optimization problem has multiple local solutions. Convergence towards the one and only global optimum cannot be achieved with the usual Newton-style descent algorithms.

Because of the different approaches towards risk measurement the composition of the efficient portfolios should differ significantly. Asset classes with more negatively skewed or leptokurtic return distributions are expected to receive lower weightings in the shortfall risk and the Corning–Fisher framework. We will focus on the composition and risk/return profile of three portfolios with very special characteristics (Figure 10.2). The minimum

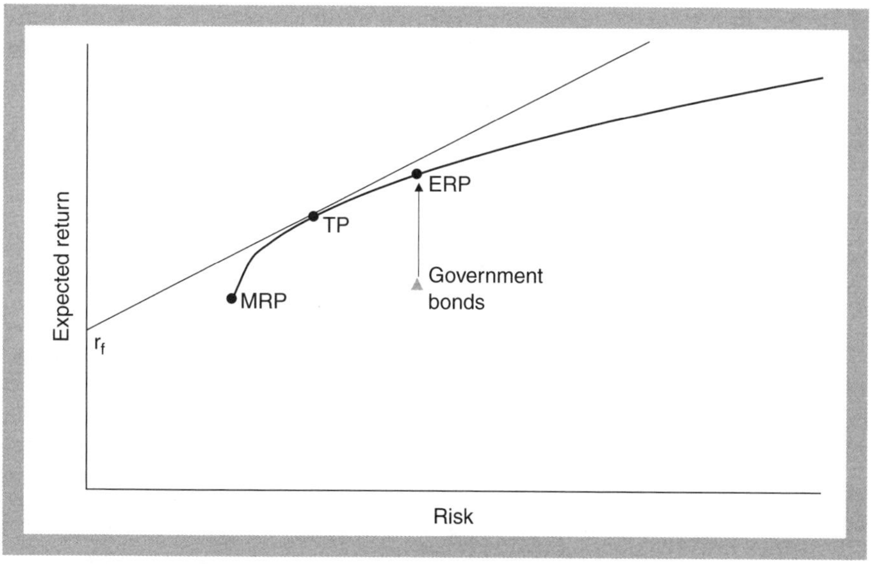

Figure 10.2 Efficient frontier with minimum risk portfolio (MRP), tangency portfolio (TP) and equal risk portfolio (ERP)

Source: Union Investment

risk portfolio (MRP) minimizes the risk subject to the imposed short sales constraint. Furthermore, the tangency portfolio (TP) and an equal risk portfolio (ERP) are examined. The TP maximizes the ratio of excess return over the risk-free rate to portfolio risk, known as the Sharpe ratio. On a depiction of the efficient frontier the TP is determined by a tangency to the efficient frontier through the risk-free rate r_f. As suggested by its name the ERP is designed to maximize return for a given level of risk, for example the volatility of a pure government portfolio. From the perspective of a government bond investor, it highlights the opportunity costs of neglecting the return opportunities associated with credits.

Table 10.2 displays the composition of the optimized portfolios. As a comparison the market capitalization weights should be kept in mind. Roughly speaking, the market weights of government bonds, agencies and mortgage-backed securities with respect to the US bond market are 26, 12, and 32 percent. Investment grade and high-yield corporate bonds are responsible for 23 and 7 percent of the market value of outstanding US bonds. In this context, municipal bonds are excluded because they do not play a significant role in the portfolios of international investors.

Across all of our optimization approaches, the MRPs and TPs are mainly made up of agencies and mortgage-backed securities, whereas government bonds are not represented in any of the portfolios. Despite its high volatility the high-yield sector seems to provide significant diversification benefits. However, it should be noted that the high-yield weight decreases when skewness and kurtosis are considered during the process of portfolio construction. In the sample period investors willing to accept the risk of a pure government portfolio would have been best off to invest a large part of their assets in a broadly diversified portfolio of investment grade and high-yield corporate bonds. Thus, they would have earned an excess return of 6–8 bp per month over government bonds.

Table 10.2 Composition of MRPs, TPs and ERPs based on the mean–variance (MV), shortfall risk (LPM) and Corning–Fisher (CF) framework for the sample period Jan. 1987–Sep. 2003

	Minimum risk portfolio			Tangency portfolio			Equal risk portfolio		
	MV	LPM	CF	MV	LPM	CF	MV	LPM	CF
Government	—	—	—	—	—	—	—	—	—
Agency	39.9	—	47.5	20.2	—	26.0	—	—	—
MBS	44.8	91.6	45.3	57.6	82.0	62.5	—	—	14.4
Corporate	—	—	—	—	—	—	66.3	54.1	75.5
High Yield	15.3	8.4	7.2	22.2	18.0	11.5	33.7	45.9	10.1

Source: Union Investment

Table 10.3 Risk/return characteristics of MRPs, TPs and ERPs based on the mean–variance (MV), shortfall risk (LPM) and Corning–Fisher (CF) framework for the sample period January 1987 to September 2003

	Minimum risk portfolio			**Tangency portfolio**			**Equal risk portfolio**			**Govt. bonds**
	MV	**LPM**	**CF**	**MV**	**LPM**	**CF**	**MV**	**LPM**	**CF**	
Mean	0.668	0.668	0.662	0.675	0.675	0.667	0.716	0.718	0.706	0.642
Standard deviation	1.019	1.047	1.033	1.034	1.041	1.024	1.368	1.427	1.299	1.368
Sharpe ratio	0.223	0.217	0.214	0.226	0.225	0.221	0.201	0.195	0.204	0.147
LPM_1	0.308	0.300	0.312	0.311	0.304	0.304	0.430	0.446	0.404	0.446
Reward to LPM_1	0.738	0.757	0.708	0.753	0.769	0.744	0.641	0.622	0.656	0.451
VaR_{CF}	2.904	2.920	2.842	3.068	3.028	2.877	4.147	4.561	3.563	3.563
Reward to VaR_{CF}	0.078	0.078	0.078	0.076	0.077	0.079	0.066	0.061	0.074	0.057

Note: The highlighted fields were optimized subject to the constraints described in the text. All numbers are based on monthly percentage returns

Source: Union Investment

For a comparison Table 10.3 contains the risk/return characteristics of a US government portfolio. By definition, all of the optimized portfolios offer a more attractive risk/reward profile than treasury bonds. In addition to the mean and the risk measures we also provide risk-adjusted performance numbers. They are defined as the ratio of excess return over the risk-free rate to portfolio risk. When risk is measured by the standard deviation of returns we get the Sharpe (1966) ratio. Ang and Chua (1979) provide an overview of composite measures of investment performance when alternative concepts of risk measurement are used.

Levy (1992) points out that lower partial moments of first order are consistent with second-order stochastic dominance. The concept of stochastic dominance has several important advantages. It requires no distributional assumptions, takes all the moments of the return distributions into account and requires only very mild assumptions about investor behavior. With respect to the comparison of the performance of several investment choices, it allows to create two different groups. The efficient set contains the desirable alternatives, the inefficient set those investments that are found to be stochastically dominated by at least one other investment (Figure 10. 3). The preference criteria are that the investor prefers more to less, is risk averse and prefers positive skewness. For all utility functions, investment G dominates F stochastically

- by first order, if $F(x) \geq G(x)$ for all x (with at least one strict inequality),

- by second order, if $\int_{-\infty}^{x} [G(t) - F(t)]\, dt \leq 0$ for all x (with at least one strict inequality),
- by third order, if $\int_{-\infty}^{x} \int_{-\infty}^{v} [G(t) - F(t)]\, dt\, dv \leq 0$ for all x (with at least one strict inequality).

The algorithm for second-order stochastic dominance with borrowing and lending developed by Levy and Kroll (1979) indicates that the government bond index is dominated by all of our optimized portfolios. It also shows that only the three TPs and the MRPs and ERPs, computed in the mean–variance approach, are second-order stochastically efficient. When borrowing and lending are not allowed, the second-order efficient set comprises all optimized portfolios.

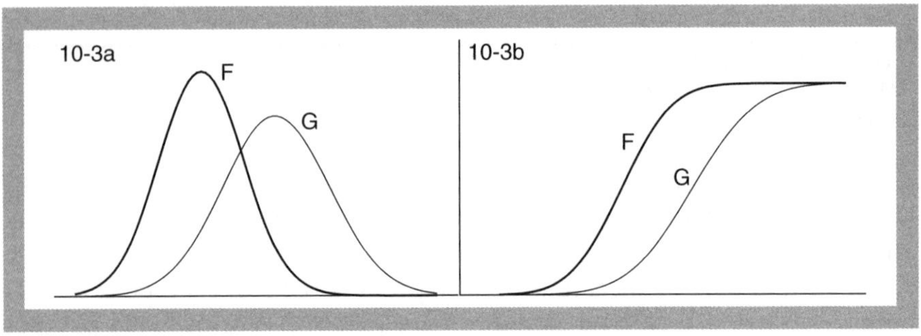

Figure 10.3 Return distributions and cumulative return distributions of two investment alternatives F and G

Source: Union Investment

10.4 ILLIQUIDITY AND PORTFOLIO CONSTRUCTION

All of the examined asset classes exhibit significant positive autocorrelation. There are two main reasons that should be noted. As mentioned earlier, one reason is the illiquidity of certain segments of the international bond markets. The high-yield sector is a typical example for a rather illiquid market segment. Broad high-yield indices represent the investment universe of institutional investors with regard to speculative grade corporate bonds. There are several qualitative criteria that benchmark indices generally have to satisfy. Among the most important are transparency, stability and representativeness. With respect to the adequate mapping of short- and medium-term fluctuations of high-yield bond prices, the last point is critical. The low liquidity of many high-yield bonds causes irregular and nonsynchronous trading. Rajan (2000) points out that about three-quarters of the index constituents are traded less than once per month. Information that is relevant for the valuation is comprised in the prices of those bonds with a significant time lag. Thus, price changes of individual bonds may seem uncorrelated even if they were caused by a common factor. This nonsynchronicity induces positive serial correlation in index returns and biases the traditional estimates of index volatility such as the annualized standard deviation of returns.

Analyses that deal with the integration of high-yielding instruments in bond portfolios must take into account the market inefficiencies mentioned above. Otherwise, false conclusions cannot be ruled out. Because of the biased correlations between individual bonds, historical estimates of the volatility of high-yield indices are too low. Generally, this causes suboptimal portfolio weights that are too high for the risk incurred. Occasionally this effect is also observed for small cap stock indices and real estate indices. Subsequently, we will transfer a technique Blundell and Ward (1987) proposed for the desmoothing of appraisal based real-estate indices to the high-yield sector. The method presumes that the serial correlation in high-yield index returns is exclusively caused by nonsynchronous trading and that the "true" time series follows a random walk. Firstenberg *et al.* (1988) and Geltner (1993) propose alternative approaches to desmooth empirical time series.

Herold and Maurer (2003) note that according to the Blundell/Ward methodology firstly the observed time series R has to be regressed on its lagged values

$$R_t = \alpha + \beta R_{t-1} + \varepsilon.$$

Afterwards the slope coefficient β is used to derive the adjusted return series in the following way:

$$R_t^{adj.} = \frac{1}{1-\beta} R_t - \frac{\beta}{1-\beta} R_{t-1}.$$

The implementation of the desmoothing methodology increases portfolio risk. We already mentioned that there is a permanent and relatively stable component in bond (index) returns resulting from interest accrual, roll down and yield-curve effects. Therefore we apply the desmoothing technique only to the series of monthly changes in the price indices, and afterwards add the other three components to derive the adjusted return series. It can be stated that the higher the degree of first-order serial correlation in monthly changes of the price indices the more portfolio risk surges. Figure 10.4 shows that the high-yield sector is most exposed to this effect. Interestingly though, in mean–variance space the risk/return profile of government bonds is dominated by mortgage-backed securities and agencies before as well as after adjustment for serial correlation. That said, it is no surprise that government bonds do not receive a significant weighting in any of the optimal portfolios.

For the sample period the first-order serial correlation coefficient for the Merrill Lynch US High Yield Index is 0.26. Brown (1985) notes that 0.25 represents the upper bound for the serial correlation that may be introduced by a valuation process characterized by nonsynchronous trading. Even after considering the effect of relatively stable components in index returns such as interest accrual, roll down and yield-curve effects it can be claimed that the US high-yield market suffers seriously from illiquidity. The desmoothing process described above increases the volatility of the high-yield index by considerable 63 bp per month.

Figure 10.4 demonstrates that the increase of high-yield volatility effected by the desmoothing of the monthly return series moves the asset classes and the efficient frontier in a risk/return chart to the right. Table 10.4 shows that consequently the composition and the risk-return profile of the optimal portfolios also change. While the weight of high yield reduces by 2–13 percentage points, mortgage-backed securities and investment grade corporate bonds become more important in a portfolio context. In the ERPs diversified corporate bond sub-portfolios receive a weighting of about 75 percent. Except for the portfolio based on the mean–variance framework, investment grade corporate bonds are also part of the TP. Investors looking

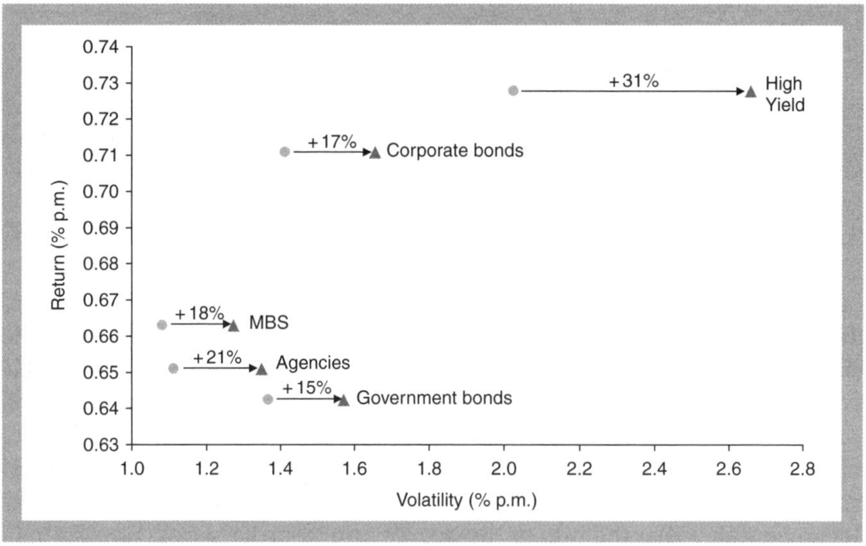

Figure 10.4 Effect of desmoothing (serial correlation adjustment) of index time series on the risk/return profiles of the considered asset classes

Source: Union Investment

Table 10.4 Composition of MRPs, TPs and ERPs based on the mean–variance (MV), shortfall risk (LPM) and Corning–Fisher (CF) framework for the sample period Jan. 1987–Sep. 2003 after adjustment for serial correlation in index returns

	Minimum risk portfolio			Tangency portfolio			Equal risk portfolio		
	MV	LPM	CF	MV	LPM	CF	MV	LPM	CF
Government	—	—	—	—	—	—	—	—	—
Agency	22.4	0.1	19.4	6.8	3.2	—	—	—	—
MBS	67.1	93.5	76.2	76.7	84.0	80.1	8.3	—	17.9
Corporate	—	—	—	—	0.2	12.7	71.0	73.3	74.7
High yield	10.5	6.4	4.4	16.5	12.6	7.2	20.7	26.7	7.4

Source: Union Investment

for a particularly attractive risk/return profile or willing to maximize their return for a given level of risk, seriously should consider corporate bonds as an alternative. Even for investors who are averse to negative skewness and leptokurtosis – as modeled by the Corning–Fisher approach – the admixture of a small high-yield portfolio can improve the risk/reward profile of their fixed income portfolio.

Again, the risk/return characteristics of the optimized portfolios are summarized in Table 10.5. We noted before that in comparison to a pure government portfolio the presented portfolios offer a more attractive investment opportunity. This observation is supported by the results of the stochastic dominance algorithm. As in the case without adjustment for serial correlation the government portfolio is dominated by all optimized portfolios. The results of the stochastic dominance algorithm also indicate that after the desmoothing process only one portfolio is excluded from the second-order stochastic dominance set: the minimum risk portfolio based on the Corning–Fisher approach.

10.5 OUT-OF-SAMPLE PERFORMANCE OF OPTIMIZED PORTFOLIOS

So far three methodologies for a quantitatively driven process of portfolio construction have been examined. The results of the empirical study show that the way of accounting for skewness, kurtosis and autocorrelation in return series has significant impact on portfolio weights. Measured by risk-adjusted performance numbers as well as stochastic dominance criteria, the identified differences between the risk/return profiles of the optimized portfolios seem marginal. However, it has to be considered that so far the

Table 10.5 Risk/return characteristics of MRPs, TPs and ERPs based on the mean–variance (MV), shortfall risk (LPM) and Corning–Fisher (CF) framework for the sample period Jan. 1987–Sep. 2003 after adjustment for serial correlation in index returns

	Minimum risk portfolio			Tangency portfolio			Equal risk portfolio			Govt. bonds
	MV	LPM	CF	MV	LPM	CF	MV	LPM	CF	
Mean	0.669	0.669	0.665	0.675	0.673	0.676	0.713	0.718	0.706	0.642
Standard Deviation	1.211	1.223	1.221	1.226	1.219	1.253	1.566	1.635	1.518	1.566
Sharpe Ratio	0.189	0.187	0.184	0.191	0.190	0.187	0.174	0.170	0.175	0.130
LPM_1	0.365	0.359	0.366	0.368	0.363	0.375	0.493	0.515	0.475	0.515
Reward to LPM_1	0.626	0.635	0.614	0.635	0.639	0.626	0.552	0.538	0.559	0.396
VaR_{CF}	3.384	3.363	3.341	3.524	3.437	3.448	4.480	4.786	4.125	4.125
Reward to VaR_{CF}	0.068	0.068	0.067	0.066	0.068	0.068	0.061	0.058	0.064	0.049

Note: The highlighted fields were optimized subject to the constraints described above

Source: Union Investment

process of portfolio optimization and performance measurement has been based on the same sample period. Implicitly perfect foresight has been assumed. There is no doubt that this assumption does not reflect a realistic investment decision-making process under uncertainty. In practice, first a decision about asset allocation is made and implemented. And afterwards the risk and return characteristics of the portfolio are measured either in absolute terms or relative to a benchmark index.

To simulate a realistic decision-making process we apply a backtesting methodology. Sample means and risk measures are estimated for the sub-period January 1987 to September 1998. In those cases where the return series is adjusted for autocorrelation the estimation of the desmoothing parameters is also based on the shortened sample period. Then the portfolios are optimized. With the obtained weights the series of monthly out-of-sample returns for each portfolio is calculated for the period October 1998 to September 2003. Based on this out-of-sample period the risk-return characteristics of the optimized portfolios and the benefits of the optimization approaches are examined.

To determine the set of efficient portfolios, pairwise tests for second-order stochastic dominance are conducted. When borrowing and lending are allowed and considered in the stochastic dominance algorithm the efficient set contains only one portfolio. It was obtained by minimizing portfolio risk in a shortfall risk framework (Table 10. 6). This portfolio does

Table 10.6 Second-order stochastic dominance efficient sets for the out-of-sample performance of optimized portfolios

	Efficient set			Inefficient set		
	MV	LPM	CF	MV	LPM	CF
No autocorrelation adjustment				MRP TP ERP	MRP TP ERP	MRP TP ERP
Autocorrelation adjustment		MRP TP*	MRP* ERP*	MRP TP ERP	ERP	TP

Note: * indicates portfolios that are in the second-order stochastic efficient set only when no borrowing and lending are allowed

Source: Union Investment

not only dominate the performance of the other optimized portfolios but also of every single asset class. Obviously the approaches that take into account skewness and kurtosis of the return distributions yield portfolios with a superior risk-return profile. Three more portfolios that result from using the shortfall risk or Corning–Fisher approach are contained in the efficient set when borrowing and lending constraints are imposed. Furthermore it should be noted that adjusting for autocorrelation during the process of portfolio construction has a positive effect on the out-of-sample performance of the chosen portfolios.

What conclusions can be drawn from these observations? Portfolios that are optimized with regard to risk seem to do better than those that additionally rely on return forecasts. Sample means are not a good predictor for future returns of bond portfolios. In this context Jorion (1986) argues, that the sample mean is exposed to considerable estimation risk whereas variances and correlations are generally more stable over time. The high influence of the return vector on the weights of the tangency and equal risk portfolios can lead to extreme and volatile portfolio returns. Kallberg and Ziemba (1984) point out that errors in estimating future returns have a ten times higher impact on the out-of-sample performance of the optimized portfolio than errors in estimating the variance–covariance matrix. Similar conclusions apply when using adjusted value at risk or lower partial moments as a risk measure.

In Figure 10.5 we have highlighted a solid black line that represents the "true" efficient frontier. It is estimated with the "true" means and variance–covariance matrix of asset returns, thus neglecting skewness and kurtosis of the underlying return distributions. However, for the assessment of the effect of errors in parameter estimation on realized risk/return profiles this plays a minor role. First, we generated a set of returns by resampling the historical return series. Randomly single observations are

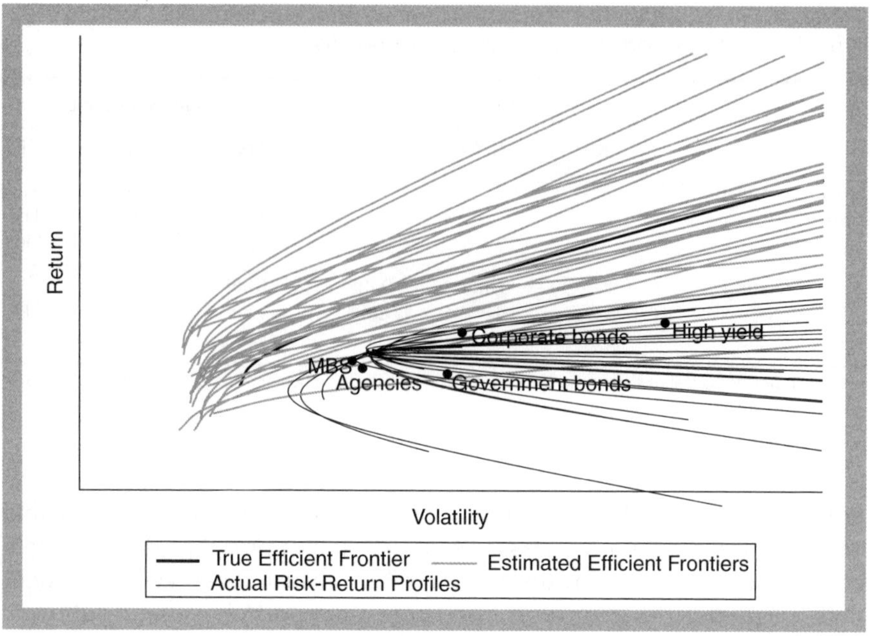

Figure 10.5 Resampled efficient frontiers. Light grey lines show the expected risk-return profile of the optimized portfolios, thin lines the actual risk-return profiles under the assumption that in the out-of-sample period the "true" means, variances and correlations are realized

(*Source:* Union Investment)

chosen, others dropped, until time series of the same length as the original series are created. Of course, this methodology involves repetitions in the resampled return series. Estimating the parameters based on the resampled time series, we then calculate the estimated efficient frontiers that are represented by the light grey lines in Figure 10.5. This is the best estimate of where the efficient frontier lies or, in other words, what risk-return tradeoff can be achieved through proper diversification. Unfortunately, the realized returns will differ from our resampled time series. Assuming that the actual realizations equal our "true" underlying return series, we obtained the thin lines. They indicate the risk-return profiles of the optimized portfolios. The results are shown by the thin lines in Figure 10.5. In fact, not only are the volatilities of the "optimal portfolios" higher than expected, the returns are lower than expected. Hence, they are entirely within the interior of the efficient frontier, thus inefficient. It is important to note that the actual risks of the minimal risk portfolios are slightly higher than expected, but the returns do not differ materially from the expected returns. Yet, portfolios that are optimized with respect to the maximization of return for a given level of risk or the maximization of the risk-adjusted performance suffer highly from estimation risk.

The results of our analyses show that accurate return forecasts are essential when employing portfolio optimization approaches. However, there are various techniques that account for uncertainty in parameter estimation. One method that is particularly popular among theoreticians as well as practitioners is Bayesian optimization. Empirical studies have yielded mixed results for this methodology. For international stock and bond portfolios Maurer and Mertz (2000) show that the out-of-sample performance of portfolios that are obtained by using Bayesian estimators in a mean–variance framework is not necessarily superior. Sophisticated forecasting models might be one way out of this dilemma. Alternative approaches suggest that the skill in directional forecasts should be higher than in precise return forecasts. Dynkin *et al.* (2003) proposed a risk budgeting framework that relies on directional forecasts, but additionally requires the estimation of the investor's skill with regard to the dimensions of his investment decisions.

10.6 LONG-TERM CHARACTERISTICS OF CORPORATE BOND PORTFOLIOS

In the course of this chapter, we have seen that bond returns not only show significant deviations from a normal distribution, but also that they are correlated across time. This is an important observation in the context of long-term investments, because mean reversion of the performance of an asset class lowers its risk in the long term. So far the issue of time diversification has generated considerable interest and controversy in particular with regard to equity investments. Theoreticians such as Merton argue that markets are efficient and security returns independent and identically distributed. As a consequence the risk-return profile of a given portfolio should not alter with the investment horizon and portfolio weights should be independent from the investment horizon.

Among practitioners, however, there is a strong belief that the risk-return profile of equities as well as corporate bonds gets more favorable with a lengthening of the planned investment period. In this case the optimal mix of assets to be held in the portfolio changes with the length of the investment horizon. From a statistical point of view, those practitioners claim that there is negative autocorrelation in the returns of equities and corporate bonds. In other words, in the long run, these asset classes show a pattern of mean reversion. This assumption seems to contradict the statistical properties of bond index returns displayed in Table 10.1. On a monthly basis all examined asset classes exhibit positive autocorrelation. Yet, annual total returns of US equities and corporate bonds collected from the Ibbotson Associates database are negatively autocorrelated.

Numerous studies examine the effect of time diversification for equities relative to treasuries. Most of them are based on the classical mean–variance framework and yield quite conflicting results. If the practitioners' view is right and there is mean reversion in the long-run behavior of one of the examined asset classes, methodologies that use the whole distribution of asset returns should yield more instructive results. Albrecht (1998) demonstrates the problems arising from the use of the mean–variance methodology for nonnormal return distributions.

A study by Hodges *et al.* (2002) employs the previously introduced concept of stochastic dominance to compare the risk-return profiles of small stocks, common stocks, corporate bonds and treasury bills in the long run. A simulation is run to compare two scenarios. Assuming no autocorrelation in asset class returns the first one rejects the hypothesis that equities are a superior longer-term investment. Actually, the efficient set contains all examined asset classes. Even treasury bills are not dominated by small or common stocks. This corresponds with the assumptions and findings formulated by the aforementioned theoreticians like Merton and Samuelson.

When the historical pattern of autocorrelation is considered the results change dramatically. Now, the membership in the stochastic dominance efficient set becomes dependent upon the investment horizon. For periods up to 7 years stocks, corporate bonds and bills are contained in the efficient set (Figure 10.6). In other words, for risk-averse investors there is no

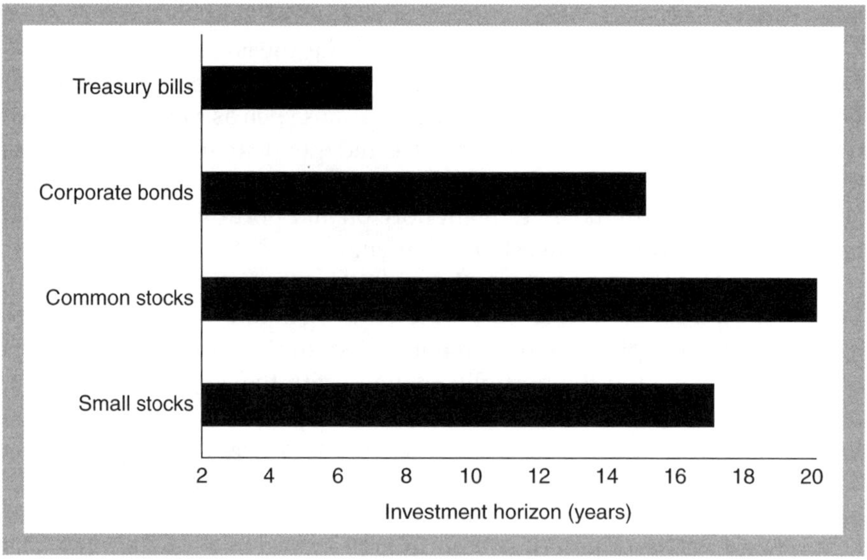

Figure 10.6 Membership in the second-order stochastic dominance efficient set under the assumption of autocorrelated returns

Source: Hodges *et al.* [2002]

indication that for the short to medium term equities are superior investments. This is counterintuitive in that it contradicts the historical return experience. Over historical 7-year periods small and common stocks returned 16.3 and 11.9 percent per annum, corporate bonds 6.7 percent and treasury bills only 4.2 percent. Yet, equity portfolios possess a significantly higher volatility than bonds and bills. When introducing the Corning–Fisher expansion we also showed that investors prefer positive to negative skewness. On an annual return basis, especially broad corporate bond portfolios benefit from this preference. For holding periods between 2 and 20 years they show consistently high positive skewness of 1.0–1.6.

Assuming risk aversion it is therefore not possible to establish a clear ranking between equities and corporate bonds for investment horizons of up to 15 years. Only for longer time horizons the benefits of investing in stocks, especially diversified portfolios of common stocks, unfold. Taking into account the considerably lower volatility of diversified corporate bond portfolios in comparison to equity portfolios, corporate bonds should be an integral part of any savings plan, especially if there is uncertainty about the effective length of the investment horizon.

CHAPTER 11

Total and Absolute Return Strategies with Credits

11.1 MULTICURRENCY INVESTING

The introduction of the Euro has reduced the opportunities for Euro fixed income investors to generate an excess return over government bonds, for example, by earning risk premia or adding currency exposure to their portfolios. Therefore, they have increasingly focused on credit as the primary source of alpha. However, after the massive credit spread tightening in 2003 the potential for outperformance seems rather limited. Including investments in foreign currencies can be a viable way to earn excess returns for corporate bond investors. Yet many portfolio managers are restricted from taking on currency risk, leaving them only with the possibility to exploit inefficiencies in the pricing of credit across currencies. The crucial question then is whether there is a global corporate bond market, that is, whether there is sufficient comovement between the major credit markets that allows to identify mispricings between bonds from one issuer but in various currencies and to benefit from an eventual correction of this inefficiency. Hence, one has to address the issue of the degree of integration of credit markets, in particular the US, Euro, Sterling and Yen markets.

In general the following relationship holds: the more integrated various markets are, the more is their performance determined by common systematic risk factors. Usually, highly integrated markets tend to move together, exhibiting high correlations. Therefore they offer few diversification. In segmented markets, conversely, there is a low degree of comovement across markets. While in this case the benefits of diversification can unfold completely, exploiting differences in credit spreads across markets and currencies is extremely difficult. Even if spread differences between the Libor spreads of bonds from one issuer, denominated in various currencies, are observed, profitable trading strategies require that mispricings will be corrected eventually.

In order to assess the degree of integration in international credit markets Desclée and Rosten (2002) suggest to concentrate on those issuers that have Dollar and Euro bullet bonds with a minimum size of 500 million dollar or equivalent and a maturity of 3–10 years outstanding. Thus they define a universe of "global" investment grade corporate issuers with sufficiently liquid bonds. Often the spread levels in Euro and Dollar for the same issuer and bonds with similar duration differ significantly. According to this study, the Libor spread of the Dollar bonds exceeded the spread of the Euro bonds on average by 10 bp over the period 1999 to August 2002. Typical examples include Ford where the spreads in Dollar were on average 136 bp higher than spreads in Euro at the end of 2002, and France Telecom with a spread differential of 42 bp. A cross-sectional regression of fluctuations in the Dollar–Euro spread differentials on the differential levels shows that there is highly significant evidence of a mean–reversion effect. Furthermore, the intercept of the regression, representing the average spread differential, is significant, meaning that Dollar spreads tend to be systematically higher than those in Euro. Positive average spread differentials between Dollar and Euro bonds have been persistent since 2000. Intuitively, the wider average spread and the higher volatility of the Dollar issues are not surprising, considering the more trading-oriented portfolio management style of US investors. Therefore, it is a logical consequence that the volatility of the Libor spreads of the Dollar bonds also was significantly higher than for the Euro bonds in the sample period.

Another central result from the above-mentioned study is that the average bond-by-bond correlations are higher within markets than across currencies. Investors obviously tend to compare spread levels of an issuer's bonds rather in one currency than across currencies. This suggests that there is a certain degree of segmentation in international credit markets, and that the different investor bases at least temporarily may have differing views on one name. Kercheval *et al.* (2003) argue that credit spread changes in a market largely reflect changes in the risk premium required by investors to hold securities from a certain sector and with a given credit quality. Fluctuations of the credit spread therefore should be primarily due to changes in overall economic and political conditions, which can differ substantially across markets. This explanation is consistent with their empirical observations of a high correlation across sectors and ratings within a single market.

However, the study by Desclée and Rosten (2002) also finds that correlations of bonds from one issuer, but in differing currencies, significantly depend on spread levels. The bonds of companies with a lower credit quality and higher spreads like Ford (F), tend to show a high degree of comovement across currencies, as Figure 11.1 illustrates. Despite the noise that results from using daily observations the correlation of the daily spread changes of the two selected Dollar and Euro bonds was a highly significant 0.80. For a typical low spread name like General Electric (GE) we obtained a correlation of 0.00, meaning we were not able to detect any comovement between the daily spread changes of Dollar and Euro bonds, as can be seen from Figure 11.2. If we conclude that the spread changes of low spread names typically are not significantly correlated, the empirical results suggest that issue-specific characteristics tend to have more influence on spread changes than issuer-specific information for low spread names. Conversely, the spread changes of issuers with a lower credit quality seem to depend on issuer-specific information, and thus are significantly correlated across currencies.

On the sector level, Desclée and Rosten (2002) obtained similar results. Whereas the spread changes of low spread credit sectors like agencies, foreign sovereigns or supranationals are rather uncorrelated across currencies, utilities, financials and particularly industrials exhibit positive correlations.

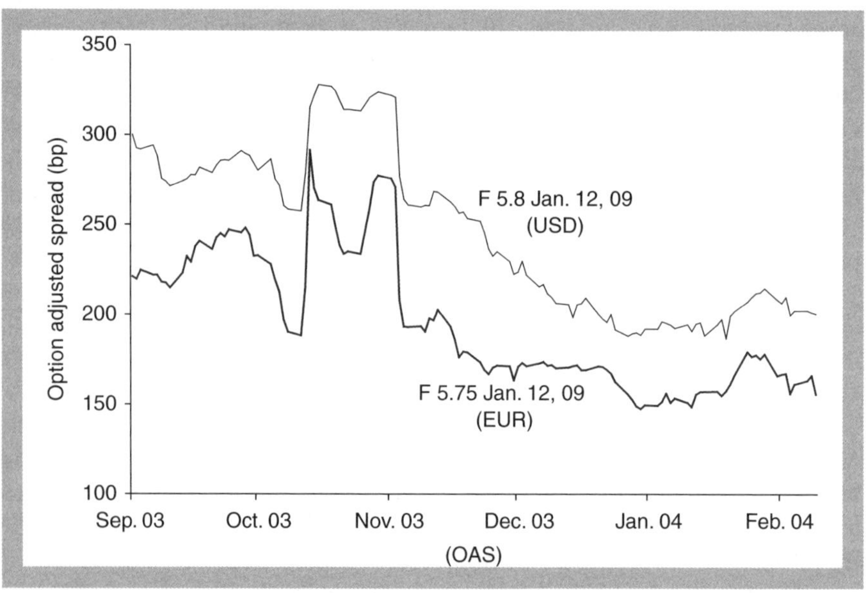

Figure 11.1 Option adjusted spreads (OAS) of Ford bonds with identical maturity and similar coupon, but in differing currencies

Sources: Bloomberg, Union Investment

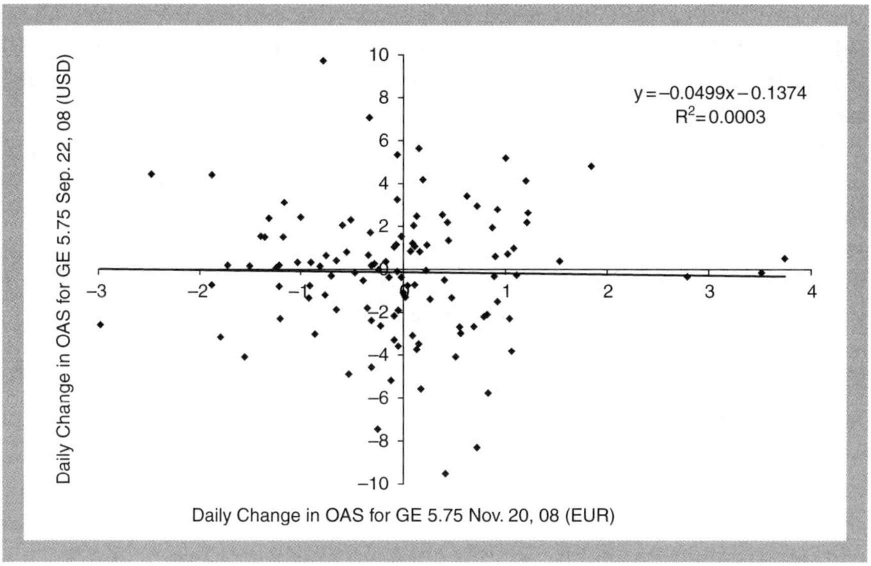

Figure 11.2 Changes in option adjusted spreads for GE bonds with similar maturity and identical coupon, but in differing currencies

Sources: Bloomberg, Union Investment

However, only the correlation of the spread changes of industrial bonds that are denominated in Dollar and Euro, respectively, is statistically significant.

From a risk-management perspective the study suggests that cross-currency correlation in credit markets is a function of spread level and industry classification. For low spread names investing across currencies increases diversification. Adding positions in foreign currency for a high spread name, conversely, increases overall risk due to the high level of correlation across currencies. Yet, considering the high bond-by-bond correlations and the mean-reverting behavior of cross-currency spread differentials, frequent trade opportunities emerge for the high spread issuers. Remember that the spread for Dollar bonds from an issuer tends to be somewhat higher than for the Euro bonds. In a stable spread environment a market-neutral position, involving a short position in the Euro bond and a long position in the Dollar bond, would benefit from the positive carry while the high cross-currency correlation will mitigate the risk of the position.

The construction of cross-currency spread trades requires assembling a curve neutral position in a common base currency. This way it is possible to isolate the relative movement of credit spreads across currencies from changes in the price of the underlying and currency fluctuations. In order to benefit from higher spreads of foreign currency bonds an investor would have to sell an asset-swapped position of the bond in base currency and buy an asset-swapped position of the bond in foreign currency. Additionally, the currency exposure has to be hedged. While this trade involves short selling and therefore usually cannot be implemented by real money managers, it is often possible to construct such a position relative to the benchmark index.

At inception the two legs of the trade have the same PV01 expressed in base currency while the two market values may differ. Yet, this difference is limited when pairs of bonds with similar durations are selected. The trade is equivalent to a view on the difference in Libor spread between a pair of bonds in two currencies. That view has to be strong enough to compensate for a hurdle rate made up by the sum of the following terms:

- costs of the asset swaps,
- costs of the currency hedge,
- transaction costs involved in setting up and unwinding the trade.

It seems that this approach is likely to represent a trading opportunity that can be exploited profitably. An unpublished study by Desclée and Rosten (2003) without and with transaction costs indicates positive information ratios for trading strategies where investors go long a particular issuer in the currency where its spread is highest and short it where its spread is lowest. In an unfunded strategy, however, transaction costs and financing considerations must be taken into account. Furthermore, the performance of the strategy has varied substantially over time. In general, the number of trading opportunities has improved steadily since 2000 due to the broadened universe of truly global issuers, with multiple securities outstanding in various markets. High spread levels and spread volatility tend to raise the potential for implementing the strategy. Especially investors that are benchmarked relative to a global credit index may benefit from frequent trading opportunities.

11.2 ASYMMETRIC RISK MANAGEMENT FOR CORPORATE BOND PORTFOLIOS*

The protracted baisse in the equity markets from 2000 to mid-2003 has reminded investors that absolute return products can be a valuable supplement to private as well as institutional investment portfolios. Asset managers consequently have created numerous absolute and total return products. Despite their asymmetric risk profile corporate bonds, too, can be managed in an absolute return framework. The approach presented here illustrates a dynamic protection strategy and its peculiarities when introducing corporate bond risk.

* Thanks are due to Thomas Bossert for his input on asymmetric risk management strategies for corporate bond portfolios

The goal of asymmetric risk management is to generate positive absolute returns. There are two main reasons for this. First, when you have lost half your money the rest has to double before you only break even. If you are able to minimize losses, it is easier to earn decent money as your capital base is bigger. Second, as Tversky and Kahneman (1991) point out, behavioral finance has found out that investors suffer twice as much from losses as they do from foregone profits of equal magnitude. This means that avoiding losses not only leaves investors with more money in their pockets but also that they feel more comfortable with less volatile portfolios. Of course, these investors also want to earn high returns, but in the end fear dominates greed.

Basically, there are two different types of absolute return management: asymmetric and symmetric strategies. Asymmetric strategies, which are often referred to as protection strategies, focus on avoiding losses in falling markets and participate in rising markets. The payout profile of these strategies is asymmetric or, to be more precise, it is convex, that is, a line connecting two points on its graph is never below the graph. In a falling market, portfolio value does not fall at all or at least falls at a slower rate than the market. In a rising market it participates in the opportunities either at a slower rate than the market, in line with the market or even at a higher rate when the portfolio can take higher risks than the market.

Symmetric strategies try to make money independent of the direction of markets as a whole. Typical examples include different types of arbitrage strategies which are usually employed by hedge funds. The goal is to earn a return above the risk-free rate in any market environment. If this could be realized it would be a risk-free rate above the risk-free rate which is a contradiction in itself. Therefore, the seemingly dominating returns of hedge funds should be analyzed very carefully. Brooks and Kat (2001) argue that these excess returns over money market are only earned because there is a hidden risk involved. These portfolios are short event risk. They earn above-average returns in rather stable markets, but pay for it when rare events finally strike. The most impressive example for this argument was Long-Term Capital Management (LTCM) which earned stable excess returns for a number of years before the dramatic spread increases in 1998 materialized that finally led to the collapse of the fund.

In this chapter, we focus on asymmetric risk-management strategies. These strategies appeal to a number of investors. They are utility-maximizing for investors whose risk aversion becomes infinitely high when their wealth goes below a minimum threshold, but declines with rising wealth. According to Leland (1980) they exhibit a HARA (hyperbolic absolute risk aversion) utility function. In general, the strategies that try to protect portfolio value in falling markets come in different forms. There are two broad categories, namely static and dynamic strategies (see Figure 11.3). Static strategies are characterized by an engineering process or a simple stop-loss mechanism. In the engineering process the initial portfolio structure

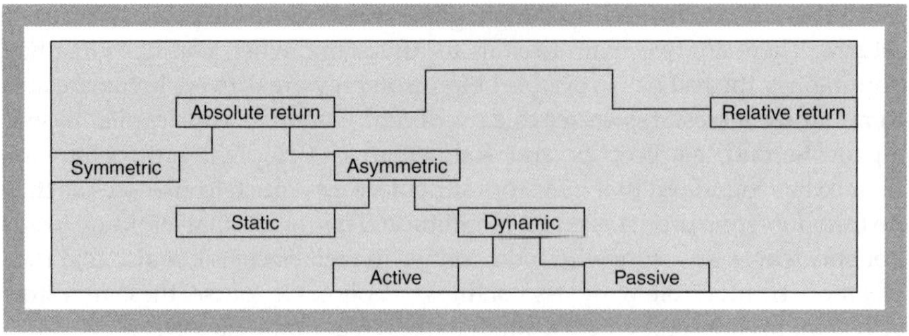

Figure 11.3 Classification of investment styles
Source: Union Investment

is calculated as a mixture of assets and derivatives. This structure is bought and left untouched until it matures, except for cash flows that have to be invested or generated by proportional reduction of the structure.

Dynamic strategies generate their asymmetric payout by a portfolio management process which involves constant adjustment of the risky positions in the portfolio. These processes are very systematic and quantitative in the sense that the portfolio manager has to calculate the maximum affordable risk and compare it to the ever-changing risk of his portfolio. These constant calculations and adjustments are either part of a passive or an active investment process. In a passive approach, risky and riskless assets are mechanistically allocated according to a hard-coded algorithm. The most prominent example of this kind of strategy is the Constant Proportion Portfolio Insurance (CPPI) which boils down to one simple formula, as Black and Jones (1987) have shown:

$$e = mc,$$

where e denotes exposure, m is multiple and c denotes the cushion, that is, the difference between the value of the portfolio and a defined floor. If we assume that a portfolio with an initial value of 100 is not supposed to fall below 90 and the multiple was defined as 5, the resulting cushion is 10, and 50 units are invested in stocks. If the value of the portfolio goes down to 95, the cushion reduces to 5. Equity exposure is reduced to 25. In a rising market the value of the portfolio might go up to 105. The new cushion is 15 and the resulting equity exposure is 75. This example highlights a characteristic of any asymmetric portfolio management approach. In a falling market risk is reduced, while in a rising market the risk exposure is increased. This is due to the fact that the portfolio manager of a dynamic protection portfolio is short gamma and must sell risk when risks are going against him, that is, when the market is going down and buy risk in a friendly market. Implicitly this represents a procyclical pattern.

In an active approach, forecasts influence the management process. Return expectations play a minor role in this asymmetric risk management. The focus is clearly on risk forecasts. Expectations on volatilities and correlations are used to finally arrive at a portfolio structure which allocates risk to various risk factors (equity market risk, interest rate risk, idiosyncratic risk, etc.) in order to be compensated by earning risk premia, but strictly within the bounds of the current risk budget of the portfolio. But, in contrast to a traditional, forecast-based management approach, disciplined risk control dominates forecasts, even risk forecasts. The approach is flexible enough to easily factor in subordinate goals and restrictions. Because it is active in a nonmechanistic sense, it is also capable of handling the different risk sources present in a corporate bond portfolio.

Dynamic portfolio insurance tries to cut off the left-hand side of the return distribution, which is equivalent to avoiding bonds that experience a massive spread widening, in other words the credit blowups. Figure 11.4 illustrates that the distribution of corporate bond spread changes is skewed to the right. Large spread widenings occur more often than would be implied by a normal distribution, and of course are not compensated by spread tightenings of the same magnitude. Therefore one of the major characteristics of the distribution of corporate bond is the dreaded fat tail on the left-hand side of the return distribution.

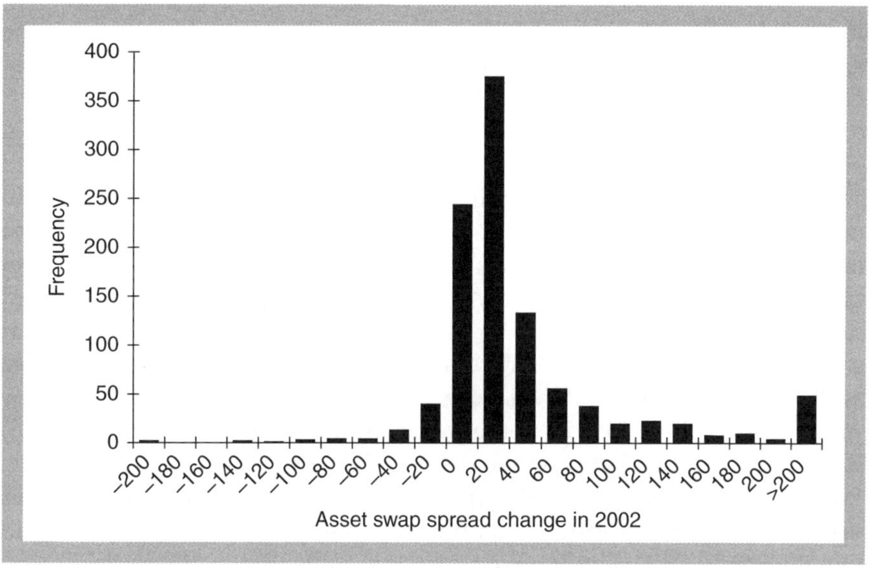

Figure 11.4 Spread changes of the constituents of the Merrill Lynch EMU Corporate Index as of Dec. 31, 2001 over the course of the year 2002

Sources: Merrill Lynch, Union Investment

First of all, this shows that following an asymmetric strategy does make sense for a corporate bond portfolio since it focuses exactly on the downside risk. On the other hand, it is clear that using dynamic protection on a credit portfolio is a challenging task. The purpose of portfolio protection is clearly to provide investors with a defined minimum portfolio value even when markets are going down. In other words, investors buy the asymmetric payout of a portfolio insured with a put option.

It is no coincidence that the title of the revolutionary article in which Fisher Black and Myron Scholes presented the Black/Scholes option pricing formula is "The Pricing of Options and Corporate Liabilities" (1973). It clearly shows the tight link between corporate bonds and options. Merton (1974) shows explicitly in a simple derivation that a corporate bond can be split into a default-free bond and a short put on the assets of the company.

We start with a company with a simple capital structure consisting of equity and debt in the form of a bond. When the bond matures the bond investor normally gets the nominal value of his investment back. In case the company is not able to repay the bond, the company's asset will be liquidated and paid out to the bondholder. The value of the corporate bond (C) is therefore the minimum of the debt (D, equivalent to nominal value of the bond) and the value of the assets of the company (A).

$$C = \min(D, A) = D + \min(A - D, 0).$$

If we look at the nominal debt value as the strike price and the value of the assets as the value of the underlying, the equation above can be rewritten as

$$C = D - \max(D - A, 0).$$

Thus a corporate bond is a combination of a risk-free bond and a short put on the company's assets. The risk of default can be extracted from the price of the put. The put price in turn depends on the asset value of the firm (price of the underlying) and its debt (strike price of the option), interest rate, maturity of the debt and the volatility of the company value. This is where the link between implied volatility and corporate spreads originates, as the implied volatility of the stock can help to estimate the volatility of the firm's asset value. Based on this relationship Galai and Masulis (1976) derive a formal link between the degree of debt financing and equity risk. With constant operational risk, equity risk rises when debt financing goes up. This link was confirmed in a number of studies and extended to operational leverage, the fact that fixed costs cannot be reduced very fast when demand turns weak, as Schwert (1989), Ferguson (1994) and Franks and Schwartz (1988) point out.

In the context of an asymmetric risk management the embedded short put option of a corporate bond means that the portfolio manager faces additional negative gamma. Dynamic risk management for a corporate bond

spread change should reflect the estimate on when one could realistically exit the position.

- The maximum weighted duration can be calculated as Maximum weighted duration = Maximum loss/spread widening.
- Finally, calculate the maximum position weight using the duration of each position Maximum position size = Maximum weighted duration/ Bond's duration.

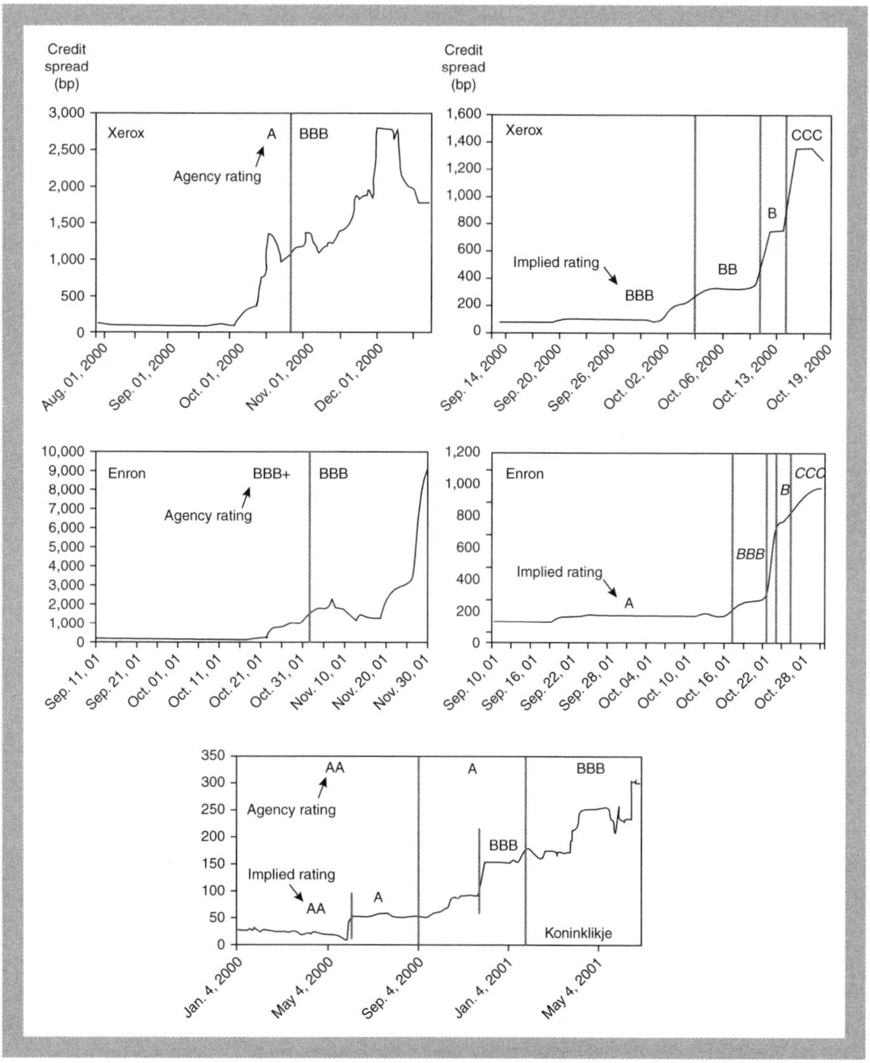

Figure 11.5 Agency ratings and implied ratings as alternative indicators of credit risk

Source: Breger *et al.* (2003)

Let us assume that the maximum loss for the portfolio at a certain point in time is 50 bp. If the potential spread widening before we will be able to get out of a bond with an implied rating of BBB is estimated to be 500 bp, the maximum weighted duration would be 0.1. For a 10-year bond with a duration of 7 years this would mean that the weight of this bond should be less than 1.4 percent (see Table 11.1).

Note that these position limits do not cover the risk of a general spread widening. Assume a pure AAA portfolio in which there are five positions with a 20 percent weight and a duration of 5 years each. A general AAA spread widening by 20 bp would cause the portfolio to lose approximately 1 percent.

To control concentration in an absolute return-oriented corporate bond portfolio at a glance the concentration ratio or Herfindahl index is a useful metric. Originally it was introduced to measure the concentration of an industry. There are other concentration indices like the Rosenbluth index. The Herfindahl index is the most popular, though. It has been used in credit studies and also plays a role in the Basle framework (see Diez-Canedo and Castanon (1999), Finger (2001) or Gordy (2002)). The Herfindahl index is calculated simply by summing the squares of the portfolio weights. Its main advantage is that it is rather intuitive. The more the value approaches zero the lower the concentration in the portfolio. The maximum value is

Table 11.1 Maximum position limits for corporate bonds with an implied investment grade rating in an absolute return portfolio with a maximum drawdown of 0.5 percent

Duration	Implied rating/Potential spread widening			
	AAA (20 bp) (%)	AA (50 bp) (%)	A (100 bp) (%)	BBB (500 bp) (%)
1	250.0	100.0	50.0	10.0
2	125.0	50.0	25.0	5.0
3	83.3	33.3	16.7	3.3
4	62.5	25.0	12.5	2.5
5	50.0	20.0	10.0	2.0
6	41.7	16.7	8.3	1.7
7	35.7	14.3	7.1	1.4
8	31.3	12.5	6.3	1.3
9	27.8	11.1	5.6	1.1
10	25.0	10.0	5.0	1.0

Source: Union Investment

one. This means that the whole portfolio is concentrated in only one bond. Table 11.2 shows that the index is not only a function of the number of bonds in the portfolio. A portfolio of ten bonds can have significantly different index values depending on how the weights are distributed.

It is important to monitor the evolution of the index over time as this might give a hint on whether concentration in the portfolio is going up or down and where in the portfolio this is happening. It also makes sense to watch the Herfindahl index for the single rating baskets as well as for the total portfolio and its average rating. Dynkin *et al.* (2002) note that empirical data supports the hypothesis that higher quality bonds' downgrade risk is more related to specific events while lower qualities are mainly affected by deteriorating economic conditions. In dynamically protected portfolios which focus on absolute return, corporate bonds are often complemented by other risky assets. It is important to find out how these assets react to events that drive corporate bond risk and how strong the link to the risk in the single parts of the corporate portfolio is. For example, if the corporate bond subportfolio is of higher quality a recession might lead to a general spread widening but not necessarily to a higher risk of downgrades. Risk-free interest rates might go down enough to compensate for this when government bonds are added to the portfolio.

The issue of diversification is of utmost importance in absolute-return management. The return distribution of single corporate bonds exhibits significant fat tails especially on the negative side. However, if we combine many bonds in a portfolio the law of large numbers leads to a distribution of portfolio returns which converges towards a normal distribution. So the risk hot spot in corporate portfolios can at least be partially diversified away. This makes it easier to control total portfolio risk in an asymmetric portfolio.

The degree of normality in portfolio return distribution depends very much on the correlation between the single bonds as the law of large numbers assumes independent variables. However, bond-specific outliers, for instance, due to downgrades, are independent events which affect the market as a whole only marginally. This influence on the distribution can be reduced by diversification. However, when spread widenings due to downgrades of different issuers are increasingly correlated absolute risk will increase no matter how many bonds are included in the portfolio. In index-oriented portfolios, the portfolio is affected in a similar manner by correlated risks as the benchmark itself. Relative risk depends on the issuer-specific deviations between portfolio and benchmark, and the degree of correlation of these active positions. In general, good estimates of correlations of the spread widening risks of different issuers are more important for absolute-return portfolios than for index-oriented portfolios.

The different risk structure of index- and absolute return-oriented mandates is not just a matter of different research focus. It also massively affects

Table 11.2 Examples for the calculation of the Herfindahl index

Bond 1 (%)	Bond 2 (%)	Bond 3 (%)	Bond 4 (%)	Bond 5 (%)	Bond 6 (%)	Bond 7 (%)	Bond 8 (%)	Bond 9 (%)	Bond 10 (%)	Herfindahl Index
100										1.0000
50	50									0.5000
10	10	10	10	10	10	10	10	10	10	0.1000
91	1	1	1	1	1	1	1	1	1	0.8290
91	5	0.5	0.5	0.5	0.5	0.5	0.5	0.5	0.5	0.8308

Source: Union Investment

day-to-day portfolio management. If the value of the corporate bond portfolio falls, for example, due to rising bond yields that are not fully compensated by narrowing credit spreads, an index-oriented portfolio manager will stick to his current portfolio structure. The absolute-return manager, however, has to react. All other things being equal, he has to reduce portfolio risk by reducing credit or interest rate exposure.

Credit risk often goes hand in hand with liquidity risk. However, liquidity is quite a difficult risk to grasp. Research is not as advanced in this area as it is in other areas of risk management. It seems to emerge from current research that liquidity risk cannot be captured with quantitative indicators alone. Fernandez (1999) points out that the analysis of liquidity risk has to be supplemented with a certain amount of qualitative input. In general, liquidity risk arises when everybody suddenly wants to leave the party through the same door. In a dynamic portfolio protection strategy, this problem is a very important one as the discipline inherent in such a strategy forces the portfolio manager to reduce portfolio risk when portfolio value goes down. During some periods it is next to impossible to get out of a credit position at a reasonable price, though. In September 1998, during the Russia/LTCM crisis, liquidity suddenly evaporated from the market (see Figure 11.6). The dramatic increase in corporate spreads was not only a materialization of credit risk, but was very much driven by liquidity risk as

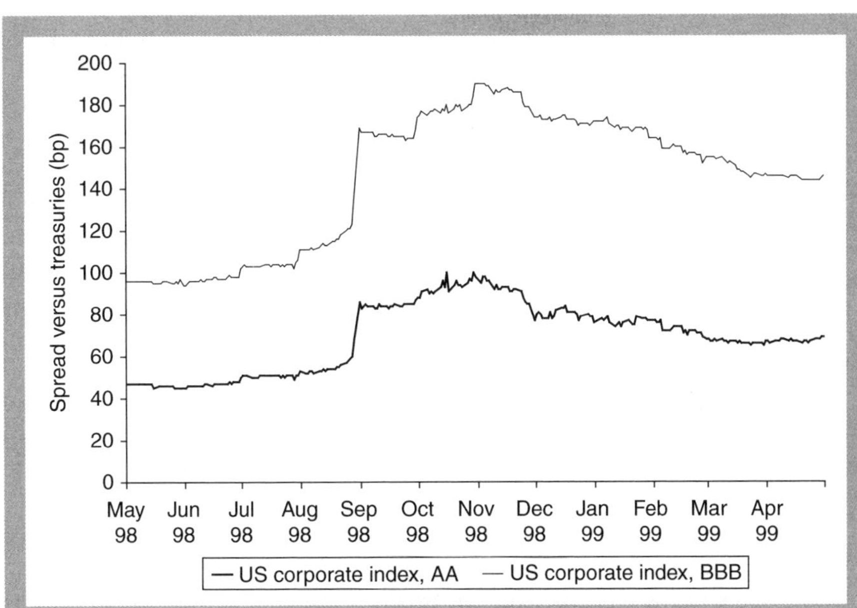

Figure 11.6 US corporate bond spreads during the Russia/LTCM crisis

Source: Union Investment

well. Pagès (2001) notes that simply subsuming liquidity risk under the heading of credit risk can lead to a false model of where risk is coming from. In periods where liquidity might become a problem the portfolio manager has to mark up the risk of the portfolio. In case of doubt, you would rather mark up your position's riskiness one time too often. This comes at the cost of opportunity losses as your portfolio was structured with less risk than it could actually have taken. But remember that under no circumstances portfolio value may fall below target minimum portfolio value.

Another area which depends very much on the knowledge and experience of the fund manager is the question of how assets should be liquidated in case of trouble. This is one of the key topics in a dynamically insured portfolio. As there are quite a number of different risks present in such a portfolio there are numerous possible combinations of which risk to exit with special regard to liquidity risk. One intuitive approach often used by portfolio managers in general is to sell the most liquid assets first, wait for liquidity to come back to the market and sell the less liquid assets later. Another one would be to sell the position that causes the trouble first. But it might also be advantageous to sell rather illiquid assets earlier, keeping a reserve of liquid assets in case the market becomes even worse. Duffie and Ziegler (2001) show that this approach also has its merits. They find this approach to be usually effective, although it increases trading costs and might not work if asset returns and bid-ask spreads have fat tails.

Of course, credit exposure cannot be reduced only by selling risky assets. The most common way to hedge credit risk is the use of credit default swaps (CDS). However, depending on the legal framework of the portfolio, it is not always possible to use CDS. German mutual funds, for example, are currently not allowed to use credit derivatives. One alternative that has become popular recently is the use of equity puts to hedge the tails, that is, cover the risk of large negative price moves. A company approaching default is very likely not to repay its bonds or at least not in full. Meanwhile the price of its stock will also fall and approach zero. This correlation between stock and bond price is normally strong enough that the long put on the stock can cover the losses of the bond. A convenient feature of a put hedge is that volatility works in favor of the hedge. Not only does the price of the stock fall. In addition to that realized volatility goes up and implied volatility follows suit as many investors are hurrying to buy protection forcing put prices up.

The puts used are far out-of-the-money with a low delta and a low put premium. This kind of hedge is also applied by portfolio managers who could trade CDS as well, as using puts is sometimes the more cost-efficient alternative. According to Kassam and Grebnev (2002) the price of a put option on the equity of an issuer and the price of a credit default swaps are related to each other through the following equation:

$$P\left(U, S, t, \sigma_{K,B,t}\right) = S \cdot t \cdot \frac{CDS}{1 - R} + P\left(U, S, t, \sigma_{ATMF}\right),$$

where P denotes the price of the put, U is the price of the underlying, S the strike price of the option, and t the option's time to maturity. CDS, R and σ denote the price of the credit default swap, recovery rate and implied volatility, respectively. The price of the put on the right-hand side is adjusted in such a way that a no-default value is approximated. The equation above generates curves which show the fair implied volatility of a put compared to a CDS for different recovery rates. The comparison of these curves with implied volatilities traded in the market serves to identify comparatively cheap and expensive puts for the purpose of substituting CDS.

Besides credit risk, the second major source of risk in a corporate bond portfolio is interest rate risk. Both risks are related. Expectations on the development of the state of the economy lead to interest rate moves, on the one hand, and spread widenings or tightenings, on the other. Again, there is a big difference in the management of absolute-return portfolios compared to index-oriented portfolios. The latter will try to estimate which effect outweighs the other and tilt the portfolio accordingly. If the portfolio manager has no conviction on how these risks will develop or affect portfolio performance he simply chooses a structure that is neutral relative to the benchmark.

The task of the absolute-return portfolio manager is not to loose any money and earn as much absolute return as possible. He cannot stay out of the market most of the time as he wants to earn a risk premium on interest rate and credit risk in order to widen the distance between a dreaded loss and the current performance. He needs the inflow of the risk premium to support his performance cushion, which allows to include other risks as well, or to up the current risks. The absolute-return manager therefore seeks a balance between the risk components in the portfolio in such a way that the different risks keep each other in check and allow him to stay in the market. Good news on the economy might lead to rising interest rates, on the one hand, and to tightening credit spreads, on the other. In order to keep interest rate risk under control the fastest, cheapest and most efficient way is the use of futures. Swaps can be a viable alternative if interest rate risk is referenced against swap, not government rates. Curve risk is a rather small risk source on a stand-alone basis. However, the steepness of the yield curve is another expression of the macroeconomic expectations of market participants.

To sum it up, when corporate bonds are included in a dynamically protected portfolio the portfolio manager has to adjust the structure constantly to get as much low or negative correlation to spread widening risk as possible. The challenge is therefore to permanently work on the complete risk structure in the portfolio in order to have the risk balanced in such a way that a fast spread widening will at least be partially offset by favorable moves in other risk sources. The exposure to idiosyncratic risk has to be controlled by sufficient diversification and adequate position sizes, as well as by hedging credit risk on a single name basis.

CHAPTER 12

Risk Management

12.1 MANAGEMENT OF SYSTEMATIC RISK IN CREDIT PORTFOLIOS

During the last few years ex ante risk management tools have gained widespread acceptance among institutional investors, because high volatility in the capital markets caused an increased degree of uncertainty in portfolio management decisions. State-of-the-art models help to quantify and decompose portfolio risk and, in a second step, attribute it to various risk factors. Since the risk/return profile of credit instruments and insufficiently diversified credit portfolios is highly asymmetric, credit investors may benefit particularly from sophisticated risk management tools. They can help to generate consistently favorable risk/return profiles over the medium to longer term. Basically, a good risk model should provide the portfolio manager on an ongoing basis with the information detailed in the following paragraphs.

- The risk model must quantify overall portfolio risk in absolute terms and relative to a benchmark. For credit portfolios risk measures that refer to downside risk may prove more useful than traditional symmetric risk measures like volatility or tracking error. As pointed out in Chapter 10 transformations of value at risk as well as shortfall probability, expected shortfall and tail conditional expectation are appropriate downside risk measures.
- A decomposition of overall portfolio risk should include risk contributions for asset classes, sectors, industries, issuers and single securities. Again,

absolute risk as well as risk relative to the benchmark must be provided. This allows a correct risk budgeting. Given that the return distribution of single corporate bonds gets more asymmetric with a declining credit quality of the issuer, especially risk models for high-yield portfolios need to estimate the distribution of future returns on a single issuer basis. To combine the empirically estimated return distributions for the issuers in the portfolio context, usually copula functions are used (cf. section 12.3).

- Especially for credit portfolios sufficient diversification is essential. There are several methods to quantify the degree of diversification in a portfolio. Commonly applied measures include the diversity score and the Herfindahl index. Although the latter is particularly easy to implement it is inferior since it does not take into account the correlation structure of the investments.

- Having quantified and decomposed portfolio risk, the risk model should try to explain it by various systematic risk factors. While the issue of diversification focuses on the control of non-systematic, issuer-specific risk, sophisticated risk models primarily aim to explain variations of excess returns that are due to systematic risk factors. Generally, the analyzed risk factors should correspond with the parameters that are actively managed throughout the investment process. In global credit portfolios, usually currency exposure, duration and yield curve bets as well as sector allocations are actively controlled. In portfolios with aggregate benchmarks the exposure to changes in swap spreads and the credit allocation are additional decision parameters. However, we have seen so far, that duration and yield curve bets often only play a minor role in pure credit portfolios. A large part of the alpha generated in credit portfolios results from issuer selection. As we will see subsequently, most risk models assume that the return component that is not explained by clearly defined systematic risk factors, is due to issuer and security selection.

- The simulation of the effect of certain trade ideas on the magnitude as well as on the composition of portfolio risk is another important feature. Since a simulation helps to quantify the risk associated with any benchmark deviation, or, in absolute return products, any position, it allows to allocate risks in concordance with the risk profile of the portfolio and the skills of the portfolio manager.

- Scenario analyses with respect to the identified systematic risk factors help to gain insights into the portfolio sensitivity to medium to longer term macroeconomic or market developments. A scenario-based risk modeling approach requires forecasts of changes in systematic factors. Risk management tools might derive possible changes in the risk factors from historical behavior and current factor levels. Additionally it should be possible to feed the risk model with the portfolio manager's own scenarios.

- Under extreme market conditions not only the volatility of securities, but also the pairwise dependence between them changes dramatically. Stress testing is a commonly applied methodology to estimate the magnitude of losses in worst-case scenarios. Since value at risk only quantifies risk under normal market conditions, a different approach is needed. Keeping the weights constant, a stress covariance matrix is applied to estimate possible losses in stress periods. For this purpose risk management tools often rely on a library of stress covariance matrices that have been observed historically in times of exogeneous or endogeneous shocks to the market. Suitable periods for the estimation of stress covariance matrices are, for example, the bond market crash in 1994, the Asian crisis in 1997, the Russian default and the failure of Long Term Capital Management (LTCM) in 1998, and the time following September 11, 2001. A second kind of stress tests imposes extreme assumptions on future volatility and correlation of asset returns to simulate permanent structural breaks in market variables or temporary deviations from historically observed market behavior. Monte Carlo simulation allows to create scenarios that have not been experienced historically. One scenario might, for example, assume that the volatility for certain assets or asset classes multiplies by a certain factor, and/or that all assets exhibit perfect correlation. Berkowitz (2000) outlines a coherent framework for stress testing.
- Many risk management tools include portfolio optimization. While the aforementioned issues have touched upon the subject of the analysis and control of portfolio risk, portfolio optimization directly moves on to the process of portfolio construction. Sound estimates of the sources of portfolio risk are the best basis for the construction of risk minimizing portfolios. However, to obtain a certain risk/return profile in the portfolio, return forecasts for all assets are required additionally. Especially for less liquid asset classes like high yield it is essential that transaction costs are considered during the process of portfolio optimization. This avoids the recommendation of trades that are not efficient from a cost/reward perspective.

State-of-the-art risk models like Lehman Brothers' Global Risk Model are based on a multifactor regression model. The general idea is that the total return of any bond can be decomposed into various systematic components and an idiosyncratic component. This framework is applicable across all asset classes, because it can be tailored to the characteristics of any asset class via the selection of specific risk factors. Empirical studies have shown that the variation in credit returns may be explained by five systematic risk factors: foreign exchange rates, yield curve, volatility, credit spreads and swap spreads. The remaining return component that is not captured by these factors, is attributed to issuer and security-specific risks. For a thorough overview of risk management processes interested readers may refer to Beckers (1996).

12.2 REDUCING NONSYSTEMATIC RISK THROUGH DIVERSIFICATION

Widening credit spreads and rising default rates characterized the credit environment of the years 1997–2002. Attracted by historically high yield pickups, many new investors have entered the arena in this period. Many of them suffered significant losses due to one or more of the credit blowups like WorldCom, Enron and TXU Europe. Therefore, the demand for risk management tools for credit portfolios has increased rapidly. But cases of fraud and corporate malfeasance suggest that risk management tools that capture systematic sources of variations in returns are not enough. Sufficient diversification of investments provides effective protection against credit events. Subsequently we will discuss how relative and absolute portfolio risk are related to diversification. Yet, too much diversification reduces the potential to generate alpha. A study by Dynkin *et al.* (2002) suggests that there is an optimal level of diversification that depends upon the skill in credit research.

Idiosyncratic risk is defined as the variation in (excess) returns that cannot be explained by systematic risk factors. In portfolios that are managed against a benchmark index, it results from active deviations from the index compositions. Large deviations from benchmark weights make a portfolio vulnerable to credit events for a particular issuer. In general, the broader a portfolio is diversified, the less it is exposed to idiosyncratic risk. Therefore, issuer-specific risk is often called a diversifiable risk. When portfolios are managed in an absolute-return fashion, over- or underweights relative to a benchmark index clearly do not matter. Risk is caused by the absolute exposure to a certain issuer. This is particularly true for structured credit products like collateralized debt obligations (CDOs), as we have pointed out in Chapter 7.

The absolute and relative risk of a credit portfolio consequently is a function of the number of bonds and the magnitude of the benchmark deviations in a portfolio. Yet, the overall credit environment, or more exactly the volatility of spreads and the level of default rates, largely determines the level of risk. As figure 12.1 illustrates, investors should have expected equally weighted portfolios of 50 corporate bonds to realize a tracking error between 0.9 and 1.3 percent during the volatile credit environment of 2002. Keeping the portfolios constant for the next three months those portfolios actually would have averaged tracking errors between 0.8 and 1.5 percent (Figure 12.2).

Sophisticated approaches like stratified sampling or optimization techniques, primarily used in passive investing, try to generate portfolios that closely track the performance of broad indices. Figure 12.3 displays the risk characteristics of portfolios that were optimized with respect to historical tracking error. The analysis is based on the Merrill Lynch EMU Corporate Index. Comprising 1,200 issues, the index is broadly diversified and thus

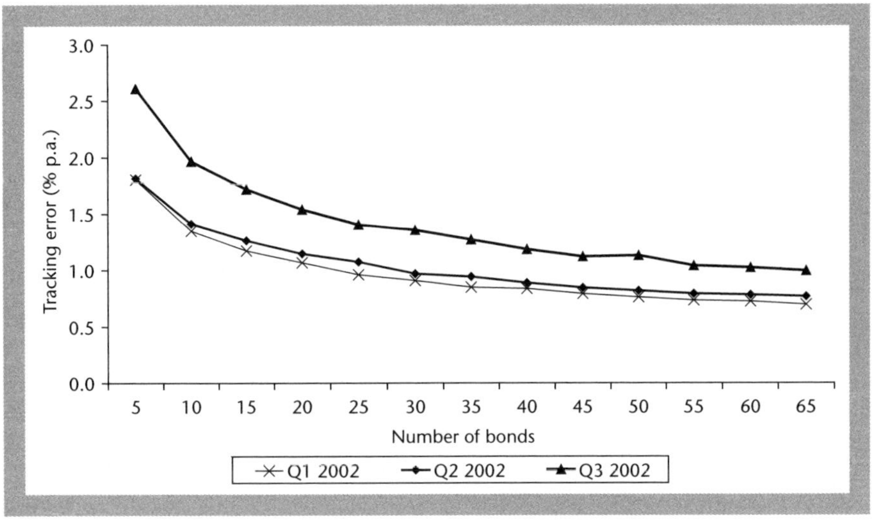

Figure 12.1 Expected tracking error of equally weighted Euro corporate bond portfolios versus Merrill Lynch EMU Corporate Index

Source: Union Investment

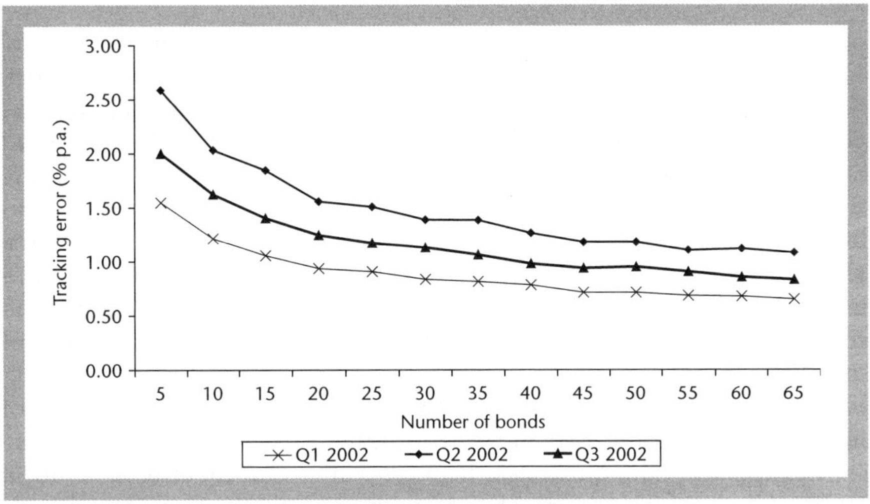

Figure 12.2 Realized tracking error of equally weighted Euro corporate bond portfolios versus Merrill Lynch EMU Corporate Index

Source: Union Investment

represents the performance of the investment grade Euro corporate bond market very well. Because of the low liquidity of a significant portion of the index bonds, replication of the index performance is only possible via the application of sampling techniques. In our case, the constituents of the

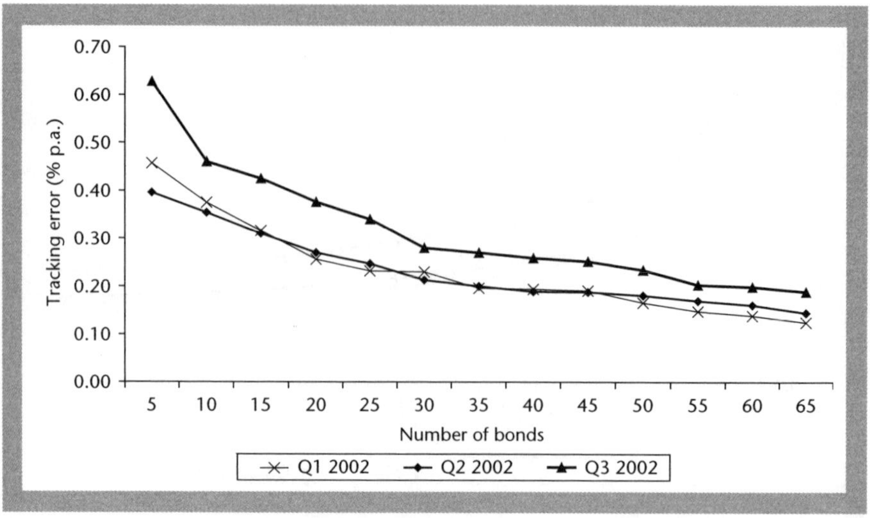

Figure 12.3 Expected tracking error of ex ante optimal Euro corporate bond portfolios versus Merrill Lynch EMU Corporate Index

Source: Union Investment

optimized portfolios are exclusively taken from the index universe. Taking into account the historical volatility and correlation structure the portfolio constituents and weights are chosen in order to minimize tracking error. The graph shows that the expected tracking error of the optimized portfolios is substantial if less than 50 securities are chosen to replicate index performance, but significantly lower than that of the naively diversified portfolios (Figure 2.3). However, although the ex post analysis of the realized performance shows lower tracking error of the optimized portfolios than the equally weighted portfolios, the realized tracking error in the out-of sample period is significantly higher than expected because of the impact of idiosyncratic risks on the performance of narrow portfolios. A minimum of 50–60 issuers seems to be necessary to reduce the effect of idiosyncratic risk to an acceptable level (Figure 12.4).

A simple example illustrates this observation. Consider a portfolio of 40 equally weighted corporate bonds, each one trading at par. Assuming a flat yield curve and an average spread over government bonds of 50 bp, the investor expects to earn an excess return of 0.5 percent, if the yield curve remains unchanged and there is no credit event. If the total return on one of the bonds is −19.5 or worse, the expected outperformance turns into a loss. The costs of portfolio management are neglected in this example. Considering a historical frequency of 6.2 percent of the issuers that have on average migrated from investment grade to high yield every year since 1970, this scenario seems quite realistic. One way to create a more favorable

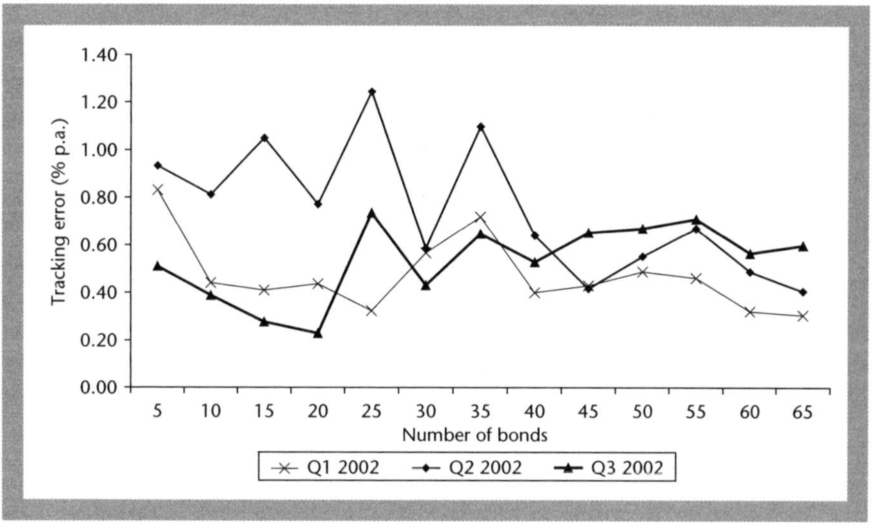

Figure 12.4 Realized tracking error of ex ante optimal Euro corporate bond portfolios versus Merrill Lynch EMU Corporate Index

Source: Union Investment

risk/reward profile might be to increase the average spread of the portfolio. But if credit spreads are accepted as useful indicators for credit risk, the probability of potential credit events should also increase. Moreover, the heightened aggressiveness of the portfolio serves to increase the spread volatility of the portfolio.

Consequently, a disciplined risk management is required for all credit portfolios. Applying strict rules for how to handle blowups does not only help to avoid large losses, but also allows for a quick decision-making in stress scenarios. During the years 2001 and 2002 that were characterized by high and still rising default rates, often the first loss proved to be the lowest one. Nevertheless, the critical point is how to determine stop loss limits. There is no simple solution for this problem. Generally, stop loss limits should depend on the risk budget of the portfolio and the volatility of the issue. Hence, high-yield managers tend to define their stop loss limits wider than pure investment grade portfolio managers. Therefore, the stop loss limits displayed in Figure 12.5 are somewhat arbitrary. They might correspond to the risk profile of a rather conservatively managed portfolio, for example, a short-term corporate bond fund.

The controlled admixture of formerly stressed credits may be an important source of alpha, especially in an ameliorating credit environment. Buying bonds that trade on cash price gives the opportunity to benefit from the asymmetric risk profile of corporate bonds. Careful fundamental analysis is essential to pick issuers with an improving credit story. Investments in

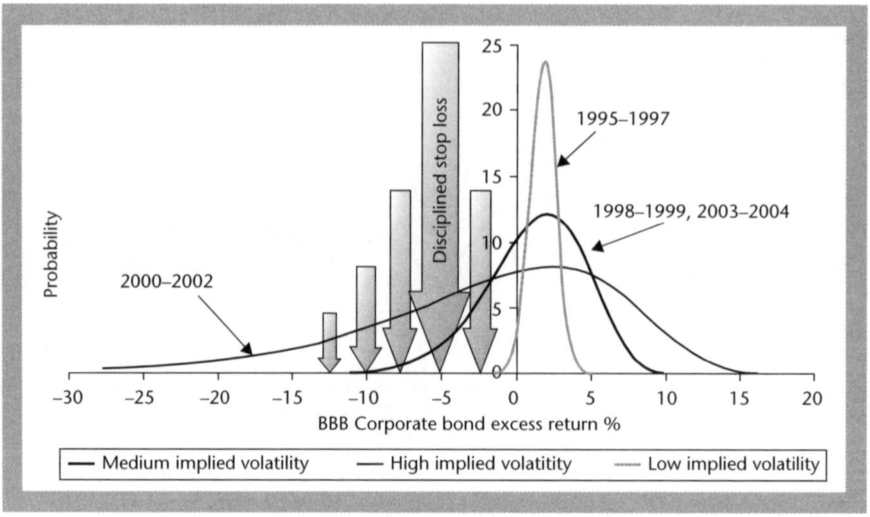

Figure 12.5 Schematic stop loss approach for investment grade corporate bonds

Source: CSFB and Union Investment

crossover or high-yield bonds have to be tracked closely because of the high volatility. Again, the key to success is diversification. Instead of buying only one name, it is recommended to create a diversified portfolio of riskier investments. The weight of the high-yield and crossover subportfolio depends on how much of the overall risk budget may be allocated to riskier asset classes. For single names, upper limits of 0.25–0.5 percent have proven useful. Clearly the application of disciplined stop loss marks helps to reduce risks.

12.3 MODELING DEFAULT RISK IN CREDIT BASKETS

So far, we have focused on the modeling of default risk on a single-issuer basis. Because of the asymmetric risk profile of corporate bonds, that is, limited upside, but a (small) probability of incurring large losses, credit risk should be managed in a portfolio context. Like in basket credit derivatives that may be tailored to the needs and the risk budget of the investor, portfolio credit risk is determined by the weighting of the issuers in the portfolio, their credit quality and default correlation between the issuers. As the previous section has shown, broader diversification significantly reduces the impact of single-issuer credit risk on the overall risk profile of the portfolio. Alike, higher credit quality on the single-name level leads to less risky credit portfolios. The impact of default correlation is largely on tail risk, that is, the probability and magnitude of extreme losses. It is natural to expect companies that share certain characteristics to have a higher probability of defaulting together. Firms from the same country are exposed to the same exchange rate and interest rate regimes. Companies from one industry face the same competition and prices for raw materials. Although there is not enough empirical evidence to support the hypothesis, it is logical to assume higher default correlations for companies from the same country or industry.

Most credit portfolios are benchmarked against a credit index. Consequently, investors try to maximize relative performance with respect to the index. In this relative investment framework, risk is determined by the active exposures to individual credits and industries. Because of tracking error limits that have to be satisfied, and liquidity considerations, the weights of issuers and sectors are largely driven by their market capitalizations. Although often not benchmark oriented, the investment process of insurance companies, too, fits into the category of relative investment approaches. In their asset liability management, insurance companies have to match portfolio cash flows to correspond with the forecasted liabilities. Issuer selection and sector allocation are the tools to generate stable and secure income streams that suffice the investment constraints and risk budget.

Structured credit instruments, such as synthetic baskets and CDOs, focus on the generation of absolute returns. Hence, portfolio weights are independent from index weights or market capitalizations. In order to minimize exposure to any individual issuer in the basket, usually equal weights are chosen. Risk, as considered in the portfolio context, is mostly due to defaults of individual issuers in the basket. Price volatility on an issuer basis is not the main concern. Especially for tranched portfolios, the occurrence of extreme losses on the portfolio level affects valuation. The assessment of default correlations is essential for the modeling of extreme loss events and the valuation of structured credit products.

It is important to note that default correlation does not influence the expected number of defaults in a credit portfolio, but rather the shape of the default distribution. High default correlations lead to a high probability of a very small or very large number of defaults, thus reflecting a high likelihood of extreme events. Figures 12.6–12.8 show for an example portfolio of 100 issuers that the default distribution becomes more fat-tailed with an increasing level of default correlation. The figures assume a 10 percent default probability for each individual issuer and either 1, 4 or 8 percent default correlation.

As we have seen the performance of credit is highly dependent upon the stage of the business cycle and the leverage cycle. Historically, it has been found that corporate bond issuers tend to default in clusters, at times when business conditions are difficult and leverage is high. This implies correlation between the defaults, or more exactly the times of default of corporate bond issuers. Figures 12.6–12.8 have highlighted that the assumption of

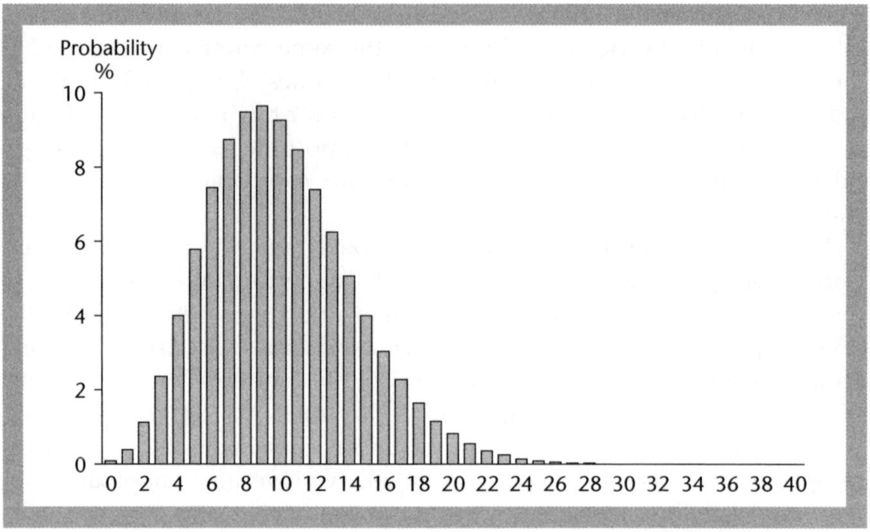

Figure 12.6 Default distribution for a portfolio of 100 issuers with a default probability of 10 percent and pairwise default correlations of 1 percent

Source: Morgan Stanley

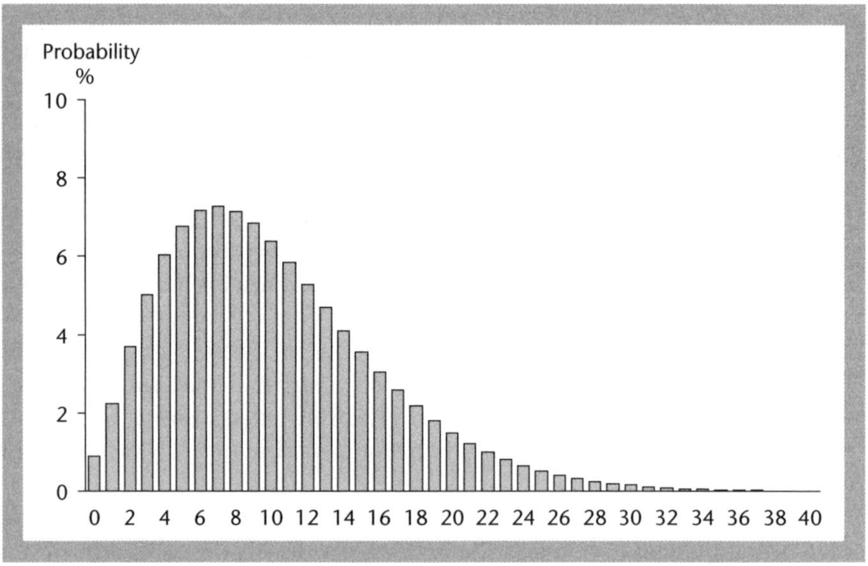

Figure 12.7 Default distribution for a portfolio of 100 issuers with a default probability of 10 percent and pairwise default correlations of 4 percent

Source: Morgan Stanley

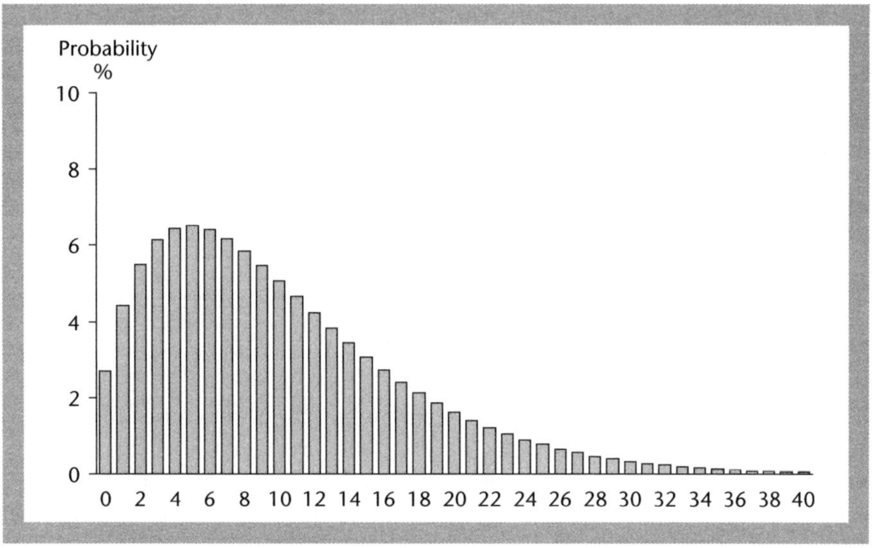

Figure 12.8 Default distribution for a portfolio of 100 issuers with a default probability of 10 percent and pairwise default correlations of 8 percent

Source: Morgan Stanley

independence of default may lead to an underestimation of the aggregate loss in a corporate bond portfolio. Yet, default correlations cannot be easily observed from history, because historical evidence is scarce. Moreover, historical evidence need not be a good guide for the future. Empirical studies suggest that default correlations are not stable over time. Like default rates they rather depend on the state of the economy. Modeling correlated defaults therefore has become the standard approach for the evaluation of risk in a portfolio of credit market instruments, and for the pricing of instruments subject to joint default risk.

Until recently the most popular approach of modeling dependent defaults was the structural approach. Several well-known multivariate models, for example KMV and CreditMetrics, assume a joint normal distribution of asset returns. Within this framework default occurs as soon as the asset value falls under a certain barrier that is defined by the firm's liabilities. The understanding of the default distribution of a credit basket first requires the assessment of individual issuer default risk. As presented in Chapter 2, models like KMV, CreditGrades or CUSP are commonly applied for this purpose. Yet, the key to the estimation of portfolio risk for a particular credit basket lies in the estimation of the dependence of default events. Consider n companies that are subject to default risk. If $\tau_1, \dots, \tau_n$ denote their respective default times, according to Duffie and Singleton (2003) default correlation can be expressed as

- correlation between $I_{\{\tau_i<T\}}$ and $I_{\{\tau_j<T\}}$, where the indicator function I is defined as

$$I = \begin{cases} 1 & \text{if default occurs before time } T, \\ 0 & \text{else} \end{cases}$$

- correlation between τ_i and τ_j;
- correlation between default probabilities over time.

The joint default of two companies occurs when the asset values of both fall under their respective barriers. Dependence is taken into account by assuming correlated stochastic processes for the asset values. The popularity of the multivariate normal distribution is explained by the simplicity of the dependence structure, which is fully characterized by a correlation matrix. The simulation of multidimensional normal-distributed asset returns uses the Cholesky decomposition. If $X_1, \dots, X_n$ are jointly normal distributed random variables with means $\mu_1, \dots, \mu_n$ and covariance matrix Σ, the Cholesky decomposition of Σ is $\mathbf{CC}^{\mathrm{T}}$, for some matrix $\mathbf{C}$.

The asset return of firm i is modeled as

$$X_i = \mu_i - C_{i,1}Z_1 + \cdots + C_{i,n}Z_n,$$

where $Z_1, \dots, Z_n$ are independent standard normal variables and $C_{i,j}$ denotes the ith and jth element of the Cholesky matrix $\mathbf{C}$. The covariance between the asset returns of firm i and j is thus given by

$$\sigma_{i,j} = [\mathbf{CC}^{\mathrm{T}}]_{i,j} = \sum_{i,j}.$$

For two issuers default correlation can be inferred easily. First, the implied default threshold for each issuer has to be calculated so that it matches the individual default probability. Assuming a default probability of 5 percent for issuer 1 would yield a default threshold of $z_1 = N^{-1}(0.05) = -1.645$. N^{-1} denotes the inverse of the cumulative standard normal distribution. In the second step the joint probability that both companies default is computed using a bivariate normal distribution for the joint behavior of asset values. The joint default probability is then given by the bivariate normal distribution function M as

$$p_{1 \text{ and } 2} = M(Z_1, Z_2, \text{asset correlation}_{1,2}).$$

If, for example, $p_1 = 0.05$, $p_2 = 0.01$, and asset correlation$_{1,2}$ is 0.5 then the joint probability of default $p_{1 \text{ and } 2} = 0.36$ percent. Using the formula

$$\rho_{1,2} = \frac{p_{1 \text{ and } 2} - p_1 p_2}{\sqrt{p_1(1 - p_1)p_2(1 - \rho_2)}}$$

the default correlation $\rho_{1,2}$ equals 14.3 percent. Hence, default correlation is markedly lower than asset correlation which is a typical observation. The critical point in this calculation is the estimation of asset correlation. Since asset correlation is not directly observable, it is often inferred from equity correlations. Yet, the estimation of the joint behavior of asset returns from equity returns is often criticized because of the different leverage of equity and assets. Generally, the approach is therefore only accepted for high grade issuers, where asset values are far from the respective default thresholds. This is due to the fact that for high grade issuers variations in asset values are almost one by one mirrored by changes in market valuations of equity, whereas the market value of debt is relatively stable. For high-yield issuers, changes in asset values can also cause large changes in the market value of debt, because asset values of those companies are much closer to the default threshold. This leverage effect may generate significant divergencies in the dependence structure of equity and asset returns. It should also be kept in mind that the approximation is not suitable for interest rate sensitive issuers like financial or utility companies.

Studies by Mashal and Naldi (2002) and Mashal and Zeevi (2002) have shown that fat-tailed Student *t*-copulas are better suited to describe the joint behavior of equity returns than multivariate normal distributions. Correlation matrices are therefore not sufficient to capture the full dependence structure of the joint behavior of equity returns. As an introduction to the subject of copulae we will nevertheless start with the presentation of an example using a Gaussian copula function. Assuming n correlated default times $\tau_1, \dots, \tau_n$ the respective survival functions are given by $p_1(\tau_1), \dots, p_n(\tau_n)$. The correlation of the default times is transferred into the survival function. If it is possible to simulate uniformly distributed variables $U_1, \dots, U_n$ with the same distribution function as $p_1(\tau_1), \dots, p_n(\tau_n)$, then the survival functions can be inverted to obtain a simulation of the default times.

Generally, copula functions are a device for generating multivariate distributions with given one-dimensional marginal distributions. Given the joint probability distribution of the correlated uniforms, the copula function satisfies

$$C(u_1, \dots, u_n) = P(U_1 \le u_1, \dots, U_n \le u_n).$$

Three examples in the two-dimensional case illustrate the use of copula functions:

- independent default times: $C(u, v) = P(U \leq u, V \leq u) = P(U \leq u). P(V \leq v) = uv$;
- perfectly correlated default times: $C(u,v) = P(U \leq u,V \leq v) = P(U \leq u, U \leq v) = \min(u,v)$
- Gaussian copula with correlation ρ: $C(u,V) = P(N(X) \geq u,N(Y) \leq v)$, where X and Y are standard joint normal with correlation ρ.

The fact that any multivariate distribution can be specified via a set of marginal distributions that are linked using a copula function, allows the modeling of dependent equity or asset returns. At the same time a copula function might be viewed as removing the effect of the marginals from a multivariate distribution, thus concentrating on the dependence structure. The Student *t*-copula function has the advantage that it is based on the concept of correlation, but through the variation of the degrees of freedom additionally offers the ability to model fat tails. For degrees of freedom greater than 30, it is very close to the Gaussian copula function.

Clearly, the choice of the survival probability functions and the copula function is essential. If a model is specified to obtain the survival probability functions, then the copula function should approximate the model-implied default probabilities as close as possible. Additionally, it should be calibrated thus that it matches the implied default probabilities not only over a 1-year horizon, but over several years. While typically the form of the joint density distribution for the default times is unknown Li (2000) explains a copula-based technique to impose one with the correct marginal distributions. This method allows to price CDO tranches as well as *n*th to default baskets accurately. For a general discussion of credit derivatives the reader may refer to Chapter 7.

References

Albrecht, P. and Maurer, R. *Investment- und Risikomanagement* (Schäffer-Poeschel, 2002).

Albrecht, T. "The Mean-Variance Framework and Long Horizons", in *Financial Analysts Journal* **54** (4), 44–9, 1998.

Alessandrini, F. "Credit Risk, Interest Rate Risk, and the Business Cycle", in *Journal of Fixed Income* **9** (2), 42–53, 1999.

Alexander, C. *Market Models* (Wiley, 2001).

Alexander, C. *The Handbook of Risk Management and Analysis* (Wiley, 1996).

Allen, L. and Saunders, A. "A Survey of Cyclical Effects in Credit Risk Measurement Models", BIS Working Paper 126, 2003.

Altman, E.I. "Measuring corporate bond mortality and performance", in *The Journal of Finance* **44** (3), 909–22, 1989.

Altman, E.I. "Financial Ratios, Discriminant Analysis and the Prediction of Corporate Bankruptcy", in *The Journal of Finance* **23** (4), 589–609, 1968.

Altman, E.I. and Kao, D.L. "The Implications of Corporate Bond Ratings Drift", in *Financial Analysts Journal* **48** (3), 64–75, 1992.

Altman, E.I. and Kishore, V. "Almost Everything You Wanted to Know About Recoveries on Defaulted Bonds", in *Financial Analysts Journal* **52** (6), 57–64, 1996.

Altman, E.I. and Saunders, A. "Credit Risk Measurement: Developments over the Last 20 Years", in *Journal of Banking and Finance* **21** (11–12), 1721–42, 1998.

Anderson, N., Breedon, F., Derry, A. and Murphy, G. *Estimating and Interpreting the Yield Curve* (Wiley, 1996).

Anderson, R. and Sundaresan, S. "A Comparative Study of Structural Models of Corporate Bond Yields: An Exploratory Investigation", in *Journal of Banking and Finance* **24** (1–2), 255–69, 2000.

Anderson, T.W. *An Introduction to Multivariate Statistical Analysis* (Wiley, 1984).

Ang, J.S. and Chua, J.H. "Composite Measures for the Evaluation of Investment Performance", in *Journal of Financial and Quantitative Analysis* **14** (2), 361–84, 1979.

Arnott, R. and Bernstein, P. "What Risk Premium is Normal?", in *Financial Analysts Journal* **58** (2), 64–85, 2002.

Arnott, R. and Ryan, R. "The Death of the Risk Premium", in *Journal of Portfolio Management* **27** (3), 61–75, 2001.

Artzner, P., Delbaen, F., Eber, J.M. and Heath, D. "Coherent Measures of Risk", in *Mathematical Finance* **9** (3), 203–28, 1999.

Artzner, P., Delbaen, F., Eber, J.M. and Heath, D. "Thinking Coherently", in *Risk* **10** (11), 68–71, 1997.

Atchison, M., Butler, K. and Simonds, R. "Nonsynchronous Security Trading and Market Index Autocorrelation", in *The Journal of Finance* **42** (1), 111–8, 1987.

Bangia, A., Diebold, F., Kronimus, A., Schagen, C. and Schuermann, T. "Ratings Migration and the Business Cycle, with Applications to Credit Portfolio Stress Testing", in *Journal of Banking and Finance* **26** (2–3), 445–74, 2002.

Bahar, R. and Nagpal, K. "Measuring default correlation", in *Risk* **14** (3), 129–32, 2001.

Barry, C.B. "Portfolio Analysis under Uncertain Means, Variances and Covariances", in *The Journal of Finance* **29** (2), 515–22, 1974.

Basle Committee on Banking Supervision "Capital Adequacy Framework", Consultation Document, Bank for International Settlements, 1999.

Basle Committee on Banking Supervision "The New Basel Capital Accord", Report, Bank for International Settlements, 2003.

Bawa, V.S. "Optimal Rules for Ordering Uncertain Prospects", in *Journal of Financial Economics* **2** (1), 95–121, 1975.

Bawa, V.S. and Lindenberg, E.B. "Capital Market Equilibrium in a Mean-Lower Partial Moment-Framework", in *Journal of Financial Economics* **5** (2), 189–200, 1977.

Bawa, V.S. "Safety-First, Stochastic Dominance and Optimal Portfolio Choice", in *Journal of Financial and Quantitative Analysis* **13** (2), 255–71, 1978.

Beckers, S. "A Survey of Risk Management: Theory and Practice", in *The Handbook of Risk Management and Analysis* (Wiley, 1996).

Berkowitz, J. "A Coherent Framework for Stress Testing", in *Journal of Risk* **2** (4), 5–15, 2000.

Bevan, A. and Garzarelli, F. "Corporate Bond Spreads and the Business Cycle: Introducing the GS-SPREAD", in *The Journal of Fixed Income* **9** (4), 8–18, 2000.

Bey, R.P. "Estimating the Optimal Stochastic Dominance Efficient Set with a Mean-Semivariance Algorithm", in *Journal of Financial and Quantitative Analysis* **14** (5), 1059–70, 1979.

Black, F. and Cox, J.C. "Valuing corporate securities: some effects of bond indenture provisions", in *The Journal of Finance* **31** (2), 351–67, 1976.

Black, F. and Jones, R. "Simplifying Portfolio Insurance", in *Journal of Portfolio Management* **14** (1), 48–51, 1987.

Black, F. and Scholes, M. "On the Pricing of Options and Corporate Liabilities", in *Journal of Political Economy* **81** (3), 637–59, 1973.

Blume, M.E., Lim, F. and MacKinlay, A.C. "The declining credit quality of US corporate debt: Myth or Reality?", in *The Journal of Finance* **53** (4), 1389–1413, 1998.

Blundell, G.F. and Ward, C.W.R. "Property Portfolio Allocation: a Multi-Factor Model", in *Land Development Studies* **4** (2), 145–56, 1987.

Box, G.E.P. "A General Distribution Theory for a Class of Likelihood Criteria", in *Biometrika* **36**, 317–46, 1949.

Brealey R. A. and Myers, S. C., *Principles of Corporate Finance* (McGraw Hill, 5th Edition 1996)

Breger, L., Goldberg, L. and Cheyette, O. "Market-implied ratings", in *Risk* **16** (7), 85–9, 2003.

Brooks, C. and Kat, H. "The Statistical Properties of Hedge Fund Index Returns and Their Implications for Investors", ISMA Centre Working paper, University of Reading, 2001.

Brown, G.R. "The Information Content of Property Valuations", in *Journal of Valuation* **3** (3), 350–62, 1985.
Burghardt, G.D., Belton, T.M., Lane, M. and Papa, J. (eds) *The Treasury Bond Basis: An In-Depth Analysis For Hedgers, Speculators and Arbitrageurs* (Irwin, 1994).
Campbell, J.Y., Lo, A.W. and MacKinlay, A.C. *The Econometrics of Financial Markets* (Princeton University Press, 1997).
Campbell, J.Y. and Taksler, G.B. "Equity volatility and corporate bond yields", Working paper, http://papers.ssrn.com, 2002.
Campbell, J.Y. and Viceira, L.M. *Strategic Asset Allocation* (Oxford University Press, 2002).
Chen, N.F. "Financial Investment Opportunities and the Macroeconomy", in *The Journal of Finance* **46** (2), 529–54, 1991.
Chunhachinda, P., Dandapani, K., Hamid, S. and Prakash, A.J. "Portfolio Selection and Skewness: Evidence from International Stock Markets", in *Journal of Banking and Finance* **21** (2), 143–67, 1997.
Clarke, R., de Silva, H. and Thorley, S. "Portfolio Constraints and the Fundamental Law of Active Management", in *Financial Analysts Journal* **58** (5), 48–66, 2002.
Collin-Dufresne, P. and Goldstein, R.S. "Do credit spreads reflect stationary leverage ratios?", in *Journal of Finance* **56** (5), 1929–57, 2001.
Collin-Dufresne, P., Goldstein, R.S. and Martin, J.S. "The determinants of credit spread changes", in *Journal of Finance* **56** (6), 2177–207, 2001.
Cornish, E.A. and Fisher, R.A. "Moments and Cumulants in the Specification of Distributions", in *Extrait de la Revue de l'Institute International de Statistique* **4**, 1–14, 1937.
Crabbe, L.E. and Fabozzi, F.J. *Corporate Bond Portfolio Management* (Wiley, 2002).
Damodaran, A. *Investment Valuation, Tools and Techniques for Determining the Value of Any Asset* (Wiley, 1996).
Das, S. *Credit Derivatives* (Wiley, 1998).
Denis, D.J., Denis, D.K. and Yost, K. "Global Diversification, Industrial Diversification and Firm Value", in *The Journal of Finance* **57** (5), 1951–79, 2002.
Desclée, A. and Rosten, J. "Are Credit Markets Globally Integrated? An Initial Assessment", in *Lehman Brothers Quantitative Credit Research Quarterly* **4**, 2002.
Diez-Castanedo, J.M. and Castanon, C.L. "Concentration Risk in Bank Loan Portfolios: Measurement, Single Obligor Limits, and Capital Adequacy," Central Bank of Mexico Preprint, 1999.
Diwald, H. *Zinsfutures und Zinsoptionen: Erfolgreicher Einsatz an DTB und LIFFE* (Beck, 1994).
Duffee, G.R. "Estimating the price of default risk", in *Review of Financial Studies* **12** (1), 197–226, 1999.
Duffee, G.R. "The relation between treasury yields and corporate bond yield spreads", in *The Journal of Finance* **53** (6), 2225–41, 1998.
Duffie, D. and Pan, J. "An Overview of Value at Risk", in *The Journal of Derivatives* **4** (3), 7–49, 1997.
Duffie, D. and Singleton, K.J. *Credit Risk: Pricing, Measurement, and Management* (Princeton University Press, 2003).
Duffie, D. and Ziegler, A. "Liquidation risk", HEC Lausanne Working paper No. 29, August 2001.
Dynkin, L., Hyman, J. and Konstantinovsky, V. "Sufficient Diversification in Credit Portfolios", in *Journal of Portfolio Management* **29** (1), 89–114, 2002.
Ederington, H.L., Yawitz, J.B. and Roberts, B.E. "The Informational Content of Bond Ratings", in *Journal of Financial Research* **10**, 211–26, 1987.
Eller, R. (ed.) *Handbuch des Risikomanagements* (Schäffer-Poeschel, 2002).
Elton, E.J., Gruber, M.J., Agrawal, D. and Mann, C. "Explaining the Rate Spread on Corporate Bonds", in *The Journal of Finance* **56** (1), 247–77, 2001.

Elton, E.J. and Gruber, M.J. *Modern Portfolio Theory and Investment Analysis* (Wiley, 1995).
Epstein B. J., Mirza A.A. *Interpretation and Application of International Accounting Standards* (Wiley, 2000).
Fabozzi, F.J. *Fixed Income Securities* (Wiley, 2002).
Fabozzi, F.J. *Handbook of Fixed Income Securities* (McGraw-Hill, 2001).
Fabozzi, F.J. *Bond Markets, Analyses and Strategies* (Prentice-Hall, 2000).
Fabozzi, F.J. *Fixed Income Mathematics* (McGraw-Hill, 1997).
Fama, E.F. and French, K. "Business Conditions and Expected Returns on Stocks and Bonds", in *Journal of Financial Economics* **25** (1), 23–49, 1989.
Farrell, J. *Portfolio Management: Theory and Application* (McGraw-Hill, 1997).
Ferguson, R. "The danger of leverage and volatility", in *Journal of Investing* **3**, 52–6, Winter 1994.
Fernandez, F.A. "Liquidity risk – New approaches to measurement and monitoring", in Securities Industry Association, Working paper, December 1999.
Fiebach, G. *Risikomanagement mit Zins-Futures und Futures-Optionen* (Haupt, 1994).
Finger, C.C. "The one-factor CreditMetrics model in the new Basel capital accord", in *RiskMetrics Journal*, 9–18, Spring 2001.
Firstenberg, P. A. Ross, S. A. and Zisler, R. C. "Real estate: the whole story", in *Journal of Portfolio Management* **14** (3), 22–34, 1988.
Fishburn, P.C "Stochastic Dominance and Moments of Distributions", in *Mathematics of Operations Research* **5** (1), 94–100, 1980.
Fishburn, P.C. "Mean-Risk Analysis with Risk Associated with Below-Target Returns", in *The American Economic Review* **67** (2), 116–126, 1977.
Francis, J.C. and Wolf A. *The Handbook of Interest Rate Risk Management* (Irwin, 1994).
Franks, J.R. and Schwartz, E.S. "The Stochastic Behavior of Market Variance Implied in the Prices of Index Options: Evidence on Leverage, Volume, and Other Effects", UCLA Anderson School Reprint 10–88, June 1988.
Galai, D. and Masulis, R.W. "The Option Pricing Model and the Risk Factors of Stock", in *Journal of Financial Economics* **3** (1–2), 53–81, 1976.
Gehrig, B. and Zimmermann, H. *Fit for Finance* (Verlag Neue Züricher Zeitung, 1999).
Geltner, D.M. "Estimating Market Values from Appraised Values without Assuming an Efficient Market", in *Journal of Real Estate Research* **8** (3), 325–45, 1993.
Gordy, M.B. "A risk-factor model foundation for ratings-based bank capital rules", Federal Reserve Board, Finance and Economics Discussion Series, 2002, 55.
Greenbaum, S.I. and Thakor, A.V. *Contemporary Financial Intermediation* (Dryden Press, 1995).
Grinold, R.C. "Are Benchmark Portfolios Efficient?", in *The Journal of Portfolio Management* **19** (1), 34–40, 1992.
Grinold, R.C. "The Fundamental Law of Active Management," in *Journal of Portfolio Management* **15** (3), 30–37, 1989.
Grinold, R.C. and Kahn, R. *Active Portfolio Management* (McGraw-Hill, 1995).
Gyoengyoesi, I. "Auswirkung von Aktienkursen auf Credit Spreads", unpublished diploma thesis, Hochschule fuer Bankwirtschaft Frankfurt, 2002.
Hadar, J. and Russell, W.R. "Rules for Ordering Uncertain Prospects", in *The American Economic Review* **59** (1), 25–34, 1969.
Hagenstein, F. "Verschiedene Arten der Volatilität bei standardisierten bzw. OTC-Bundoptionen", in *Handbuch des Risikomanagements* (Schäffer-Poeschel, 2002), 485–502.
Hagenstein, F. and Bangemann, T. *Aktives Rentenmanagement* (Schäffer-Poeschel, 2001).
Hagenstein, F. and Bangemann, T. *Active Fixed Income and Credit Management* (Palgrave, 2002).
Hagenstein, F. and Mertz, A. "Investmentprozess Corporate Bonds", in *Handbuch Asset Management* (Schäffer-Poeschel, 2003), 171–88.

Hagenstein, F. and Seifert, J. "Der Investmentprozess für Unternehmensanleihen", in *Handbuch des Risikomanagements* (Schäffer-Poeschel, 2002), 755–814.

Hand, J.M, Holthausen, R.W. and Leftwich, R.W. "The Effect of Bond Rating Agency Announcements on Bond and Stock Prices", in *The Journal of Finance* **47** (2), 733–752, 1992.

Harlow, W.V. "Asset Allocation in a Downside-Risk Framework", in *Financial Analysts Journal* **47** (5), 28–40, 1991.

Heinke, V. "Credit Ratings im Bond-Portfoliomanagement", in *Handbuch Portfoliomanagement* (Uhlenbruch-Verlag, 2002), 495–524.

Herold, U. and Maurer, R. "How Much Credit?", in *Journal of Fixed Income* **12** (4) 49–56, 2003.

Hodges, C.W., Levy, H. and Yoder, J.A. "Time Diversification and Stochastic Dominance", Working Paper, State University of West Georgia, 2002.

Holthausen, D.M. "A Risk-Return Model with Risk and Return Measured as Deviations from a Target Return", in *The American Economic Review* **71** (1), 182–88, 1981.

Huang, J. and Huang, M. "How much of the corporate-treasury yield spread is due to credit risk?", unpublished paper, Graduate School of Business, 2000.

Hull, J.C. *Options, Futures and Other Derivatives* (Prentice-Hall, 1997).

Hull, J.C. and White, A. "The Impact of Default Risk on the Prices of Options and Other Derivative Securities", in *Journal of Banking and Finance* **19** (2), 299–322, 1995.

Ilmanen, A. and Sayood, R. "Quantitative Forecasting Models and Active Diversification for International Bonds", in *The Journal of Fixed Income* **12** (3), 40–51, 2002.

Ingersoll, J.E. "A contingent-claims valuation of convertible securities", in *Journal of Financial Economics* **4** (4), 289–321, 1977.

International Monetary Fund "When bubbles burst", World Economic Outlook, 61–94, April 2003.

Ivaschenko, I. "How much leverage is too much, or does corporate risk determine the severity of a recession?", *IMF Working Paper No. 3*, 2003.

Jackson, P., Perraudin, W. and Saporta, V. "Setting Minimum Capital for Internationally Active Banks", Paper presented at the Bank of England Conference on Banks and Systemic Risks, London, 2001.

Jarque, C.M. and Bera, A.K. "A test for normality of observations and regression residuals", in *International Statistical Review* **55** (2), 163–72, 1987.

Jensen, M. and Meckling, W. "Theory of the Firm: Managerial Behavior, Agency Costs and Ownership Structure", in *Journal of Financial Economics* **3** (4), 305–60, 1976.

Jobson, J.D., Korkie, B.M. and Ratti, V. "Improved Estimation for Markowitz Portfolios Using James-Stein Type Estimators", in *Proceedings of the American Statistical Association, Business and Economic Statistics Section*, 279–82, 1979.

Jones, E.P., Mason, S.P. and Rosenfeld, E. "Contingent claims analysis of corporate capital structures: An empirical investigation", in *The Journal of Finance* **39** (2), 611–25, 1984.

Jorion, P. *Value at Risk: The New Benchmark for Controlling Market Risk* (Irwin, 1997).

Jorion, P. "Bayes-Stein Estimation for Portfolio Analysis", in *Journal of Financial and Quantitative Analysis* **21** (3), 279–92, 1986.

Kahneman, D. and Tversky, A. "Prospect Theory: An Analysis of Decision Making under Risk", in *Econometrica* **47** (2), 263–291, 1979.

Kallberg, J.G. and Ziemba, W.T. "Misspecification in Portfolio Selection Problems", in *Risk and Capital* **227**, 74–87, 1984.

Kassam, A. and Grebnev, A. "Using equity options for credit protection", in Goldman Sachs European Equity Derivatives, 8–9, May 2002.

Keanan, S. et al. "Predicting Default Rates", Moody's Investor Service, 1999.

Kercheval, A., Goldberg, L. and Breger, L. "Modeling credit risk: currency dependence in global credit markets", in *The Journal of Portfolio Management* **29** (2), 90–100, 2003.

Kindleberger, C. *Manias, Panics and Crashes: A History of Financial Crises* (Basic Books, 1978).

King, M. "Portfolio Diversification: How Much is Enough?", J. P. Morgan Credit Research Alert, March 2003.

King, M., McGinty, L. and Due, J. "Credit Spreads, Default Rates and the Business Cycle", J. P. Morgan Credit Research, August 2002.

Klein, R.W. and Bawa, V.S. "The Effect of Estimation Risk on Optimal Portfolio Choice", in *Journal of Financial Economics* **3**, 215–31, 1976.

Kliger, D. and Sarig, O. "The Information Value of Bond Ratings", in *The Journal of Finance* **55** (6), 2879–902, 2000.

Koopman, S.J. and Lucas, A. "Business and Default Cycles for Credit Risk", Tinbergen Institute Discussion Paper 03-062/2, 2003.

Kotler, P. *Marketing Management – Analysis, Planning, Implementation, and Control* (Prentice Hall International Editions, 8th Edition 1994).

Kumar, M.S. and Persaud, A. "Pure Contagion and Investors' Shifting Risk Appetite: Analytical Issues and Empirical Evidence", IMF Working Paper WP/01/134, 2001.

Lee, W. *Theory and Methodology of Tactical Asset Allocation* (FJF, 2000).

Leland, H.E. "Who should buy Portfolio Insurance?", in *The Journal of Finance* **35** (2), 581–96, 1980.

Leland, H.E. "Corporate Debt Value, Bond Covenants, and Optimal Capital Structure", in *The Journal of Finance* **49** (4), 1213–52, 1994.

Levy, H. *Stochastic Dominance: Investment Decision Making under Uncertainty* (Kluwer, 1992).

Levy, H. and Hanoch, G. "Relative Effectiveness of Efficiency Criteria for Portfolio Selection", in *Journal of Financial and Quantitative Analysis* **5**, 63–76, 1970.

Levy, H. and Kroll, Y. "Stochastic Dominance with Riskless Assets", in *Journal of Financial and Quantitative Analysis* **11**, 743–77, 1976.

Levy, H. and Kroll, Y. "Efficiency Analysis with Borrowing and Lending Criteria: and their Effectiveness", in *Review of Economics and Statistics* **61** (1), 125–30, 1979.

Li, D. "On Default Correlation: A Copula Function Approach", in *Journal of Fixed Income* **9** (4), 43–54, 2000.

Lo, A.W. and MacKinlay, C.A. "An Econometric Analysis of Non-synchronous Trading", in *Journal of Econometrics* **45** (1–2), 181–211, 1990.

Lucas, D. "Default correlation and credit analysis", in *Journal of Fixed Income*, 76–87, March 1995.

Markowitz, H. "Portfolio Selection", in *The Journal of Finance* **7** (1), 77–91, 1952.

Mashal, R. and Naldi, M. "Extreme Events and Default Baskets", in *Risk* **15** (7), 119–22, 2002.

Mashal, R. and Zeevi, A. "Beyond Correlation: Extreme Co-movements between Financial Assets", Working Paper, Columbia Business School, 2002.

Maurer, R. and Mertz, A."Internationale Diversifikation von Aktien- und Anleiheportfolios aus der Perspektive deutscher Investoren", in *Die Betriebswirtschaft* **60** (4), 423–40, 2000.

Matten, C. *Managing Bank Capital. Capital Allocation and Performance Measurement* (Wiley, 1996).

Merton, R.C. "On the pricing of corporate debt: the risk structure of interest rates", in *The Journal of Finance* **29** (2), 449–70, 1974.

Merton, R.C. and Perold, A.F. "Theory of Risk Capital in Financial Firms", in *Journal of Applied Corporate Finance* **6** (3), 16–32, 1993.

Mina, J. and Ulmer, A. "Delta-Gamma Four Ways", in Risk Metrics Group, 1999.

Modigliani, F. and Miller, M. "The cost of capital, corporation finance and the theory of investment", in *American Economic Review* **53** (3), 261–97, 1958.

Moody's Investor Service, *Moody's Ratings Methodology Handbook*, June 2002.

Nantell, T.J. and B. Price "An Analytical Comparison of Variance and Semivariance Capital Market Theories", in *Journal of Financial and Quantitative Analysis* **14** (2), 221–42, 1979.

Natenberg, S. *Option Volatility and Pricing: Advanced Trading Strategies and Techniques* (Irwin, 1994).

Nawrocki, D.N. and Staples, K. "A Customized LPM Risk Measure for Portfolio Analysis", in *Applied Economics* **21** (2), 205–18, 1989.

Nawrocki, D.N. "Optimal Algorithms and Lower Partial Moment: Ex Post Results", in *Applied Economics* **23** (3), 465–70, 1991.

Nickell, P., Perraudin, W. and Varotto, S. "Stability of rating transitions", in *Journal of Banking and Finance* **24** (1–2), 203–27, 2000.

Pagès, H. "Can liquidity risk be subsumed in credit risk? A case study from Brady bond prices", Bank for International Settlements, Working paper No. 101, July 2001.

Phoa, W. *Advanced Fixed Income Analytics* (FJF, 1998).

Pinches, G.E. and Mingo, K.A. "A multivariate analysis of industrial bonds ratings" in *The Journal of Finance* **28** (1), 1–16, 1973.

Plona, C. *The European Bond Basis: An In-Depth Analysis for Hedgers, Speculators and Arbitrageurs* (Irwin, 1997).

Pogue, T.F. and Soldofsky, R.M. "What's in a bond rating?", in *Journal of Financial and Quantitative Analysis* **4**, 201–28, June 1969.

Porter, R.B. "Semivariance and Stochastic Dominance: A Comparison", in *The American Economic Review* **64** (1), 200–03, 1974.

Porter, R.B., Wart J.R. and Ferguson D.L. "Efficient Algorithms for Conducting Stochastic Dominance Tests on Large Numbers of Portfolios", in *Journal of Financial and Quantitative Analysis* **8** (1), 71–81, 1973.

Price, K., Price, B. and Nantell, T.J. "Variance and Lower Partial Moment Measures of Systematic Risk: Some Analytical and Empirical Results", in *The Journal of Finance* **37** (3), 843–55, 1982.

Rahl, L. (ed.) *Risk Budgeting – A New Approach to Investing* (Risk Waters Group, 2000).

Rajan, A. "The Impact of Liquidity on Measured Historical Volatility", Salomon Smith Barney, 2000.

Ray, C.I. *The Bond Market: Trading and Risk Management* (Irwin, 1993).

Reilly, F.K. and Brown, K.C. *Investment Analysis and Portfolio Management* (Thomson South-Western, 7th Edition 2003).

Saita, F. "Allocation of Risk Capital in Financial Institutions", in *Financial Management* **28** (3), 95–111, 1999.

Schmidt-von Rhein, A. "Portfoliooptimierung mit der Ausfallvarianz", Handbuch Portfoliomanagement (Uhlenbruch, 1998), 591–625.

Schubert, L. "Lower Partial Moments in Mean-Varianz-Portefeuilles", in *Finanzmarkt und Portfolio Management* **10** (4), 496–509, 1997.

Schwert, G.W. "Why Does Stock Market Volatility Change Over Time?", in *The Journal of Finance* **44** (5), 1115–53, 1989.

Servigny, A. de and Renault, O. "Correlation evidence", in *Risk* **6** (7), 90–4, 2003.

Sharpe, W. "Mutual Fund Performance", in *Journal of Business* **39** (1), Part 2: Supplement on Security Prices, 119–38, 1966.

Sharpe, W. "The Arithmetic of Active Management", in *Financial Analysts Journal* **47** (1), 7–9, 1991.

Shiller, R.J. "Human Behavior and the Efficiency of the Financial System", NBER Working Paper No. 6375, 1998.

Sortino, F.A. and Price, L.N. "Performance Measurement in a Downside Risk Framework", in *The Journal of Investing* **3** (3), 59–64, 1994.

Stock, J. and Watson, M.W. "New Indexes of Coincident and Leading Economic Indicators", in *NBER Macroeconomic Annual*, 357–94, 1989.

Taylor, A. and Perraudin, W. "Credit risk orderings implicit in ratings and bond market yields", Working paper, http://www.ssrn.com, 2001.

Thomas, L.R. "Active Management", in *Journal of Portfolio Management* **26** (2), 25–32, 2000.

Tompkins, R. *Options explained* (McMillan, 1994).

Tversky, A. and Kahneman, D. "Loss aversion in riskless choice: A reference dependent model", in *Quarterly Journal of Economics* **106** (4), 1039–61, 1991.

Tversky, A. and Kahneman, D. "Prospect Theory: An Analysis of Decision Making Under Risk", in *Econometrica* **47** (2), 263–94, 1979.

Tversky, A. and Kahneman, D. "Judgement under Uncertainty: Heuristics and Biases" in *Science* **185**, No. 4157, 1124–31, 1974.

Unser, M. "Lower Partial Moments as Measures of Perceived Risk: An Experimental Study", in *Journal of Economic Psychology* **21** (3), 253–80, 2000.

Veld-Merkoulova, Y.V. "The Effects of Divestitures on the Bondholder's Value", Working Paper, University of Rotterdam, 2002.

Waring, M. B. and Siegel, L.B. "The Dimensions of Active Management", in *Journal of Portfolio Management* **29** (3), 35–51, 2003.

Weinstein, M. "The Effect of a Rating Change Announcement on Bond Price", in *Journal of Financial Economics* **5** (December), 329–50, 1977.

West, R. "Bond ratings, bond yields and financial regulation: some findings", in *Journal of Law and Economics* **16** (1), 159–68, 1973.

Wilson, T. "Portfolio Credit Risk (Part I and II)", in *Risk* **10** (9 and 10), 111–17 and 56–61, 1997.

Index